TEN DAYS THAT

SHOOK THE WORLD

TEN DAYS
THAT SHOOK
THE WORLD

BY JOHN REED

With a Foreword by V. I. Lenin
Edited with Introduction and
Notes by Bertram D. Wolfe

**THE
MODERN
LIBRARY**   NEW YORK

DK
265
.R38
1960

14952265

CONTENTS

CONTENTS

INTRODUCTION

BY BERTRAM D. WOLFE

John Reed was as American as apple pie and store cheese. Yet he was one of the founders of the Communist International, and his ashes lie under the Kremlin Wall. From a mansion on Cedar Hill in Portland, Oregon, to the Kremlin Wall at the heart of Moscow and Russia—such is the trajectory of his life. Except that his further evolution was cut short by untimely death, it was the trajectory, too, of much of the pre-1914 Greenwich Village radicalism of which he was an integral part. Indeed, to follow his adventures of flesh and spirit is to learn more about native American Bohemianism than about Russian communism, more about the Village

> Twixt Broadway and Sixth Avenue
> And West perhaps a block or two
> From Third Street up, and Ninth Street down
> Between Fifth Avenue and the town*

than about the *Kitai-Gorod,* a Chinatown without Chinese, that abuts the Kremlin Wall.

John Silas Reed, as he was christened in Portland's fashionable Trinity Episcopal Church, was born on October 20, 1887, in the sumptuous mansion of his maternal grandparents. His childhood memories center around their lordly hilltop home, "a French chateau, with immense

* From *The Day in Bohemia,* by John Reed.

park, formal gardens, lawns, stables, greenhouses, glass grape-arbor, tame deer . . . Chinese servants . . . idols, strange customs and ceremonies . . . pig-tails and gongs and fluttering red paper." The owner of the mansion was a Portland pioneer who had prospered mightily, owned the gas works, the water works, the iron works, in short, on a Portland scale, was "big business." The mansion's mistress had a reputation for gay parties and defiance of convention, raised by wealth and power above the wash of Portland gossip. An uncle, too, brought color into the boy's life by mysterious comings and goings and tall tales of far-off places where he had filibustered, planted coffee, become Secretary of State of a short-lived Guatemalan revolutionary government, spent all its treasury on a single banquet for his friends, declared war on Germany in revenge for his having flunked a college course in German.

But Jack's father and mother, the C. J. Reeds, were neither so rich nor so colorful. They owned a little home in Portland, in later years moving to an apartment hotel. C. J. Reed did well as agent for an Eastern agricultural implement company—until it was swallowed up by the International Harvester trust. Thereafter he struggled along as an insurance salesman. He strove to give his two sons the education proper to Portland "society" (private school, Eastern prep school, Harvard), never letting his boys know the effort it cost him. In his later years, he became a crusader against many of the deeds of the great Portland families of which his father-in-law was a leading representative. Some of Oregon's business leaders were preempting the forests (to say Oregon was to say lumber). When Theodore Roosevelt began his battle for conservation of our vanishing forest preserves, C. J. Reed was appointed United States Marshal to fight the despoilers of the Oregon forests, with William J. Burns as chief detective, Francis J. Heney as prosecutor, and Lincoln Steffens as "muckraker." The split in Portland society, the excitements of the crusade, the friendship between Jack's father and Lincoln Steffens—such was the political heritage which John Reed took with him to Harvard and Greenwich Village.

Jack's boyhood was troubled by illness, particularly a kidney ailment, by a sense of physical weakness, a fear of older and tougher boys. He was never really well and strong until his sixteenth year. His way to Portland Academy lay through Goose Hollow, inhabited by "brutal Irish boys." He fought when he had to, ran when he could, paid monetary tribute to his tormentors, finally got himself accepted precariously as one of the less valued members of the Fourteenth Street Gang. Then as now gangs had their domains, but they used less lethal weapons to defend them.

The boy's happiness was not in the world of fights and sports, but, his mother having early taught him to read, in the world of books and dreams. He began to write boyish verses, tell fanciful tales to younger listeners, see in every personable girl a Guinevere and in himself Sir Galahad aquest for the Holy Grail. "History was my passion, kings strutting about and armored ranks of men." Mark Twain, Bill Nye, *Lorna Doone, Webster's Unabridged,* Malory, the *Arabian Nights*—this assortment he characteristically selects as dearest to him. Echoes of these predilect works recur in all his later imaginative writing. At nine he began a "Comic History of the United States." At twenty-six he did his humorous *Day in Bohemia,* showed his continued love for lexicons in an ode "On First Looking into *Roget's Thesaurus,*" started but never finished a fantastic drama with such characters as God Almighty, Gertrude Stein, and a Chorus of Pederasts. In Florence, that same year, he saw a "field of Dragon's Teeth, where turbulent armies bred" and in Venice was lost in the beauty of history. "The things *Men* have done!" he murmured over and over again to Mabel Dodge. "But I wish that *I* could have been there at the *doing* of it, or that they were doing it *now*." It was as the ardent chronicler of the things *Men* were doing, as a poet in love with history and there at the *doing* of it, that John Reed would make his name.

As a sickly boy at the Portland Academy, Jack was an outsider. "I wasn't good at the things the other boys were, and their codes of honor and conduct didn't hold me. . . . They had a good-natured contempt for me. . . . That is why my impression of boyhood is an unhappy one, and why I have so few close friends in Portland, and don't ever want to live there again."

Only at swimming did he excel, spending long hours in the Willamette outdiving and outracing his companions. Not belonging to the world of the "normal" boys, he took refuge in staging plays of his own writing, founding and managing juvenile journals, filling them with his own stuff. Since his education was what is today called "permissive" and his reading wide-ranging and disorderly, his mind would be to the end as amazing for what he didn't know as for what he did, most amazing for the things he knew that weren't quite so. In 1917, just before he left for his look at the Russian Revolution, he wrote a brief memoir from which we have been quoting, a backward glance at the first twenty-nine years of his life. Of the temper of his spirit he wrote:

I never stuck long at anything I didn't like. . . . On the other hand, there are few things I don't get some fun out of, if only the novelty of experience. I love people, except the

well-fed smug, and am interested in all new things and all
the beautiful old things they do. I love beauty and chance and
change. . . . I suppose I'll always be a Romanticist.

No one could put better what his friends meant when
they said, "Jack is a poet."

Obsessed with the sense of being an outsider, his youth
was absorbed with an attempt to belong. In the Eastern
prep school to which his folks sent him to prepare for
Harvard, he felt more successful. His health was better,
though his kidney never ceased to give trouble; he played
football, ran the quarter-mile and excelled in swimming.
Where all were strangers, they were more willing to accept
him.

But in Harvard, which he entered in 1906, he felt the
desperation of an outsider once more. Of the 744 young
men in his entering class, it seemed that all had friends
but Jack. How to make friends, get into the clubs, become
a part of all the visible gayety? To make the freshman
crew he stayed all through a lonely vacation in Cambridge
to practice alone on the rowing machine, only to be the
last man kicked off the squad before the meets began. He
tried out for the college papers, sought a desirable room-
mate but was snubbed, snubbing in turn a Jewish boy who
asked to room with him—for which he sought and won
forgiveness later. Through it all he felt terribly alone.

As an upperclassman, his status began to improve. He
made some college papers as managing editor, though the
top posts eluded him "because the aristocrats blackballed
me." As a freshman, he had actually prayed to God to
make his fellow students like him: now his prayers were
on the way to being fulfilled. To be sure, he never made
the "better" clubs—except Hasty Pudding in his senior
year when it needed someone capable of composing comic

lyrics for its annual show. But he became president of the
Cosmopolitan Club, outsiders banded together from forty-
three lands, where the boy from Portland could find a
heady brew of ideas and ideologies. He got various administrative posts: manager of the Dramatic Club, manager
of two music clubs, captain of the Water Polo Team, song
leader of Harvard's cheering section, where "I had the
blissful sensation of swaying two thousand voices in great
crashing choruses during the big football games." His apprenticeship to Bill Nye and Mark Twain and his fecundity
in thinking up sophomoric jokes and comic rhymes won
him second place on the *Lampoon.* He got on the *Monthly,*
but could not make the *Crimson,* Harvard's daily. He felt
almost, but not quite, in.

When a fight developed between "aristocrats" and
"commoners," Reed wavered. The commoners lived in the
dormitories in Harvard Yard, the aristocrats on Mt. Au-
burn Street, whence the fight was known as one between
Yard and Street. Tempted by the symbols of status, Jack
had taken a room on the Street. That, plus a modicum of
acceptance from the "insiders" in his senior year, made
him choose to run on their ticket—which went down to defeat.

Even then, the aristocrats did not altogether accept
him. When he did get invited to their Back Bay drawing
rooms, a perverse, defiant streak made him play some
prank, affront some great personage, denounce some cher-
ished institution, behave as badly as possible. When his
companions were invited to the next affair without him,
he would feel sorry for himself. To reject while yearning
to belong, this was always to be the squaring of the circle
for John Reed.

Being a Harvard man remained important to him in
later years. The Harvard Club in New York, Harvard

men in Washington and Paris, rooming with Harvard men,
continued to matter. It was at a Harvard gathering in
Washington that he dramatized his opposition to conscrip-
tion and to America's entrance into the war, by refusing
to stand up when "The Star-Spangled Banner" was sung.
Afterwards it wounded him deeply when fellow alumni
hesitated to speak to him. This concern with Harvard was
part of the life-long boyishness in Reed, a boyishness noted
by all who have written of him, but misinterpreted by
those who have set him down as a "playboy."

The Harvard of his day was in a ferment of intellectual
radicalism. The war was to mark a decline in campus radicalism—one need only compare the prewar Intercollegiate
Socialist Society with its postwar offspring, the League for
Industrial Democracy, to convince oneself of that. The
Socialist Club, where Walter Lippmann then held forth
as pundit, got Jack to come to some of its meetings, but he
would not join. His reasons, truth in jest, are in his lines
describing Lippmann as one

> Who builds a world, and leaves out all the fun,
> Who dreams a pageant, gorgeous, infinite,
> And then leaves all the color out of it,
> Who wants to make the human race, and me,
> March to a geometric Q.E.D.

Reed shopped around at the Single Tax and Anarchist
Clubs, the Harvard Men's League for Woman's Suffrage,
and the other causes then enlisting enthusiasm on the
campus: modern art, thesis drama, anti-puritanism, sexual
freedom, atheism—an apprenticeship for life in Greenwich
Village.

Harvard's one remembered teacher was "Copey," who
"stimulated me to find color and strength and beauty in
books and in the world, and to express it." Professor Cope-

land, in turn, led him back to his father's old friend and comrade-in-arms, Lincoln Steffens, destined to influence him more deeply than any other man for the rest of his days.

Lincoln Steffens was attracted to younger men and greatly enjoyed the influence he could exercise over them. As a top-flight journalist, he was always being made an editor of some magazine or daily paper, yet he hated a desk and four walls, was no editor at all—except for his uncanny ability to think up assignments for himself, and his love of scouting for young writers. He had gone to Harvard to ask Copeland for the names of some promising young men. Copey's list included Lippmann, whom Steffens placed on the staff of *Everybody's*, and the son of his old friend C. J. Reed, for whom he got a job on the *American Magazine*.

Jack's ambitions were modest: "To make a million dollars . . . to get married . . . to write my name in letters of fire against the sky." When he confided some of this, "Steffens looked at me with that lovely smile: 'You can do anything you want to,' he said. . . . There are two men who give me confidence in myself—Copeland and Steffens. . . . More than any other, Steff has influenced my mind."

In 1911, Steffens was at the zenith of his reputation—though the foundations on which it was built were already eroding. For a few years, America had been much taken with crusades against Big Business, and against political corruption. Leading magazines vied with each other to publish exposés. Their articles crowded out murders, love nests and sports in conversation. Wrongly credited with being "the inventor of muckraking," Steffens was surely its most celebrated practitioner. To this busy trade he contributed a unique off-beat note: liking for the "crooks and grafters," and dislike of the men of his own class, the reformers to whose crusades his able articles contributed. This inversion of feeling gave his writings a special dimension. His *Shame of the Cities* was the recognized classic of the genre. By the time he published it, however, he was heartily tired of the whole business by which he had won his fame—in this a jump ahead of the American people, who would soon weary of it, too.

Publicly, Steffens was beginning to affirm that he admired Tammany Boss Croker more than any of his respectable enemies, and thought J. B. Dill, who had framed the New Jersey loophole laws for corporations, "about the wisest, and, yes, about the rightest man I ever met." Invited to Harvard by President Eliot, Steff offered to give a "course in corruption," not to teach the young how to avoid it but "how to succeed in their professions," whereupon President Eliot turned on his heel and walked right out of his own office.*

Wearied of repetitious detection and exposure (wasn't it everywhere the same?), Steffens was chagrined when editors would not let him switch from muckraking to didactic essays to teach that "intelligence was above morality," that there was no science or certainty to morals, that if you "threw the grafters out" they were bound to get right back in again. He wanted to explain that it was "the system" which corrupted, and that the cure was quite simple: nationalize all industry and then industry will be government, hence no longer able to corrupt it. His valedictory was fittingly entitled "An Apology for Graft," its thesis being that "a strong man, however bad, is socially better than a weak man, however good."

---

* All the direct quotations concerning Lincoln Steffens are taken from his published articles, *Letters* and *Autobiography*.

With no patience for the sobering thought that good fights have to be fought again and again, Steffens' undisciplined, cocksure, arrogant mind cast about for a swift and simple solution. He set out to formulate "the scientific laws of revolution," as previously he had worked out "the scientific laws of corruption." History was kind to him. South of the border there was a succession of revolutions in Mexico. But scientists "need more than a single case." How good of History to offer another revolution in Russia in 1917, and yet another in Italy in 1922. He made a pious scientific pilgrimage to each of the three. John Reed followed him on the first two expeditions, but was no longer alive to go on the third.

"I would like to spend the evening of my life," Steffens wrote of his new love, "watching the morning of a new world." It was a long evening. Born twenty-one years before Reed, Steffens died sixteen years after him. To the end, influencing and propagandizing young people in favor of revolution remained his ruling passion.

As he had admired Croker and Dill and felt contempt for their opponents and victims, so now he avowed his admiration for the strong and ruthless men who were shaping, or misshaping, our age. His admiration for Lenin is too well known to require comment. No less instructive, however, was his apostrophe to Mussolini:

It was as if the Author of all things had looked down upon this little planet of His, and seeing the physical, mental, moral confusion, said: "I will have a political thunderstorm, big enough for all men to notice and not too big for them to comprehend, and through it I will shoot a blazing thunderbolt that will strike down all their foolish old principles, burn up their dead ideas, and separate the new light I am creating from the darkness men have made." And so he formed Mussolini out of the rib of Italy.

After his study of three revolutions, Steffens was more than ever sure that "it is useless—it is almost wrong—to fight for the right under our system; petty reforms in politics . . . were impossible, unintelligent, immoral."

He urged young people to go to Russia. Personally, he lingered long in a lovely villa in Mussolini's Italy, then settled in "corrupt" old Paris and finally in California's Carmel-by-the-Sea. He "had been to Heaven" (Moscow), but was "so accustomed to Hell" (Paris) that for himself he preferred the infernal regions. He could "recognize salvation, but could not be saved." To an inquiring student he wrote: "Our old culture is finished. We have all got to turn to welcome the new culture, which covers everything —the arts, science, business, life." When other, more engaged Village radicals, like Max Eastman for instance, took a closer look and then became critical of the new Heaven, Steffens declaimed: "The intelligentsia! They shoot 'em in Russia; and I know why: they have to be shot every time the World moves, shot or crushed." Yet privately he acknowledged in a letter to a friend: "That's my belief. But I don't want to live there. It's too much like serving in an army at war, with no mercy for the weak and no time for the wounded. Youth can stand it; youth loves it; but for me who am ruined by an easy life of the old culture, Russia is impossible. My service to it has to be outside here."

Such was the temper and mind of the celebrated journalist and man of the world who in 1911 took young Reed under his tutelage, introducing him to life and art and the men, women and *isms* of Greenwich Village.

At first sight, Jack fell in love with New York: the Village, where he roomed, the theaters, Chinatown, the Fulton Fish Market, the soaring towers, the two rivers smelling of spice and far-off places and things of the sea, the teeming life of the Jewish East Side and Little Italy, Bowery drifters, cheap lodging houses, restaurants where the foods of the entire world could be found, dope peddlers, streetwalkers, gangsters that killed for hire, Coney Island's tinsel glitter—all was enchantment. In verses, derivative but bespeaking an eye and a heart all his own, Jack celebrated "the monuments uncouth" of this city's "wild ungovernable youth," the splendors of her achievements and of her still unfulfilled dreams, and the excitements of his own adventures in this splendid and chaotic setting. "In New York I first loved, and first wrote of the things I saw with a fierce joy of creation. . . . I was not happy or well long, away from New York. . . . I am not now for that matter." *

Best of all places in the beloved city was his beloved Village. Here were famous men and women, impassioned talk, unflagging excitement, physical and spiritual adventure. And truly, when Reed and three comrades from Harvard took rooms in a seedy old building at 42 Washington Square South (and Lincoln Steffens, to revel in their youth and admiration, forsook his accustomed luxury to move into rooms on the floor below), Greenwich Village was one of the most exciting places in the world. The Villagers were creators or devotees of the arts, propounders and disciples of the *isms,* advocates and exemplars of life lived adventurously, recklessly, free from the trammels of puritanism, respectability or convention. The Village in 1911 was Freud and Margaret Sanger; Big Bill Haywood, Carlo Tresca and Emma Goldman; Marx, Henry George, Tolstoy and Benjamin Tucker; Alfred Steiglitz and Isadora Duncan, and all the other heads of all sorts of movements, some of them with their whole movement in a single head.

* Written in Croton, New York, in 1917.

Editors scouted there for artists and writers. Alongside the established journals new ones sprang up that could not pay a penny, taking funds instead from their contributors to keep going. Reed tried to write things that would sell and make that million dollars. But as solace for rejection slips he found that the Village had an open-hearted, empty-treasuried, joyous magazine: the *Masses*. At that moment, Max Eastman presided over it. Nose-thumbing, vaguely modern, radical, experimental, it was more a Catherine wheel of artists, poets, light and heavy thinkers, and literary pranksters than a cause or tendency—worlds apart from the *New Masses* and the un-Reed-like "John Reed Clubs" of the thirties. Like the Village itself, the old *Masses* was a home for personal rebels, esthetic rebels, anarchists, socialists, feminists, any *ists* whatsoever. It was perpetually dying for lack of funds, perpetually springing into new life out of the abundance of high spirits which was its real capital.

Before long, as he had been at Harvard, John Reed was the managing editor. For one of its phoenixlike resurrections, he wrote:

We refuse to commit ourselves to any course of action, except this: to do with the Masses exactly what we please. . . . We don't even intend to conciliate our readers. . . . Poems, stories, drawings rejected by the capitalistic press on account of their excellence will find a welcome. . . . We intend to be arrogant, impertinent, in bad taste, but not vulgar . . . to attack old systems, old morals, old prejudices . . . to set up new ones in their places. . . . Bound by no creed or theory of social reform, we will express them all, providing they be radical. . . .

It was a credo for the Village of 1913, for the *Masses,* and a good personal statement of Jack's own radicalism.

Notable in it was the sense of beleaguered comradeship among these assorted rebels. Though they disputed endlessly with each other and scornfully demolished each other's pet theories, they stood shoulder to shoulder against the established. They could write without mockery of "the good love of comrades." However much they might disagree with each other's creeds, they defended each other's right to utter and publish and otherwise give expression to what to each might seem good. None thought in those days that his heresy might one day become a new orthodoxy, directing inquisition, persecution, anathema and death at all who continued to be rebels. Something of this comradeship in diverse rebellion continued to sweeten Village life until the thirties, when the blood purges would cleave a chasm between those who identified themselves with the driver of the juggernaut and those who felt compassion for the victims over whom it rolled.

The Village's conception of "the Revolution" was more esthetic than social. Its high point was the Armory Show of 1913. Mabel Dodge, whose $500 check and busy visits to owners of "advanced" art to get loans of pictures, did much to make the show possible, characterized it with her usual uninhibited precision:

I felt as though the Exhibition were mine. I really did. It became overnight my own little Revolution. *I* would upset America. . . . It was tragic—I was able to admit that—but the old ways must go, and with them their priests. . . . My hand would not shake nor could I allow my personal feelings of pity to halt me. *I* was going to dynamite New York. . . .

(In 1917, the vanguard artists and writers of St. Petersburg would make the same pathetic error of confounding their revolution in art with Lenin's revolution in the power structure, for which confusion some have long paid and others are still paying.)

In 1913 the salon of Mabel Dodge was a unifier of Village life. Like V. F. Calverton in the postwar generation, she had a rare gift for bringing together the atomized particles of our decentralized culture.

Born Mabel Ganson in Buffalo in 1879 (which made her eight years Jack's senior), she had become Mabel Evans in 1900, Mabel Dodge in 1903, would marry the painter Maurice Sterne in 1916, and the Hispano-Indian, Antonio Luhan, in 1923. Between the second marriage and the third, she came to play a large role in the Village, and in the life of John Reed.

Having returned from three years in her elegant Florentine villa to "ugly, ugly America" and being on the way to becoming estranged from her loyal, conventional second husband, she sought to fill the void in her spirit by turning her luxuriously furnished apartment at 23 Fifth Avenue, with a wall broken through to an apartment on Ninth Street, into an open house for everybody that was anybody, and for many a nobody. Wealthy, gracious, openhearted, beautiful, intellectually curious and quite without any sense of discrimination, she was Bohemia's most successful lion hunter. "I wanted to know the Heads of things, Heads of movements, Heads of newspapers, Heads of all kinds of groups . . . anything that showed above the tribal pattern." Her hospitality, her capacity for listening, her quiet, encouraging smile, brought together the great, the near-great, and those who came to dream of greatness.

Steffens was one of her lions. With him on occasion he brought three young Harvard classmates of the class of 1910: Lee Simonson, Walter Lippmann and John Reed. There they could meet of a Wednesday evening the Hapgoods, Jo Davidson, Margaret Sanger, Alexander Berkman, Emma Goldman, Max Eastman, Frances Perkins, Andrew Dasburg, Charles Demuth, Marsden Hartley, Amos Pinchot, Amy Lowell, Edward Arlington Robinson, Carl Van Vechten, Harry Kemp, Frank Harris, George Sylvester Viereck, John Collier . . . an inexhaustible *Who's Who* in the flesh. The kaleidoscope shifted each Wednesday night, but to young Reed all the variegated patterns were attractive and beautiful.

Sometimes Mrs. Dodge set the subject and selected an opening speaker. Sometimes she shifted the night to make sure of a more uniform, specially invited group. More often, however, the talk flowed out of the diversity of personalities and attitudes or convictions. Here, from her *Intimate Memoirs,* is her account of one of her "special" evenings:

I switched from the usual Wednesday to a Monday, so that none but more or less radical sympathizers would be there. People who believed that others had the right to kill on principle, if they thought it Right: The Live and Let Live Kind of People.

One evening she took her guests to hear Bill Haywood ("a great battered hulk of a man, with one eye gone, and an eminent look in the other") at the home of his mistress, a Village schoolteacher. He talked of the desperate Paterson Silk Strike, of police brutality and the silence of the metropolitan press.

"Why don't you bring the strike to New York and *show* it?" asked Mabel Dodge. "In Madison Square Garden, why not?"

"I'll do it!" cried a voice—and a young man detached himself from the group and assumed a personality before my

eyes. . . . His olive-green eyes glowed softly, his high forehead was like a baby's with light-brown curls rolling away
from it and two spots of shining light on his temples, making
him lovable. His chin was the best . . . the real poet's
jawbone . . . eyebrows always lifted . . . generally breathless!

(Max Eastman has affectionately described Jack as having a face "rather like a potato." Curiously, we who knew
him found both descriptions, each in its way, correct).

Reed went to Paterson, spent three weeks in the midst
of the strike, led the foreign-born workers, as once he had
the Harvard cheering section, in revolutionary song,
listened excitedly to I.W.W. speakers, got locked up in a
Paterson jail. When the police, who had arrested him for
"resisting an officer" (refusing to "move on"), found that
he was embarrassing them by articles on prison conditions,
they threw him out after four days of his thirty-day term.
He headed straight for Mabel Dodge's home. Since it had
been her idea, he somehow took it for granted that she
would work with him on bringing the strike to Madison
Square Garden. His exuberance dragged her into an enter-
prise alien to her nature. Thus was born "The Pageant of
the Paterson Strike," and thus John Reed became an ad-
herent of the I.W.W.

His scenario was rather bare and simple, but the novelty of mass scenes with real strikers and I.W.W. leaders
as actors gave the performance an intensity beyond the
strength of the script. Of course, Jack appeared in his own
pageant, to lead the strikers—and the audience—in singing revolutionary songs.

It is hard work to fill Madison Square Garden. The
dollar and two-dollar seats remained almost empty, until
workingmen and strikers were let in to fill them free, or at

ten cents a seat. Instead of making money, the pageant ended with a deficit. The long strike, too, was finally lost. But Jack did not stay to learn the results. The day after the pageant, before the accounting was in, he and Mabel left on the same boat for Europe.

When he came to the Village he had a girl whom he had wanted to marry. "For the first five months, I was sentimental about it and remained chaste." Then she was forgotten, and he followed a roving eye and fancy into a succession of affairs, all "wonderful" but none deep. When he told his current love, "Rose, I don't love you; I love Mabel Dodge," she shed a few tears on his shoulder and sobbed, "I am so unhappy," then suddenly raised her eyes in surprise and said, "Why no, I'm not!"

But the love for Mabel Dodge was different. By her own account it must have been a possessive, even an oppressive passion. She was jealous of the stones of Venice, of the way he felt about history, and the way he said: "The things *Men* have done!" ("Past or present, I did not care what they had done. . . . I jumped into the automobile and returned to Florence, leaving him there to it.") She was jealous of the Harvard friends who came to take him out on stag explorations. Later, when Steffens had Reed sent to Mexico to report on the revolution there, she was jealous of his life with Villa's band. And she was jealous of the Great War which took her away from him when he became a correspondent in Europe.

Good-bye, my darling [he wrote after one such quarrel]: You smother me. You crush me. You want to kill my spirit. I love you better than life but do not want to die in my spirit. I am going away to save myself. Forgive me. I love you. I love you. Reed.

Yet always he returned, and the contest continued. Then suddenly, after a year and some months, love for Reed in Mabel Dodge died as swiftly as it had flared up. Yet for some time he continued to count on it, had editors send her reports on him, wrote her of brief affairs with other girls and of his enduring love for her.

For her part, she could not see why they "should not continue to be close friends." She even tried to house him as her guest in the attic of the farmhouse she took with Maurice Sterne, but he could not act out this desperate Village convention. "Why can't people *live* their theories, anyway?" she protested.

Not until December of 1915 was Jack able to break the spell. Then he wrote to a friend:

I think I've found her at last. She's wild, brave and straight —and graceful and lovely to look at. In this spiritual vacuum, this unfertilized soil [he was writing from Portland where he was visiting his mother], she has grown (how I can't imagine) into an artist. She is coming to New York to get a job—with me, I hope. I think she is the first person I ever loved without reservation.

The new love was Louise Bryant Trullinger, wife of a Portland dentist, unhappy with Portland and with him, hungering for New York and the promise of adventure. Thus began a stormy love, broken by quarrels, separations and intermittent affairs on both sides, yet continuing. In November, 1916, when Jack went to the hospital to get his ailing kidney removed, they were married. In 1917, and again in 1919, she went to Russia when Reed was there, and wrote as a correspondent in her own right. She accompanied him in most of his adventures of those ten autumn days of 1917 that "shook the world." She was at his bedside in Moscow when he died.

In November, 1913, John Reed went to Mexico to report for the *Metropolitan* and the *World*. To him the Mexican Revolution was a pageant, a succession of thrilling adventures, a delight to the eye, a chance to make the reassuring discovery that he was not afraid of a hail of bullets. His reports flowed with life and movement: simple, savage men, capricious cruelty, warm comradeship, splashes of color, bits of marching and campfire song, fragments of social and political dreams, gay humor, personal peril, reckless daring. Neither Steffens, who attached himself to Carranza, nor Reed, who celebrated the pastoral dreams and bloody deeds of Pancho Villa, had any real understanding of the Mexican maze. But Reed's mixture of personal adventure and camera-eye close-ups lighted by a poet's vision, made superb reporting. The book that came of it, *Insurgent Mexico,* despite its careless ignorance of men, events and forces, and even of Spanish, which he mangled in the snatches of ballad, was closer to the feel of Mexico in revolution than most things Americans have written on it. When he returned to New York, he found he had a reputation as a top war correspondent.

When war broke out in Europe in 1914, he was assigned to cover it by the *Metropolitan*. He went to Italy—nothing worthy of his pen. Then France, which had settled down to the stalemate of trench warfare. It seemed dull and gloomy, with none of the excitement of Pancho Villa's hard-riding band. He tried England—no story there either.

"The real war," he wrote, parroting Steffens, "is a clash of traders." Like most Village radicals, he was inclined to sympathy with Germany as the "underdog," the latecomer among trading and colonizing nations, who had arrived on the scene when everything was pre-empted. Not much to choose between the sides, but the Entente seemed to him "more hypocritical." His most violent language he reserved for England, who

grips the Red Sea, sucks the blood from India, menaces a half billion human beings from Hong Kong, owns all Australia, half North America, and half of Africa . . . the great intriguer, sitting like a spider in the web of nations. . . . It was England's will that Germany should be destroyed.

The *Metropolitan* did not print the article.

Since America was neutral, he headed next for the German side, and its front in occupied France. His reports were in general favorable to the occupiers. In the foremost trench, where he could see the French lines and the dead in No-Man's Land, he spent a night under fire. After a night in rain and mud and a downfall of shrapnel and shells, he was asked by a German lieutenant whether he would like to have a shot. With a rifle borrowed from a German soldier, he fired two shots at daybreak in the general direction of the French line. This escapade, reported by a fellow correspondent, was to cause trouble for him later in Tsarist Russia, be held against him in Washington, cause him to be barred from France. That is how John Reed came to be transferred from the Western to the Eastern Front.

His work as a European war correspondent was a disappointment to editors, friends, and to Jack himself. His recklessness, poet's vision, camera-eye and shallow explanations concerning the "traders' war" were not enough to work with in the grim, vast, irreducible stalemate. "I have come to hate Europe," he wrote to his mother.

The Eastern Front proved little more rewarding. Having worked his way up through the Balkans into Russia, without permission from the Russian authorities and pursued by the story of two shots from a Mauser, he landed in a Russian jail. It was sixteen days before American officials could arrange his ignominious departure. With his usual boyish exuberance, he had written on his passport for the benefit of the Russian authorities: "I am a German and an Austrian spy. I do it for money. Reed."

Yet, despite his misadventures, his brief stay in Russia had made him a complete Russophile. He felt at home in the esthetic intensity and disorder as he had felt at home in Mexico:

Russian ideals are the most exhilarating, Russian thought the freest, Russian art the most exuberant; Russian food and drink are to me the best, and Russians themselves are, perhaps, the most interesting human beings that exist. . . . There the people live as if they know it was a Great Empire. . . . Everyone acts just as he feels like acting, and says just what he wants to. There are no particular times for getting up or going to bed or eating dinner, and there is no conventional way of murdering a man, or of making love.

It was Tsarist Russia of late 1915 that he was celebrating.

Back in America in early 1916, Reed grew alarmed by his country's drift toward war. With Henrietta Rodman, Franklin Giddings, Carlton Hayes, John Dewey, he signed an appeal to Socialists to vote for Wilson because "he has kept us out of war." When George Creel organized a group of writers to re-elect Wilson, including Steffens, Howe, Zona Gale, Hutch Hapgood, George Cram Cook, Susan Glaspell, Reed joined that, too. America's swift entrance into the war on the side of the Allies a few months later, even before Wilson had delivered his Second Inaugural Address, goes far to explain the subsequent alienated fury of Village radicalism.

After the removal of his long-ailing kidney, the publication of a slender volume of undistinguished poems, the writing of his backward glance over the first twenty-nine years of his life, Jack sought an assignment to Russia where the Tsar had just fallen. In his *Almost Thirty*, he wrote:

I must find myself again. Some men seem to get their direction early. . . . I have no idea what I shall be or do one month from now. Whenever I have tried to become some one thing, I have failed . . . only by drifting with the wind I have found myself. . . . I wish with all my heart that the proletariat would rise and take their rights. . . . But I am not sure any more that the working class is capable of revolution, peaceful or otherwise. The War has been a terrible shatterer of faith. . . . And yet, I cannot give up the idea that out of democracy will be born the new world—richer, braver, freer, more beautiful. . . . And I don't know what I can do to help. . . . My happiness is built on the misery of other people . . . that fact poisons me, disturbs my serenity, makes me write propaganda when I would rather play.

This was his mood when, on August 17, 1917, having been exempted from the draft because of his kidney operation, John Reed set sail with Louise for Russia.

He arrived in Petrograd late that August predisposed to witness a miracle. The Russophile, the minstrel of Villa's revolution, the I.W.W. enthusiast, the disillusioned Socialist and Wilsonian pacifist, the poet who wanted to belong but could not find out to what—suddenly fused into one. The civilization he both rejected and loved was in un-

deniable crisis, and his own country had joined in the
universal madness. Any cause that promised to take
Russia out of war, and, he hoped, put an end forever to
"the system that made wars possible," could enlist his
ardor. He was ready to give himself completely to this
simple, comforting and by no means ignoble belief. Of the
awesome disputations of Russia's intelligentsia he knew
nothing. Of Lenin's authoritarian party structure and organization machine even less: so much the freer was his
fancy to endow the conflict and chaos he was to witness
with the form and substance of his own dream. To Boardman Robinson, since 1915 the illustrator of his war articles, he wrote: "We are in the middle of things and
believe me it's thrilling. For color and terror and grandeur
this makes Mexico look pale."

His Russian was even sketchier than his Spanish, but no
matter. For worker and peasant there was a gay smile
and the sputter of *Ya amerikanskii sotsialist!* And all the
politically active people seemed to know some French or
German, or had been to America or England and could
speak English. Since all Russia was talking and unburden-
ing its soul, any number of officers, political leaders, intellectuals, were ready to talk to him. Makers of history and
those being unmade by history, veteran fighters for freedom
smarting under the new-found insult of "counter-revolutionist"—who would refuse to talk to an American reporter who was so ardent, attractive and boyish a listener?

No dearth of those who spoke English and would offer
themselves as interpreters: Alex Gomberg, unofficial fixer
for so many unofficial Americans in Petrograd; Gomberg's brother, Zorin, high in the councils of Bolshevism;
Albert Rhys Williams, Socialist always ready with "theo-
retical explanations" of everything; Boris Reinstein, who
had been in the Socialist Labor Party in America; Volo-

darsky, another emigré back from America to become one of Bolshevism's top leaders; Melnichansky, Bolshevik leader whom Reed had known as George Melcher in Bayonne, New Jersey; Bill Shatov, returned from Village anarchism and I.W.W. membership, filled with the certainty that Lenin was about to inaugurate anarchy by "withering away the state" the moment he got hold of it. Besides, in the back of every meeting into which Jack shouldered his way, there was always someone to answer his perpetual, breathless "Say, what's going on here?"

Sometimes with Gomberg, Williams, Louise, and Bessie Beatty (another American correspondent), and sometimes alone, he made his way into every institution, meeting, skirmish: into the Smolny Institute, where from October 25* on the Bolsheviks had their military headquarters; into the City Duma, stronghold of liberal democracy; into the Soviets of Workers and Soldiers and the Soviets of Peasants; into barracks, factory meetings, street processions, meeting halls, courtrooms; into the Winter Palace when it was being defended by student officer candidates and a woman's battalion; and again when it was being overrun by the Red Guard and looted; to Moscow to see what damage had been done to the architectural monuments of the Kremlin; to the shifting battlefront at Tsarskoe Selo and Gatchina, where armies dissolved and reformed and changed sides in the midst of a hail of propaganda and negotiations more than bullets. In October, November and December, all Russia was meeting and John Reed was meeting with it.

If two shots from a German Mauser did not make him cease to be a neutral in The Great War, in this "class war pure and simple," as he called it, he strove to be a par-

---

* Following John Reed's procedure in *Ten Days*, I have used the dates of the Reformed, New Style or Western calendar. The "October 25" here referred to is thus two weeks before the Bolshevik seizure of power.

ticipant as well as an observer. Twice he addressed crowds in the Cirque Moderne, bringing fraternal greetings (from whom?), being introduced as a spokesman for the American Socialist Party (which he was not), and as a man under indictment in far-off capitalist America (which, as an editor of the antiwar *Masses,* he was). He addressed Bolshevik factory meetings, careened around the city on one of their trucks hurling out leaflets he could not read, joined the looting throng in the Winter Palace, carrying off some notes of a doomed Minister and a jewel-handled sword concealed under his coat.* With his poet's blood and rebel's heart he decided what to believe, then with the artist's gift for selection, heightening and unifying, he assimilated all the chaotic impressions into a picture more unitary, impressive, satisfying than the chaos he was witnessing.

When Boardman Robinson reproached him once with "but it didn't happen that way!"—his answer was an *ad hominem* of one artist to another. "What the hell difference does it make?" he cried, and, seizing one of Robinson's sketches: "She didn't have a bundle as big as that . . . he didn't have so full a beard." But drawing—Robinson explained—was not a matter of photographic accuracy but of overall impression. "Exactly!" Reed cried in triumph. "That is just what I am trying to do!"

Yet there is nothing of the mean deliberate lie about John Reed's book. A good reporter, always in the thick of things, his sense of vivid detail often makes one page refute another and establishes many a to him unpalatable truth. He was vulnerable to gossip, rumor and conjecture

* Louise Bryant speaks of "a silver Caucasian dagger, a short sword presented by the Tsar" as secured in an "exchange of keepsakes" with some *Junkers* (military cadets) before the Bolshevik capture of the Winter Palace, and she denies that there was any looting. Granville Hicks, who used interviews with Louise, with Bessie Beatty, Alex Gomberg, and Albert Rhys Williams, gives the story as I have told it here.

tian may believe that on the night that celebrates the Savior's birth "no spirit dares stir abroad; the nights are wholesome, then no planets strike, nor fairy takes, nor witch hath power to charm, so hallow'd and so gracious is the time"—so Reed writes of the night Lenin seized power: "On that night not a single hold-up occurred, not a single robbery." And three days later: "Quiet the city lay, not a hold-up, not a robbery, not even a drunken fight." Yet this does not prevent him from quoting Trotsky on the all-embracing wave of drunkenness which followed the seizure of power. Nor prevent his reproducing a *Prikaz* showing that the drunken revelry continued into late December and was then to be met by dynamiting wine cellars without prior warning to those engaged in their pillage. It is instructive to compare Reed's "Quiet the city lay" with the plaint of Antonov-Ovseenko, leader of the attack on the Winter Palace:

The Preobrazhensky regiment got completely drunk while guarding the wine cellars of the Palace. . . . The Pavlovsky regiment did not withstand the temptation either. . . . Mixed picked guards were sent; they, too, got drunk. Members of the regimental committees were assigned. . . . These succumbed, too. Men of the armored brigades were ordered to disperse the crowds—they paraded up and down, then began to sway suspiciously. . . . An attempt was made to flood the cellars. The fire brigades got drunk. . . . At dusk the mad bacchanals would spread. "Let us finish off these Tsarist remnants!" This gay slogan took hold of the crowd. . . . The whole city was infected by this drinking madness. . . . The Council of People's Commissars appointed a special commissar with emergency powers. . . . But the commissar too proved unreliable. . . .[*]

[*] Antonov-Ovseenko, *Zapiski o Grazhdanskoi Voine*, I, pp. 19-20.

that accorded with his preconceptions, but what he actually
saw with his own eyes he did his best to record faithfully.

He idealized the masses. He believed the ridiculous
legend, born perhaps of his own fantasy, that the Bolshevik
Central Committee, after having rejected the idea of insurrection, was made to reverse itself by a single speech
of a rank and file workingman. (There was such a reversal,
but the "rank and file workingman" was Lenin!) Though
literacy had been declining all through the war, and would
continue to decline for years after, Reed wrote sincerely:
"All Russia was learning to read." A few pages later,
without any sense of contradiction, comes this vivid scene:

We did not notice a change in the attitude of the soldiers
and Red Guards around us. . . . A small group followed us.
. . . By the time we reached the picture gallery about a
hundred men surged in after us. One giant of a soldier stood
in our path, his face dark with sullen suspicion. "Who are
you?" he growled. The others massed slowly around, staring
and beginning to mutter. . . . I produced our passes from
the Military Revolutionary Committee. The soldier took them
gingerly, turned them upside down and looked at them without comprehension. Evidently he could not read. *"Bumagi*
[papers]!" he said with contempt. The mass began to close in
like wild cattle around a cowpuncher on foot. . . .

It was an officer, from that intelligentsia which Reed
professed to despise, who—frightened and sweating—
managed to save Jack and Louise from instant lynching.
At the front he was nearly lynched by a detachment of
Red Guards, none of whom could read his Russian cre-
dential, and again he was saved by an officer. But he
never permitted himself to doubt that the mob was just
and wise and lynchings salutary.

For Reed the revolution was holy. As a devout Chris-

Yet Jack did not see it until actual shooting between the drunken soldiers and the Helsingfors sailors sent to dynamite the barrels and bottles in the cellars of the Winter Palace.* Reed puts the beginning of the looting of wine cellars as "toward the end of November" and accepts the legend that the soldiers drank only on the instigation of "counter-revolutionists." But Trotsky found it necessary to make his first speech on the wave of drunkenness on the fourth day after the seizure of power, that is, after the very night of which Reed wrote "Quiet the city lay." Only one completely possessed by his dream could have written that sentence.

Though this dream revolution obscured his vision at times, his eyes were everywhere. And his person, too. He tried to see it all, put it all on paper. If he did not comprehend the meaning of the large events, what observer or participant did? He understood less and misunderstood more than many, so that one of the personages of whom he wrote would say to me of his book: "The work of an innocent who did not know whether he was attending a wedding or a funeral!" ** It was a funeral—of Russia's newly won liberties, achieved after a century of struggle. If Jack thought he was witnessing the wedding of liberty and justice destined to live together happily ever after, so well does he report that we can see the acts of burial even as he sings of nuptials.

As a record of significant detail, as a repository of facts for the historian, his book is crammed with precious material: interviews, speeches, resolutions, press accounts. One of his habits was to tear down a specimen of every poster or proclamation for future translation. The book is

* This information concerning the moment of Reed's awareness comes from Bessie Beatty, *The Red Heart of Russia*, p. 329 ff.
** The words are those of Wladimir Woytinsky (Voitinsky), in his later years one of America's most distinguished economists.

full of quotations from such documents, and illustrated by photos of many of them—a priceless opportunity for the historian to enter into a time that has passed.

Whether because of or despite the dream which possessed him, as literature Reed's book is the finest piece of eyewitness reporting the revolution produced. It is his true monument, more enduring than the ashes and the name carved on the Kremlin Wall.

After the *Ten Days*, the rest of John Reed's life is anti-climax. He tried to become a Communist politician, but as a politician he was out of his element. He sat on tiresome committees and toured the country, speaking on the Russian Revolution. Politics as politics was dull but he found excitement in the possibility of martyrdom. Though the country was in the grip of wartime fever and hysteria, somehow officials, courts and juries rejected the idea that Reed was suitable as a symbolic martyr. Officials returned the posters and notebooks they had seized from him when he landed in America; the indictments against him as a *Masses* editor, an opponent of war, an "inciter to riot," a preacher of sedition, all were quashed, or dismissed, or ended in acquittal. When he was in a Finnish jail, as earlier in the jail of Tsarist Russia, American officials, a little reluctantly perhaps, intervened on his behalf. He helped to split the Socialist Party, got caught up in the frustrating splits of the nascent Communist Party, all the while longing to get back to the old life of poetry and adventure. Twice he fled from cheerless meetings to seek out Sherwood Anderson. "If I were dead sure I had something on the ball as a poet . . ." he said to Anderson wistfully.

Candor compelled him as he read his own verses to recognize that he did not have much on the ball as a poet.

He wrote propaganda articles on America, the world situation, communism. Except for a challenging title and an occasional impudently humorous phrase, they are dull, foolish, barely readable. His spirits rose only when there was some chance of excitement, as when he and Eadmonn MacAlpine secretly forged a parody replica of the New York *Socialist* and managed to place it on sale at Socialist headquarters until the prank was discovered. He spent the autumn of 1919 in Provincetown. "I wish I could stay here," he told Susan Glaspell, "but I have promised too many people . . ."

Then came the chance to return to adventure. The occasion was petty: to present the faction case of one of the splinters of the new Communist movement as against the other, before the Communist International. To get to the Red Mecca was a quest perilous. Fearful of the contagion of revolution, the West had set up a *cordon sanitaire* around Russia, as later the Kremlin would set up its own *iron curtain* against the contagion of freedom. Denied a passport, Jack sailed with forged papers as Jim Gormley, stoker on a Scandinavian vessel. Though his health had been weakened by the kidney operation and by irregular habits of eating, drinking and sleeping, Gormley did his work satisfactorily as a stoker—until he jumped ship in Norway. From there he stowed away in a greasy pile of rags on a ship bound to Finland, and was smuggled across the Finnish frontier into Russia.

It was not the Russia he had dreamed of. He was hurt by the spectacle of hunger, misery, breakdown, apathy, above all by the way the new official class was beginning to lavish care on itself in the midst of universal misery. He strove to preserve the fragments of his dreams by attributing everything to the civil war and blockade, and

ignoring the contribution to the breakdown made by
Lenin's absurd outlawing of trade between town and country and his nationalization of everything "down to the last
inkwell." *

"From every trip," wrote Angelica Balabanoff, then
Secretary of the Communist International, "he would come
back to the capital less and less cheerful, more and more
sad and preoccupied . . . because of the superfluous sufferings of the people, those which could have been
avoided."

He made two attempts to return to America. On the
second, he was caught in Finland, and, after more than
two months of hunger and filth in a Finnish jail, was de-
ported back to Moscow. He had scurvy, his arms and legs
were swollen from malnutrition, but he continued, as before, to insist on living like the ordinary Russian.

Now he decided to wait for the Second Congress, the
first genuine congress of the Communist International.
From its sessions came another sort of disillusion to which
his heart was peculiarly vulnerable.

The order of business for the congress had been determined by Lenin. Having concluded that the great push
for world revolution had failed, and with it the attempt to
smash the old Socialist parties and trade unions, Lenin
set it down as the immediate task of all revolutionaries to
return to, or infiltrate, the old trade unions. As always,
Lenin took it for granted that whatever conclusion he had
come to in evaluation, in strategy, and in tactics, was
infallibly right. In the Comintern, as in his own party, his
word was law and wisdom.

But the British delegates had worked out their own
attitude toward the Labor Party, while the Americans
were hostile to the American Federation of Labor and

* The phrase is Bukharin's.

favorable to the I.W.W. As for Reed, he had been brought
to the labor movement by the I.W.W.'s strike in Paterson.
The leaders of the I.W.W. had gone to jail *en masse* for
opposing the war, while the A.F. of L. had been pro-war
and supported "the system." The A.F. of L. must be
smashed and the I.W.W. supported.

That Lenin had made up his mind for America did not
impress Jack. It was the Americans who knew their land
and had to determine the policies they were to carry out
in it. He prepared for a fight. On behalf of thirty delegates
from the English-speaking countries, Reed introduced two
motions: to put the trade union question at the top of the
order of business, and to add English to the already
adopted German, French and Russian, as an official
language of debate. With Zinoviev in the chair, the motions were not voted down but simply ruled out.

As I was the only translator [writes Angelica Balabanoff] I
remember the protest of the English-speaking delegations because the Chair decided not to have the speeches translated
into English. I was naïve enough to believe that this "omis-
sion" was to save time or translation work. When I said that I
would gladly translate into English, too, my offer was not
taken into consideration.

Thus Reed could neither have his arguments seriously
presented to other delegations, nor find out what was being
said against them. He had seen steamrollers before, but
never one like this. Shunted to the Trade Union Commission, he was told bluntly that the matter was "settled"
and he must obey discipline. Radek charged him with
"sabotage." Zinoviev mocked him for believing that America could be taken from the Rockefellers and Morgans,
but not the A.F. of L. from the Gomperses. As boss of

the *apparat,* Zinoviev mobilized obedient henchmen, lined up delegations on the basis of loyalty to the Russians, held meetings without notifying the recalcitrant Reed of time or place.

Still Jack would not give in. A rebel not a robot, he was not made to be a cog in a machine. The Comintern, even then, was on its way to becoming a "monolith," appropriate symbol not of the diversity of rebellious humanity, but of the solid block of granite which might serve as tombstone over men's hope of freedom. Of the impatient and ardent rebels who had flocked to Moscow from all over the world, not one would long endure in the Comintern. Even Angelica Balabanoff, despite her decades of activity in two parties and in the Second and Third Internationals, would last only a few months longer. By the time the congress was over, Angelica was the only Russian leader to whom Jack could talk, or confide his doubts and sorrows. Yet he still had fight in him. He wrote an article for his party's journal in which he said: "Nobody in Russia seems to understand industrial unionism. . . . At the next Congress these theses must be altered." But for him there was to be no next congress.

"When he came to me after the Congress," Dr. Balabanoff wrote, "he was in a terrible state of depression. He looked old and exhausted. The experience had been a terrible blow." Either during the congress, or right after it, Reed resigned his post as member of the Executive of the International, as a protest, his Communist biographers have circumspectly said, "on an organization question." Somehow he was persuaded to withdraw his resignation, and somehow made to go with Zinoviev, Radek and a trainload of delegates and officials to a "Congress of the Toiling Peoples of the East" in Baku. The variegated temperaments, traits and costumes of the men from the East fascinated him; their sudden drawing and brandishing of curved scimitars to approve a resolution, captivated his romantic imagination. But the demagogy of Zinoviev and Radek, and the ostentatious luxury on the official train running through a land of famine, sickened him.

Back in Moscow, Jack took to his bed with typhus. How much the virus, how much the ravaged body, how much the broken spirit contributed, we can only guess. To Angelica Balabanoff, and to Louise Bryant who had just managed to come to Moscow from America, it seemed—as Angelica was to write—that the "moral and nervous shock had deprived him of the wish to live, of that love of life that was so prominent in his character."

When Kobetski, technical secretary of the International, wrote to Lenin that Reed was dead, Lenin answered:

Comrade Kobetski!

1. Your report (that is the report of the physician you sent me) and the note, should be sent abroad.

2. Who is in charge of the Hotel Lux? Its remodeling for the Comintern? The management part?

                              Lenin   18/X

With his death, all rebellion ended. As the author of what Lenin rightly esteemed to be the best book on his seizure of power, Reed was given a state funeral. Feeling that she could not speak of him without speaking of the sadness of his last days, Angelica Balabanoff refused to deliver an address or even attend his funeral. "I knew Reed would have understood. . . . Most of the people who commemorated him were not entitled to do so. Their speeches *had* to be cold, official, conventional." Like Lenin's note.

A decade passed and Reed's ashes lay forgotten, along with his sturdy example of independence. Then Stalin began to find use for the names of the safely dead while he was purging the living, including most of the men who figure so prominently in Reed's book: Trotsky, Antonov-Ovseenko, Kamenev, Zinoviev, Bukharin, Radek, Shliapnikov, and so many more. *Ten Days That Shook the World* kept them alive in its pages, so it, too, was suppressed, first in Russia, then wherever the Comintern owned the copyright through a manipulated publisher. But in America, John Reed's name was exploited through the John Reed Clubs. A biography was invented for him in which his rebellious spirit and manly opposition to dictatorial authority found no place.

Suddenly, in the middle thirties, the "line" changed once more. In the new "Popular Fronts," revolution and hostility to liberal and democratic intellectuals was to be played down. Since Reed's name was inseparable from the events, the attitudes and the very idea of the October Revolution, it was dropped as remorselessly as it had been previously used. Overnight, the John Reed Clubs became the League of American Writers.

With Stalin's death, the wheel of fortune took yet another turn. Reed's book reappeared in Russia. It contains, as before, Lenin's foreword of unqualified praise, but an anonymous postcript discreetly contradicts it:

The book does not sufficiently reflect the stubborn struggle conducted by Lenin and his closest companions against the capitulators and against the tactical line of Trotsky. . . .

John Reed's text is actually tampered with in only one passage. Where, in his preliminary "Notes and Explanations," he had listed as among the leaders of the Bolsheviks

"Lenin, Trotsky, Lunacharsky," this trinity has been omitted.* But Trotsky's ghost is not so easily laid. Where his name is first introduced by Reed, a footnote now describes him as a

> Menshevik who headed the centrist trend (Trotskyism) in the Russian Social Democratic Movement . . . a concealed liquidator, during the first World War occupied the chauvinistic position of 'defense of the fatherland,' propagating the slogan, 'Neither victory nor defeat' . . . expelled from the Party in 1927 for anti-Party and counter-revolutionary activities. In 1929 he was sent abroad where he continued to wage a struggle against the Soviet Union and the Communist Parties.

Of his murder in Mexico, not a word.

But Trotsky haunts so many pages of Reed's book. At the point where he appears as spokesman for the Bolsheviks, Chairman of the Petrograd Soviet and of the Military Revolutionary Committee, another footnote explains:

> The inexorable logic of historical events sometimes forced the representatives of the capitulating line to talk and act against their own convictions. This happened to Trotsky in the period of the uprising, when, as Chairman of the Petersburg Soviet, forced by the objective development of the Revolution, he had to pursue the Leninist tactics of uprising. At the meeting of the Petrograd Soviet of October 25 [November 7], faced with the accomplished fact of the victory of the rising people, Trotsky was compelled to answer in the spirit of Leninist tactics. . . . 'The will of the All-Russian Congress of Soviets has been anticipated by the rising of the Petrograd workers and soldiers.' He was compelled to say

* I am indebted for this information to Mr. Leopold Labedz, an editor of *Soviet Survey,* who made a comparison of the latest edition with the original text.

what was contrary to what he had said two days before at the Plenum of the Petrograd Soviet on October 23. . . .

Thus John Reed's spirit still evades official control and goes its own way. It will escape the bonds of such foot-notes to stir the young in Russia, as it has outlasted a quarter of a century—actually twenty-seven years—of suppression. It lives on in the record of his rebellious, adventurous, generously romantic, perpetually immature, brave poet's life. And in his colorful *Insurgent Mexico*. And, at its enduring best, in *Ten Days That Shook the World*.

* * * *

The present edition follows the first edition as prepared by John Reed personally and published early in 1919, with the following changes:

1. It includes Lenin's foreword, written by him in 1919, but first published in America as a foreword to the edition of 1926.

2. I have corrected obvious typographical errors and errors in Russian; made more self-consistent the trans-literation of Russian names, corrected errors in the initials of identifiable personages. But where Reed has mistakenly substituted one personage for another as, for example, where he attributes a speech made by Ehrlich of the Bund to Abramovich of the same organization, his text has been kept, the correction being indicated in a footnote. Where Reed's transcription of a name differs from that which has become subsequently familiar, I have used the more familiar transcription. With less well known people, where his spelling of Russian names differs from the stand-ard of the Library of Congress now generally followed in America, but his transliteration has an inner consistency of its own, I have generally retained Reed's spelling. Thus

his Tchernov, which follows the French method of trans-
literating, is here written Chernov, but from his Colpinno,
now generally written Kolpino, I have eliminated the
double *n*, but retained the *C* since it is just as logical for
pronunciation purposes as the more generally used *K*.

3. Most of Reed's footnotes to the first edition were
relegated to an appendix at the back of the book. For
greater convenience I have put them immediately after
the chapter to which they belong. Where Reed put brief
notes at the bottom of a page, that procedure has been
retained. Where I have ventured to add an occasional
clarifying footnote of my own, it is followed by the indication: "—*Ed.*"

FOREWORD

With the greatest interest and with never slackening attention I read John Reed's book, *Ten Days That Shook the World*. Unreservedly do I recommend it to the workers of the world. Here is a book which I should like to see published in millions of copies and translated into all languages. It gives a truthful and most vivid exposition of the events so significant to the comprehension of what really is the Proletarian Revolution and the Dictatorship of the Proletariat. These problems are widely discussed, but before one can accept or reject these ideas, he must understand the full significance of his decision. John Reed's book will undoubtedly help to clear this question, which is the fundamental problem of the international labor movement.

V. I. LENIN

End of 1919 *

* Lenin wrote this foreword after reading a presentation copy which Reed gave him during the year 1919. It was first published in Russian in the edition of 1923, and in English in 1926. But as early as December 16, 1924, presumably under pressure from Stalin and his associates, Krupskaya (Lenin's wife) published a statement in *Pravda* to the effect that the book contained "legends and inaccuracies" and had been praised by Lenin only because it gave an admirable picture of the spirit of the revolution.—*Ed.*

AUTHOR'S PREFACE

This book is a slice of intensified history—history as I saw it. It does not pretend to be anything but a detailed account of the November Revolution, when the Bolsheviki, at the head of the workers and soldiers, seized the state powei of Russia and placed it in the hands of the Soviets.

Naturally most of it deals with "Red Petrograd," the capital and heart of the insurrection. But the reader must realize that what took place in Petrograd was almost exactly duplicated, with greater or lesser intensity, at different intervals of time, all over Russia.

In this book, the first of several which I am writing, I must confine myself to a chronicle of those events which I myself observed and experienced, and those supported by reliable evidence; preceded by two chapters briefly outlining the background and causes of the November Revolution. I am aware that these two chapters make difficult reading, but they are essential to an understanding of what follows.

Many questions will suggest themselves to the mind of the reader. What is Bolshevism? What kind of a governmental structure did the Bolsheviki set up? If the Bolsheviki championed the Constituent Assembly before the November Revolution, why did they disperse it by force of arms afterward? And if the bourgeoisie opposed the Constituent Assembly until the danger of Bolshevism became apparent, why did they champion it afterward?

These and many other questions cannot be answered here. In another volume, *Kornilov to Brest-Litovsk*,* I

* Reed never finished or never published this work.—*Ed.*

trace the course of the Revolution up to and including the
German peace. There I explain the origin and functions of
the Revolutionary organisations, the evolution of popular
sentiment, the dissolution of the Constituent Assembly,
the structure of the Soviet state, and the course and outcome of the Brest-Litovsk negotiations. . . .

In considering the rise of the Bolsheviki it is necessary
to understand that Russian economic life and the Russian
army were not disorganised on November 7th, 1917, but
many months before, as the logical result of a process
which began as far back as 1915. The corrupt reactionaries in control of the Tsar's Court deliberately undertook
to wreck Russia in order to make a separate peace with
Germany. The lack of arms on the front, which had
caused the great retreat of the summer of 1915, the lack
of food in the army and in the great cities, the break-down
of manufactures and transportation in 1916—all these we
know now were part of a gigantic campaign of sabotage.[1]
This was halted just in time by the March Revolution.

For the first few months of the new régime, in spite of
the confusion incident upon a great Revolution, when one
hundred and sixty millions of the world's most oppressed
peoples suddenly achieved liberty, both the internal situation and the combative power of the army actually improved.

But the "honeymoon" was short. The propertied classes
wanted merely a political revolution, which would take
the power from the Tsar and give it to them. They wanted
Russia to be a constitutional Republic, like France or the
United States; or a constitutional Monarchy, like England.
On the other hand, the masses of the people wanted real
industrial and agrarian democracy.

William English Walling, in his book, *Russia's Message,* an account of the Revolution of 1905, describes

very well the state of mind of the Russian workers, who were later to support Bolshevism almost unanimously.

They (the working people) saw it was possible that even under a free Government, if it fell into the hands of other social classes, they might still continue to starve. . . .

The Russian workman is revolutionary, but he is neither violent, dogmatic, nor unintelligent. He is ready for barricades, but he has studied them, and alone of the workers of the world he has learned about them from actual experience. He is ready and willing to fight his oppressor, the capitalist class, to a finish. But he does not ignore the existence of other classes. He merely asks that the other classes take one side or the other in the bitter conflict that draws near. . . .

They (the workers) were all agreed that our (American) political institutions were preferable to their own, but they were not very anxious to exchange one despot for another (i.e., the capitalist class). . . .

The workingmen of Russia did not have themselves shot down, executed by hundreds in Moscow, Riga and Odessa, imprisoned by thousands in every Russian jail, and exiled to the deserts and the arctic regions, in exchange for the doubtful privileges of the workingmen of Goldfields and Cripple Creek. . . .

And so developed in Russia, in the midst of a foreign war, the Social Revolution on top of the Political Revolution, culminating in the triumph of Bolshevism.

Mr. A. J. Sack, director in this country of the Russian Information Bureau, which opposes the Soviet Government, has this to say in his book, *The Birth of the Russian Democracy*:

The Bolsheviks organised their own cabinet, with Nicholas[2] Lenin as Premier and Leon Trotsky—Minister of Foreign Affairs. The inevitability of their coming into power became evident almost immediately after the March Revolution. The history of the Bolsheviki, after the Revolution, is a history of their steady growth. . . .

Foreigners, and Americans especially, frequently emphasise the "ignorance" of the Russian workers. It is true they lacked the political experience of the peoples of the West, but they were very well trained in voluntary organisation. In 1917 there were more than twelve million members of the Russian consumers' Cooperative societies; and the Soviets themselves are a wonderful demonstration of their organising genius. Moreover, there is probably not a people in the world so well educated in Socialist theory and its practical application.

William English Walling thus characterises them:

The Russian working people are for the most part able to read and write. For many years the country has been in such a disturbed condition that they have had the advantage of leadership not only of intelligent individuals in their midst, but of a large part of the equally revolutionary educated class, who have turned to the working people with their ideas for the political and social regeneration of Russia. . . .

Many writers explain their hostility to the Soviet Government by arguing that the last phase of the Russian Revolution was simply a struggle of the "respectable" elements against the brutal attacks of Bolshevism. However, it was the propertied classes, who, when they realised the growth in power of the popular revolutionary organisations, undertook to destroy them and to halt the Revolution. To this end the propertied classes finally resorted to desperate measures. In order to wreck the Kerensky Ministry and the Soviets, transportation was disorganised and internal troubles provoked; to crush the Factory-Shop

Committees, plants were shut down, and fuel and raw materials diverted; to break the Army Committees at the
front, capital punishment was restored and military defeat
connived at.[3]

This was all excellent fuel for the Bolshevik fire. The
Bolsheviki retorted by preaching the class war, and by
asserting the supremacy of the Soviets.

Between these two extremes, with the other factions
which whole-heartedly or half-heartedly supported them,
were the so-called "moderate" Socialists, the Mensheviki
and Socialist Revolutionaries, and several smaller parties.
These groups were also attacked by the propertied classes,
but their power of resistance was crippled by their theories.

Roughly, the Mensheviki and Socialist Revolutionaries[4]
believed that Russia was not economically ripe for a social
revolution—that only a *political* revolution was possible.
According to their interpretation, the Russian masses were
not educated enough to take over the power; any attempt
to do so would inevitably bring on a reaction, by means of
which some ruthless opportunist might restore the old
régime. And so it followed that when the "moderate"
Socialists were forced to assume the power, they were
afraid to use it.

They believed that Russia must pass through the stages
of political and economic development known to Western
Europe, and emerge at last, with the rest of the world,
into full-fledged Socialism. Naturally, therefore, they
agreed with the propertied classes that Russia must first
be a parliamentary state—though with some improve-
ments on the Western democracies. As a consequence,
they insisted upon the collaboration of the propertied
classes in the Government.

From this it was an easy step to supporting them. The
"moderate" Socialists needed the bourgeoisie. But the

bourgeoisie did not need the "moderate" Socialists. So it resulted in the Socialist Ministers, being obliged to give way, little by little, on their entire program, while the propertied classes grew more and more insistent.

And at the end, when the Bolsheviki upset the whole hollow compromise, the Mensheviki and Socialist Revolutionaries found themselves fighting on the side of the propertied classes. . . . In almost every country in the world to-day the same phenomenon is visible.

Instead of being a destructive force, it seems to me that the Bolsheviki were the only party in Russia with a constructive program and the power to impose it on the country. If they had not succeeded to the Government when they did, there is little doubt in my mind that the armies of Imperial Germany would have been in Petrograd and Moscow in December, and Russia would again be ridden by a Tsar. . . .

It is still fashionable, after a whole year of the Soviet Government, to speak of the Bolshevik insurrection as an "adventure." Adventure it was, and one of the most marvelous mankind ever embarked upon, sweeping into history at the head of the toiling masses, and staking everything on their vast and simple desires. Already the machinery had been set up by which the land of the great estates could be distributed among the peasants. The Factory-Shop Committees and the Trade Unions were there to put into operation workers' control of industry. In every village, town, city, district and province there were Soviets of Workers', Soldiers' and Peasants' Deputies, prepared to assume the task of local administration.

No matter what one thinks of Bolshevism, it is undeniable that the Russian Revolution is one of the great events of human history, and the rise of the Bolsheviki a phenomenon of world-wide importance. Just as historians search the records for the minutest details of the story of the Paris Commune, so they will want to know what happened in Petrograd in November, 1917, the spirit which animated the people, and how the leaders looked, talked and acted. It is with this in view that I have written this book.

In the struggle my sympathies were not neutral. But in telling the story of those great days I have tried to see events with the eye of a conscientious reporter, interested in setting down the truth.

J. R.

New York, January 1st, 1919.

EDITOR'S NOTES
TO PREFACE

1. When the Tsarist archives and the diaries and letters of the Tsar, the Tsaritsa, and the members of the Royal Household were published after 1917, the widely held view of treason at court was proved false, and the "deliberate undertaking to wreck Russia" even more so. Not a "gigantic campaign of sabotage" but the ineptness of key officials, distrust at court of public initiative from below, and the inadequacy of the political and economic structure for the strains of total war, caused the growing tension and breakdown.—*Ed.*

2. Lenin never used the name *"Nicholas."* He signed many pseudonyms in the course of his long battle with the police, and among them was *N. Lenin,* and sometimes *N.N.* But *N* in Russia, and in many other European lands, is a common sign that the name used is a pseudonym, as if to say *Not Lenin.* When Lenin seized power it occurred to some journalist to say that there was a new Nicholas on the throne in place of Nicholas II, and the legend took hold.—*Ed.*

3. Elaborate investigations first under the Provisional Government and then under Lenin yielded no evidence that "military defeat was connived at." The demand of the officers for the restoration of the death penalty was aimed at desertion and indiscipline under fire, but conditions at the front and in the rear, too, were such that the provision remained a dead letter. The death penalty was again revoked by the Provisional Government shortly before its fall.—*Ed.*

4. Reed is mistaken as to the Socialist Revolutionaries. They put much more emphasis on a social revolution, particularly the redistribution of the land, than on political forms, and historically their party diverged from the Marxists in their belief that Russia could go "directly" to socialism with-

out reaching any particular prior level of capitalist or bourgeois political and economic development. The argument
about "ripeness" was largely a discussion among the Marxists,
and until Russia entered the war, Lenin tended to repeat the
Russian Marxist dogma that Russia was neither economically,
nor politically, nor culturally ripe for anything but a "bourgeois" revolution. Traces of this dogma and of his wrestling
with it remain in his writings to the end.—*Ed.*

NOTES AND

EXPLANATIONS

To the average reader the multiplicity of Russian organisations—political groups, Committees and Central Committees, Soviets, Dumas and Unions—will prove extremely confusing. For this reason I am giving here a few brief definitions and explanations.

Political Parties

In the elections to the Constituent Assembly, there were seventeen tickets in Petrograd, and in some of the provincial towns as many as forty; but the following summary of the aims and composition of political parties is limited to the groups and factions mentioned in this book. Only the essence of their programmes and the general character of their constituencies can be noticed. . . .

1. *Monarchists,* of various shades, *Octobrists,* etc. These once-powerful factions no longer existed openly; they either worked underground, or their members joined the *Cadets,* as the *Cadets* came by degrees to stand for their political programme. Representatives in this book, Rodzianko, Shulgin.

2. *Cadets.* So-called from the initials of its name, Constitutional Democrats. Its official name is "Party of the People's Freedom." Under the Tsar composed of Liberals from the propertied classes, the *Cadets* were the great party of *political* reform, roughly corresponding to the Progressive Party in America. When the Revolution broke

out in March 1917, the *Cadets* formed the first Provisional Government. The *Cadet* Ministry was overthrown in April because it declared itself in favour of Allied imperialistic aims, including the imperialistic aims of the Tsar's Government. As the Revolution became more and more a *social economic* Revolution, the *Cadets* grew more and more conservative. Its representatives in this book are: Miliukov, Vinaver, Shatsky.

2a. *Group of Public Men.* After the *Cadets* had become unpopular through their relations with the Kornilov counter-revolution, the *Group of Public Men* was formed in Moscow. Delegates from the *Group of Public Men* were given portfolios in the last Kerensky Cabinet. The *Group* declared itself non-partisan, although its intellectual leaders were men like Rodzianko and Shulgin. It was composed of the more "modern" bankers, merchants and manufacturers, who were intelligent enough to realise that the Soviets must be fought by their own weapon—economic organisation. Typical of the *Group:* Lianozov, Konovalov.

3. *Populist Socialists,* or *Trudoviki* (Labour Group). Numerically a small party, composed of cautious intellectuals, the leaders of the Cooperative societies, and conservative peasants. Professing to be Socialists, the *Populists* really supported the interests of the petty bourgeoisie— clerks, shopkeepers, etc. By direct descent, inheritors of the compromising tradition of the Labour Group in the Fourth Imperial Duma, which was composed largely of peasant representatives. Kerensky was the leader of the *Trudoviki* in the Imperial Duma when the Revolution of March, 1917, broke out. The *Populist Socialists* are a nationalistic party. Their representatives in this book are: Peshekhonov, Chaikovsky.

4. *Russian Social Democratic Labour Party.* Originally Marxian Socialists. At a party congress held in 1903, the

party split, on the question of tactics, into two factions—
the Majority (Bolshinstvo), and the Minority (Men-
shinstvo). From this sprang the names "Bolsheviki" and
"Mensheviki"—"members of the majority" and "members
of the minority." These two wings became two separate
parties, both calling themselves "Russian Social Democratic Labour Party," and both professing to be Marxians.
Since the Revolution of 1905 the Bolsheviki were really
the minority, becoming again the majority in September,
1917.

a. *Mensheviki.* This party includes all shades of Socialists who believe that society must progress by natural
evolution toward Socialism, and that the working-class
must conquer political power first. Also a nationalistic
party.* This was the party of the Socialist intellectuals,
which means: all the means of education having been in
the hands of the propertied classes, the intellectuals instinctively reacted to their training, and took the side of
the propertied classes. Among their representatives in this
book are: Dan, Lieber, Tseretelli.

b. *Mensheviki Internationalists.* The radical wing of the
Mensheviki, internationalists and opposed to all coalition
with the propertied classes; yet unwilling to break loose
from the conservative Mensheviki, and opposed to the
dictatorship of the working-class advocated by the Bolsheviki. Trotsky was long a member of this group. Among
their leaders: Martov, Martynov.

c. *Bolsheviki.* Now call themselves the *Communist
Party,* in order to emphasise their complete separation
from the tradition of "moderate" or "parliamentary"
Socialism, which dominates the Mensheviki and the so-

* Like the socialist parties generally, the Mensheviki were "internationalists." During the war, and especially after the downfall of the Tsar, their
majority became "defensist," i.e., in favor of the defense of Russia. This is
presumably what Reed means by the words, "also a nationalistic party."—*Ed.*

called Majority Socialists in all countries. The *Bolsheviki* proposed immediate proletarian insurrection, and seizure of the reins of Government, in order to hasten the coming of Socialism by forcibly taking over industry, land, natural resources and financial institutions. This party expresses the desires chiefly of the factory workers, but also of a large section of the poor peasants. The name "Bolshevik" can *not* be translated by "Maximalist." The Maximalists are a separate group. (See paragraph 5b). Among the leaders: Lenin, Trotsky, Lunacharsky.

d. *United Social Democrats Internationalists.* Also called the *Novaya Zhizn* (New Life) group, from the name of the very influential newspaper which was its organ. A little group of intellectuals with a very small following among the working-class, except the personal following of Maxim Gorky, its leader. Intellectuals, with almost the same programme as the *Mensheviki Internationalists,* except that the *Novaya Zhizn* group refused to be tied to either of the two great factions. Opposed the Bolshevik tactics, but remained in the Soviet Government. Other representatives in this book: Avilov, Kramarov.

e. *Yedinstvo.* A very small and dwindling group, composed almost entirely of the personal following of Plekhanov, one of the pioneers of the Russian Social Democratic movement in the 80's, and its greatest theoretician. Now an old man, Plekhanov was extremely patriotic, too conservative even for the Mensheviki. After the Bolshevik *coup d'etat, Yedinstvo* disappeared.

5. *Socialist Revolutionary party.* Called *Essaires* from the initials of their name. Originally the revolutionary party of the peasants, the party of the Fighting Organisations—the Terrorists. After the March Revolution, it was joined by many who had never been Socialists. At that time it stood for the abolition of private property in land

only, the owners to be compensated in some fashion.*
Finally the increasing revolutionary feeling of peasants
forced the *Essaires* to abandon the "compensation" clause,
and led to the younger and more fiery intellectuals breaking off from the main party in the fall of 1917 and forming
a new party, the *Left Socialist Revolutionary party.* The
Essaires, who were afterward always called by the radical
groups *"Right Socialist Revolutionaries,"* adopted the political attitude of the Mensheviki, and worked together
with them. They finally came to represent the wealthier
peasants, the intellectuals, and the politically uneducated
populations of remote rural districts. Among them there
was, however, a wider difference of shades of political and
economic opinion than among the Mensheviki. Among
their leaders mentioned in these pages: Avksentiev, Gotz,
Kerensky, Chernov, "Babushka" Breshkovskaya.

a. *Left Socialist Revolutionaries.* Although theoretically
sharing the Bolshevik programme of dictatorship of the
working-class, at first were reluctant to follow the ruthless
Bolshevik tactics. However, the *Left Socialist Revolutionaries* remained in the Soviet Government, sharing the
Cabinet portfolios, especially that of Agriculture. They
withdrew from the Government several times, but always
returned. As the peasants left the ranks of the *Essaires*
in increasing numbers, they joined the *Left Socialist Revolutionary party,* which became the great peasant party
supporting the Soviet Government standing for confiscation without compensation of the great landed estates, and

* No faction of the Socialist Revolutionary Party was in favor of com-
pensating the landowners. In fact, no socialist party favored compensation.
Only the Cadets (Liberal Democrats), who also favored an expropriation of
the landowners' land, added the words "with just compensation." The very
decree which Lenin finally promulgated concerning the land was taken from
the program of the Socialist Revolutionary Party, as he acknowledged on
November 8 in presenting it to the Second Congress of Soviets the day after
he had seized power.—*Ed.*

their disposition by the peasants themselves. Among the leaders: Spiridonova, Karelin, Kamkov, Kalagayev.

b. *Maximalists.* An off-shoot of the *Socialist Revolutionary party* in the Revolution of 1905, when it was a powerful peasant movement, demanding the immediate application of the maximum Socialist programme. Now an insignificant group of peasant anarchists.

Parliamentary Procedure

Russian meetings and conventions are organised after the continental model rather than our own. The first action is usually the election of officers and the *presidium*.

The *presidium* is a presiding committee, composed of representatives of the groups and political factions represented in the assembly, in proportion to their numbers. The *presidium* arranges the Order of Business, and its members can be called upon by the President to take the chair *pro tem.*

Each question (*vopros*) is stated in a general way and then debated, and at the close of the debate resolutions are submitted by the different factions, and each one voted on separately. The Order of Business can be, and usually is, smashed to pieces in the first half hour. On the plea of "emergency," which the crowd almost always grants, anybody from the floor can get up and say anything on any subject. The crowd controls the meeting, practically the only functions of the speaker being to keep order by ringing a little bell, and to recognise speakers. Almost all the real work of the session is done in caucuses of the different groups and political factions, which almost always cast their votes in a body and are represented by floor-leaders. The result is, however, that at every important new point, or vote, the session takes a recess to enable the different groups and political factions to hold a caucus.

The crowd is extremely noisy, cheering or heckling speakers, overriding the plans of the *presidium*. Among the customary cries are: "*Prosim!* Please! Go on!" "*Pravilno!*" or "*Eto vierno!* That's true! Right!" "*Dovolno!* Enough!" "*Doloi!* Down with him!" "*Pozor!* Shame!" and "*Teeshe!* Silence! Not so noisy!"

Popular Organizations

1. *Soviet*. The word *soviet* means "council." Under the Tsar the Imperial Council of State was called *Gosudarstvennyi Soviet*. Since the Revolution, however, the term *Soviet* has come to be associated with a certain type of parliament elected by members of working-class economic organisations—the Soviet of Workers', of Soldiers', or of Peasants' Deputies. I have therefore limited the word to these bodies, and wherever else it occurs I have translated it "Council."

Besides the local *Soviets,* elected in every city, town and village of Russia—and in large cities, also Ward (*Raionny*) *Soviets*—there are also the *oblastnoi* or *gubiernsky* (district or provincial) *Soviets,* and the Central Executive Committee of the All-Russian *Soviets* in the capital, called from its initials *Tsay-ee-kah.** (See below, "Central Committees.")

Almost everywhere the *Soviets* of Workers' and of Soldiers' Deputies combined very soon after the March Revolution. In special matters concerning their peculiar interests, however, the Workers' and the Soldiers' Sections continued to meet separately. The *Soviets* of Peasants' Deputies did not join the other two until after the

* The Russians did not call the Central Executive Committee of the Soviets *Tsay-ee-kah* but *Tsik,* and after the first national Soviet Congress was held and an all-Russian Central Executive formed, they called it VTsik. However, since Reed has used *Tsay-ee-kah* consistently throughout, it has been left so.—*Ed.*

Bolshevik *coup d'etat*. They, too, were organised like the
workers and soldiers, with an Executive Committee of the
All-Russian Peasants' *Soviets* in the capital.

2. *Trade Unions*. Although mostly industrial in form,
the Russian labour unions were still called Trade
Unions,* and at the time of the Bolshevik Revolution
had from three to four million members. These Unions
were also organised in an All-Russian body, a sort of
Russian Federation of Labour, which had its Central
Executive Committee in the capital.

3. *Factory-Shop Committees*. These were spontaneous
organisations created in the factories by the workers in
their attempt to control industry, taking advantage of the
administrative break-down incident upon the Revolution.
Their function was by revolutionary action to take over
and run the factories. The *Factory-Shop Committees* also
had their All-Russian organisation, with a Central Committee at Petrograd, which co-operated with the Trade
Unions.**

4. *Dumas*. The word *duma* means roughly "delibera-
tive body." The old Imperial Duma, which persisted six
months after the Revolution, in a democratised form, died
a natural death in September, 1917. The *City Duma* referred to in this book was the reorganised Municipal Council, often called "Municipal Self-Government." It was
elected by direct and secret ballot, and its only reason for
failure to hold the masses during the Bolshevik Revolu-

---

* The Russian unions were not called Trade Unions but Professional
Unions, or, for short, *Profsoyuzy*. This was because the first public unions
formed in the 1905 period were unions of professional men, professors,
doctors, lawyers, etc., and the labor unions adopted the same name.—*Ed.*

** Factory-Shop Committees were set up on Bolshevik initiative to offset
the weakness of the Bolsheviks in the organized labor movement. As Bolshevism began to gain strength in some unions in the autumn of 1917, they
neglected the task of setting up a functioning all-Russian Shop Committee
organization. The Shop Committees did not as a rule cooperate with the
unions but were used to bypass or to split them.—*Ed.*

tion was the general decline in influence of all purely *political* representation in the face of the growing power of organisations based on *economic* groups.

5. *Zemstvos*. May be roughly translated "county councils." Under the Tsar semi-political, semi-social bodies with very little administrative power, developed and controlled largely by intellectual Liberals among the landowning classes. Their most important function was education and social service among the peasants. During the war the *Zemstvos* gradually took over the entire feeding and clothing of the Russian Army, as well as the buying from foreign countries, and work among the soldiers generally corresponding to the work of the American Y. M. C. A. at the Front.* After the March Revolution the *Zemstvos* were democratized, with a view to making them the organs of local government in the rural districts. But like the *City Dumas,* they could not compete with the *Soviets*.

6. *Cooperatives*. These were the workers' and peasants' Consumers' Cooperative societies, which had several million members all over Russia before the Revolution. Founded by Liberals and "moderate" Socialists, the Cooperative movement was not supported by the revolutionary Socialist groups, because it was a substitute for the complete transference of means of production and distribution into the hands of the workers. After the March Revolution the *Cooperatives* spread rapidly, and were dominated by Populist Socialists, Mensheviki and Socialist Revolutionaries, and acted as a conservative political force until the Bolshevik Revolution. However, it was the *Cooperatives* which fed Russia when the old structure of commerce and transportation collapsed.

* The Zemstvos and other public committees supplemented, but did not "take over" the work of feeding and clothing the Russian Army, nor that of getting its equipment abroad.—*Ed.*

7. *Army Committees.* The *Army Committees* were formed by the soldiers at the front to combat the reactionary influence of the old regime officers. Every company, regiment, brigade, division and corps had its committee, over all of which was elected the *Army Committee.* The *Central Army Committee* cooperated with the General Staff. The administrative break-down in the army incident upon the Revolution threw upon the shoulders of the *Army Committees* most of the work of the Quartermaster's Department, and in some cases, even the command of troops.

8. *Fleet Committees.* The corresponding organisations in the Navy.

Central Committees

In the spring and summer of 1917, All-Russian conventions of every sort of organisation were held at Petrograd. There were national congresses of Workers', Soldiers' and Peasants' Soviets, Trade Unions, Factory-Shop Committees, Army and Fleet Committees—besides every branch of the military and naval service, Cooperatives, Nationalities, etc. Each of these conventions elected a Central Committee, or a Central Executive Committee, to guard its particular interests at the seat of Government. As the Provisional Government grew weaker, these Central Committees were forced to assume more and more administrative powers.

The most important Central Committees mentioned in this book are:

Union of Unions. During the Revolution of 1905, Professor Miliukov and other Liberals established unions of professional men—doctors, lawyers, physicians, etc. These were united under one central organisation, the *Union of Unions.* In 1905 the *Union of Unions* acted with the revolutionary democracy; in 1917, however, the *Union of Unions* opposed the Bolshevik uprising, and united the Government employees who went on strike against the authority of the Soviets.

Tsay-ee-kah. All-Russian Central Executive Committee of the Soviets of Workers' and Soldiers' Deputies. So called from the initials of its name.

Tsentroflot. "Centre-Fleet"—the Central Fleet Committee.

Vikzhel. All-Russian Central Committee of the Railway Workers' Union. So called from the initials of its name.

Other Organizations

Red Guards. The armed factory workers of Russia. The *Red Guards* were first formed during the Revolution of 1905, and sprang into existence again in the days of March, 1917, when a force was needed to keep order in the city. At that time they were armed, and all efforts of the Provisional Government to disarm them were more or less unsuccessful. At every great crisis in the Revolution the *Red Guards* appeared on the streets, untrained and undisciplined, but full of Revolutionary zeal.

White Guards. Bourgeois volunteers, who emerged in the last stages of the Revolution, to defend private property from the Bolshevik attempt to abolish it. A great many of them were University students.

Tekhintsi. The so-called "Savage Division" in the army, made up of Mohametan tribesmen from Central Asia, and personally devoted to General Kornilov. The *Tekhintsi* were noted for their blind obedience and their savage cruelty in warfare.*

* The *Tekhintsi* and the Savage Division were not identical, although both were from the Caucasus and both under the direct command of General Kornilov. Although Reed uses them interchangeably in his work, it has not been necessary to determine which he meant in each case as the general picture is not altered by substituting the one for the other.—*Ed.*

Death Battalions. Or *Shock Battalions.* The Women's Battalion is known to the world as the *Death Battalion,* but there were many *Death Battalions* composed of men. These were formed in the summer of 1917 by Kerensky, for the purpose of strengthening the discipline and combative fire of the army by heroic example. The *Death Battalions* were composed mostly of intense young patriots. These came for the most part from among the sons of the propertied classes.

Union of Officers. An organisation formed among the reactionary officers in the army to combat politically the growing power of the Army Committees.

Knights of St. George. The Cross of St. George was awarded for distinguished action in battle. Its holder automatically became a *"Knight of St. George."* The predominant influence in the organisation was that of the supporters of the military idea.

Peasants' Union. In 1905, the *Peasants' Union* was a revolutionary peasants' organisation. In 1917, however, it had become the political expression of the more prosperous peasants, to fight the growing power and revolutionary aims of the Soviets of Peasants' Deputies.*

Chronology and Spelling

I have adopted in this book our Calendar throughout, instead of the former Russian Calendar, which was thirteen days earlier.

* The Peasants' Unions were set up in the 1905 period by Socialist Revolutionaries as the popular mass organization of the peasants under the slogan "Land through Freedom; Freedom through Land." They were later suppressed or died as the 1905-07 turmoil came to an end. When an attempt was made to revive them in 1917 by rural moderates, the Socialist Revolutionary Party set up Peasant Soviets which easily reduced the new Peasant Unions to nullity. The Peasant Soviets remained the undisputed domain of the Socialist Revolutionary Party until it and the Peasant Soviet Congress itself were split with Bolshevik encouragement after Lenin took power.—*Ed.*

In the spelling of Russian names and words, I have made no attempt to follow any scientific rules for transliteration, but have tried to give the spelling which would lead the English-speaking reader to the simplest approximation of their pronunciation.

Sources

Much of the material in this book is from my own notes. I have also relied, however, upon a heterogeneous file of several hundred assorted Russian newspapers, covering almost every day of the time described, of files of the English paper, the *Russian Daily News,* and of the two French papers, *Journal de Russie* and *Entente*. But far more valuable than these is the *Bulletin de la Presse* issued daily by the French Information Bureau in Petrograd, which reports all important happenings, speeches and the comment of the Russian press. Of this I have an almost complete file from the spring of 1917 to the end of January, 1918.

Besides the foregoing, I have in my possession almost every proclamation, decree and announcement posted on the walls of Petrograd from the middle of September, 1917, to the end of January, 1918. Also the official publication of all Government decrees and orders, and the official Government publication of the secret treaties and other documents discovered in the Ministry of Foreign Affairs when the Bolsheviki took it over.

CHAPTER I

BACKGROUND

Toward the end of September, 1917, an alien Professor of Sociology visiting Russia came to see me in Petrograd. He had been informed by business men and intellectuals that the Revolution was slowing down. The Professor wrote an article about it, and then travelled around the country, visiting factory towns and peasant communities—where, to his astonishment, the Revolution seemed to be speeding up. Among the wage-earners and the land-working people it was common to hear talk of "all land to the peasants, all factories to the workers." If the Professor had visited the front, he would have heard the whole Army talking Peace. . . .

The Professor was puzzled, but he need not have been; both observations were correct. The property-owning classes were becoming more conservative, the masses of the people more radical.

There was a feeling among business men and the *intelligentsia* generally that the Revolution had gone quite far enough, and lasted too long; that things should settle down. This sentiment was shared by the dominant "moderate" Socialist groups, the *oborontsi*[1] Mensheviki and Socialist Revolutionaries, who supported the Provisional Government of Kerensky.

[1] Footnote references will be found in "Notes" at end of each chapter.

On October 14th the official organ of the "moderate" Socialists said:

The drama of Revolution has two acts; the destruction of the old régime and the creation of the new one. The first act has lasted long enough. Now it is time to go on to the second, and to play it as rapidly as possible. As a great revolutionist put it, "Let us hasten, friends, to terminate the Revolution. He who makes it last too long will not gather the fruits. . . ."

Among the worker, soldier and peasant masses, however, there was a stubborn feeling that the "first act" was not yet played out. On the front the Army Committees were always running foul of officers who could not get used to treating their men like human beings; in the rear the Land Committees elected by the peasants were being jailed for trying to carry out Government regulations concerning the land; and the workmen[2] in the factories were fighting black-lists and lockouts. Nay, furthermore, returning political exiles were being excluded from the country as "undesirable" citizens; and in some cases, men who returned from abroad to their villages were prosecuted and imprisoned for revolutionary acts committed in 1905.*

To the multiform discontent of the people the "moderate" Socialists had one answer: Wait for the Constituent Assembly, which is to meet in December. But the masses were not satisfied with that. The Constituent Assembly was all well and good; but there were certain definite things for which the Russian Revolution had been made, and for which the revolutionary martyrs rotted in their stark Brotherhood Grave on Mars Field, that must be achieved Constituent Assembly or no Constituent Assembly: Peace,

---

* No political exiles were excluded from Russia after the Tsar fell, nor was any one prosecuted or imprisoned in 1917 for participation in the revolutionary movement of 1905.—*Ed.*

Land, and Workers' Control of Industry. The Constituent Assembly had been postponed and postponed—would probably be postponed again, until the people were calm enough—perhaps to modify their demands! At any rate, here were eight months of the Revolution gone, and little enough to show for it. . . .

Meanwhile the soldiers began to solve the peace question by simply deserting, the peasants burned manor-houses and took over the great estates, the workers sabotaged and struck. . . . Of course, as was natural, the manufacturers, land-owners and army officers exerted all their influence against any democratic compromise. . . .

The policy of the Provisional Government alternated between ineffective reforms and stern repressive measures. An edict from the Socialist Minister of Labour ordered all the Workers' Committees henceforth to meet only after working hours. Among the troops at the front, "agitators" of opposition political parties were arrested, radical newspapers closed down, and capital punishment applied—to revolutionary propagandists.[3] Attempts were made to disarm the Red Guard. Cossacks were sent to keep order in the provinces. . . .

These measures were supported by the "moderate" Socialists and their leaders in the Ministry, who considered it necessary to cooperate with the propertied classes. The people rapidly deserted them, and went over to the Bolsheviki, who stood for Peace, Land, and Workers' Control of Industry, and a Government of the working-class. In September, 1917, matters reached a crisis. Against the overwhelming sentiment of the country, Kerensky and the "moderate" Socialists succeeded in establishing a Government of Coalition with the propertied classes; and as a result, the Mensheviki and Socialist Revolutionaries lost the confidence of the people forever.

An article in *Rabochi Put* (Workers' Way)* about the middle of October, entitled "The Socialist Ministers," expressed the feeling of the masses of the people against the "moderate" Socialists:

Here is a list of their services.[4]

Tseretelli: disarmed the workmen with the assistance of General Polovtsev, checkmated the revolutionary soldiers, and approved of capital punishment in the army.

Skobelev: commenced by trying to tax the capitalists 100% of their profits,, and finished—and finished by an attempt to dissolve the Workers' Committees in the shops and factories.

Avksentiev: put several hundred peasants in prison, members of the Land Committees, and suppressed dozens of workers' and soldiers' newspapers.

Chernov: signed the "Imperial" manifest, ordering the dissolution of the Finnish Diet.

Savinkov: concluded an open alliance with General Kornilov. If this savior of the country was not able to betray Petrograd, it was due to reasons over which he had no control.

Zarudny: with the sanction of Alexinsky and Kerensky, put some of the best workers of the Revolution, soldiers and sailors, in prison.

Nikitin: acted as a vulgar policeman against the Railway Workers.

Kerenksy: it is better not to say anything about him. The list of his services is too long. . . .

A Congress of delegates of the Baltic Fleet, at Helsingfors, passed a resolution which began as follows:

We demand the immediate removal from the ranks of the Provisional Government of the "Socialist," the political adventurer—Kerensky, as one who is scandalising and ruining the great Revolution, and with it the revolutionary masses,

* Official organ of the Bolsheviks.—*Ed.*

by his shameless political blackmail on behalf of the bourgeoisie. . . .

The direct result of all this was the rise of the Bolsheviki. . . .

Since March, 1917, when the roaring torrents of workmen and soldiers beating upon the Tauride Palace compelled the reluctant Imperial Duma to assume the supreme
power in Russia, it was the masses of the people, workers,
soldiers and peasants, which forced every change in the
course of the Revolution. They hurled the Miliukov Ministry down; it was their Soviet which proclaimed to the world
the Russian peace terms—"No annexations, no indemnities, and the right of self-determination of peoples"; and
again, in July, it was the spontaneous rising of the un-
organised proletariat which once more stormed the Tauride
Palace, to demand that the Soviets take over the Government of Russia.

The Bolsheviki, then a small political sect, put themselves at the head of the movement. As a result of the
disastrous failure of the rising, public opinion turned
against them, and their leaderless hordes slunk back into
the Vyborg Quarter, which is Petrograd's *St. Antoine*.
Then followed a savage hunt of the Bolsheviki; hundreds
were imprisoned, among them Trotsky, Madame Kollontai
and Kamenev; Lenin and Zinoviev went into hiding, fugi-
tives from justice; the Bolshevik papers were suppressed.
Provocators and reactionaries raised the cry that the Bolsheviki were German agents, until people all over the world
believed it.

But the Provisional Government found itself unable
to substantiate its accusations; the documents proving pro-
German conspiracy were discovered to be forgeries;* and

* Part of the famous "Sisson Documents."

one by one the Bolsheviki were released from prison without trial, on nominal or no bail—until only six remained. The impotence and indecision of the ever-changing Provisional Government was an argument nobody could refute. The Bolsheviki raised again the slogan so dear to the masses, "All Power to the Soviets!"—and they were not merely self-seeking, for at that time the majority of the Soviets was "moderate" Socialist, their bitter enemy.

But more potent still, they took the crude, simple desires of the workers, soldiers and peasants, and from them built their immediate programme. And so, while the *oborontsi* Mensheviki and Socialist Revolutionaries involved themselves in compromise with the bourgeoisie, the Bolsheviki rapidly captured the Russian masses. In July they were hunted and despised; by September the metropolitan workmen, the sailors of the Baltic Fleet, and the soldiers, had been won almost entirely to their cause. The September municipal elections in the large cities[5] were significant; only 18 per cent of the returns were Menshevik and Socialist Revolutionary, against more than 70 per cent in June. . . .

There remains a phenomenon which puzzled foreign observers: the fact that the Central Executive Committees of the Soviets, the Central Army and Fleet Committees,* and the Central Committees of some of the Unions—notably, the Post and Telegraph Workers and the Railway Workers—opposed the Bolsheviki with the utmost violence. These Central Committees had all been elected in the middle of the summer, or even before, when the Mensheviki and Socialist Revolutionaries had an enormous following; and they delayed or prevented any new elections. Thus, according to the constitution of the Soviets of Workers' and Soldiers' Deputies, the All-Russian Congress *should have been called in September;* but the *Tsay-ee-*

* See Notes and Explanations.

*kah** would not call the meeting, on the ground that the Constituent Assembly was only two months away, at which time, they hinted, the Soviets would abdicate. Meanwhile, one by one, the Bolsheviki were winning in the local Soviets all over the country, in the Union branches and the ranks of the soldiers and sailors. The Peasants' Soviets remained still conservative, because in the sluggish rural districts political consciousness developed slowly, and the Socialist Revolutionary party had been for a generation the party which had agitated among the peasants. . . . But even among the peasants a revolutionary wing was forming. It showed itself clearly in October, when the left wing of the Socialist Revolutionaries split off, and formed a new political faction, the Left Socialist Revolutionaries.

At the same time there were signs everywhere that the forces of reaction were gaining confidence.[6] At the Troitsky Farce theatre in Petrograd, for example, a burlesque called *Sins of the Tsar* was interrupted by a group of Monarchists, who threatened to lynch the actors for "insulting the Emperor." Certain newspapers began to sigh for a "Russian Napoleon." It was the usual thing among bourgeois *intelligentsia* to refer to the Soviets of Workers' Deputies (Rabotchikh Deputatov) as *Sobatchikh* Deputatov—Dogs' Deputies.

On October 15th I had a conversation with a great Russian capitalist, Stepan Georgevitch Lianozov, known as the "Russian Rockefeller"—a Cadet by political faith.

"Revolution," he said, "is a sickness. Sooner or later the foreign powers must intervene here—as one would intervene to cure a sick child, and teach it how to walk. Of course it would be more or less improper, but the nations must realise the danger of Bolshevism in their own coun-

* See Notes and Explanations.

tries—such contagious ideas as 'proletarian dictatorship,' and 'world social revolution' . . . There is a chance that this intervention may not be necessary. Transportation is demoralised, the factories are closing down, and the Germans are advancing. Starvation and defeat may bring the Russian people to their senses. . . ."

Mr. Lianozov was emphatic in his opinion that whatever happened, it would be impossible for merchants and manufacturers to permit the existence of the workers' Shop Committees, or to allow the workers any share in the management of industry.

"As for the Bolsheviki, they will be done away with by one of two methods. The Government can evacuate Petrograd, then a state of siege declared, and the military commander of the district can deal with these gentlemen without legal formalities. . . . *Or if, for example, the Constituent Assembly manifests any Utopian tendencies, it can be dispersed by force of arms. . . .*"

Winter was coming on—the terrible Russian winter. I heard business men speak of it so: "Winter was always Russia's best friend. Perhaps now it will rid us of Revolution." On the freezing front miserable armies continued to starve and die, without enthusiasm. The railways were breaking down, food lessening, factories closing. The desperate masses cried out that the bourgeoisie was sabotaging the life of the people, causing defeat on the Front. Riga had been surrendered just after General Kornilov said publicly, "Must we pay with Riga the price of bringing the country to a sense of its duty?"

To Americans it is incredible that the class war should develop to such a pitch. But I have personally met officers on the Northern Front who frankly preferred military disaster to cooperation with the Soldiers' Committees. The secretary of the Petrograd branch of the Cadet party told

me that the break-down of the country's economic life
was part of a campaign to discredit the Revolution. An
Allied diplomat, whose name I promised not to mention,
confirmed this from his own knowledge. I know of certain
coal-mines near Kharkov which were fired and flooded by
their owners, of textile factories at Moscow whose engineers put the machinery out of order when they left, of
railroad officials caught by the workers in the act of crip-
pling locomotives. . . .

A large section of the propertied classes preferred the
Germans to the Revolution—even to the Provisional Government—and didn't hesitate to say so. In the Russian
household where I lived, the subject of conversation at the
dinner-table was almost invariably the coming of the
Germans, bringing "law and order." . . . One evening I
spent at the house of a Moscow merchant; during tea we
asked the eleven people at the table whether they preferred
"Wilhelm or the Bolsheviki." The vote was ten to one for
Wilhelm . . .

The speculators took advantage of the universal disorganisation to pile up fortunes, and to spend them in fantastic revelry or the corruption of Government officials.
Foodstuffs and fuel were hoarded, or secretly sent out of
the country to Sweden.* In the first four months of the
Revolution, for example, the reserve food-supplies were
almost openly looted from the great Municipal warehouses of Petrograd, until the two-years' provision of grain
had fallen to less than enough to feed the city for one
month. . . . According to the official report of the last
Minister of Supplies in the Provisional Government, coffee
was bought wholesale in Vladivostok for two rubles a
pound, and the consumer in Petrograd paid thirteen. In

* There is no evidence to support this inherently absurd charge that foodstuffs were sent to Sweden.—Ed.

all the stores of the large cities were tons of food and clothing; but only the rich could buy them.

In a provincial town I knew a merchant family turned speculator—*marodior* (bandit, ghoul) the Russians call it. The three sons had bribed their way out of military service. One gambled in foodstuffs. Another sold illegal gold from the Lena mines to mysterious parties in Finland. The third owned a controlling interest in a chocolate factory, which supplied the local Cooperative societies—on condition that the Cooperatives furnished him everything he needed. And so, while the masses of the people got a quarter pound of black bread on their bread cards, he had an abundance of white bread, sugar, tea, candy, cake and butter. . . . Yet when the soldiers at the front could no longer fight from cold, hunger and exhaustion, how indignantly did this family scream "Cowards!"—how "ashamed" they were "to be Russians" . . . When finally the Bolsheviki found and requisitioned vast hoarded stores of provisions, what "Robbers" they were.

Beneath all this external rottenness moved the old-time Dark Forces, unchanged since the fall of Nicholas the Second, secret still and very active. The agents of the notorious *Okhrana* still functioned, for and against the Tsar, for and against Kerensky—whoever would pay. . . . In the darkness, underground organisations of all sorts, such as the Black Hundreds, were busy attempting to restore reaction in some form or other.

In this atmosphere of corruption, of monstrous half-truths, one clear note sounded day after day, the deepening chorus of the Bolsheviki, "All Power to the Soviets! All power to the direct representatives of millions on millions of common workers, soldiers, peasants. Land, bread, an end to the senseless war, an end to secret diplomacy, speculation, treachery. . . . The Revolution is in danger, and with it the cause of the people all over the world!"

The struggle between the proletariat and the middle class, between the Soviets and the Government, which had begun in the first March days, was about to culminate. Having at one bound leaped from the Middle Ages into the twentieth century, Russia showed the startled world two systems of Revolution—the political and the social—in mortal combat.

What a revelation of the vitality of the Russian Revolution, after all these months of starvation and disillusionment! The bourgeoisie should have better known its Russia. Not for a long time in Russia will the "sickness" of Revolution have run its course. . . .

Looking back, Russia before the November insurrection seems of another age, almost incredibly conservative. So quickly did we adapt ourselves to the newer, swifter life; just as Russian politics swung bodily to the Left—until the Cadets were outlawed as "enemies of the people," Kerensky became a "counter-revolutionist," the "middle" Socialist leaders, Tseretelli, Dan, Lieber, Gotz and Avksentiev, were too reactionary for their following, and men like Victor Chernov, and even Maxim Gorky, belonged to the Right Wing. . . .

About the middle of December, 1917, a group of Socialist Revolutionary leaders paid a private visit to Sir George Buchanan, the British Ambassador, and implored him not to mention the fact that they had been there, because they were "considered too far Right."

"And to think," said Sir George. "One year ago my Government instructed me not to receive Miliukov, because he was so dangerously Left!"

September and October are the worst months of the Russian year—especially the Petrograd year. Under dull grey skies, in the shortening days, the rain fell drenching, incessant. The mud underfoot was deep, slippery and clinging, tracked everywhere by heavy boots, and worse than usual because of the complete break-down of the Municipal administration. Bitter damp winds rushed in from the Gulf of Finland, and the chill fog rolled through the streets. At night, for motives of economy as well as fear of Zeppelins, the street-lights were few and far between; in private dwellings and apartment-houses the electricity was turned on from six o'clock until midnight, with candles forty cents apiece and little kerosene to be had. It was dark from three in the afternoon to ten in the morning. Robberies and housebreakings increased. In apartment houses the men took turns at all-night guard duty, armed with loaded rifles. This was under the Provisional Government.

Week by week food became scarcer. The daily allowance of bread fell from a pound and a half to a pound, then three-quarters, half, and a quarter-pound. Toward the end there was a week without any bread at all. Sugar one was entitled to at the rate of two pounds a month—if one could get it at all, which was seldom. A bar of chocolate or a pound of tasteless candy cost anywhere from seven to ten rubles—at least a dollar. There was milk for about half the babies in the city; most hotels and private houses never saw it for months. In the fruit season apples and pears sold for a little less than a ruble apiece on the street-corner. . . .

For milk and bread and sugar and tobacco one had to stand in *queue* long hours in the chill rain. Coming home from an all-night meeting I have seen the *khvost* (tail) beginning to form before dawn, mostly women, some with babies in their arms. . . . Carlyle, in his *French Revolution,* has described the French people as distinguished above all others by their faculty of standing in *queue.* Russia had accustomed herself to the practice, begun in the reign of Nicholas the Blessed as long ago as 1915, and from then continued intermittently until the summer of 1917, when it settled down as the regular order of things. Think of the poorly-clad people standing on the iron-white streets of Petrograd whole days in the Russian winter! I have listened in the bread-lines, hearing the bitter, acrid note of discontent which from time to time burst up through the miraculous goodnature of the Russian crowd. . . .

Of course all the theatres were going every night, including Sundays. Karsavina appeared in a new Ballet at the Marinsky, all dance-loving Russia coming to see her. Shaliapin was singing. At the Alexandrinsky they were reviving Meyerhold's production of Tolstoy's "Death of Ivan the Terrible"; and at that performance I remember noticing a student of the Imperial School of Pages, in his dress uniform, who stood up correctly between the acts and faced the empty Imperial box, with its eagles all erased. . . . The *Krivoye Zerkalo* staged a sumptuous version of Schnitzler's "Reigen."

Although the Hermitage and other picture galleries had been evacuated to Moscow, there were weekly exhibitions of paintings. Hordes of the female *intelligentsia* went to hear lectures on Art, Literature and the Easy Philosophies. It was a particularly active season for Theosophists. And the Salvation Army, admitted to Russia for the first time in history, plastered the walls with announcements of gospel meetings, which amused and astounded Russian audiences. . . .

As in all such times, the petty conventional life of the

city went on, ignoring the Revolution as much as possible. The poets made verses—but not about the Revolution. The realistic painters painted scenes from mediæval Russian history—anything but the Revolution. Young ladies from the provinces came up to the capital to learn French and cultivate their voices, and the gay young beautiful officers wore their gold-trimmed crimson *bashlyki** and their elaborate Caucasian swords around the hotel lobbies. The ladies of the minor bureaucratic set took tea with each other in the afternoon, carrying each her little gold or silver or jewelled sugar-box, and half a loaf of bread in her muff, and wished that the Tsar were back, or that the Germans would come, or anything that would solve the servant problem. . . . The daughter of a friend of mine came home one afternoon in hysterics because the woman street-car conductor had called her "Comrade!"

All around them great Russia was in travail, bearing a new world. The servants one used to treat like animals and pay next to nothing, were getting independent. A pair of shoes cost more than a hundred rubles, and as wages averaged about thirty-five rubles a month the servants refused to stand in *queue* and wear out their shoes. But more than that. In the new Russia every man and woman could vote; there were working-class newspapers, saying new and startling things; there were the Soviets; and there were the Unions. The *izvoshchiki* (cab-drivers) had a Union; they were also represented in the Petrograd Soviet. The waiters and hotel-servants were organised, and refused tips. On the walls of restaurants they put up signs which read, "No tips taken here—" or, "Just because a man has to make his living waiting on table is no reason to insult him by offering him a tip!"

At the Front the soldiers fought out their fight with the

* A *bashlyk* is a Caucasian hood.—*Ed.*

officers, and learned self-government through their committees. In the factories those unique Russian organisations, the Factory-Shop Committees,* gained experience
and strength and a realisation of their historical mission
by combat with the old order. All Russia was learning to
read, and *reading*—politics, economics, history—because
the people wanted to *know*. . . . In every city, in most
towns, along the Front, each political faction had its newspaper—sometimes several. Hundreds of thousands of
pamphlets were distributed by thousands of organisations,
and poured into the armies, the villages, the factories, the
streets. The thirst for education, so long thwarted, burst
with the Revolution into a frenzy of expression. From
Smolny Institute alone, the first six months, went out
every day tons, car-loads, train-loads of literature, sat-
urating the land. Russia absorbed reading matter like hot
sand drinks water, insatiable. And it was not fables, falsi-
fied history, diluted religion, and the cheap fiction that
corrupts—but social and economic theories, philosophy,
the works of Tolstoy, Gogol, and Gorky. . . .

Then the Talk, beside which Carlyle's "flood of French
speech" was a mere trickle. Lectures, debates, speeches—
in theatres, circuses, school-houses, clubs, Soviet meeting-
rooms, Union headquarters, barracks. . . . Meetings in the
trenches at the Front, in village squares, factories. . . .
What a marvelous sight to see Putilovsky Zavod (the
Putilov factory) pour out its forty thousand to listen to
Social Democrats, Socialist Revolutionaries, Anarchists,
anybody, whatever they had to say, as long as they would
talk! For months in Petrograd, and all over Russia, every
street-corner was a public tribune. In railway trains,
street-cars, always the spurting up of impromptu debate,
everywhere. . . .

* See Notes and Explanations.

And the All-Russian Conferences and Congresses, drawing together the men of two continents—conventions of
Soviets, of Cooperatives, Zemstvos,* nationalities, priests,
peasants, political parties; the Democratic Conference, the
Moscow Conference, the Council of the Russian Republic.
There were always three or four conventions going on in
Petrograd. At every meeting, attempts to limit the time of
speakers voted down, and every man free to express the
thought that was in him. . . .

We came down to the front of the Twelfth Army, back
of Riga, where gaunt and bootless men sickened in the
mud of desperate trenches; and when they saw us they
started up, with their pinched faces and the flesh showing
blue through their torn clothing, demanding eagerly, "Did
you bring anything to *read*?"

What though the outward and visible signs of change
were many, what though the statue of Catharine the Great
before the Alexandrinsky Theatre bore a little red flag in
its hand, and others—somewhat faded—floated from all
public buildings; and the Imperial monograms and eagles
were either torn down or covered up; and in place of the
fierce *gorodovoye* (city police) a mild-mannered and unarmed citizen militia** patrolled the streets—still, there
were many quaint anachronisms.

For example, Peter the Great's *Tabel o Rangov*—Table
of Ranks—which he rivetted upon Russia with an iron
hand, still held sway. Almost everybody from the school-
boy up wore his prescribed uniform, with the insignia of
the Emperor on button and shoulder-strap. Along about
five o'clock in the afternoon the streets were full of sub-

---

* See Notes and Explanations.
** The militia carried side arms, which Reed does not seem to have noticed until later.—*Ed.*

dued old gentlemen in uniform, with portfolios, going home from work in the huge, barrack-like Ministries or Government institutions, calculating perhaps how great a mortality among their superiors would advance them to the coveted *chin* (rank) of Collegiate Assessor, or Privy Councillor, with the prospect of retirement on a comfortable pension, and possibly the Cross of St. Anne. . . .

There is the story of Senator Sokolov, who in full tide of Revolution came to a meeting of the Senate one day in civilian clothes, and was not admitted because he did not wear the prescribed livery of the Tsar's service!

It was against this background of a whole nation in ferment and disintegration that the pageant of the Rising of the Russian Masses unrolled. . . .

NOTES TO CHAPTER I

1

Oborontsi—"Defenders." All the "moderate" Socialist groups adopted or were given this name, because they consented to the continuation of the war under Allied leadership, on the ground that it was a war of National Defence. The Bolsheviki, the Left Socialist Revolutionaries, the Mensheviki Internationalists (Martov's faction), and the Social Democrats Internationalists (Gorky's group) were in favour of forcing the Allies to declare democratic war aims, and to offer peace to Germany on those terms.

2 Wages and Cost of Living Before and During the Revolution

The following tables of wages and costs were compiled, in October, 1917, by a joint Committee from the Moscow Chamber of Commerce and the Moscow section of the Ministry of Labour, and published in *Novaya Zhizn,* October 26th, 1917:

Wages Per Day—(Rubles and kopeks)

Trade	July 1914	July 1916	August 1917
Carpenter, Cabinet-maker	1.60 — 2.	4. — 6.	8.50
Terrassier	1.30 — 1.50	3. — 3.50	
Mason, plasterer	1.70 — 2.35	4. — 6.	8.
Painter, upholsterer	1.80 — 2.20	3. — 5.50	8.
Blacksmith	1. — 2.25	4. — 5.	8.50
Chimney-sweep	1.50 — 2.	4. — 5.50	7.50
Locksmith	.90 — 2.	3.50 — 6.	9.
Helper	1. — 1.50	2.50 — 4.50	8.

In spite of numerous stories of gigantic advances in wages immediately following the Revolution of March, 1917, these figures, which were published by the Ministry of Labour as characteristic of conditions all over Russia, show that wages did not rise immediately after the Revolution, but little by little. On an average, wages increased slightly more than 500 per cent. . . .

But at the same time the value of the ruble fell to less than one-third its former purchasing power, and the cost of the necessities of life increased enormously.

The following table was compiled by the Municipal Duma of Moscow, where food was cheaper and more plentiful than in Petrograd:

Cost of Food—(Rubles and kopeks)

		August 1914	August 1917	% Increase
Black bread	(Fund)	.02½	.12	330
White bread	"	.05	.20	300
Beef	"	.22	1.10	400
Veal	"	.26	2.15	727
Pork	"	.23	2.	770
Herring	"	.06	.52	767
Cheese	"	.40	3.50	754
Butter	"	.48	3.20	557
Eggs	(Doz.)	.30	1.60	443
Milk	(Krushka)	.07	.40	471

On an average, food increased in price 566 per cent, or 51 per cent more than wages.

As for the other necessities, the price of these increased tremendously.

The following table was compiled by the Economic section of the Moscow Soviet of Workers' Deputies, and accepted as correct by the Ministry of Supplies of the Provisional Government.

Cost of Other Necessities—*(Rubles and kopeks)*

		August 1914	August 1917	% Increase
Calico	(*Arshin*)	.11	1.40	1173
Cotton Cloth	"	.15	2.	1233
Dress Goods	"	2.	40.	1900
Castor Cloth	"	6.	80.	1233
Men's Shoes	(Pair)	12.	144.	1097
Sole Leather		20.	400.	1900
Rubbers	(Pair)	2.50	15.	500
Men's Clothing	(Suit)	40.	400. — 455.	900 — 1109
Tea	(*Fund*)	4.50	18.	300
Matches	(Carton)	.10	.50	400
Soap	(*Pood*)	4.50	40.	780
Gasoline	(*Vedro*)	1.70	11.	547
Candles	(*Pood*)	8.50	100.	1076
Caramel	(*Fund*)	.30	4.50	1400
Fire Wood	(Load)	10.	120.	1100
Charcoal		.80	13.	1525
Sundry Metal Ware ..		1.	20.	1900

On an average, the above categories of necessities increased about 1,109 per cent in price, more than twice the increase of salaries. The difference, of course, went into the pockets of speculators and merchants.

In September, 1917, when I arrived in Petrograd, the average daily wage of a skilled industrial worker—for example, a steelworker in the Putilov Factory—was about 8 rubles. At the same time, profits were enormous. . . . I was told by one of the owners of the Thornton Woollen Mills, an English concern on the outskirts of Petrograd, that while wages had increased about 300 per cent in his factory, his profits had gone up *900 per cent*.

3 The Death Penalty

The death penalty was officially re-established on July 12 under the pressure of the high command, who wanted it as an instrument to stop mass desertions and refusals to advance or hold a line under fire, but the officers no longer enjoyed the prestige and power to command a firing squad, and the measure was not applied. As General Brussilov put it: "The officers, from the Company Commander to the Commander-in-Chief, have no power." And General Klembovsky asked: "The death penalty? But is it possible to put to death whole divisions?" Particularly after the attempted *coup* of Kornilov the problem was how to prevent soldiers from shooting their officers rather than the reverse. The Bolsheviks, however, used the mere existence of the death penalty as a powerful talking point in the army. The day they took power, while Lenin was busy in another room, Kamenev introduced a formal resolution into the Soviet Congress for the abolition of the death penalty. It passed unanimously, but when Lenin heard of it he was furious. "This is madness," he is reported by Trotsky to have said. "How can we accomplish a revolution without shooting?"

"Kamenev," Trotsky continues, "tried to show that it was a question of the repeal of the death penalty that Kerensky had introduced especially for deserting soldiers, but Lenin was not to be appeased." (Trotsky, *Lenin,* New York, 1925, pp. 133-34). On November 11, Trotsky announced that the Military Revolutionary Committee was holding the Cadets (student officers) as hostages, and would shoot five of them for every revolutionary worker or soldier shot." (Speech to the Petrograd Soviet, November 11, 1917).—*Ed.*

4   The Socialist Ministers

The history of the efforts of the Socialists in the Provisional Government of July to realise their programme in coalition with the bourgeois Ministers, is an illuminating example of class struggle in politics. Says Lenin, in explanation of this phenomenon:

"The capitalists, . . . seeing that the position of the Government was untenable, resorted to a method which since 1848 has been for decades practised by the capitalists in order to befog, divide, and finally overpower the working-class. This method is the so-called 'Coalition Ministry,' composed of bourgeois and of renegades from the Socialist camp.

"In those countries where political freedom and democracy have existed side by side with the revolutionary movement of the workers—for example in England and France—the capitalists make use of this subterfuge, and very successfully too. The 'Socialist' leaders, upon entering the Ministries, invariably prove mere figure-heads, puppets, simply a shield for the capitalists, a tool with which to defraud the workers. The 'democratic' and 'republican' capitalists in Russia set in motion this very same scheme. The Socialist Revolutionaries and Mensheviki fell victim to it, and on June 1st a 'Coalition' Ministry, with the participation of Chernov, Tseretelli, Skobelev, Avksentiev, Savinkov, Zarudny and Nikitin became an accomplished fact. . . ."—*Problems of the Revolution.*

5 September Municipal Elections in Moscow

In the first week of October, 1917, *Novaya Zhizn* published the following comparative table of election results, pointing out that this meant the bankruptcy of the policy of Coalition with the propertied classes. "If civil war can yet be avoided, it can only be done by a united front of all the revolutionary democracy. . . ."

Elections for the Moscow Central and Ward Dumas

	June 1917	September 1917
Socialist Revolutionaries	58 Members	14 Members
Cadets	17 "	30 "
Mensheviki	12 "	4 "
Bolsheviki	11 "	47 "

6 Growing Arrogance of the Reactionaries

September 18th. The Cadet Shulgin, writing in a Kiev newspaper, said that the Provisional Government's declaration that Russia was a Republic constituted a gross abuse of its powers. "We cannot admit either a Republic, or the present Republican Government. . . . And we are not sure that we want a Republic in Russia. . . ."

October 23d. At a meeting of the Cadet party held at Riazan, M. Dukhonin declared, "On March 1st we must establish a Constitutional Monarchy. We must not reject the legitimate heir to the throne, Mikhail Alexandrovitch. . . ."

October 27th. Resolution passed by the Conference of Business Men at Moscow:

"The Conference . . . insists that the Provisional Government take the following immediate measures in the Army:

"1. Forbidding of all political propaganda; the Army must be out of politics.

"2. Propaganda of antinational and international ideas and theories deny the necessity for armies, and hurt discipline; it should be forbidden, and all propagandists punished. . . .

"3. The function of the Army Committees must be limited to

economic questions exclusively. All their decisions should be confirmed by their superior officers, who have the right to dissolve the
Committees at any time. . . .

"4. The salute to be reestablished, and made obligatory. Full
reestablishment of disciplinary power in the hands of officers, with
right of review of sentence. . . .

"5. Expulsion from the Corps of Officers of those who dishonour
it by participating in the movement of the soldier-masses, which
teaches them disobedience. . . . Reestablishment for this purpose
of the Courts of Honor. . . .

"6. The Provisional Government should take the necessary measures to make possible the return to the army of Generals and other
officers unjustly discharged under the influence of Committees, and
other irresponsible organisations. . . ."

CHAPTER II

THE COMING STORM

In September General Kornilov marched on Petrograd to make himself military dictator of Russia. Behind him was suddenly revealed the mailed fist of the bourgeoisie, boldly attempting to crush the Revolution. Some of the Socialist Ministers were implicated; even Kerensky was under suspicion.[1] Savinkov, summoned to explain to the Central Committee of his party, the Socialist Revolutionaries, refused and was expelled. Kornilov was arrested by the Soldiers' Committees. Generals were dismissed, Ministers suspended from their functions, and the Cabinet fell.

Kerensky tried to form a new Government, including the Cadets, party of the bourgeoisie. His party, the Socialist Revolutionaries, ordered him to exclude the Cadets. Kerensky declined to obey, and threatened to resign from the Cabinet if the Socialists insisted. However, popular feeling ran so high that for the moment he did not dare oppose it, and a temporary Directorate of Five of the old Ministers, with Kerensky at the head, assumed the power until the question should be settled.

The Kornilov affair drew together all the Socialist groups—"moderates" as well as revolutionists—in a passionate impulse of self-defence. There must be no more Kornilovs. A new Government must be created, responsible to the elements supporting the Revolution. So the *Tsay-ee-kah* invited the popular organisations to send delegates to a Democratic Conference, which should meet at Petrograd in September.

In the *Tsay-ee-kah* three factions immediately appeared. The Bolsheviki demanded that the All-Russian Congress of Soviets be summoned, and that they take over the power. The "centre" Socialist Revolutionaries, led by Chernov, joined with the Left Socialist Revolutionaries, led by Kamkov and Spiridonova, the Mensheviki Internationalists under Martov, and the "centre" Mensheviki,* represented by Bogdanov and Skobelev, in demanding a purely Socialist Government. Tseretelli, Dan and Lieber, at the head of the right wing Mensheviki, and the right Socialist Revolutionaries under Avksentiev and Gotz, insisted that the propertied classes must be represented in the new Government.

Almost immediately the Bolsheviki won a majority in the Petrograd Soviet, and the Soviets of Moscow, Kiev, Odessa and other cities followed suit.

Alarmed, the Mensheviki and Socialist Revolutionaries in control of the *Tsay-ee-kah* decided that after all they feared the danger of Kornilov less than the danger of Lenin. They revised the plan of representation in the Democratic Conference,[2] admitting more delegates from the Cooperative Societies and other conservative bodies. Even this packed assembly at first voted for a *Coalition Government without the Cadets*. Only Kerensky's open threat of resignation, and the alarming cries of the "moderate" Socialists that "the Republic is in danger" persuaded the Conference, by a small majority, to declare in favour of the principle of coalition with the bourgeoisie, and to sanction the establishment of a sort of consultative

* See Notes and Explanations.

Parliament, without any legislative power, called the Provisional Council of the Russian Republic. In the new Ministry the propertied classes practically controlled, and in the Council of the Russian Republic they occupied a disproportionate number of seats.

The fact is that the *Tsay-ee-kah* no longer represented the rank and file of the Soviets, and had illegally refused to call another All-Russian Congress of Soviets, due in September. It had no intention of calling this Congress or of allowing it to be called. Its official organ, *Izvestia* (News), began to hint that the function of the Soviets was nearly at an end,[3] and that they might soon be dissolved. . . . At this time, too, the new Government announced as part of its policy the liquidation of "irresponsible organisations" —i.e. the Soviets.

The Bolsheviki responded by summoning the All-Russian Soviets to meet at Petrograd on November 2, and take over the Government of Russia. At the same time they withdrew from the Council of the Russian Republic, stating that they would not participate in a "Government of Treason to the People." [4]

The withdrawal of the Bolsheviki, however, did not bring tranquillity to the ill-fated Council. The propertied classes, now in a position of power, became arrogant. The Cadets declared that the Government had no legal right to declare Russia a republic. They demanded stern measures in the Army and Navy to destroy the Soldiers' and Sailors' Committees, and denounced the Soviets. On the other side of the chamber the Mensheviki Internationalists and the Left Socialist Revolutionaries advocated immediate peace, land to the peasants, and workers' control of industry— practically the Bolshevik programme.

I heard Martov's speech in answer to the Cadets. Stooped over the desk of the tribune like the mortally sick man he was, and speaking in a voice so hoarse it could hardly be heard, he shook his finger toward the right benches:

"You call us defeatists; but the real defeatists are those who wait for a more propitious moment to conclude peace, insist upon postponing peace until later, until nothing is left of the Russian army, until Russia becomes the subject of bargaining between the different imperialist groups. . . . You are trying to impose upon the Russian people a policy dictated by the interests of the bourgeoisie. The question of peace should be raised without delay. . . . You will see then that not in vain has been the work of those whom you call German agents, of those Zimmer-waldists* who in all the lands have prepared the awakening of the conscience of the democratic masses. . . ."

Between these two groups the Mensheviki and Socialist Revolutionaries wavered, irresistibly forced to the left by the pressure of the rising dissatisfaction of the masses. Deep hostility divided the chamber into irreconcilable groups.

This was the situation when the long-awaited announcement of the Allied Conference in Paris brought up the burning question of foreign policy. . . .

Theoretically all Socialist parties in Russia were in favour of the earliest possible peace on democratic terms. As long ago as May, 1917, the Petrograd Soviet, then under control of the Mensheviki and Socialist Revolutionaries, had proclaimed the famous Russian peace-conditions. They had demanded that the Allies hold a conference to discuss war-aims. This conference had been promised for August; then postponed until September;

---

* Members of the revolutionary internationalist wing of the Socialists of Europe, so-called because of their participation in the International Conference held at Zimmerwald, Switzerland, in 1915.

then until October; and now it was fixed for November 10th.

The Provisional Government suggested two representatives—General Alexeyev, reactionary military man, and Tereshchenko, Minister of Foreign Affairs.* The Soviets chose Skobelev to speak for them and drew up a manifesto, the famous *nakaz*[5]—instructions. The Provisional Government objected to Skobelev and his *nakaz;* the Allied ambassadors protested and finally Bonar Law in the British House of Commons, in answer to a question, responded coldly, "As far as I know the Paris Conference will not discuss the aims of the war at all, but only the methods of conducting it. . . ."

At this the conservative Russian press was jubilant, and the Bolsheviki cried, "See where the compromising tactics of the Mensheviki and Socialist Revolutionaries have led them!"

Along a thousand miles of front the millions of men in Russia's armies stirred like the sea rising, pouring into the capital their hundreds upon hundreds of delegations, crying "Peace! Peace!"

I went across the river to the Cirque Moderne, to one of the great popular meetings which occurred all over the city, more numerous night after night. The bare, gloomy amphitheatre, lit by five tiny lights hanging from a thin wire, was packed from the ring up the steep sweep of grimy benches to the very roof—soldiers, sailors, workmen, women, all listening as if their lives depended upon it. A soldier was speaking—from the Five Hundred and

---

* The Provisional Government would naturally have sent its Minister of Foreign Affairs (Tereshchenko assumed this post on May 16), and the Commander-in-Chief of the Army. But on May 10, General Alexeyev attacked the "longing for peace" which "has replaced the old traditional loyalty to the country," and on June 4 he was dismissed. Consequently, the new Commander-in-Chief or his deputy would have been the military expert. In any case, if a full-scale conference had been held, these would not have constituted the entire delegation.—*Ed.*

Forty-eighth Division, wherever and whatever that was:

"Comrades," he cried, and there was real anguish in his drawn face and despairing gestures. "The people at the top are always calling upon us to sacrifice more, sacrifice more, while those who have everything are left unmolested.

"We are at war with Germany. Would we invite German generals to serve on our Staff? Well we're at war with the capitalists too, and yet we invite them into our Government. . . .

"The soldier says, 'Show me what I am fighting for. Is it Constantinople, or is it free Russia? Is it the democracy, or is it the capitalist plunderers? If you can prove to me that I am defending the Revolution then I'll go out and fight without capital punishment to force me.'

"When the land belongs to the peasants, and the factories to the workers, and the power to the Soviets, then we'll know we have something to fight for, and we'll fight for it!"

In the barracks, the factories, on the street-corners, endless soldier speakers, all clamouring for an end to the war, declaring that if the Government did not make an energetic effort to get peace, the army would leave the trenches and go home.

The spokesman for the Eighth Army:

"We are weak, we have only a few men left in each company. They must give us food and boots and reinforcements, or soon there will be left only empty trenches. Peace or supplies . . . either let the Government end the war or support the Army. . . ."

For the Forty-sixth Siberian Artillery:

"The officers will not work with our Committees, they betray us to the enemy, they apply the death penalty to our agitators; and the counter-revolutionary Government

supports them. We thought that the Revolution would
bring peace. But now the Government forbids us even to
talk of such things, and at the same time doesn't give us
enough food to live on, or enough ammunition to fight
with. . . ."

From Europe came rumours of peace at the expense of
Russia.[6] . . .

News of the treatment of Russian troops in France
added to the discontent. The First Brigade had tried to
replace its officers with Soldiers' Committees, like their
comrades at home, and had refused an order to go to
Salonika, demanding to be sent to Russia. They had been
surrounded and starved, and then fired on by artillery, and
many killed.[7] . . .

On October 29th I went to the white-marble and crimson hall of the Marinsky palace, where the Council of the
Republic sat, to hear Tereshchenko's declaration of the
Government's foreign policy, awaited with such terrible
anxiety by all the peace-thirsty and exhausted land.

A tall, impeccably-dressed young man with a smooth
face and high cheek-bones, suavely reading his careful,
non-committal speech.[8] Nothing . . . Only the same
platitudes about crushing German militarism with the help
of the Allies—about the "state interests" of Russia, about
the "embarrassment" caused by Skobelev's *nakaz.* He
ended with the key-note:

"Russia is a great power. Russia will remain a great
power, whatever happens. We must all defend her, we
must show that we are defenders of a great ideal, and
children of a great power."

Nobody was satisfied. The reactionaries wanted a
"strong" imperialist policy; the democratic parties wanted
an assurance that the Government would press for
peace. . . . I reproduce an editorial in *Rabochi i Soldat*

(Worker and Soldier), organ of the Bolshevik Petrograd Soviet:

The Government's Answer to the Trenches

The most taciturn of our Ministers, Mr. Tereshchenko, has actually told the trenches the following:

1. We are closely united with our Allies. (Not with the peoples, but with the Governments.)

2. There is no use for the democracy to discuss the possibility or impossibility of a winter campaign. That will be decided by the Governments of our Allies.

3. The 1st of July offensive was beneficial and a very happy affair. (He did not mention the consequences.)

4. It is not true that our Allies do not care about us. The Minister has in his possession very important declarations. (Declarations? What about deeds? What about the behaviour of the British fleet? [9] The parleying of the British king with exiled counter-revolutionary General Gurko? The Minister did not mention all this.)

5. The *nakaz* to Skobelev is bad; the Allies don't like it and the Russian diplomats don't like it. In the Allied Conference we must all 'speak one language.'

And is that all? That is all. What is the way out? The solution is, faith in the Allies and in Tereshchenko. When will peace come? When the Allies permit.

That is how the Government replied to the trenches about peace!

Now in the background of Russian politics began to form the vague outlines of a sinister power—the Cossacks. *Novaya Zhizn* (New Life), Gorky's paper, called attention to their activities:

At the beginning of the Revolution the Cossacks refused to shoot down the people. When Kornilov marched on Petrograd they refused to follow him. From passive loyalty to the Revolution the Cossacks have passed to an active political offensive (against it). From the back-ground of the Revolution they have suddenly advanced to the front of the stage. . . .

Kaledin, *ataman* of the Don Cossacks, had been dismissed by the Provisional Government for his complicity in the Kornilov affair. He flatly refused to resign, and surrounded by three immense Cossack armies lay at Novocherkask, plotting and menacing. So great was his power that the Government was forced to ignore his insubordination. More than that, it was compelled formally to recognise the Council of the Union of Cossack Armies, and to declare illegal the newly-formed Cossack Section of the Soviets. . . .

In the first part of October a Cossack delegation called upon Kerensky, arrogantly insisting that the charges against Kaledin be dropped, and reproaching the Minister-President for yielding to the Soviets. Kerensky agreed to let Kaledin alone, and then is reported to have said, "In the eyes of the Soviet leaders I am a despot and a tyrant. . . . As for the Provisional Government, not only does it not depend upon the Soviets, but it considers it regrettable that they exist at all."

At the same time another Cossack mission called upon the British ambassador, treating with him boldly as representatives of "the free Cossack people."

In the Don something very like a Cossack Republic had been established. The Kuban declared itself an independent Cossack State. The Soviets of Rostov-on-Don and Yekaterinburg were dispersed by armed Cossacks, and the headquarters of the Coal Miners' Union at Kharkov raided. In all its manifestations the Cossack movement was anti-Socialist and militaristic. Its leaders were nobles and great land-owners, like Kaledin, Kornilov, Generals Dutov, Karaulov and Bardizhe, and it was backed by the powerful merchants and bankers of Moscow. . . .

Old Russia was rapidly breaking up. In Ukraine, in Finland, Poland, White Russia, the nationalist movements gathered strength and became bolder. The local Governments, controlled by the propertied classes, claimed autonomy, refusing to obey orders from Petrograd. At Helsingfors the Finnish Senate declined to loan money to the Provisional Government, declared Finland autonomous, and demanded the withdrawal of Russian troops. The bourgeois Rada at Kiev extended the boundaries of Ukraine until they included all the richest agricultural lands of South Russia, as far east as the Urals, and began the formation of a national army. Premier Vinnichenko hinted at a separate peace with Germany—and the Provisional Government was helpless. Siberia, the Caucasus, demanded separate Constituent Assemblies.* And in all these countries there was the beginning of a bitter struggle between the authorities and the local Soviets of Workers' and Soldiers' Deputies. . . .

Conditions were daily more chaotic. Hundreds of thousands of soldiers were deserting the front and beginning to move in vast, aimless tides over the face of the land. The peasants of Tambov and Tver Governments, tired of waiting for the land, exasperated by the repressive meas-

* Reed has here confused his notes of early 1918 with those of 1917. The Ukrainian Rada was for autonomy in a free federation until the Bolshevik dictatorship and ultra-centralism made it clear that this was impossible. Vinnichenko was not yet a "premier" but Chairman of the Secretariat of the Rada. The Ukraine did not propose a separate peace with Germany until Lenin prepared to make such a separate peace at Brest-Litovsk. The boundaries of an autonomous or an independent Ukraine were naturally vague, but the Rada's proposal was for "self-determination" in a free plebiscite. The Caucasus also did not separate until the Constituent Assembly was dispersed by the Bolsheviks, when they set up their own Seim, or parliament, formed from the delegates they had just elected to the Constituent Assembly. The Siberian "Constituent Assembly" was of similar late origin.—Ed.

ures of the Government, were burning manor-houses and massacring land-owners. Immense strikes and lock-outs convulsed Moscow, Odessa and the coal-mines of the Don. Transportation was paralysed; the army was starving and in the big cities there was no bread.

The Government, torn between the democratic and reactionary factions, could do nothing: when forced to act it always supported the interests of the propertied classes. Cossacks were sent to restore order among the peasants, to break the strikes. In Tashkent, Government authorities suppressed the Soviet. In Petrograd the Economic Council, etablished to rebuild the shattered economic life of the country, came to a deadlock between the opposing forces of capital and labour, and was dissolved by Kerensky. The old régime military men, backed by Cadets, demanded that harsh measures be adopted to restore discipline in the Army and the Navy. In vain Admiral Verderevsky, the venerable Minister of Marine, and General Verkhovsky, Minister of War, insisted that only a new, voluntary, democratic discipline, based on co-operation with the soldiers' and sailors' Committees, could save the army and navy. Their recommendations were ignored.

The reactionaries seemed determined to provoke popular anger. The trial of Kornilov was coming on. More and more openly the bourgeois press defended him, speaking of him as "the great Russian patriot." Burtzev's paper, *Obshchee Dielo* (Common Cause), called for a dictatorship of Kornilov, Kaledin and Kerensky!

I had a talk with Burtzev one day in the press gallery of the Council of the Republic. A small, stooped figure with a wrinkled face, eyes near-sighted behind thick glasses, untidy hair and beard streaked with grey.

"Mark my words, young man! What Russia needs is a

Strong Man. We should get our minds off the Revolution now and concentrate on the Germans. Bunglers, bunglers, to defeat Kornilov; and back of the bunglers are the German agents. Kornilov should have won. . . ."

On the extreme right the organs of the scarcely-veiled Monarchists, Purishkevich's *Narodny Tribun* (People's Tribune), *Novaya Rus* (New Russia), and *Zhivoye Slovo* (Living Word), openly advocated the extermination of the revolutionary democracy. . . .

On the 23rd of October occurred the naval battle with a German squadron in the Gulf of Riga. On the pretext that Petrograd was in danger, the Provisional Government drew up plans for evacuating the capital. First the great munitions works were to go, distributed widely throughout Russia; and then the Government itself was to move to Moscow. Instantly the Bolsheviki began to cry out that the Government was abandoning the Red Capital in order to weaken the Revolution. Riga had been sold to the Germans; now Petrograd was being betrayed!

The bourgeois press was joyful. "At Moscow," said the Cadet paper *Rech* (Speech), "the Government can pursue its work in a tranquil atmosphere, without being interfered with by anarchists." Rodzianko, leader of the right wing of the Cadet party, declared in *Utro Rossii* (The Morning of Russia) that the taking of Petrograd by the Germans would be a blessing, because it would destroy the Soviets and get rid of the revolutionary Baltic Fleet:

Petrograd is in danger (he wrote). I say to myself, "Let God take care of Petrograd." They fear that if Petrograd is lost the central revolutionary organisations will be destroyed. To that I answer that I rejoice if all these organisations are destroyed; for they will bring nothing but disaster upon Russia. . . .

With the taking of Petrograd the Baltic Fleet will also be destroyed. . . . But there will be nothing to regret; most of the battleships are completely demoralised. . . .

In the face of a storm of popular disapproval the plan of evacuation was repudiated.

Meanwhile the Congress of Soviets loomed over Russia like a thunder-cloud, shot through with lightnings. It was opposed, not only by the Government but by all the "moderate" Socialists. The Central Army and Fleet Committees, the Central Committees of some of the Trade Unions, the Peasants' Soviets, but most of all the *Tsay-ee-kah* itself, spared no pains to prevent the meeting. *Izvestia* and *Golos Soldata* (Voice of the Soldier), newspapers founded by the Petrograd Soviet but now in the hands of the *Tsay-ee-kah,* fiercely assailed it, as did the entire artillery of the Socialist Revolutionary party press, *Dielo Naroda* (People's Cause) and *Volia Naroda* (People's Will).

Delegates were sent through the country, messages flashed by wire to committees in charge of local Soviets, to Army Committees, instructing them to halt or delay elections to the Congress. Solemn public resolutions against the Congress, declarations that the democracy was opposed to the meeting so near the date of the Constituent Assembly, representatives from the Front, from the Union of Zemstvos, the Peasants' Union, Union of Cossack Armies, Union of Officers, Knights of St. George, Death Battalions,* protesting. . . . The Council of the Russian Republic was one chorus of disapproval. The entire machinery set up by the Russian Revolution of March functioned to block the Congress of Soviets. . . .

On the other hand was the shapeless will of the pro-

* See Notes and Explanations.

letariat—the workmen, common soldiers and poor peasants. Many local Soviets were already Bolshevik; then there were the organisations of the industrial workers, the *Fabrichno-Zavodskiye Comitieti*—Factory-Shop Committees; and the insurgent Army and Fleet organisations. In some places the people, prevented from electing their regular Soviet delegates, held rump meetings and chose one of their number to go to Petrograd. In others they smashed the old obstructionist committees and formed new ones. A ground-swell of revolt heaved and cracked the crust which had been slowly hardening on the surface of revolutionary fires dormant all those months. Only a spontaneous mass-movement could bring about the All-Russian Congress of Soviets. . . .

Day after day the Bolshevik orators toured the barracks and factories, violently denouncing "this Government of civil war." One Sunday we went, on a top-heavy steam tram that lumbered through oceans of mud, between stark factories and immense churches, to *Obukhovsky Zavod,* a Government munitions-plant out on the Schlüsselburg Prospekt.

The meeting took place between the gaunt brick walls of a huge unfinished building, ten thousand black-clothed men and women packed around a scaffolding draped in red, people heaped on piles of lumber and bricks, perched high up on shadowy girders, intent and thunder-voiced. Through the dull, heavy sky now and again burst the sun, flooding reddish light through the skeleton windows upon the mass of simple faces upturned to us.

Lunacharsky, a slight, student-like figure with the sensitive face of an artist, was telling why the power must be taken by the Soviets. Nothing else could guarantee the Revolution against its enemies, who were deliberately ruining the country, ruining the army, creating opportunities for a new Kornilov.

A soldier from the Rumanian front, thin, tragical and fierce, cried, "Comrades! We are starving at the front, we are stiff with cold. We are dying for no reason. I ask the American comrades to carry word to America, that the Russians will never give up their Revolution until they die. We will hold the fort with all our strength until the peoples of the world rise and help us! Tell the American workers to rise and fight for the Social Revolution!"

Then came Petrovsky, slight, slow-voiced, implacable: "Now is the time for deeds, not words. The economic situation is bad, but we must get used to it. They are trying to starve us and freeze us. They are trying to provoke us. But let them know that they can go too far— that if they dare to lay their hands upon the organisations of the proletariat we will sweep them away like scum from the face of the earth!"

The Bolshevik press suddenly expanded. Besides the two party papers, *Rabochi Put* and *Soldat* (Soldier), there appeared a new paper for the peasants, *Derevenskaya Byednota* (Village Poorest), poured out in a daily half-million edition; and on October 17th, *Rabochi i Soldat*. Its leading article summed up the Bolshevik point of view:

The fourth year's campaign will mean the annihilation of the army and the country. . . . There is danger for the safety of Petrograd. . . . Counter-revolutionists rejoice in the people's misfortunes. . . . The peasants brought to desperation come out in open rebellion; the landlords and Government authorities massacre them with punitive expeditions; factories and mines are closing down, workmen are threatened with starvation. . . . The bourgeoisie and its Generals want

to restore a blind discipline in the army. . . . Supported by
the bourgeoisie, the Kornilovtsi are openly getting ready to
break up the meeting of the Constituent Assembly. . . .

The Kerensky Government is against the people. He will
destroy the country. . . . This paper stands for the people
and by the people—the poor classes, workers, soldiers and
peasants. The people can only be saved by the completion of
the Revolution . . . and for this purpose the full power must
be in the hands of the Soviets. . . .

This paper advocates the following:

All power to the Soviets—both in the capital and in the
provinces.

Immediate truce on all fronts. An honest peace between
peoples.

Landlord estates—without compensation—to the peasants.

Workers' control over industrial production.

A faithfully and honestly elected Constituent Assembly.

It is interesting to reproduce here a passage from that
same paper—the organ of those Bolsheviki so well known
to the world as German agents:

The German kaiser, covered with the blood of millions of
dead people, wants to push his army against Petrograd. Let us
call to the German workmen, soldiers and peasants, who want
peace not less than we do, to . . . stand up against this
damned war!

This can be done only by a revolutionary Government,
which would speak really for the workmen, soldiers and
peasants of Russia, and would appeal over the heads of the
diplomats directly to the German troops, fill the German
trenches with proclamations in the German language. . . .
Our airmen would spread these proclamations all over Germany. . . .

In the Council of the Republic the gulf between the
two sides of the chamber deepened day by day.

"The propertied classes," cried Karelin, for the Left Socialist Revolutionaries, "want to exploit the revolutionary machine of the State to bind Russia to the war-chariot of the Allies! The revolutionary parties are absolutely against this policy. . . ."

Old Nicholas Chaikovsky, representing the Populist Socialists, spoke against giving the land to the peasants, and took the side of the Cadets:

"We must have immediately strong discipline in the army. . . . Since the beginning of the war I have not ceased to insist that it is a crime to undertake social and economic reforms in war-time. We are committing that crime, and yet I am not the enemy of these reforms, because I am a Socialist."

Cries from the Left, "We don't believe you!" Mighty applause from the Right. . . .

Adzhemov, for the Cadets, declared that there was no necessity to tell the army what it was fighting for, since every soldier ought to realise that the first task was to drive the enemy from Russian territory.

Kerensky himself came twice, to plead passionately for national unity, once bursting into tears at the end. The assembly heard him coldly, interrupting with ironical remarks.

Smolny Institute, headquarters of the *Tsay-ee-kah* and of the Petrograd Soviet, lay miles out on the edge of the city, beside the wide Neva.* I went there on a street-car, moving snail-like with a groaning noise through the cobbled, muddy streets, and jammed with people. At the end

* This testifies rather to the nature of streetcar traffic than to Reed's sense of geography. Smolny is in the very heart of downtown monumental Petrograd, two blocks from the Tauride Palace where the Duma and the Provisional Government met, four longish blocks from the old American Embassy and about the same distance from the Liteiny Prospekt and the Nevsky Prospekt.—*Ed.*

of the line rose the graceful smoke-blue cupolas of Smolny Convent outlined in dull gold, beautiful; and beside it the great barracks-like façade of Smolny Institute, two hundred yards long and three lofty stories high, the Imperial arms carved hugely in stone still insolent over the entrance. . . .

Under the old régime a famous convent-school for the daughters of the Russian nobility, patronised by the Tsarina herself, the Institute had been taken over by the revolutionary organisations of workers and soldiers. Within were more than a hundred huge rooms, white and bare, on their doors enamelled plaques still informing the passerby that within was "Ladies' Class-room Number 4" or "Teachers' Bureau"; but over these hung crudely-lettered signs, evidence of the vitality of the new order: "Central Committee of the Petrograd Soviet" and *"Tsay-ee-kah"* and "Bureau of Foreign Affairs"; "Union of Socialist Soldiers," "Central Committee of the All-Russian Trade Unions," "Factory-Shop Committees," "Central Army Committee"; and the central offices and caucus-rooms of the political parties. . . .

The long, vaulted corridors, lit by rare electric lights, were thronged with hurrying shapes of soldiers and workmen, some bent under the weight of huge bundles of newspapers, proclamations, printed propaganda of all sorts. The sound of their heavy boots made a deep and incessant thunder on the wooden floor. . . . Signs were posted up everywhere: "Comrades! For the sake of your health, preserve cleanliness!" Long tables stood at the head of the stairs on every floor, and on the landings, heaped with pamphlets and the literature of the different political parties, for sale. . . .

The spacious, low-ceilinged refectory downstairs was still a dining-room. For two rubles I bought a ticket entitling me to dinner, and stood in line with a thousand others, waiting to get to the long serving-tables, where twenty men and women were ladling from immense cauldrons cabbage soup, hunks of meat and piles of *kasha,* slabs of black bread. Five kopeks paid for tea in a tin cup. From a basket one grapped a greasy wooden spoon. . . . The benches along the wooden tables were packed with hungry proletarians, wolfing their food, plotting, shouting rough jokes across the room. . . .

Upstairs was another eating-place, reserved for the *Tsay-ee-kah*—though every one went there. Here could be had bread thickly buttered and endless glasses of tea. . . .

In the south wing on the second floor was the great hall of meetings, the former ball-room of the Institute. A lofty white room lighted by glazed-white chandeliers holding hundreds of ornate electric bulbs, and divided by two rows of massive columns; at one end a dais, flanked with two tall many-branched light standards, and a gold frame behind, from which the Imperial portrait had been cut. Here on festal occasions had been banked brilliant military and ecclesiastical uniforms, a setting for Grand Duchesses. . . .

Just across the hall outside was the office of the Credentials Committee for the Congress of Soviets. I stood

ТОВАРИЩИ,
ДЛЯ ВАШЕГО-ЖЕ ЗДОРОВЬЯ,
СОБЛЮДАЙТЕ ЧИСТОТУ.

there watching the new delegates come in—burly, bearded
soldiers, workmen in black blouses, a few long-haired
peasants. The girl in charge—a member of Plekhanov's
*Yedinstvo** group—smiled contemptuously. "These are
very different people from the delegates to the first *Siezd*
(Congress)," she remarked. "See how rough and ignorant
they look! The Dark People. . . ." It was true; the depths
of Russia had been stirred, and it was the bottom which
came uppermost now. The Credentials Committee, appointed by the old *Tsay-ee-kah,* was challenging delegate
after delegate, on the ground that they had been illegally
elected. Karakhan, member of the Bolshevik Central Committee, simply grinned. "Never mind," he said, "When
the time comes we'll see that you get your seats. . . ."

Rabochi i Soldat said:

The attention of delegates to the new All-Russian Congress
is called to attempts of certain members of the Organising
Committee to break up the Congress, by asserting that it
will not take place, and that delegates had better leave Petrograd. . . . Pay no attention to these lies. . . . Great days are
coming. . . .

It was evident that a quorum would not come together
by November 2, so the opening of the Congress was postponed to the 7th. But the whole country was now
aroused; and the Mensheviki and Socialist Revolutionaries,
realising that they were defeated, suddenly changed their
tactics and began to wire frantically to their provincial
organisations to elect as many "moderate" Socialist delegates as possible. At the same time the Executive Committee of the Peasants' Soviets issued an emergency call
for a Peasants' Congress, to meet December 13th and

* See Notes and Explanations.

offset whatever action the workers and soldiers might take. . . .

What would the Bolsheviki do? Rumours ran through the city that there would be an armed "demonstration," a *vystuplenie*—"coming out" of the workers and soldiers. The bourgeois and reactionary press prophesied insurrection, and urged the Government to arrest the Petrograd Soviet, or at least to prevent the meeting of the Congress. Such sheets as *Novaya Rus* advocated a general Bolshevik massacre.

Gorky's paper, *Novaya Zhizn,* agreed with the Bolsheviki that the reactionaries were attempting to destroy the Revolution, and that if necessary they must be resisted by force of arms; but all the parties of the revolutionary democracy must present a united front.

As long as the democracy has not organised its principal forces, so long as the resistance to its influence is still strong, there is no advantage in passing to the attack. But if the hostile elements appeal to force, then the revolutionary democracy should enter the battle to seize the power, and it will be sustained by the most profound strata of the people. . . .

Gorky pointed out that both reactionary and Government newspapers were inciting the Bolsheviki to violence. An insurrection, however, would prepare the way for a new Kornilov. He urged the Bolsheviki to deny the rumours. Potresov, in the Menshevik *Dien* (Day), published a sensational story, accompanied by a map, which professed to reveal the secret Bolshevik plan of campaign.

As if by magic, the walls were covered with warnings,[10] proclamations, appeals, from the Central Committees of the "moderate" and conservative factions and the *Tsay-ee-kah,* denouncing any "demonstrations," imploring the workers and soldiers not to listen to agitators. For instance, this from the Military Section of the Socialist Revolutionary party:

Again rumours are spreading around the town of an intended *vystuplenie*. What is the source of these rumors? What organisation authorizes these agitators who preach insurrection? The Bolsheviki, to a question addressed to them in the *Tsay-ee-kah,* denied that they have anything to do with it. . . . But these rumours themselves carry with them a great danger. It may easily happen that, not taking into consideration the state of mind of the majority of the workers, soldiers and peasants, individual hot-heads will call out part of the workers and soldiers on the streets, inciting them to an uprising. . . . In this fearful time through which revolutionary Russia is passing, any insurrection can easily turn into civil war, and there can result from it the destruction of all organisations of the proletariat, built up with so much labour. . . . The counter-revolutionary plotters are planning to take advantage of this insurrection to destroy the Revolution, open the front to Wilhelm, and wreck the Constituent Assembly. . . . Stick stubbornly to your posts! Do not come out!

On October 28th, in the corridors of Smolny, I spoke with Kamenev, a little man with a reddish pointed beard and Gallic gestures. He was not at all sure that enough delegates would come. "If there *is* a Congress," he said, "it will represent the overwhelming sentiment of the people. If the majority is Bolshevik, as I think it will be, we shall demand that the power be given to the Soviets, and the Provisional Government must resign. . . ."

Volodarsky, a tall, pale youth with glasses and a bad complexion, was more definite. "The 'Lieber-Dans' and the other compromisers are sabotaging the Congress. If they succeed in preventing its meeting,—well, then we are realists enough not to depend on *that!*"

Under date of October 29th I find entered in my note-book the following items culled from the newspapers of the day:

Moghilev (General Staff Headquarters). Concentration here of loyal Guard Regiments, the Savage Division, Cossacks and Death Battalions.*

The *yunkers* of the Officers' Schools of Pavlovsk, Tsarskoye Selo and Peterhof ordered by the Government to be ready to come to Petrograd. Oranienbaum *yunkers* arrive in the city.

Part of the Armoured Car Division of the Petrograd garrison stationed in the Winter Palace.

Upon orders signed by Trotsky, several thousand rifles delivered by the Government Arms Factory at Sestroretsk to delegates of the Petrograd workmen.

At a meeting of the City Militia of the Lower Liteiny Quarter, a resolution demanding that all power be given to the Soviets.

This is just a sample of the confused events of those feverish days, when everybody knew that something was going to happen, but nobody knew just what.

At a meeting of the Petrograd Soviet in Smolny, the night of October 30th, Trotsky branded the assertions of the bourgeois press that the Soviet contemplated armed insurrection as "an attempt of the reactionaries to discredit and wreck the Congress of Soviets. . . . The Petrograd Soviet," he declared, "had not ordered any *vystuplenie*. If it is necessary we shall do so, and we will be supported by the Petrograd garrison. . . . They (the Government) are preparing a counter-revolution; and we shall answer with an offensive which will be merciless and decisive."

It is true that the Petrograd Soviet had not ordered a demonstration, but the Central Committee of the Bolshe-

* See Notes and Explanations.

vik party was considering the question of insurrection. All
night long the 23d they met. There were present all the
party intellectuals, the leaders—and delegates of the Petrograd workers and garrison. Alone of the intellectuals
Lenin and Trotsky stood for insurrection. Even the military men opposed it. A vote was taken. Insurrection was
defeated!

Then arose a rough workman, his face convulsed with
rage. "I speak for the Petrograd proletariat," he said,
harshly. "We are in favour of insurrection. Have it your
own way, but I tell you now that if you allow the Soviets
to be destroyed, *we're through with you!*" Some soldiers
joined him. . . . And after that they voted again—insurrection won. . . .

However, the right wing of the Bolsheviki, led by
Riazanov, Kamenev and Zinoviev, continued to campaign
against an armed rising. On the morning of October 31st
appeared in *Rabochi Put* the first instalment of Lenin's
"Letter to the Comrades," one of the most audacious pieces
of political propaganda the world has ever seen. In it
Lenin seriously presented the arguments in favour of
insurrection, taking as text the objections of Kamenev
and Riazanov. "Either . . . openly renouncing the slogan,
'All Power to the Soviets,' " he wrote, "or an uprising.
There is no middle course. . . ."

That same afternoon Paul Miliukov, leader of the
Cadets, made a brilliant, bitter speech[11] in the council of
the Republic, branding the Skobelev *nakaz* as pro-German, declaring that the "revolutionary democracy" was
destroying Russia, sneering at Tereshchenko, and openly
declaring that he preferred German diplomacy to Russian. . . . The Left benches were one roaring tumult all
through. . . .

On its part the Government could not ignore the significance of the success of the Bolshevik propaganda. On the 29th a joint commission of the Government and the Council of the Republic hastily drew up two laws, one for giving the land temporarily to the peasants, and the other for pushing an energetic foreign policy of peace. The next day Kerensky suspended capital punishment in the army. That same afternoon was opened with great ceremony the first session of the new "Commission for Strengthening the Republican Régime and Fighting Against Anarchy and Counter-Revolution"—of which history shows not the slightest further trace. . . . The following morning with two other correspondents I interviewed Kerensky[12]—the last time he received journalists.

"The Russian people," he said, bitterly, "are suffering from economic fatigue—and from disillusionment with the Allies! The world thinks that the Russian Revolution is at an end. Do not be mistaken. The Russian Revolution is just beginning. . . ." Words more prophetic, perhaps, than he knew.

Stormy was the all-night meeting of the Petrograd Soviet the 30th of October, at which I was present. The "moderate" Socialist intellectuals, officers, members of Army Committees, the *Tsay-ee-kah,* were there in force. Against them rose up workmen, peasants and common soldiers, passionate and simple.

A peasant told of the disorders in Tver, which he said were caused by the arrest of the Land Committees. "This Kerensky is nothing but a shield to the *pomieshchiki* (landowners)," he cried. "They know that at the Constituent Assembly we will take the land anyway, so they are trying to destroy the Constituent Assembly!"

A machinist from the Putilov works described how the superintendents were closing down the departments one by one on the pretext that there was no fuel or raw materials. The Factory-Shop Committee, he declared, had discovered huge hidden supplies.

"It is a *provocatzia*," said he. "They want to starve us—or drive us to violence!"

Among the soldiers one began, "Comrades! I bring you greetings from the place where men are digging their graves and call them trenches!"

Then arose a tall, gaunt young soldier, with flashing eyes, met with a roar of welcome. It was Chudnovsky, reported killed in the July fighting, and now risen from the dead.

"The soldier masses no longer trust their officers. Even the Army Committees, who refused to call a meeting of our Soviet, betrayed us. . . . The masses of the soldiers want the Constituent Assembly to be held exactly when it was called for, and those who dare to postpone it will be cursed—and not only platonic curses either, for the Army has guns too. . . ."

He told of the electoral campaign for the Constituent now raging in the Fifth Army. "The officers, and especially the Mensheviki and the Socialist Revolutionaries, are trying deliberately to cripple the Bolsheviki. Our papers are not allowed to circulate in the trenches. Our speakers are arrested——"

"Why don't you speak about the lack of bread?" shouted another soldier.

"Man shall not live by bread alone," answered Chudnovsky, sternly. . . .

Followed him an officer, delegate from the Vitebsk Soviet, a Menshevik *oboronetz*. "It isn't the question of who has the power. The trouble is not with the Government, but with the war . . . and the war must be won before any change—" At this, hoots and ironical cheers. "These Bolshevik agitators are demagogues!" The hall rocked with laughter. "Let us for a moment forget the class struggle—" But he got no farther. A voice yelled, "Don't you wish we would!"

Petrograd presented a curious spectacle in those days. In the factories the committee-rooms were filled with stacks of rifles, couriers came and went, the Red Guard* drilled. . . . In all the barracks meetings every night, and all day long interminable hot arguments. On the streets the crowds thickened toward gloomy evening, pouring in slow voluble tides up and down the Nevsky, fighting for the newspapers. . . . Hold-ups increased to such an extent that it was dangerous to walk down side streets. . . . On the Sadovaya one afternoon I saw a crowd of several hundred people beat and trample to death a soldier caught stealing. . . . Mysterious individuals circulated around the shivering women who waited in *queue* long cold hours for bread and milk, whispering that the Jews had cornered the food supply—and that while the people starved, the Soviet members lived luxuriously. . . .

At Smolny there were strict guards at the door and the outer gates, demanding everybody's pass. The committee-rooms buzzed and hummed all day and all night, hundreds of soldiers and workmen slept on the floor, wherever they could find room. Upstairs in the great hall a thousand people crowded to the uproarious sessions of the Petrograd Soviet. . . .

Gambling clubs functioned hectically from dusk to dawn, with champagne flowing and stakes of twenty thousand rubles. In the centre of the city at night prostitutes in jewels and expensive furs walked up and down, crowded the cafés. . . .

Monarchist plots, German spies, smugglers hatching schemes. . . .

* See Notes and Explanations.

And in the rain, the bitter chill, the great throbbing city under grey skies rushing faster and faster toward—what?

NOTES TO CHAPTER II

1

The Kornilov revolt is treated in detail in my forthcoming volume, "Kornilov to Brest-Litovsk." The responsibility of Kerensky for the situation which gave rise to Kornilov's attempt is now pretty clearly established. Many apologists for Kerensky say that he knew of Kornilov's plans, and by a trick drew him out prematurely, and then crushed him. Even Mr. A. J. Sack, in his book, "The Birth of the Russian Democracy," says:

"Several things . . . are almost certain. The first is that Kerensky knew about the movement of several detachments from the Front toward Petrograd, and it is possible that as Prime Minister and Minister of War, realising the growing Bolshevist danger, he called for them. . . ."

The only flaw in that argument is that there was no "Bolshevist danger" at that time, the Bolsheviki still being a powerless minority in the Soviets, and their leaders in jail or hiding.

2 Democratic Conference

When the Democratic Conference was first proposed to Kerensky, he suggested an assembly of all the elements in the nation— "the live forces," as he called them—including bankers, manufacturers, land-owners, and representatives of the Cadet party. The Soviet refused, and drew up the following table of representation, which Kerensky agreed to:

100 delegates	....	All-Russian Soviets Workers' and Soldiers' Deputies
100	"	....All-Russian Soviets Peasants' Deputies
50	"	....Provincial Soviets Workers' and Soldiers' Deputies
50	"	....Peasants' District Land Committees
100	"	....Trade Unions
84	"	....Army Committees at the Front

150	"	....Workers' and Peasants' Cooperative Societies
20	"	....Railway Workers' Union
10	"	....Post and Telegraph Workers' Union
20	"	....Commercial Clerks
15	"	....Liberal Professions—Doctors, Lawyers, Journalists, etc.
50	"	....Provincial Zemstvos
59	"	....Nationalist Organisations—Poles, Ukrainians, etc.

This proportion was altered twice or three times. The final disposition of delegates was:

300 delegates		....All-Russian Soviets Workers', Soldiers' & Peasants' Deputies
300	"	....Cooperative Societies
300	"	....Municipalities
150	"	....Army Committees at the Front
150	"	....Provincial Zemstvos
200	"	....Trade Unions
100	"	....Nationalist Organisations
200	"	....Several small groups

3   The Function of the Soviets is Ended

On September 28th, 1917, *Izvestia,* organ of the *Tsay-ee-kah,* published an article which said, speaking of the last Provisional Ministry:

"At last a truly democratic government, born of the will of all classes of the Russian people, the first rough form of the future liberal parliamentary régime, has been formed. Ahead of us is the Constituent Assembly, which will solve all questions of fundamental law, and whose composition will be essentially democratic. The function of the Soviets is at an end, and the time is approaching when they must retire, with the rest of the revolutionary machinery, from the stage of a free and victorious people, whose weapons shall hereafter be the peaceful ones of political action."

The leading article of *Izvestia* for October 23d was called, "The Crisis in the Soviet Organisations." It began by saying that travellers reported a lessening activity of local Soviets everywhere. "This is natural," said the writer. "For the people are becoming

interested in the more permanent legislative organs—the Municipal
Dumas and the Zemstvos. . . .

"In the important centres of Petrograd and Moscow, where the
Soviets were best organised, they did not take in all the democratic
elements. . . . The majority of the intellectuals did not participate,
and many workers also; some of the workers because they were
politically backward, others because the centre of gravity for them
was in their Unions. . . . We cannot deny that these organisations
are firmly united with the masses, whose everyday needs are better
served by them. . . .

"That the local democratic administrations are being energetically organised is highly important. The City Dumas are elected
by universal suffrage, and in purely local matters have more authority than the Soviets. Not a single democrat will see anything
wrong in this. . . .

". . . Elections to the Municipalities are being conducted in a
better and more democratic way than the elections to the Soviets.
. . . All classes are represented in the Municipalities. . . . And
as soon as the local Self-Governments begin to organise life in the
Municipalities, the rôle of the local Soviets naturally ends. . . .

". . . There are two factors in the falling off of interest in the
Soviets. The first we may attribute to the lowering of political interest in the masses; the second, to the growing effort of provincial
and local governing bodies to organise the building of new Russia.
. . . The more the tendency lies in this latter direction, the sooner
disappears the significance of the Soviets. . . .

"We ourselves are being called the 'undertakers' of our own
organisation. In reality, we ourselves are the hardest workers in
constructing the new Russia. . . .

"When autocracy and the whole bureaucratic régime fell, we set
up the Soviets as a barracks in which all the democracy could find
temporary shelter. Now, instead of barracks, we are building the
permanent edifice of a new system, and naturally the people will
gradually leave the barracks for more comfortable quarters."

4 Trotsky's Speech at the Council of the Russian Republic

"The purpose of the Democratic Conference, which was called
by the *Tsay-ee-kah,* was to do away with the irresponsible personal
government which produced Kornilov, and to establish a responsible government which would be capable of finishing the

war, and ensure the calling of the Constituent Assembly at the given time. In the meanwhile, behind the back of the Democratic Conference, by trickery, by deals between Citizen Kerensky, the Cadets, and the leaders of the Menshevik and Socialist Revolutionary parties, we received the opposite result from the officially announced purpose. A power was created around which and in which we have open and secret Kornilovs playing leading parts. The irresponsibility of the Government is officially proclaimed, when it is announced that the Council of the Russian Republic is to be a *consultative* and not a *legislative* body. In the eighth month of the Revolution, the irresponsible Government creates a cover for itself in this new edition of Bieligen's Duma.

"The propertied classes have entered this Provisional Council in a proportion which clearly shows, from elections all over the country, that many of them have no right here whatever. In spite of that the Cadet Party, which until yesterday wanted the Provisional Government to be responsible to the State Duma—this same Cadet party secured the independence of the Government from the Council of the Republic. In the Constituent Assembly the propertied classes will no doubt have a less favourable position than they have in this Council, and they will not be able to be irresponsible to the Constituent Assembly.

"If the propertied classes were really getting ready for the Constituent Assembly six weeks from now, there could be no reason for establishing the irresponsibility of the Government at this time. The whole truth is that the bourgeoisie, which directs the policies of the Provisional Government, has for its aim to break the Constituent Assembly. At present this is the main purpose of the propertied classes, which control our entire national policy—external and internal. In the industrial, agrarian and supply departments the politics of the propertied classes, acting with the Government, increases the natural disorganisation caused by the war. The propertied classes, which are provoking a peasants' revolt! The propertied classes, which are provoking civil war, and openly hold their course on the bony hand of hunger, with which they intend to overthrow the Revolution and finish with the Constituent Assembly!

"No less criminal also is the international policy of the bourgeoisie and its Government. After forty months of war, the capital is threatened with mortal danger. In reply to this arises a plan to move the Government to Moscow. The idea of abandoning the capital does not stir the indignation of the bourgeoisie. Just the opposite. It is accepted as a natural part of the general policy designed to promote counter-revolutionary conspiracy. . . . Instead of recognising that the salvation of the country lies in concluding peace, instead of throwing openly the idea of immediate peace to all the worn-out peoples, over the heads of diplomats and imperialists, and making the continuation of the war impossible,—the Provisional Government, by order of the Cadets, the Counter-Revolutionists and the Allied Imperialists, without sense, without purpose and without a plan, continues to drag on the murderous war, sentencing to useless death new hundreds of thousands of soldiers and sailors, and preparing to give up Petrograd, and to wreck the Revolution. At a time when Bolshevik soldiers and sailors are dying with other soldiers and sailors as a result of the mistakes and crimes of others, the so-called Supreme Commander (Kerensky) continues to suppress the Bolshevik press. The leading parties of the Council are acting as a voluntary cover for these policies.

"We, the faction of Social Democrats Bolsheviki, announce that with this Government of Treason to the People we have nothing in common. We have nothing in common with the work of these Murderers of the People which goes on behind official curtains. We refuse either directly or indirectly to cover up one day of this work. While Wilhelm's troops are threatening Petrograd, the Government of Kerensky and Kornilov is preparing to run away from Petrograd and turn Moscow into a base of counter-revolution!

"We warn the Moscow workers and soldiers to be on their guard. Leaving this Council, we appeal to the manhood and wisdom of the workers, peasants and soldiers of all Russia. Petrograd is in danger! The Revolution is in danger! The Government has increased the danger—the ruling classes intensify it. Only the people themselves can save themselves and the country.

"We appeal to the people. Long live immediate, honest, democratic peace! All power to the Soviets! All land to the people! Long live the Constituent Assembly!"

5   The "Nakaz" to Skobelev

Résumé

(Passed by the *Tsay-ee-kah* and given to Skobelev as an instruction for the representative of the Russian Revolutionary democracy at the Paris Conference.)

The peace treaty must be based on the principle, "No annexations, no indemnities, the right of self-determination of peoples."

Territorial Problems

(1) Evacuation of German troops from invaded Russia. Full right of self-determination to Poland, Lithuania and Livonia.

(2) For Turkish Armenia autonomy, and later complete self-determination, as soon as local Governments are established.

(3) The question of Alsace-Lorraine to be solved by a plebiscite, after the withdrawal of all foreign troops.

(4) Belgium to be restored. Compensation for damages from an international fund.

(5) Serbia and Montenegro to be restored, and aided by an international relief fund. Serbia to have an outlet on the Adriatic. Bosnia and Herzegovina to be autonomous.

(6) The disputed provinces in the Balkans to have provisional autonomy, followed by a plebiscite.

(7) Rumania to be restored, but forced to give complete self-determination to the Dobrudja. . . . Rumania must be forced to execute the clauses of the Berlin Treaty concerning the Jews, and recognise them as Rumanian citizens.

(8) In Italia Irridenta a provisional autonomy, followed by a plebiscite to determine state dependence.

(9) The German colonies to be returned.

(10) Greece and Persia to be restored.

Freedom of the Seas

All straits opening into inland seas, as well as the Suez and Panama Canals, are to be neutralised. Commercial shipping to be free. The right of privateering to be abolished. The torpedoing of commercial ships to be forbidden.

Indemnities

All combatants to renounce demands for any indemnities, either direct or indirect—as, for instance, charges for the maintenance of prisoners. Indemnities and contributions collected during the war must be refunded.

Economic Terms

Commercial treaties are not to be a part of the peace terms. Every country must be independent in its commercial relations, and must not be obliged to, or prevented from, concluding an economic treaty, by the Treaty of Peace. Nevertheless, all nations should bind themselves, by the Peace Treaty, not to practise an economic blockade after the war, nor to form separate tariff agreements. The right of most favoured nation must be given to all countries without distinction.

Guarantees of Peace

Peace is to be concluded at the Peace Conference by delegates elected by the national representative institutions of each country. The peace terms are to be confirmed by these parliaments.

Secret diplomacy is to be abolished; all parties are to bind themselves not to conclude any secret treaties. Such treaties are declared in contradiction to international law, and void. All treaties, until confirmed by the parliaments of the different nations, are to be considered void.

Gradual disarmament both on land and sea, and the establishment of a militia system. The "League of Nations" advanced by President Wilson may become a valuable aid to international law, provided that (a), all nations are to be obliged to participate in it with equal rights, and (b), international politics are to be democratised.

Ways to Peace

The Allies are to announce immediately that they are willing to open peace negotiations as soon as the enemy powers declare their consent to the renunciation of all forcible annexations.

The Allies must bind themselves not to begin any peace negotiations, nor to conclude peace, except in a general Peace Conference with the participation of delegates from all the neutral countries.

All obstacles to the Stockholm Socialist Conference are to be removed, and passports are to be given immediately to all delegates of parties and organisations who wish to participate.

(The Executive Committee of the Peasants' Soviets also issued a *nakaz*, which differs little from the above.)

6 Peace at Russia's Expense

The Ribot revelations of Austria's peace-offer to France; the so-called "Peace Conference" at Berne, Switzerland, during the summer of 1917, in which delegates participated from all belligerent countries, representing large financial interests in all these countries; and the attempted negotiations of an English agent with a Bulgarian church dignitary; all pointed to the fact that there were strong currents, on both sides, favourable to patching up a peace at the expense of Russia. In my next book, "Kornilov to Brest-Litovsk," I intend to treat this matter at some length, publishing several secret documents discovered in the Ministry of Foreign Affairs at Petrograd.

7 Russian Soldiers in France

Official Report of the Provisional Government

"From the time the news of the Russian Revolution reached Paris, Russian newspapers of extreme tendencies immediately began to appear; and these newspapers, as well as individuals, freely circulated among the soldier masses and began a Bolshevik propaganda, often spreading false news which appeared in the French journals. In the absence of all official news, and of precise details, this campaign provoked discontent among the soldiers. The result was a desire to return to Russia, and a hatred toward the officers.

"Finally it all turned into rebellion. In one of their meetings, the soldiers issued an appeal to refuse to drill, since they had decided to fight no more. It was decided to isolate the rebels, and General Zankevich ordered all soldiers loyal to the Provisional Government to leave the camp of Courtine, and to carry with them all ammunition. On June 25th the order was executed; there remained at the camp only the soldiers who said they would submit 'conditionally' to the Provisional Government. The soldiers at the camp of Courtine received several times the visit of the Commander-in-Chief of the Russian Armies abroad, of Rapp, the Commissar of the Ministry of War, and of several distinguished former exiles who wished to influence them, but these attempts were unsuccessful, and finally Commissar Rapp insisted that the rebels lay down their arms, and, in sign of submission, march in good order to a place called Clairvaux. The order was only partially obeyed; first 500 men went out, of whom 22 were arrested; 24 hours later about 6,000 followed. . . . About 2,000 remained. . . .

"It was decided to increase the pressure; their rations were diminished, their pay was cut off, and the roads toward the village of Courtine were guarded by French soldiers. General Zankevich, having discovered that a Russian artillery brigade was passing through France, decided to form a mixed detachment of infantry and artillery to reduce the rebels. A deputation was sent to the rebels; the deputation returned several hours later, convinced of the futility of the negotiations. On September 1st General Zankevich sent an ultimatum to the rebels demanding that they lay down their arms, and menacing in case of refusal, to open fire with artillery if the order was not obeyed by September 3d at 10 o'clock.

"The order not being executed, a light fire of artillery was opened on the place at the hour agreed upon. Eighteen shells were fired, and the rebels were warned that the bombardment would become more intense. In the night of September 3d 160 men surrendered. September 4th the artillery bombardment recommenced, and at 11 o'clock, after 36 shells had been fired, the rebels raised two white flags and began to leave the camp without arms. By evening 8,300 men had surrendered. 150 soldiers who remained in the camp opened fire with machine-guns that night. The 5th of September, to make an end of the affair, a heavy barrage was laid on the camp, and our soldiers occupied it little by little. The rebels kept up a heavy fire with their machine-guns. September 6th, at 9 o'clock, the camp was entirely occupied. . . . After the disarmament of the rebels, 81 arrests were made. . . ."

Thus the report. From secret documents discovered in the Ministry of Foreign Affairs, however, we know that the account is not strictly accurate. The first trouble arose when the soldiers tried to form Committees, as their comrades in Russia were doing. They demanded to be sent back to Russia, which was refused; and then, being considered a dangerous influence in France, they were ordered to Salonika. They refused to go, and the battle followed. . . . It was discovered that they had been left in camp without officers for about two months, and badly treated, before they became rebellious. All attempts to find out the name of the "Russian artillery brigade" which had fired on them were futile; the telegrams discovered in the Ministry left it to be inferred that French artillery was used. . . .

After their surrender, more than two hundred of the mutineers were shot in cold blood.

8 Tereshchenko's Speech

Résumé

". . . The questions of foreign policy are closely related to those of national defence. . . . And so, if in questions of national defence you think it is necessary to hold session in secret, also in our foreign policy we are sometimes forced to observe the same secrecy. . . .

"German diplomacy attempts to influence public opinion. . . . Therefore the declarations of directors of great democratic organisations who talk loudly of a revolutionary Congress, and the impossibility of another winter campaign, are dangerous. . . . All these declarations cost human lives. . . .

"I wish to speak merely of governmental logic, without touching the questions of the honour and dignity of the State. From the point of view of logic, the foreign policy of Russia ought to be based on a real comprehension of the *interests* of Russia. . . . These interests mean that it is impossible that our country remain alone, and that the present alignment of forces with us, (the Allies), is satisfactory. . . . All humanity longs for peace, but in Russia no one will permit a humiliating peace which would violate the State interests of our fatherland!"

The orator pointed out that such a peace would for long years, if not for centuries, retard the triumph of democratic principles in the world, and would inevitably cause new wars.

"All remember the days of May, when the fraternisation on our Front threatened to end the war by a simple cessation of military operations, and lead the country to a shameful separate peace . . . and what efforts it was necessary to use to make the soldier masses at the front understand that it was not by this method that the Russian State must end the war and guarantee its interest. . . ."

He spoke of the miraculous effect of the July offensive, what strength it gave to the words of Russian ambassadors abroad, and the despair in Germany caused by the Russian victories. And also, the disillusionment in Allied countries which followed the Russian defeat. . . .

"As to the Russian Government, it adhered strictly to the formula of May, 'No annexations and no punitive indemnities.'

We consider it essential not only to proclaim the self-determination of peoples, but also to renounce imperialist aims. . . ."

Germany is continually trying to make peace. The only talk in Germany is of peace; she knows she cannot win.

"I reject the reproaches aimed at the Government which allege that Russian foreign policy does not speak clearly enough about the aims of the war. . . .

"If the question arises as to what ends the Allies are pursuing, it is indispensable first to demand what aims the Central Powers have agreed upon. . . .

"The desire is often heard that we publish the details of the treaties which bind the Allies; but people forget that, up to now, we do not know the treaties which bind the Central Powers. . . ."

Germany, he said, evidently wants to separate Russia from the West by a series of weak buffer-states.

"This tendency to strike at the vital interests of Russia must be checked. . . .

"And will the Russian democracy, which has inscribed on its banner the rights of nations to dispose of themselves, allow calmly the continuation of oppression upon the most civilised peoples (in Austria-Hungary)?

"Those who fear that the Allies will try to profit by our difficult situation, to make us support more than our share of the burden of war, and to solve the questions of peace at our expense, are entirely mistaken. . . . Our enemy looks upon Russia as a market for its products. The end of the war will leave us in a feeble condition, and with our frontier open the flood of German products can easily hold back for years our industrial development. Measures must be taken to guard against this. . . .

"I say openly and frankly: the combination of forces which unites us to the Allies is *favourable to the interests of Russia.* . . . It is therefore important that our views on the questions of war and peace shall be in accord with the views of the Allies as clearly and precisely as possible. . . . To avoid all misunderstanding, I must say frankly that Russia must present at the Paris Conference *one point of view . . .*"

He did not want to comment on the *nakaz* to Skobelev, but he referred to the Manifesto of the Dutch-Scandinavian Committee, just published in Stockholm. This Manifesto declared for the autonomy of Lithuania and Livonia; "but that is clearly impossible," said Tereshchenko, "for Russia must have free ports on the Baltic all the year round. . . .

"In this question the problems of foreign policy are also closely related to interior politics, for if there existed a strong sentiment of unity of all great Russia, one would not witness the repeated manifestations, everywhere, of a desire of peoples to separate from the Central Government. . . . Such separations are contrary to the interests of Russia, and the Russian delegates cannot raise the issue. . . ."

9 The British Fleet (etc.)

At the time of the naval battle of the Gulf of Riga, not only the Bolsheviki, but also the Ministers of the Provisional Government, considered that the British Fleet had deliberately abandoned the Baltic, as one indication of the attitude so often expressed publicly by the British press, and semi-publicly by British representatives in Russia, "Russia's finished! No use bothering about Russia!"

See interview with Kerensky (Note 12, p. 67).

GENERAL GURKO was a former Chief of Staff of the Russian armies under the Tsar. He was a prominent figure in the corrupt Imperial Court. After the Revolution, he was one of the very few persons exiled for his political and personal record. The Russian naval defeat in the Gulf of Riga coincided with the public reception, by King George in London, of General Gurko, a man whom the Russian Provisional Government considered dangerously pro-German as well as reactionary! *

* General Gurko was not suspected of being pro-German. He was dismissed for his stubborn and outspoken criticism of the Provisional Government, of its Decree on the Rights of the Soldier, which he insisted would demoralize the discipline and fighting capacity of the army, of the July Offensive as improperly prepared and sure to end in defeat, of the communiqués issued during the offensive as communiqués which revealed too much to the enemy, etc. At first denied the right to resign his post he was later arrested on Kerensky's personal order, but could not be tried because he had committed no punishable offense. He was finally exiled without trial by an administrative order issued by the Premier and the Minister of War. He was permitted to go to England, and the Provisional Government asked the English Government to give him refuge.—Ed.

10 Appeals Against Insurrection

To Workers and Soldiers

"Comrades! The Dark Forces are increasingly trying to call forth in Petrograd and other towns DISORDERS AND *Pogroms.* Disorder is necessary to the Dark Forces, for disorder will give them an opportunity for crushing the revolutionary movement in blood. Under the pretext of establishing order, and of protecting the inhabitants, they hope to establish the domination of Kornilov, which the revolutionary people succeeded in suppressing not long ago. Woe to the people if these hopes are realised! The triumphant counter-revolution will destroy the Soviets and the Army Committees, will disperse the Constituent Assembly, will stop the transfer of the land to the Land Committees, will put an end to all the hopes of the people for a speedy peace, and will fill all the prisons with revolutionary soldiers and workers.

"In their calculations, the counter-revolutionists and Black Hundred leaders are counting on the serious discontent of the unenlightened part of the people with the disorganisation of the food-supply, the continuation of the war, and the general difficulties of life. They hope to transform every demonstration of soldiers and workers into a *pogrom,* which will frighten the peaceful population and throw it into the arms of the Restorers of Law and Order.

"Under such conditions every attempt to organise a demonstration in these days, although for the most laudable object, would be a crime. All conscious workers and soldiers who are displeased with the policy of the Government will only bring injury to themselves and to the Revolution if they indulge in demonstrations.

"THEREFORE THE *Tsay-ee-kah* ASKS ALL WORKERS NOT TO OBEY ANY CALLS TO DEMONSTRATE.

"WORKERS AND SOLDIERS! DO NOT YIELD TO PROVOCATION! REMEMBER YOUR DUTY TO YOUR COUNTRY AND TO THE REVOLUTION! DO NOT BREAK THE UNITY OF THE REVOLUTIONARY FRONT BY DEMONSTRATIONS WHICH ARE BOUND TO BE UNSUCCESSFUL!"

The Central Executive Committee of the Soviets of Workers' and Soldiers' Deputies (Tsay-ee-kah)

*   *   *   *

Russian Social Democratic Labour Party
THE DANGER IS NEAR!
To All Workers and Soldiers

(Read and Hand to Others)

Comrades Workers and Soldiers!

"Our country is in danger. On account of this danger our freedom and our Revolution are passing through difficult days. The enemy is at the gates of Petrograd. The disorganisation is growing with every hour. It becomes more and more difficult to obtain bread for Petrograd. All, all from the smallest to the greatest, must redouble their efforts, must endeavour to arrange things properly. . . . We must save our country, save freedom. . . . More arms and provisions for the Army! Bread—for the great cities. Order and organisation in the country. . . .

"And in these terrible critical days rumours creep about that SOMEWHERE a demonstration is being prepared, that SOME ONE is calling on the soldiers and workers to destroy revolutionary peace and order. . . . *Rabochi Put,* the newspaper of the Bolsheviki, is pouring oil on the flames: it is flattering, trying to please the unenlightened people, tempting the workers and soldiers, urging them on against the Government, promising them mountains of good things. . . . The confiding, ignorant men believe, they do not reason. . . . And from the other side come also rumours—rumours that the Dark Forces, the friends of the Tsar, the German spies, are rubbing their hands with glee. They are ready to join the Bolsheviki, and with them fan the disorders into civil war.

"The Bolsheviki and the ignorant soldiers and workers seduced by them cry senselessly: 'Down with the Government! All power to the Soviets!' And the Dark servants of the Tsar and the spies of Wilhelm will egg them on; 'Beat the Jews, beat the shopkeepers, rob the markets, devastate the shops, pillage the wine stores! Slay, burn, rob!'

"And then will begin a terrible confusion, a war between one part of the people and the other. All will become still more disorganised, and perhaps once more blood will be shed on the streets of the capital. And then—what then?

"Then, the road to Petrograd will be open to Wilhelm. Then, no bread will come to Petrograd, the children will die of hunger. Then, the Army at the front will remain without support, our brothers in the trenches will be delivered to the fire of the enemy. Then, Russia will lose all prestige in other countries, our money will lose its value; everything will be so dear as to make life impossible. Then, the long awaited Constituent Assembly will be postponed —it will be impossible to convene it in time. And then—Death to the Revolution, Death to our Liberty. . . .

"Is it this that you want, workers and soldiers? No! If you do not, then go, go to the ignorant people seduced by the betrayers, and tell them the whole truth, which we have told you!

"Let all know that EVERY MAN WHO IN THESE TERRIBLE DAYS CALLS ON YOU TO COME OUT IN THE STREETS AGAINST THE GOVERN-MENT, IS EITHER A SECRET SERVANT OF THE TSAR, A PROVOCATOR, OR AN UNWISE ASSISTANT OF THE ENEMIES OF THE PEOPLE, OR A PAID SPY OF WILHELM!

"Every conscious worker revolutionist, every conscious peasant, every revolutionary soldier, all who understand what harm a demonstration or a revolt against the Government might cause to the people, must join together and not allow the enemies of the people to destroy our freedom."

The Petrograd Electoral Committee of the Mensheviki-oborontsi.

11 Miliukov's Speech

Résumé

"Every one admits, it seems, that the defence of the country is our principal task, and that, to assure it, we must have discipline in the Army and order in the rear. To achieve this, there must be a power capable of daring, not only by persuasion, but also by force. . . . The germ of all our evils comes from the point of view, original, truly Russian, concerning foreign policy, which passes for the Internationalist point of view.

"The noble Lenin only imitates the noble Keroyevsky when he holds that from Russia will come the New World which shall resuscitate the aged West, and which will replace the old banner of doctrinary Socialism by the new direct action of starving masses—and that will push humanity forward and force it to break in the doors of the social paradise. . . ."

These men sincerely believed that the decomposition of Russia would bring about the decomposition of the whole capitalist régime. Starting from that point of view, they were able to commit the unconscious treason, in wartime, of calmly telling the soldiers to abandon the trenches, and instead of fighting the external enemy, creating internal civil war and attacking the proprietors and capitalists. . . .

Here Miliukov was interrupted by furious cries from the Left, demanding what Socialist had ever advised such action. . . .

"Martov says that only the revolutionary pressure of the proletariat can condemn and conquer the evil will of imperialist cliques and break down the dictatorship of these cliques. . . . Not by an accord between Governments for a limitation of armaments, but by the disarming of these Governments and the radical democratisation of the military system. . . ."

He attacked Martov viciously, and then turned on the Mensheviki and Socialist Revolutionaries, whom he accused of entering the Government as Ministers with the avowed purpose of carrying on the class-struggle!

"The Socialists of Germany and of the Allied countries contemplated these gentlemen with ill-concealed contempt, but they decided that it was for Russia, and sent us some apostles of the Universal Conflagration. . . .

"The formula of our democracy is very simple; no foreign policy, no art of diplomacy, an immediate democratic peace, a declaration to the Allies, 'We want nothing, we haven't anything to fight with!' And then our adversaries will make the same declaration, and the brotherhood of peoples will be accomplished!"

Miliukov took a fling at the Zimmerwald Manifesto, and declared that even Kerensky has not been able to escape the influence of "that unhappy document which will forever be your indictment." He then attacked Skobelev, whose position in foreign assemblies, where he would appear as a Russian delegate, yet opposed to the foreign policy of his Government, would be so strange that people would say, "What's that gentleman carrying, and what shall we talk to him about?" As for the *nakaz*, Miliukov said that he himself was a pacifist; that he believed in the creation of an International Arbitration Board, and the necessity for a limitation of armaments, and parliamentary control over secret diplomacy, which did not mean the abolition of secret diplomacy.

As for the Socialist ideas in the *nakaz*, which he called "Stockholm ideas"—peace without victory, the right of self-determination of peoples, and renunciation of the economic war—

"The German successes are directly proportionate to the successes of those who call themselves the revolutionary democracy. I do not wish to say, 'to the successes of the Revolution,' because I believe that the defeats of the revolutionary democracy are victories for the Revolution. . . .

"The influence of the Soviet leaders abroad is not unimportant. One had only to listen to the speech of the Minister of Foreign Affairs to be convinced that, in this hall, the influence of the revolutionary democracy on foreign policy is so strong, that the Minister does not dare to speak face to face with it about the honour and dignity of Russia!

"We can see, in the *nakaz* of the Soviets, that the ideas of the Stockholm Manifesto have been elaborated in two directions—that of Utopianism, and that of German interests. . . ."

Interrupted by the angry cries of the Left, and rebuked by the President, Miliukov insisted that the proposition of peace concluded by popular assemblies, not by diplomats, and the proposal to undertake peace negotiations as soon as the enemy had renounced annexations, were pro-German. Recently Kuhlman said that a personal declaration bound only him who made it. . . . "Anyway, we will imitate the Germans before we will imitate the Soviet of Workers' and Soldiers' Deputies. . . ."

The sections treating of the independence of Lithuania and Livonia were symptoms of nationalist agitation in different parts of Russia, supported, said Miliukov, by German money. . . . Amid bedlam from the Left, he contrasted the clauses of the *nakaz* concerning Alsace-Lorraine, Rumania, and Serbia, with those treating of the nationalities in Germany and Austria. The *nakaz* embraced the German and Austrian point of view, said Miliukov.

Passing to Tereshchenko's speech, he contemptuously accused him of being afraid to speak the thought in his mind, and even afraid to think in terms of the greatness of Russia. The Dardanelles must belong to Russia. . . .

"You are continually saying that the soldier does not know why he is fighting, and that when he does know, he'll fight. . . . It is true that the soldier doesn't know why he is fighting, but now you have told him that there is no reason for him to fight, that we have no national interests, and that we are fighting for alien ends. . . ."

Paying tribute to the Allies, who, he said, with the assistance of America, "will yet save the cause of humanity," he ended:

"Long live the light of humanity, the advanced democracies of the West, who for a long time have been travelling the way we now only begin to enter, with ill-assured and hesitating steps! Long live our brave Allies!"

12   Interview with Kerensky

The Associated Press man tried his hand. "Mr. Kerensky," he began, "in England and France people are disappointed with the Revolution——"

"Yes, I know," interrupted Kerensky, quizzically. "Abroad the Revolution is no longer fashionable!"

"What is your explanation of why the Russians have stopped fighting?"

"That is a foolish question to ask." Kerensky was annoyed. "Russia entered the war first of all the Allies, and for a long time she bore the whole brunt of it. Her losses have been inconceivably greater than those of all the other nations put together. Russia has now the right to demand of the Allies that they bring greater force of arms to bear." He stopped for a moment and stared at his interlocutor. "You are asking why the Russians have stopped fighting, and the Russians are asking where is the British fleet—with German battle-ships in the Gulf of Riga?" Again he ceased suddenly, and as suddenly burst out. "The Russian Revolution hasn't failed and the revolutionary Army hasn't failed. It is not the Revolution which caused disorganisation in the army—that disorganisation was accomplished years ago, by the old régime. Why aren't the Russians fighting? I will tell you. Because the masses of the people are economically exhausted,—and because they are disillusioned with the Allies!"

The interview of which this is an excerpt was cabled to the United States, and in a few days sent back by the American State Department, with a demand that it be "altered." This Kerensky refused to do; but it was done by his secretary, Dr. David Soskice—and, thus purged of all offensive references to the Allies, was given to the press of the world. . . .

CHAPTER III

ON THE EVE

In the relations of a weak Government and a rebellious people there comes a time when every act of the authorities exasperates the masses, and every refusal to act excites their contempt. . . .

The proposal to abandon Petrograd raised a hurricane; Kerensky's public denial that the Government had any such intention was met with hoots of derision.

Pinned to the wall by the pressure of the Revolution (cried *Rabochi Put*), the Government of "provisional" bourgeois tries to get free by giving out lying assurances that it never thought of fleeing from Petrograd, and that it didn't wish to surrender the capital. . . .

In Kharkov thirty thousand coal miners organised, adopting the preamble of the I. W. W. constitution: "The working class and the employing class have nothing in common." Dispersed by Cossacks, some were locked out by the mine-owners, and the rest declared a general strike. Minister of Commerce and Industry Konovalov appointed his assistant, Orlov, with plenary powers, to settle the trouble. Orlov was hated by the miners. But the *Tsay-ee-kah* not only supported his appointment, but refused to demand that the Cossacks be recalled from the Don Basin. . . .*

This was followed by the dispersal of the Soviet at Kaluga. The Bolsheviki, having secured a majority in the Soviet, set free some political prisoners. With the sanction of the Government Commissar the Municipal Duma called in troops from Minsk, and bombarded the Soviet headquarters with artillery. The Bolsheviki yielded, but as they left the building Cossacks attacked them, crying, "This is what we'll do to all the other Bolshevik Soviets, including those of Moscow and Petrograd!" This incident sent a wave of panic rage throughout Russia. . . .

In Petrograd was ending a regional Congress of Soviets of the North, presided over by the Bolshevik Krylenko. By an immense majority it resolved that all power should be assumed by the All-Russian Congress; and concluded by greeting the Bolsheviki in prison, bidding them rejoice, for the hour of their liberation was at hand. At the same time the first All-Russian Conference of Factory-Shop Committees[1] declared emphatically for the Soviets, and continued significantly,

After liberating themselves politically from Tsardom, the working-class wants to see the democratic régime triumphant in the sphere of its productive activity. This is best expressed by Workers' Control over industrial production, which naturally arose in the atmophere of economic decomposition created by the criminal policy of the dominating classes. . . .

The Union of Railwaymen was demanding the resignation of Liverovsky, Minister of Ways and Communications. . . .

* The Don Basin was the home of the Don Cossacks, and neither the Central Executive Committee of the Soviets nor the Provisional Government could conceivably have demanded that they "be recalled from the Don. Compare on this John Reed's own account in Chapter II of the Government's recognition of the Council of the Union of Cossack Armies.—Ed.

In the name of the *Tsay-ee-kah,* Skobelev insisted that the *nakaz* be presented at the Allied Conference, and formally protested against the sending of Tereshchenko to Paris. Tereshchenko offered to resign. . . .

General Verkhovsky, unable to accomplish his reorganisation of the army, only came to Cabinet meetings at long intervals. . . .

On November 3d Burtzev's *Obshchee Dielo* came out with great headlines:

Citizens! Save the fatherland!

I have just learned that yesterday, at a meeting of the Commission for National Defence, Minister of War General Verkhovsky, one of the principal persons responsible for the fall of Kornilov, proposed to sign a separate peace, independently of the Allies.

That is treason to Russia!

Tereshchenko declared that the Provisional Government had not even examined Verkhovsky's proposition.

"You might think," said Tereshchenko, "that we were in a madhouse!"

The members of the Commission were astounded at the General's words.

General Alexeyev wept.

No! It is not madness! It is worse. It is direct treason to Russia!

Kerensky, Tereshchenko and Nekrasov must immediately answer us concerning the words of Verkhovsky.

Citizens, arise!

Russia is being sold!

Save her!

What Verkhovsky really said was that the Allies must be pressed to offer peace, because the Russian army could fight no longer. . . .

Both in Russia and abroad the sensation was tremendous. Verkhovsky was given "indefinite leave of absence for ill-health," and left the Government. *Obshchee Dielo* was suppressed. . . .

Sunday, November 4th, was designated as the Day of the Petrograd Soviet, with immense meetings planned all over the city, ostensibly to raise money for the organisation and the press; really, to make a demonstration of strength. Suddenly it was announced that on the same day the Cossacks would hold a *Krestny Khod*—Procession of the Cross—in honour of the Ikon of 1612, through whose miraculous intervention Napoleon had been driven from Moscow. The atmosphere was electric; a spark might kindle civil war. The Petrograd Soviet issued a manifesto, headed "Brothers—Cossacks!"

You, Cossacks, are being incited against us, workers and soldiers. This plan of Cain is being put into operation by our common enemies, the oppressors, the privileged classes— generals, bankers, landlords, former officials, former servants of the Tsar. . . . We are hated by all grafters, rich men, princes, nobles, generals, including your Cossack generals. They are ready at any moment to destroy the Petrograd Soviet and crush the Revolution. . . .

On the 4th of November somebody is organising a Cossack religious procession. It is a question of the free consciousness of every individual whether he will or will not take part in this procession. We do not interfere in this matter, nor do we obstruct anybody. . . . However, we warn you, Cossacks! Look out and see to it that under the pretext of a *Krestni Khod,* your Kaledins do not instigate you against workmen, against soldiers. . . .

The procession was hastily called off. . . .

In the barracks and the working-class quarters of the

town the Bolsheviki were preaching, "All Power to the Soviets!" and agents of the Dark Forces were urging the people to rise and slaughter the Jews, shop-keepers, Socialist leaders. . . .

On one side the Monarchist press, inciting to bloody repression—on the other Lenin's great voice roaring, "Insurrection! . . . We cannot wait any longer!"

Even the bourgeois press was uneasy.[2] *Birzhevya Viedomosti* (Exchange Gazette) called the Bolshevik propaganda an attack on "the most elementary principles of society—personal security and the respect for private property."

But it was the "moderate" Socialist journals which were the most hostile.[3] "The Bolsheviki are the most dangerous enemies of the Revolution," declared *Dielo Naroda*. Said the Menshevik *Dien,* "The Government ought to defend itself and defend us." Plekhanov's paper, *Yedinstvo* (Unity),[4] called the attention of the Government to the fact that the Petrograd workers were being armed, and demanded stern measures against the Bolsheviki.

Daily the Government seemed to become more helpless. Even the Municipal administration broke down. The columns of the morning papers were filled with accounts of the most audacious robberies and murders, and the criminals were unmolested.

On the other hand armed workers patrolled the streets at night, doing battle with marauders and requisitioning arms wherever they found them.

On the first of November Colonel Polkovnikov, Military Commander of Petrograd, issued a proclamation:

Despite the difficult days through which the country is passing, irresponsible appeals to armed demonstrations and

БРАТЬЯ-КАЗАКИ!

Петроградскій совѣтъ солдатскихъ и рабочихъ депутатовъ обращается къ вамъ свое слово.

Васъ, казаки, хотятъ возстановить противъ насъ, рабочихъ и солдатъ. Эту гнусную работу совершаютъ наши общіе враги, насильники-дворяне, банкиры, помѣщики, старые чиновники, бывшіе слуги царскіе. Они всегда были сильны и властны раздѣленіемъ народа. Направляли солдатъ на рабочихъ и крестьянъ. Казаковъ напускали на солдатъ. Какими средствами достигали они этого? Ложью, клеветой. Казакъ, солдатъ, матросъ, рабочій, крестьянинъ — родные братья. Всѣ они труженики, всѣ бѣдны, всѣ тянутъ лямку, всѣ придавлены и ограблены войною.

Кому нужна война? Кто ея затѣялъ? Не казакъ и не солдатъ, не рабочій и не крестьянинъ. Война нужна генераламъ, банкирамъ, царямъ, помѣщикамъ. Они увеличиваютъ на войнѣ свою власть, свою силу, свои богатства. Народную кровь они превращаютъ въ болото своихъ барышей.

Народъ хочетъ мира. Во всѣхъ странахъ солдаты и рабочіе жаждутъ мира. Петроградскій совѣтъ рабочихъ и солдатскихъ депутатовъ говоритъ буржуямъ и генераламъ: „Отойдите въ сторону, насильники! Пусть власть перейдетъ въ руки самого народа, и тогда народъ немедленно же заключитъ честный миръ".

Правильно ли это, товарищи-казаки? Мы не сомнѣваемся, что вы всѣ скажете правильно! Но именно поэтому насъ ненавидятъ всѣ ростовщики, богачи, князья, дворяне, генералы, и въ ихъ числѣ ваши, казачьи генералы. Они готовы въ любой часъ уничтожить петроградскій совѣтъ, задушить революцію, надѣть оковы на народъ, какъ было при царѣ.

Поэтому они вамъ клевещутъ на насъ. Они обманываютъ васъ. Они говорятъ, будто Совѣтъ хочетъ отобрать ваши земли. Не вѣрьте, казаки! Совѣтъ хочетъ отобрать землю помѣщичью и передать ихъ крестьянамъ, хлѣборобамъ и въ частности бѣднымъ казакамъ. У кого это поднимется рука, отобрать землю у труженика-казака?

Вамъ говорятъ, будто Совѣтъ собирается 22-го октября устроить какое-то возстаніе, сраженіе съ вами, стрѣльбу на улицахъ, рѣзню. Тѣ, кто сказалъ вамъ это — негодяи и провокаторы. Такъ и закатите имъ! На 22-е октября Совѣтъ назначилъ мирные митинги, собранія, концерты, гдѣ рабочіе и солдаты, матросы и крестьяне будутъ слушать и обсуждать рѣчи о войнѣ и мирѣ, о народной долѣ. На эти мирные, братскіе митинги мы приглашаемъ и васъ. Добро пожаловать, братья-казаки!

Кто изъ васъ сомнѣвается пусть зайдетъ въ Смольный, гдѣ помѣщается Совѣтъ. Тутъ всегда много солдатъ, есть и казаки. Они объяснятъ сомнѣвающемуся, чего хочетъ Совѣтъ, каковы его цѣли и пути. Для того народъ и скинулъ царя, чтобъ свободно обсуждать свои нужды и брать свои дѣла въ собственныя руки. Сбросьте и вы, казаки, повязку, которую надѣваютъ вамъ на глаза Калединцы, Бардижи, Карауловы и прочіе враги трудового казачества.

22-го октября устраивается тѣмъ то казачій крестный ходъ. Дѣло свободной совѣсти каждаго казака участвовать или не участвовать въ крестномъ ходѣ. Мы въ это дѣло не вмѣшиваемся и никакихъ препятствій никому не чинимъ.

Однако, мы васъ предупреждаемъ, казаки: глядите зорко, какъ бы, подъ видомъ крестнаго хода, не попытались ваши Калединцы натравить васъ на рабочихъ, на солдатъ. Ихъ цѣль — вызвать кровопролитіе и въ братской крови утопить вашу и нашу свободу.

Знайте твердо. 22-го октября — день Петроградскаго Совѣта, день мирныхъ митинговъ, собраній и денежнаго сбора на солдатскія и рабочія газеты. Приходите къ намъ, казаки,—въ общую семью трудового народа, для общей борьбы за волю и счастье.

Братскую руку протягиваетъ вамъ, казаки,

Петроградскій Совѣтъ Рабочихъ и Солдатскихъ Депутатовъ.

Типографія «Копѣйка», Петроградъ, Садовая ул., д. соб. домъ.

Appeal of the Petrograd Soviet to the Cossacks to call off their *Krestny Khod*—the religious procession planned for November 4th (our calendar). "Brothers—Cossacks!" it begins. "The Petrograd Soviet of Workers' and Soldiers' Deputies addresses you."

massacres are still being spread around Petrograd, and from day to day robbery and disorder increase.

This state of things is disorganising the life of the citizens, and hinders the systematic work of the Government and the Municipal Institutions.

In full consciousness of my responsibility and my duty before my country, I command:

1. Every military unit, in accordance with special instructions and within the territory of its garrison, to afford every assistance to the Municipality, to the Commissars, and to the militia, in the guarding of Government institutions.

2. The organisation of patrols, in co-operation with the District Commander and the representatives of the city militia, and the taking of measures for the arrest of criminals and deserters.

3. The arrest of all persons entering barracks and inciting to armed demonstrations and massacres, and their delivery to the headquarters of the Second Commander of the city.

4. To suppress any armed demonstration or riot at its start, with all armed forces at hand.

5. To afford assistance to the Commissars in preventing unwarranted searches in houses and unwarranted arrests.

6. To report immediately all that happens in the district under charge to the Staff of the Petrograd Military District.

I call upon all Army Committees and organisations to afford their help to the commanders in fulfilment of the duties with which they are charged.

In the Council of the Republic Kerensky declared that the Government was fully aware of the Bolshevik preparations, and had sufficient force to cope with any demonstration.[5] He accused *Novaya Rus* and *Rabochi Put* of both doing the same kind of subversive work. "But owing to the absolute freedom of the press," he added, "the Government is not in a position to combat printed lies.*

---

* This was not quite candid. The Provisional Government had suppressed Bolshevik papers before, in July, and was planning to do so again.

. . ." Declaring that these were two aspects of the same propaganda, which had for its object the counter-revolution, so ardently desired by the Dark Forces, he went on:

"I am a doomed man, it doesn't matter what happens to me, and I have the audacity to say that the other enigmatic part is that of the unbelievable provocation created in the city by the Bolsheviki!"

On November 2d only fifteen delegates to the Congress of Soviets had arrived. Next day there were a hundred, and the morning after that a hundred and seventy-five, of whom one hundred and three were Bolsheviki. . . . Four hundred constituted a quorum, and the Congress was only three days off. . . .

I spent a great deal of time at Smolny. It was no longer easy to get in. Double rows of sentries guarded the outer gates, and once inside the front door there was a long line of people waiting to be let in, four at a time, to be questioned as to their identity and their business. Passes were given out, and the pass system was changed every few hours; for spies continually sneaked through. . . .

One day as I came up to the outer gate I saw Trotsky and his wife just ahead of me. They were halted by a soldier. Trotsky searched through his pockets, but could find no pass.

"Never mind," he said finally. "You know me. My name is Trotsky."

"You haven't got a pass," answered the soldier stubbornly. "You cannot go in. Names don't mean anything to me."

"But I am the president of the Petrograd Soviet."

"Well," replied the soldier, "if you're as important a fellow as that you must at least have one little paper."

Trotsky was very patient. "Let me see the Commandant," he said. The soldier hesitated, grumbling something

Военно-Революціон.
Комитет
при
ПЕТР. С. Р. и С. Д:

Комендантскій отдѣлъ.

16 ноября 1917 г.

№ 955

Смольный институтъ.

Пропускъ.

Дано, сіе _Джонъ Ридъ_
Кореси. амер. соц. прессы

срокомъ по _1 Декабря._

на право свободнаго входа въ Смоль-

ный Институтъ.

Комендантъ

Ф. Дзержинскій

Дѣлопроизводитель

Pass to Smolny Institute, issued by the Military Revolutionary Committee, giving me the right of entry at any time.

TRANSLATION:

Military Revolutionary Committee
attached to the
Petrograd Soviet of W. & S. D.
Commandant's office
16th November, 1917
No. 955
Smolny Institute

PASS

Is given by the present to John Reed, correspondent of the
American Socialist press, until December 1, the right of free
entry into Smolny Institute.

Commandant*
Adjutant

* The signature of the Commandant on Reed's pass is that of F. Dzerzhinsky, soon to be named by Lenin head of the *Cheka*. Thus Reed's document establishes that Dzerzhinsky was even then assuming police functions
as Commandant of Smolny which had been militarized on becoming the headquarters of the Military Revolutionary Committee.—*Ed.*

about not wanting to disturb the Commandant for every devil that came along. He beckoned finally to the soldier in command of the guard. Trotsky explained matters to him. "My name is Trotsky," he repeated.

"Trotsky?" The other soldier scratched his head. "I've heard the name somewhere," he said at length. "I guess it's all right. You can go on in, comrade. . . ."

In the corridor I met Karakhan, member of the Bolshevik Central Committee, who explained to me what the new Government would be like.

"A loose organisation, sensitive to the popular will as expressed through the Soviets, allowing local forces full play. At present the Provisional Government obstructs the action of the local democratic will, just as the Tsar's Government did. The initiative of the new society shall come from below. . . . The form of the Government will be modelled on the Constitution of the Russian Social Democratic Labour Party. The new *Tsay-ee-kah,* responsible to frequent meetings of the All-Russian Congress of Soviets, will be the parliament; the various Ministries will be headed by *collegia*—committees—instead of by Ministers, and will be directly responsible to the Soviets. . . ."

On October 30th, by appointment, I went up to a small, bare room in the attic of Smolny, to talk with Trotsky. In the middle of the room he sat on a rough chair at a bare table. Few questions from me were necessary; he talked rapidly and steadily, for more than an hour. The substance of his talk, in his own words, I give here:

"The Provisional Government is absolutely powerless. The bourgeoisie is in control, but this control is masked by a fictitious coalition with the *oborontsi* parties. Now, during the Revolution, one sees revolts of peasants who are tired of waiting for their promised land; and all over the country, in all the toiling classes, the same disgust is evident. This domination by the bourgeoisie is only possible by means of civil war. The Kornilov method is the only way by which the bourgeoisie can control. But it is force which the bourgeoisie lacks. . . . The Army is with us. The conciliators and pacifists, Socialist Revolutionaries and Mensheviki, have lost all authority—because the struggle between the peasants and the landlords, between the workers and the employers, between the soldiers and the officers, has become more bitter, more irreconcilable than ever. Only by the concerted action of the popular mass, only by the victory of proletarian dictatorship, can the Revolution be achieved and the people saved. . . .

"The Soviets are the most perfect representatives of the people—perfect in their revolutionary experience, in their ideas and objects. Based directly upon the army in the trenches, the workers in the factories, and the peasants in the fields, they are the backbone of the Revolution.

"There has been an attempt to create a power without the Soviets—and only powerlessness has been created. Counter-revolutionary schemes of all sorts are now being hatched in the corridors of the Council of the Russian Republic. The Cadet party represents the counter-revolution militant. On the other side, the Soviets represent the cause of the people. Between the two camps there are no groups of serious importance. . . . It is the *lutte finale*. The bourgeois counter-revolution organises all its forces and waits for the moment to attack us. Our answer will be decisive. We will complete the work scarcely begun in March, and advanced during the Kornilov affair. . . ."

He went on to speak of the new Government's foreign policy:

"Our first act will be to call for an immediate armistice
on all fronts, and a conference of peoples to discuss democratic peace terms. The quantity of democracy we get in
the peace settlement depends on the quantity of revolutionary response there is in Europe. If we create here a Government of the Soviets, that will be a powerful factor for
immediate peace in Europe; for this Government will
address itself directly and immediately to all peoples,
over the heads of their Governments, proposing an armistice. At the moment of the conclusion of peace the
pressure of the Russian Revolution will be in the direction of 'no annexations, no indemnities, the right of self-
determination of peoples,' and a *Federated Republic of
Europe*. . . .

"At the end of this war I see Europe recreated, not by
the diplomats, but by the proletariat. The Federated Republic of Europe—the United States of Europe—that is
what must be. National autonomy no longer suffices.
Economic evolution demands the abolition of national
frontiers. If Europe is to remain split into national groups,
then Imperialism will recommence its work. Only a Federated Republic of Europe can give peace to the world."
He smiled—that fine, faintly ironical smile of his. "But
without the action of the European masses, these ends
cannot be realised—now. . . ."

Now while everybody was waiting for the Bolsheviki
to appear suddenly on the streets one morning and begin
to shoot down people with white collars on, the real insurrection took its way quite naturally and openly.

The Provisional Government planned to send the Petrograd garrison to the front.

The Petrograd garrison numbered about sixty thousand

men, who had taken a prominent part in the Revolution. It was they who had turned the tide in the great days of March, created the Soviets of Soldiers' Deputies, and hurled back Kornilov from the gates of Petrograd.

Now a large part of them were Bolsheviki. When the Provisional Government talked of evacuating the city, it was the Petrograd garrison which answered, "If you are not capable of defending the capital, conclude peace; if you cannot conclude peace, go away and make room for a People's Government which can do both. . . ."

It was evident that any attempt at insurrection depended upon the attitude of the Petrograd garrison. The Government's plan was to replace the garrison regiments with "dependable" troops—Cossacks, Death Battalions. The Army Committees, the "moderate" Socialists and the *Tsay-ee-kah* supported the Government. A wide-spread agitation was carried on at the Front and in Petrograd, emphasizing the fact that for eight months the Petrograd garrison had been leading an easy life in the barracks of the capital, while their exhausted comrades in the trenches starved and died.

Naturally there was some truth in the accusation that the garrison regiments were reluctant to exchange their comparative comfort for the hardships of a winter campaign. But there were other reasons why they refused to go. The Petrograd Soviet feared the Government's intentions, and from the Front came hundreds of delegates, chosen by the common soldiers, crying, "It is true we need reinforcements, but more important, we must know that Petrograd and the Revolution are well-guarded. . . . Do you hold the rear, comrades, and we will hold the front!"

On October 25th, behind closed doors, the Central Committee of the Petrograd Soviet discussed the formation of a special Military Committee to decide the whole question. The next day a meeting of the Soldiers' Section of the Petrograd Soviet elected a Committee, which immediately proclaimed a boycott of the bourgeois newspapers, and condemned the *Tsay-ee-kah* for opposing the Congress of Soviets. On the 29th, in open session of the Petrograd Soviet, Trotsky proposed that the Soviet formally sanction the Military Revolutionary Committee. "We ought," he said, "to create our special organisation to march to battle, and if necessary to die. . . ." It was decided to send to the front two delegations, one from the Soviet and one from the garrison, to confer with the Soldiers' Committees and the General Staff.

At Pskov, the Soviet delegates were met by General Cheremissov, commander of the Northern Front, with the curt declaration that he had ordered the Petrograd garrison to the trenches, and that was all. The garrison committee was not allowed to leave Petrograd. . . .

A delegation of the Soldiers' Section of the Petrograd Soviet asked that a representative be admitted to the Staff of the Petrograd District. Refused. The Petrograd Soviet demanded that no orders be issued without the approval of the Soldiers' Section. Refused. The delegates were roughly told, "We only recognise the *Tsay-ee-kah*. We do not recognise you; if you break any laws, we shall arrest you."

On the 30th a meeting of representatives of all the Petrograd regiments passed a resolution: *"The Petrograd garrison no longer recognises the Provisional Government. The Petrograd Soviet is our Government. We will obey only the orders of the Petrograd Soviet, through the Military Revolutionary Committee."* The local military units were ordered to wait for instructions from the Soldiers' Section of the Petrograd Soviet.

Next day the *Tsay-ee-kah* summoned its own meeting, composed largely of officers, formed a Committee to cooperate with the Staff, and detailed Commissars in all quarters of the city:

A great soldier meeting at Smolny on the 3d resolved:

Saluting the creation of the Military Revolutionary Committee, the Petrograd garrison promises it complete support in all its actions, to unite more closely the front and the rear in the interests of the Revolution.

The garrison moreover declares that with the revolutionary proletariat it assures the maintenance of revolutionary order in Petrograd. Every attempt at provocation on the part of the Kornilovtsi or the bourgeoisie will be met with merciless resistance.

Now conscious of its power, the Military Revolutionary Committee peremptorily summoned the Petrograd Staff to submit to its control. To all printing plants it gave orders not to publish any appeals or proclamations without the Committee's authorisation. Armed Commissars visited the Kronversk arsenal and seized great quantities of arms and ammunition, halting a shipment of ten thousand bayonets which was being sent to Novocherkask, headquarters of Kaledin. . . .

Suddenly awake to the danger, the Government offered immunity if the Committee would disband. Too late. At midnight November 5th Kerensky himself sent Malevsky to offer the Petrograd Soviet representation on the Staff. The Military Revolutionary Committee accepted. An hour later General Manikovsky, acting Minister of war, countermanded the offer. . . .

Tuesday morning, November 6th, the city was thrown into excitement by the appearance of a placard signed,

"Military Revolutionary Committee attached to the Petro-grad Soviet of Workers' and Soldiers' Deputies."

To the Population of Petrograd. Citizens!

Counter-revolution has raised its criminal head. The Korni-lovtsi are mobilising their forces in order to crush the All-Russian Congress of Soviets and break the Constituent Assembly. At the same time the *pogromists* may attempt to call upon the people of Petrograd for trouble and bloodshed. The Petrograd Soviet of Workers' and Soldiers' Deputies takes upon itself the guarding of revolutionary order in the city against counter-revolutionary and *pogrom* attempts.

The Petrograd garrison will not allow any violence or disorders. The population is invited to arrest hooligans and Black Hundred agitators and take them to the Soviet Commissars at the nearest barracks. At the first attempt of the Dark Forces to make trouble on the streets of Petrograd, whether robbery or fighting, the criminals will be wiped off the face of the earth!

Citizens! We call upon you to maintain complete quiet and self-possession. The cause of order and Revolution is in strong hands.

List of regiments where there are Commissars of the Military Revolutionary Committee. . . .

On the 3rd the leaders of the Bolsheviki had another historic meeting behind closed doors. Notified by Zalkind, I waited in the corridor outside the door; and Volodarsky as he came out told me what was going on.

Lenin spoke: "November 6th will be too early. We must have an all-Russian basis for the rising; and on the 6th all the delegates to the Congress will not have arrived. . . . On the other hand, November 8th will be too late. By that time the Congress will be organised, and it is difficult for a large organised body of people to take swift, decisive action. We must act on the 7th, the day the Congress meets, so that we may say to it, 'Here is the power! What are you going to do with it?' "

In a certain upstairs room sat a thin-faced, long-haired individual, once an officer in the armies of the Tsar, then revolutionist and exile, a certain Ovseenko, called Antonov, mathematician and chess-player; he was drawing careful plans for the seizure of the capital.

On its side the Government was preparing. Inconspicuously certain of the most loyal regiments, from widely-separated divisions, were ordered to Petrograd. The *yunker** artillery was drawn into the Winter Palace. Patrols of Cossacks made their appearance in the streets, for the first time since the July days. Polkovnikov issued order after order, threatening to repress all insubordination with the "utmost energy." Kishkin, Minister of Public Instruction, the worst-hated member of the Cabinet, was appointed Special Commissar to keep order in Petrograd; he named as assistants two men no less unpopular, Rutenburg and Palchinsky. Petrograd, Cronstadt and Finland were declared in a state of siege—upon which the bourgeois *Novoye Vremya* (New Times) remarked ironically:

Why the state of siege? The Government is no longer a power. It has no moral authority and it does not possess the necessary apparatus to use force. . . . In the most favourable circumstances it can only negotiate with any one who consents to parley. Its authority goes no farther. . . .

Monday morning, the 5th, I dropped in at the Marinsky Palace, to see what was happening in the Council of the

---

* *Yunker* is the official term for a student in an officers' training school, similar to our West Point cadet. During the war, so many officers perished that many such training schools were set up with students drawn from all classes of the population and soldiers and non-commissioned officers who showed exceptional promise.—*Ed.*

Russian Republic. Bitter debate on Tereshchenko's foreign policy. Echoes of the Burtzev-Verkhovski affair. All the diplomats present except the Italian ambassador, who everybody said was prostrated by the Corso disaster. . . .

As I came in, the Left Socialist Revolutionary Karelin was reading aloud an editorial from the London *Times* which said, "The remedy for Bolshevism is bullets!" Turning to the Cadets he cried, "That's what *you* think, too!"

Voices from the Right, "Yes! Yes!"

"Yes, I know you think so," answered Karelin, hotly. "But you haven't the courage to try it!"

Then Skobelev, looking like a matinée idol with his soft blond beard and wavy yellow hair, rather apologetically defending the Soviet *nakaz*. Tereshchenko followed, assailed from the Left by cries of "Resignation! Resignation!" He insisted that the delegates of the Government and of the *Tsay-ee-kah* to Paris should have a common point of view—his own. A few words about the restoration of discipline in the army, about war to victory. . . . Tumult, and over the stubborn opposition of the truculent Left, the Council of the Republic passed to the simple order of the day.

There stretched the rows of Bolshevik seats—empty since that first day when they left the Council, carrying with them so much life. As I went down the stairs it seemed to me that in spite of the bitter wrangling, no real voice from the rough world outside could penetrate this high, cold hall, and that the Provisional Government was wrecked—on the same rock of War and Peace that had wrecked the Miliukov Ministry. . . . The doorman grumbled as he put on my coat, "I don't know what is becoming of poor Russia. All these Mensheviki and Bolsheviki and Trudoviki. . . . This Ukraine and this Finland and the German imperialists and the English imperialists. I am

forty-five years old, and in all my life I never heard so
many words as in this place. . . ."

In the corridor I met Professor Shatsky, a rat-faced individual in a dapper frock-coat, very influential in the
councils of the Cadet party. I asked him what he thought
of the much-talked-of Bolshevik *vystuplenie*. He shrugged,
sneering.

"They are cattle—*canaille*," he answered. "They will not
dare, or if they dare they will soon be sent flying. From
our point of view it will not be bad, for then they will ruin
themselves and have no power in the Constituent Assembly. . . .

"But, my dear sir, allow me to outline to you my plan
for a form of Government to be submitted to the Constituent Assembly. You see, I am chairman of a commission appointed from this body, in conjunction with the
Provisional Government, to work out a constitutional
project. . . . We will have a legislative assembly of two
chambers, such as you have in the United States. In the
lower chamber will be territorial representatives; in the
upper, representatives of the liberal professions, zemstvos,
Cooperatives—and Trade Unions. . . ."

Outside a chill, damp wind came from the west, and the
cold mud underfoot soaked through my shoes. Two companies of *yunkers* passed swinging up the Morskaya,
tramping stiffly in their long coats and singing an oldtime
crashing chorus, such as the soldiers used to sing under the
Tsar. . . . At the first cross-street I noticed that the City
Militiamen were mounted, and armed with revolvers in
bright new holsters; a little group of people stood silently
staring at them. At the corner of the Nevsky I bought a
pamphlet by Lenin, "Will the Bolsheviki be Able to Hold
the Power?" paying for it with one of the stamps which did

duty for small change. The usual street-cars crawled past, citizens and soldiers clinging to the outside in a way to make Theodore P. Shonts green with envy. . . . Along the sidewalk a row of deserters in uniform sold cigarettes and sunflower seeds. . . .

Up the Nevsky in the sour twilight crowds were battling for the latest papers, and knots of people were trying to make out the multitudes of appeals[6] and proclamations pasted in every flat place; from the *Tsay-ee-kah,* the Peasants' Soviets, the "moderate" Socialist parties, the Army Committees—threatening, cursing, beseeching the workers and soldiers to stay home, to support the Government. . . .

An armoured automobile went slowly up and down, siren screaming. On every corner, in every open space, thick groups were clustered; arguing soldiers and students. Night came swiftly down, the wide-spaced street-lights flickered on, the tides of people flowed endlessly. . . . It is always like that in Petrograd just before trouble. . . .

The city was nervous, starting at every sharp sound. But still no sign from the Bolsheviki; the soldiers stayed in the barracks, the workmen in the factories. . . . We went to a moving picture show near the Kazan Cathedral—a bloody Italian film of passion and intrigue. Down front were some soldiers and sailors, staring at the screen in childlike wonder, totally unable to comprehend why there should be so much violent running about, and so much homicide. . . .

From there I hurried to Smolny. In room 10 on the top floor, the Military Revolutionary Committee sat in continuous session, under the chairmanship of a tow-headed, eighteen-year-old boy named Lazimir. He stopped, as he passed, to shake hands rather bashfully.

"Peter-Paul Fortress has just come over to us," said he, with a pleased grin. "A minute ago we got word from a regiment that was ordered by the Government to come to Petrograd. The men were suspicious, so they stopped the train at Gatchina and sent a delegation to us. 'What's the matter?' they asked. 'What have you got to say? We have just passed a resolution, "All Power to the Soviets." ' . . . The Military Revolutionary Committee sent back word, 'Brothers! We greet you in the name of the Revolution. Stay where you are until further instructions!' "

All telephones, he said, were cut off: but communication with the factories and barracks was established by means of military telephonograph apparatus. . . .

A steady stream of couriers and Commissars came and went. Outside the door waited a dozen volunteers, ready to carry word to the farthest quarters of the city. One of them, a gypsy-faced man in the uniform of a lieutenant, said in French, "Everything is ready to move at the push of a button. . . ."

There passed Podvoisky, the thin, bearded civilian whose brain conceived the strategy of insurrection;* Antonov, unshaven, his collar filthy, drunk with loss of sleep; Krylenko, the squat, wide-faced soldier, always smiling, with his violent gestures and tumbling speech; and Dybenko, the giant bearded sailor with the placid face. These were the men of the hour—and of other hours to come.

Downstairs in the office of the Factory-Shop Committees sat Seratov, signing orders on the Government Arsenal for arms—one hundred and fifty rifles for each factory. . . . Delegates waited in line, forty of them. . . .

In the hall I ran into some of the minor Bolshevik

* This overrates Podvoisky. The chief planner of the insurrection strategy was none of the four men mentioned in this paragraph, but the Chairman of the Petrograd Soviet, and *ex officio* head of the Military Revolutionary Committee, Leon Trotsky.—*Ed.*

leaders. One showed me a revolver. "The game is on," he said, and his face was pale. "Whether we move or not the other side knows it must finish us or be finished. . . ."

The Petrograd Soviet was meeting day and night. As I came into the great hall Trotsky was just finishing.

"We are asked," he said, "if we intend to have a *vystuplenie*. I can give a clear answer to that question. The Petrograd Soviet feels that at last the moment has arrived when the power must fall into the hands of the Soviets. This transfer of government will be accomplished by the All-Russian Congress. Whether an armed demonstration is necessary will depend on . . . those who wish to interfere with the All-Russian Congress. . . .

"We feel that our Government, entrusted to the personnel of the Provisional Cabinet, is a pitiful and helpless Government, which only awaits the sweep of the broom of History to give way to a really popular Government. But we are trying to avoid a conflict, even now, to-day. We hope that the All-Russian Congress will take . . . into its hands that power and authority which rests upon the organised freedom of the people. If, however, the Government wants to utilise the short period it is expected to live—twenty-four, forty-eight, or seventy-two hours—to attack us, then we shall answer with counter-attacks, blow for blow, steel for iron!" [7]

Amid cheers he announced that the Left Socialist Revolutionaries had agreed to send representatives into the Military Revolutionary Committee. . . .

As I left Smolny, at three o'clock in the morning, I noticed that two rapid-firing guns had been mounted, one on each side of the door, and that strong patrols of soldiers guarded the gates and the near-by street-corners. Bill Shatov* came bounding up the steps. "Well," he cried,

* Well known in the American labor movement.

"We're off! Kerensky sent the *yunkers* to close down our papers, *Soldat* and *Rabochi Put*. But our troops went down and smashed the Government seals, and now we're sending detachments to seize the bourgeois newspaper offices!" Exultantly he slapped me on the shoulder, and ran in. . . .

On the morning of the 6th I had business with the censor, whose office was in the Ministry of Foreign Affairs. Everywhere, on all the walls, hysterical appeals to the people to remain "calm." Polkovnikov emitted *prikaz* after *prikaz:*

I order all military units and detachments to remain in their barracks until further orders from the Staff of the Military district. . . . All officers who act without orders from their superiors will be court-martialled for mutiny. I forbid absolutely any execution by soldiers of instructions from other organisations. . . .

The morning papers announced that the Government had suppressed the papers *Novaya Rus, Zhivoye Slovo, Rabochi Put* and *Soldat,** and decreed the arrest of the leaders of the Petrograd Soviet and the members of the Military Revolutionary Committee. . . .

As I crossed the Palace Square several batteries of *yunker* artillery came through the Red Arch at a jingling trot, and drew up before the Palace. The great red building of the General Staff was unusually animated, several armoured automobiles ranked before the door, and motors full of officers were coming and going. . . . The censor was very much excited, like a small boy at a circus.

---

* *Novaya Rus* and *Zhivoye Slovo* were extreme reactionary papers and *Rabochi Put* and *Soldat* were Bolshevik.—*Ed.*

Kerensky, he said, had just gone to the Council of the Republic to offer his resignation. I hurried down to the Marinsky Palace, arriving at the end of that passionate and almost incoherent speech of Kerensky's, full of self-justification and bitter denunciation of his enemies.

"I will cite here the most characteristic passage from a whole series of articles published in *Rabochi Put* by Ulianov-Lenin, a state criminal who is in hiding and whom we are trying to find. . . . This state criminal has invited the proletariat and the Petrograd garrison to repeat the experience of the 16th-18th of July, and insists upon the immediate necessity for an armed rising. . . . Moreover, other Bolshevik leaders have taken the floor in a series of meetings, and also made an appeal to immediate insurrection. Particularly should be noticed the activity of the present president of the Petrograd Soviet, Bronstein-Trotsky. . . .

"I ought to bring to your notice . . . that the expressions and the style of a whole series of articles in *Rabochi Put* and *Soldat* resemble absolutely those of *Novaya Rus*. . . . We have to do not so much with the movement of such and such political party, as with the exploitation of the political ignorance and criminal instincts of a part of the population, a sort of organisation whose object it is to provoke in Russia, cost what it may, an inconscient movement of destruction and pillage; for given the state of mind of the masses, any movement at Petrograd will be followed by the most terrible massacres, which will cover with eternal shame the name of free Russia. . . .

". . . By the admission of Ulianov-Lenin himself, the situation of the extreme left wing of the Social Democrats in Russia is very favourable." (Here Kerensky read the following quotation from Lenin's article.):

Think of it! . . . The German comrades have only one Liebknecht, without newspapers, without freedom of meeting, without a Soviet. . . . They are opposed by the incredible hostility of all classes of society—and yet the German comrades try to act; while we, having dozens of newspapers, freedom of meeting, the majority of the Soviets, we, the best-placed international proletarians of the entire world, can we refuse to support the German revolutionists and insurrectionary organisations? . . .

Kerensky then continued:

"The organisers of rebellion recognise thus implicitly that the most perfect conditions for the free action of a political party obtain now in Russia, administered by a Provisional Government at the head of which is, in the eyes of this party, 'a usurper and a man who has sold himself to the bourgeoisie, the Minister-President Kerensky. . . .'

". . . The organisers of the insurrection do not come to the aid of the German proletariat, but of the German governing classes, and they open the Russian front to the iron fists of Wilhelm and his friends. . . . Little matter to the Provisional Government the motives of these people, little matter if they act consciously or unconsciously; but in any case, from this tribune, in full consciousness of my responsibility, I qualify such acts of a Russian political party as acts of treason to Russia!

". . . I place myself at the point of view of the Right, and I propose immediately to proceed to an investigation and make the necessary arrests." (Uproar from the Left.) "Listen to me!" he cried in a powerful voice. "At the moment when the state is in danger, because of conscious or unconscious treason, the Provisional Government, and myself among others, prefer to be killed rather than betray the life, the honour and the independence of Russia. . . ."

At this moment a paper was handed to Kerensky.

"I have just received the proclamation which they are distributing to the regiments. Here is the contents." Reading:

" '*The Petrograd Soviet of Workers' and Soldiers' Deputies is menaced. We order immediately the regiments to mobilise on a war footing and to await new orders. All delay or non-execution of this order will be considered as an act of treason to the Revolution. The Military Revolutionary Committee. For the President, Podvoisky. The Secretary, Antonov.'*

"In reality, this is an attempt to raise the populace* against the existing order of things, to break the Constituent and to open the front to the regiments of the iron fist of Wilhelm. . . .

"I say 'populace' * intentionally, because the conscious democracy and its *Tsay-ee-kah,* all the Army organisations, all that free Russia glorifies, the good sense, the honour and the conscience of the great Russian democracy, protests against these things. . . .

"I have not come here with a prayer, but to state my firm conviction that the Provisional Government, which defends at this moment our new liberty—that the new Russian state, destined to a brillant future, will find unanimous support except among those who have never dared to face the truth. . . .

". . . The Provisional Government has never violated the liberty of all citizens of the State to use their political rights. . . . But now the Provisional Government . . . declares: in this moment those elements of the Russian

* The word Kerensky used means *rabble* or *mob.—Ed.*

nation, those groups and parties who have dared to lift their hands against the free will of the Russian people, at the same time threatening to open the front to Germany, must be liquidated with decision! . . .

"Let the population of Petrograd understand that it will encounter a firm power, and perhaps at the last moment good sense, conscience and honour will triumph in the hearts of those who still possess them. . . ."

All through this speech, the hall rang with deafening clamour. When the Minister-President had stepped down, pale-faced and wet with perspiration, and strode out with his suite of officers, speaker after speaker from the Left and Centre attacked the Right, all one angry roaring. Even the Socialist Revolutionaries, through Gotz:

"The policy of the Bolsheviki is demagogic and criminal, in their exploitation of the popular discontent. But there is a whole series of popular demands which have received no satisfaction up to now. . . . The questions of peace, land and the democratization of the army ought to be stated in such a fashion that no soldier, peasant or worker would have the least doubt that our Government is attempting, firmly and infallibly, to solve them. . . .

"We Mensheviki do not wish to provoke a Cabinet crisis, and we are ready to defend the Provisional Government with all our energy, to the last drop of our blood—if only the Provisional Government, on all these burning questions, will speak the clear and precise words awaited by the people with such impatience. . . ."

Then Martov, furious:

"The words of the Minister-President, who allowed himself to speak of 'populace' when it is question of the movement of important sections of the proletariat and the army—although led in the wrong direction—are nothing but an incitement to civil war."

The order of the day proposed by the Left was voted. It amounted practically to a vote of lack of confidence.

1. The armed demonstration which has been preparing for some days past has for its object a *coup d'etat,* threatens to provoke civil war, creates conditions favourable to *pogroms* and counter-revolution, the mobilization of counter-revolutionary forces, such as the Black Hundreds, which will inevitably bring about the impossibility of convoking the Constituent, will cause a military catastrophe, the death of the Revolution, paralyse the economic life of the country and destroy Russia;

2. The conditions favourable to this agitation have been created by delay in passing urgent measures, as well as objective conditions caused by the war and the general disorder. It is necessary before everything to promulgate at once a decree transmitting the land to the peasants' Land Committees, and to adopt an energetic course of action abroad in proposing to the Allies to proclaim their peace-terms and to begin peace-parleys;

3. To cope with Monarchist manifestations and *pogromist* movements, it is indispensable to take immediate measures to suppress these movements, and for this purpose to create at Petrograd a Committee of Public Safety, composed of representatives of the Municipality and the organs of the revolutionary democracy, acting in contact with the Provisional Government. . . .

It is interesting to note that the Mensheviki and Socialist Revolutionaries all rallied to this resolution. . . . When Kerensky saw it, however, he summoned Avksentiev to the Winter Palace to explain. If it expressed a lack of confidence in the Provisional Government, he begged Avksentiev to form a new Cabinet. Dan, Gotz and Avksentiev, the leaders of the "compromisers," performed their last compromise. . . . They explained to Kerensky that it was not meant as a criticism of the Government!

At the corner of the Morskaya and the Nevsky, squads of soldiers with fixed bayonets were stopping all private automobiles, turning out the occupants, and ordering them toward the Winter Palace. A large crowd had gathered to watch them. Nobody knew whether the soldiers belonged to the Government or the Military Revolutionary Committee. Up in front of the Kazan Cathedral the same thing was happening, machines being directed back up the Nevsky. Five or six sailors with rifles came along, laughing excitedly, and fell into conversation with two of the soldiers. On the sailors' hat bands were *Avrora* and *Zaria Svobody*,—the names of the leading Bolshevik cruisers of the Baltic Fleet. One of them said, "Cronstadt is coming!" . . . It was as if, in 1792, on the streets of Paris, some one had said: "The Marseillais are coming!" For at Cronstadt were twenty-five thousand sailors, convinced Bolsheviki and not afraid to die. . . .

Rabochi i Soldat was just out, all its front page one huge proclamation:

SOLDIERS! WORKERS! CITIZENS!

The enemies of the people passed last night to the offensive. The Kornilovists of the Staff are trying to draw in from the suburbs *yunkers* and volunteer battalions. The Oranienbaum *yunkers* and the Tsarskoye Selo volunteers refused to come out. A stroke of high treason is being contemplated against the Petrograd Soviet. . . . The campaign of the counter-revolutionists is being directed against the All-Russian Congress of Soviets on the eve of its opening, against the Constituent Assembly, against the people. The Petrograd Soviet is guarding the Revolution. The Military Revolutionary Committee is directing the repulse of the conspirators' attack. The entire garrison and proletariat of Petrograd are ready to deal the enemy of the people a crushing blow.

The Military Revolutionary Committee decrees:

1. All regimental, division and battle-ship Committees, together with the Soviet Commissars, and all revolutionary organizations, shall meet in continuous session, concentrating in their hands all information about the plans of the conspirators.

2. Not one soldier shall leave his division without permission of the Committee.

3. To send to Smolny at once two delegates from each military unit and five from each Ward Soviet.

4. All members of the Petrograd Soviet and all delegates to the All-Russian Congress are invited immediately to Smolny for an extraordinary meeting.

Counter-revolution has raised its criminal head.

A great danger threatens all the conquests and hopes of the soldiers and workers.

But the forces of the Revolution by far exceed those of its enemies.

The cause of the People is in strong hands. The conspirators will be crushed.

No hesitation or doubts! Firmness, steadfastness, discipline, determination!

Long live the Revolution!

The Military Revolutionary Committee.

The Petrograd Soviet was meeting continuously at Smolny, a centre of storm, delegates falling down asleep on the floor and rising again to take part in the debate, Trotsky, Kamenev, Volodarsky speaking six, eight, twelve hours a day. . . .

I went down to room 18 on the first floor where the Bolshevik delegates were holding caucus, a harsh voice steadily booming, the speaker hidden by the crowd: "The compromisers say that we are isolated. Pay no attention to them. Once it begins they must be dragged along with us, or else lose their following. . . ."

Here he held up a piece of paper. "We are dragging

them! A message has just come from the Mensheviki and
Socialist Revolutionaries! They say that they condemn our
action, but that if the Government attacks us they will
not oppose the cause of the proletariat!" Exultant shouting. . . .

As night fell the great hall filled with soldiers and workmen, a monstrous dun mass, deep-humming in a blue haze
of smoke. The old *Tsay-ee-kah* had finally decided to welcome the delegates to that new Congress which would
mean its own ruin—and perhaps the ruin of the revolutionary order it had built. At this meeting, however, only
members of the *Tsay-ee-kah* could vote. . . .

It was after midnight when Gotz took the chair and Dan
rose to speak, in a tense silence, which seemed to me almost menacing.

"The hours in which we live appear in the most tragic
colours," he said. "The enemy is at the gates of Petrograd, the forces of the democracy are trying to organise to
resist him, and yet we await bloodshed in the streets of the
capital, and famine threatens to destroy, not only our
homogeneous Government, but the Revolution itself. . . .

"The masses are sick and exhausted. They have no interest in the Revolution. If the Bolsheviki start anything,
that will be the end of the Revolution . . ." (Cries,
"That's a lie!") "The counter-revolutionists are waiting
with the Bolsheviki to begin riots and massacres. . . .
If there is any *vystuplenie,* there will be no Constituent
Assembly. . . ." (Cries, "Lie! Shame!")

"It is inadmissible that in the zone of military operations the Petrograd garrison shall not submit to the orders
of the Staff. . . . You must obey the orders of the Staff
and of the *Tsay-ee-kah* elected by you. All Power to the
Soviets—that means death! Robbers and thieves are wait-

ing for the moment to loot and burn. . . . When you have such slogans put before you, 'Enter the houses, take away the shoes and clothes from the bourgeoisie—' " (Tumult. Cries, "No such slogan! A lie! A lie!") "Well, it may start differently, but it will end that way!

"The *Tsay-ee-kah* has full power to act, and must be obeyed. . . . We are not afraid of bayonets. . . . The *Tsay-ee-kah* will defend the Revolution with its body. . . ." (Cries, "It was a dead body long ago!")

Immense continued uproar, in which his voice could be heard screaming, as he pounded the desk, "Those who are urging this are committing a crime!"

Voice: "You committed a crime long ago, when you captured the power and turned it over to the bourgeoisie!"

Gotz, ringing the chairman's bell: "Silence, or I'll have you put out!"

Voice: "Try it!" (Cheers and whistling.)

"Now concerning our policy about peace." (Laughter.) "Unfortunately Russia can no longer support the continuation of the war. There is going to be peace, but not permanent peace—not a democratic peace. . . . To-day, at the Council of the Republic, in order to avoid bloodshed, we passed an order of the day demanding the surrender of the land to the Land Committees and immediate peace negotiations. . . ." (Laughter, and cries, "Too late!")

Then for the Bolsheviki, Trotsky mounted the tribune, borne on a wave of roaring applause that burst into cheers and a rising house, thunderous. His thin, pointed face was positively Mephistophelian in its expression of malicious irony.

"Dan's tactics prove that the masses—the great, dull, indifferent masses—are absolutely with him!" (Titanic mirth.) He turned toward the chairman, dramatically. "When we spoke of giving the land to the peasants, you were against it. We told the peasants, 'If they don't give it to you, take it yourselves!' and the peasants followed our advice. And now you advocate what we did six months ago. . . .

"I don't think Kerensky's order to suspend the death penalty in the army was dictated by his ideals. I think Kerensky was persuaded by the Petrograd garrison, which refused to obey him. . . .

"To-day Dan is accused of having made a speech in the Council of the Republic which proves him to be a secret Bolshevik. . . . The time may come when Dan will say that the flower of the Revolution participated in the rising of July 16th and 18th. . . . In Dan's resolution to-day at the Council of the Republic there was no mention of enforcing discipline in the army, although that is urged in the propaganda of his party. . . .

"No. The history of the last seven months shows that the masses have left the Mensheviki. The Mensheviki and the Socialist Revolutionaries conquered the Cadets, and then when they got the power, they gave it to the Cadets. . . .

"Dan tells you that you have no right to make an insurrection. Insurrection is the right of all revolutionists! When the down-trodden masses revolt, it is their right. . . ."

Then the long-faced, cruel-tongued Lieber, greeted with groans and laughter.

"Engels and Marx said that the proletariat had no right to take power until it was ready for it. In a bourgeois revolution like this . . . the seizure of power by the masses means the tragic end of the Revolution. . . . Trotsky, as a Social Democratic theorist, is himself opposed to what he is now advocating. . . ." (Cries, "Enough! Down with him!")

Martov, constantly interrupted: "The Internationalists

are not opposed to the transmission of power to the democracy, but they disapprove of the methods of the Bolsheviki. This is not the moment to seize the power. . . ."

Again Dan took the floor, violently protesting against the action of the Military Revolutionary Committee, which had sent a Commissar to seize the office of *Izvestia* and censor the paper. The wildest uproar followed. Martov tried to speak, but could not be heard. Delegates of the Army and the Baltic Fleet stood up all over the hall, shouting that the Soviet was *their* Government. . . .

Amid the wildest confusion Ehrlich offered a resolution, appealing to the workers and soldiers to remain calm and not to respond to provocations to demonstrate, recognising the necessity of immediately creating a Committee of Public Safety, and asking the Provisional Government at once to pass decrees transferring the land to the peasants and beginning peace negotiations. . . .

Then up leaped Volodarsky, shouting harshly that the *Tsay-ee-kah,* on the eve of the Congress, had no right to assume the functions of the Congress. The *Tsay-ee-kah* was practically dead, he said, and the resolution was simply a trick to bolster up its waning power. . . .

"As for us, Bolsheviki, we will not vote on this resolution!" Whereupon all the Bolsheviki left the hall and the resolution was passed. . . .

Toward four in the morning I met Zorin in the outer hall, a rifle slung from his shoulder.

"We're moving!"[8] said he, calmly but with satisfaction. "We pinched the Assistant Minister of Justice and the Minister of Religions. They're down cellar now. One regiment is on the march to capture the Telephone Exchange, another the Telegraph Agency, another the State Bank. The Red Guard is out. . . ."

On the steps of Smolny, in the chill dark, we first saw

the Red Guard—a huddled group of boys in workmen's clothes, carrying guns with bayonets, talking nervously together.

Far over the still roofs westward came the sound of scattered rifle fire, where the *yunkers* were trying to open the bridges over the Neva, to prevent the factory workers and soldiers of the Viborg quarter from joining the Soviet forces in the centre of the city; and the Cronstadt sailors were closing them again. . . .

Behind us great Smolny, bright with lights, hummed like a gigantic hive. . . .

NOTES TO CHAPTER III

1   Resolution of the Factory-Shop Committees

Workers' Control

1. (See page 69.)

2. The organisation of Workers' Control is a manifestation of the same healthy activity in the sphere of industrial production, as are party organisations in the sphere of politics, trade unions in employment, Cooperatives in the domain of consumption, and literary clubs in the sphere of culture.

3. The working-class has much more interest in the proper and uninterrupted operation of factories . . . than the capitalist class. Workers' Control is a better security in this respect for the interests of modern society, of the whole people, than the arbitrary will of the owners, who are guided only by their selfish desire for material profits or political privileges. Therefore Workers' Control is demanded by the proletariat not only in their own interest, but in the interest of the whole country, and should be supported by the revolutionary peasantry as well as the revolutionary Army.

4. Considering the hostile attitude of the majority of the capitalist class toward the Revolution, experience shows that proper distribution of raw materials and fuel, as well as the most

efficient management of factories, is impossible without Workers' Control.

5. Only Workers' Control over capitalist enterprises, cultivating the workers' conscious attitude toward work, and making clear its social meaning, can create conditions favourable to the development of a firm self-discipline in labour, and the development of all labour's possible productivity.

6. The impending transformation of industry from a war to a peace basis, and the redistribution of labour all over the country, as well as among the different factories, can be accomplished without great disturbances only by means of the democratic self-government of the workers themselves. . . . Therefore the realisation of Workers' Control is an indispensable preliminary to the demobilisation of industry.

7. In accordance with the slogan proclaimed by the Russian Social Democratic Labour Party (Bolsheviki), Workers' Control on a national scale, in order to bring results, must extend to all capitalist concerns, and not be organised accidentally, without system; it must be well-planned, and not separated from the industrial life of the country as a whole.

8. The economic life of the country—agriculture, industry, commerce and transport—must be subjected to one unified plan, constructed so as to satisfy the individual and social requirements of the wide masses of the people; it must be approved by their elected representatives, and carried out under the direction of these representatives by means of national and local organisations.

9. That part of the plan which deals with land-labour must be carried out under supervision of the peasants' and land-workers' organisations; that relating to industry, trade and transport operated by wage-earners, by means of Workers' Control; the natural organs of Workers' Control inside the industrial plant will be the Factory-Shop and similar Committees; and in the labour market, the Trade Unions.

10. The collective wage agreements arranged by the Trade Unions for the majority of workers in any branch of labour, must be binding on all the owners of plants employing this kind of labour in the given district.

11. Employment bureaus must be placed under the control and management of the Trade Unions, as class organisations acting within the limits of the whole industrial plan, and in accordance with it.

12. Trade Unions must have the right, upon their own initiative, to begin legal action against all employers who violate labour contracts or labour legislation, and also in behalf of any individual worker in any branch of labour.

13. On all questions relating to Workers' Control over production, distribution and employment, the Trade Unions must confer with the workers of individual establishments through their Factory-Shop Committees.

14. Matters of employment and discharge, vacations, wage scales, refusal of work, degree of productivity and skill, reasons for abrogating agreements, disputes with the administration, and similar problems of the internal life of the factory, must be settled exclusively according to the findings of the Factory-Shop Committee, which has the right to exclude from participation in the discussion any members of the factory administration.

15. The Factory-Shop Committee forms a commission to control the supplying of the factory with raw materials, fuel, orders, labour power and technical staff (including equipment), and all other supplies and arrangements, and also to assure the factory's adherence to the general industrial plan. The factory administration is obliged to surrender to the organs of Workers' Control, for their aid and information, all data concerning the business; to make it possible to verify this data, and to produce the books of the company upon demand of the Factory-Shop Committee.

16. Any illegal acts on the part of the administration discovered by the Factory-Shop Committees, or any suspicion of such illegal acts, which cannot be investigated or remedied by the workers alone, shall be referred to the district central organisation of Factory-Shop Committees charged with the particular branch of labour involved, which shall discuss the matter with the institutions charged with the execution of the general industrial plan, and find means to deal with the matter, even to the extent of confiscating the factory.

17. The union of the Factory-Shop Committees of different concerns must be accomplished on the basis of the different trades, in order to facilitate control over the whole branch of industry, so as to come within the general industrial plan; and so as to create an effective plan of distribution among the different factories of orders, raw materials, fuel, technical and labour power; and also to facilitate cooperation with the Trade Unions, which are organised by trades.

18. The central city councils of Trade Unions and Factory-Shop Committees represent the proletariat in the corresponding provincial and local institutions formed to elaborate and carry out the general industrial plan, and to organise economic relations between the towns and the villages (workers and peasants). They also possess final authority for the management of Factory-Shop Committees and Trade Unions, so far as Workers' Control in their district is concerned, and they shall issue obligatory regulations concerning workers' discipline in the routine of production—which regulations, however, must be approved by vote of the workers themselves.

2   The Bourgeois Press on the Bolsheviki

Russkaya Volia, October 28. "The decisive moment approaches. . . . It is decisive for the Bolsheviki. Either they will give us . . . a second edition of the events of July 16-18, or they will have to admit that with their plans and intentions, with their impertinent policy of wishing to separate themselves from everything consciously national, they have been definitely defeated. . . .

"What are the chances of Bolshevik success?

"It is difficult to answer that question, for their principal support is the . . . ignorance of the popular masses. They speculate on it, they work upon it by a demagogy which nothing can stop. . . .

"The Government must play its part in this affair. Supporting itself morally by the Council of the Republic, the Government must take a clearly-defined attitude toward the Bolsheviki. . . .

"And if the Bolsheviki provoke an insurrection against the legal power, and thus facilitate the German invasion, they must be treated as mutineers and traitors. . . ."

Birzhevya Viedomosti, October 28. "Now that the Bolsheviki have separated themselves from the rest of the democracy, the struggle against them is very much simpler—and it is not reasonable, in order to fight against Bolshevism, to wait until they make a manifestation. The Government should not even allow the manifestation. . . .

"The appeals of the Bolsheviki to insurrection and anarchy are acts punishable by the criminal courts, and in the freest countries, their authors would receive severe sentences. For what the Bolsheviki are carrying on is not a political struggle against the Government, or even for the power; it is propaganda for anarchy, massacres, and civil war. This propaganda must be extirpated at its roots; it would be strange to wait, in order to begin action against an agitation for *pogroms,* until the *pogroms* actually occurred. . . ."

Novoye Vremya, November 1. ". . . Why is the Government excited only about November 2d (date of calling of the Congress of Soviets), and not about September 12th, or October 3d?

"This is not the first time that Russia burns and falls in ruins, and that the smoke of the terrible conflagration makes the eyes of our Allies smart. . . .

"Since it came to power, has there been a single order issued by the Government for the purpose of halting anarchy, or has any one attempted to put out the Russian conflagration?

"There were other things to do. . . .

"The Government turned its attention to a more immediate problem. It crushed an insurrection (the Kornilov attempt) concerning which every one is now asking, 'Did it ever exist?' "

3   Moderate Socialist Press on the Bolsheviki

Dielo Naroda, October 28 (Socialist Revolutionary). "The most frightful crime of the Bolsheviki against the Revolution is that they impute exclusively to the bad intentions of the revolutionary Government all the calamities which the masses are so cruelly suffering; when as a matter of fact these calamities spring from objective causes.

"They make golden promises to the masses, knowing in advance that they can fulfil none of them; they lead the masses on a false trail, deceiving them as to the source of all their troubles. . . .

"The Bolsheviki are the most dangerous enemies of the Revolution. . . ."

Dien, October 30 (Menshevik). "Is this really 'the freedom of the press'? Every day *Novaya Rus* and *Rabochi Put* openly incite to insurrection. Every day these two papers commit in their columns actual crimes. Every day they urge *pogroms.* . . . Is that 'the freedom of the press'? . . .

"The Government ought to defend itself and defend us. We have the right to insist that the Government machinery does not remain passive while the threat of bloody riots endangers the lives of its citizens. . . ."

4 "Yedinstvo"

Plekhanov's paper, *Yedinstvo,* suspended publication a few weeks after the Bolsheviki seized the power. Contrary to popular report, *Yedinstvo* was not suppressed by the Soviet Government; an announcement in the last number admitted that it was unable to continue *because there were too few subscribers.* . . .*

5 Were the Bolsheviki Conspirators?

The French newspaper *Entente* of Petrograd, on November 15th, published an article of which the following is a part:

"The Government of Kerensky discusses and hesitates. The Government of Lenin and Trotsky attacks and acts.

"This last is called a Government of Conspirators, but that is wrong. Government of usurpers, yes, like all revolutionary Governments which triumph over their adversaries. Conspirators— no!

"No! They did not conspire. On the contrary, openly, audaciously, without mincing words, without dissimulating their intentions, they multiplied their agitation, intensified their propaganda in the factories, the barracks, at the Front, in the country, everywhere, even fixing in advance the date of their taking up arms, the date of their seizure of the power. . . .

"*They*—conspirators? Never. . . ."

6 Appeal Against Insurrection

From the Central Army Committee

". . . Above everything we insist upon the inflexible execution of the organised will of the majority of the people, expressed by the Provisional Government in accord with the Council of the Republic and the *Tsay-ee-kah,* as organ of the popular power. . . .

* This is not correct. *Yedinstvo* suffered like all nongovernmental papers for lack of funds but published in all 189 numbers as a daily after Plekhanov's return to Russia in 1917. It was suppressed by Lenin's government in the course of November but reappeared soon under the title of *Nashe Yedinstvo.* When it was suppressed again, Plekhanov moved it to Moscow, where he managed to issue only two monthly numbers. Then the combination of lack of funds and support, government harassment, and Plekhanov's shattered health, put an end to it.—*Ed.*

"Any demonstration to depose this power by violence, at a moment when a Government crisis will infallibly create disorganisation, the ruin of the country, and civil war, will be considered by the Army as a counterrevolutionary act, and repressed by force of arms. . . .

"The interests of private groups and classes should be submitted to a single interest—that of augmenting industrial production, and distributing the necessities of life with fairness. . . .

"All who are capable of sabotage, disorganisation, or disorder, all deserters, all slackers, all looters, should be forced to do auxiliary service in the rear of the Army. . . .

"We invite the Provisional Government to form, out of these violators of the people's will, these enemies of the Revolution, labour detachments to work in the rear, on the Front, in the trenches under enemy fire. . . ."

7 Offensive or Defensive

This is typical of a number of speeches and moves of Trotsky disavowing the intention to undertake the offensive while actually preparing it. In an article characteristically directed against Trotsky and entitled "Trotskyism or Leninism?" Stalin described the tactics which Reed is reporting on in the present work in the following terms: "A peculiar feature of the tactics of the revolution in this period must be noted, namely, that the revolution strove to take every, or nearly every, step in its attack in the guise of defence. Undoubtedly, the refusal to allow the troops to be withdrawn from Petrograd was an important step in the revolution's attack; nevertheless, this attack was carried out under the slogan of protecting Petrograd from possible attack by the external enemy. Undoubtedly, the formation of the Revolutionary Military Committee was a still more important step in the attack upon the Provisional Government; nevertheless, it was carried out under the slogan of organizing Soviet control over the actions of the Headquarters of the Military District. Undoubtedly, the open transfer of allegiance of the garrison to the side of the Revolutionary Military Committee and the organization of a network of Soviet Commissars [in the barracks] marked the beginning of the uprising; nevertheless, the revolution took these steps under the slogan of protecting the Petrograd Soviet from possible action by the counter-revolution. The revolution, so to speak, masked its actions in attack under the cloak of defence in order more easily to draw the irresolute, vacillating elements into its orbit. This, no doubt, explains the outwardly defensive character of the speeches, articles and slogans of that period, the inner content of which, none the less, was of a deeply offensive nature." (*Pravda,* November 26, 1924).—*Ed.*

8   Events of the Night, November 6th

Toward evening bands of Red Guards began to occupy the printing-shops of the bourgeois press, where they printed *Rabochi Put, Soldat,* and various proclamations by the hundred thousand. The City Militia was ordered to clear these places, but found the offices barricaded, and armed men defending them. Soldiers who were ordered to attack the print-shops refused.

About midnight a Colonel with a company of *yunkers* arrived at the club "Free Mind," with a warrant to arrest the editor of *Rabochi Put.* Immediately an enormous mob gathered in the street outside and threatened to lynch the *yunkers.* The Colonel thereupon begged that he and the *yunkers* be arrested and taken to Peter-Paul prison for safety. This request was granted.

At 1 A.M. a detachment of soldiers and sailors from Smolny occupied the Telegraph Agency. At 1.35 the Post Office was occupied. Toward morning the Military Hotel was taken, and at 5 o'clock the Telephone Exchange. At dawn the State Bank was surrounded. And at 10 A.M. a cordon of troops was drawn about the Winter Palace.

CHAPTER IV

THE FALL OF THE PROVISIONAL GOVERNMENT

Wednesday, November 7th, I rose very late. The noon cannon boomed from Peter-Paul as I went down the Nevsky. It was a raw, chill day. In front of the State Bank some soldiers with fixed bayonets were standing at the closed gates.

"What side do you belong to?" I asked. "The Government?"

"No more Government," one answered with a grin, "*Slava Bogu!* Glory to God!" That was all I could get out of him. . . .

The street-cars were running on the Nevsky, men, women and small boys hanging on every projection. Shops were open, and there seemed even less uneasiness among the street crowds than there had been the day before. A whole crop of new appeals against insurrection had blossomed out on the walls during the night—to the peasants, to the soldiers at the front, to the workmen of Petrograd. One read:

From the Petrograd Municipal Duma:

The Municipal Duma informs the citizens that in the extraordinary meeting of November 6th the Duma formed a

Committee of Public Safety, composed of members of the Central and Ward Dumas, and representatives of the following revolutionary democratic organizations: The *Tsay-ee-kah*, the All-Russian Executive Committee of Peasant Deputies, the Army organisations, the *Tsentroflot*, the Petrograd Soviet of Workers' and Soldiers' Deputies (!), the Council of Trade Unions, and others.

Members of the Committee of Public Safety will be on duty in the building of the Municipal Duma. Telephones No. 15-40, 223-77, 138-36.

November 7th, 1917.

Though I didn't realize it then, this was the Duma's declaration of war against the Bolsheviki.

I bought a copy of *Rabochi Put,* the only newspaper which seemed on sale, and a little later paid a soldier fifty kopeks for a second-hand copy of *Dien.* The Bolshevik paper, printed on large-sized sheets in the conquered office of the *Russkaya Volia,* had huge headlines: "ALL POWER —TO THE SOVIETS OF WORKERS, SOLDIERS AND PEASANTS! PEACE! BREAD! LAND!" The leading article was signed "Zinoviev,"—Lenin's companion in hiding. It began:

Every soldier, every worker, every real Socialist, every honest democrat realises that there are only two alternatives to the present situation.

Either—the power will remain in the hands of the bourgeois-landlord crew, and this will mean every kind of repression for the workers, soldiers and peasants, continuation of the war, inevitable hunger and death. . . .

Or—the power will be transferred to the hands of the revolutionary workers, soldiers and peasants; and in that case it will mean a complete abolition of landlord tyranny, immediate check of the capitalists, immediate proposal of a just peace. Then the land is assured to the peasants, then control of industry is assured to the workers, then bread is assured to the hungry, then the end of this nonsensical war! . . .

Dien contained fragmentary news of the agitated night. Bolsheviki capture of the Telephone Exchange, the Baltic station, the Telegraph Agency; the Peterhof *yunkers* unable to reach Petrograd; the Cossacks undecided; arrest of some of the Ministers; shooting of Chief of the City Militia Meyer; arrests, counter-arrests, skirmishes between clashing patrols of soldiers, *yunkers* and Red Guards.[1]

On the corner of the Morskaya I ran into Captain Gomberg, Menshevik *oboronetz,* secretary of the Military Section of his party. When I asked him if the insurrection had really happened he shrugged his shoulders in a tired manner and replied, *"Chort znayet!* The devil knows! Well, perhaps the Bolsheviki can seize the power, but they won't be able to hold it more than three days. They haven't the men to run a government. Perhaps it's a good thing to let them try—that will finish them. . . ."

The Military Hotel at the corner of St. Isaac's Square was picketed by armed sailors. In the lobby were many of the smart young officers, walking up and down or muttering together; the sailors wouldn't let them leave. . . .

Suddenly came the sharp crack of a rifle outside, followed by a scattered burst of firing. I ran out. Something unusual was going on around the Marinsky Palace, where the Council of the Russian Republic met. Diagonally across the wide square was drawn a line of soldiers, rifles ready, staring at the hotel roof.

"Provocatzia! Shot at us!" snapped one, while another went running toward the door.

At the western corner of the Palace lay a big armoured

car with a red flag flying from it, newly lettered in red paint: "S. R. S. D." (*Soviet Rabochikh Soldatskikh Deputatov*); all the guns trained toward St. Isaac's. A barricade had been heaped up across the mouth of Novaya Ulitza—boxes, barrels, an old bed-spring, a wagon. A pile of lumber barred the end of the Moika quay. Short logs from a neighbouring woodpile were being built up along the front of the building to form breastworks. . . .

"Is there going to be any fighting?" I asked.

"Soon, soon," answered a soldier, nervously. "Go away, comrade, you'll get hurt. They will come from that direction," pointing toward the Admiralty.

"Who will?"

"That I couldn't tell you, brother," he answered, and spat.

Before the door of the Palace was a crowd of soldiers and sailors. A sailor was telling of the end of the Council of the Russian Republic. "We walked in there," he said, "and filled all the doors with comrades. I went up to the counter-revolutionist Kornilovitz who sat in the president's chair. 'No more Council,' I says. 'Run along home now!' "

There was laughter. By waving assorted papers I managed to get around to the door of the press gallery. There an enormous smiling sailor stopped me, and when I showed my pass, just said, "If you were Saint Michael himself, comrade, you couldn't pass here!" Through the glass of the door I made out the distorted face and gesticulating arms of a French correspondent, locked in. . . .

Around in front stood a little, grey-moustached man in the uniform of a general, the centre of a knot of soldiers. He was very red in the face.

"I am General Alexeyev," he cried. "As your superior officer and as a member of the Council of the Republic

I demand to be allowed to pass!" The guard scratched his head, looking uneasily out of the corner of his eye; he beckoned to an approaching officer, who grew very agitated when he saw who it was and saluted before he realised what he was doing.

"*Vashe Vysokoprevoskhoditelstvo*—your High Excellency—" he stammered, in the manner of the old régime, "Access to the Palace is strictly forbidden—I have no right——"

An automobile came by, and I saw Gotz sitting inside, laughing apparently with great amusement. A few minutes later another, with armed soldiers on the front seat, full of arrested members of the Provisional Government. Peters, Lettish member of the Military Revolutionary Committee, came hurrying across the Square.

"I thought you bagged all those gentlemen last night," said I, pointing to them.

"Oh," he answered, with the expression of a disappointed small boy. "The damn fools let most of them go again before we made up our minds. . . ."

Down the Voskressensky Prospekt a great mass of sailors were drawn up, and behind them came marching soldiers, as far as the eye could reach.

We went toward the Winter Palace by way of the Admiralteisky. All the entrances to the Palace Square were closed by sentries, and a cordon of troops stretched clear across the western end, besieged by an uneasy throng of citizens. Except for far-away soldiers who seemed to be carrying wood out of the Palace courtyard and piling it in front of the main gateway, everything was quiet.

We couldn't make out whether the sentries were pro-Government or pro-Soviet. Our papers from Smolny had no effect, however, so we approached another part of the line with an important air and showed our American passports, saying "Official business!" and shouldered through. At the door of the Palace the same old *shveit-zari,* in their brass-buttoned blue uniforms with the red-and-gold collars, politely took our coats and hats, and we went up-stairs. In the dark, gloomy corridor, stripped of its tapestries, a few old attendants were lounging about, and in front of Kerensky's door a young officer paced up and down, gnawing his moustache. We asked if we could interview the Minister-president. He bowed and clicked his heels.

"No, I am sorry," he replied in French. "Alexander Feodorvich is extremely occupied just now. . . ." He looked at us for a moment. "In fact, he is not here. . . ."

"Where is he?"

"He has gone to the Front.[2] And do you know, there wasn't enough gasoline for his automobile. We had to send to the English Hospital and borrow some."

"Are the Ministers here?"

"They are meeting in some room—I don't know where."

"Are the Bolsheviki coming?"

"Of course. Certainly, they are coming. I expect a telephone call every minute to say that they are coming. But we are ready. We have *yunkers* in the front of the Palace. Through that door there."

"Can we go in there?"

"No. Certainly not. It is not permitted." Abruptly he shook hands all around and walked away. We turned to the forbidden door, set in a temporary partition dividing the hall and locked on the outside. On the other side were voices, and somebody laughing. Except for that the vast spaces of the old Palace were silent as the grave. An old *shveitzar* ran up. "No, *barin,* you must not go in there."

"Why is the door locked?"

"To keep the soldiers in," he answered. After a few

minutes he said something about having a glass of tea and went back up the hall. We unlocked the door.

Just inside a couple of soldiers stood on guard, but they said nothing. At the end of the corridor was a large, ornate room with gilded cornices and enormous crystal lustres, and beyond it several smaller ones, wainscoted with dark wood. On both sides of the parquetted floor lay rows of dirty mattresses and blankets, upon which occasional soldiers were stretched out; everywhere was a litter of cigarette-butts, bits of bread, cloth, and empty bottles with expensive French labels. More and more soldiers, with the red shoulder-straps of the *yunker*-schools, moved about in a stale atmosphere of tobacco-smoke and unwashed humanity. One had a bottle of white Burgundy, evidently filched from the cellars of the Palace. They looked at us with astonishment as we marched past, through room after room, until at last we came out into a series of great state-salons, fronting their long and dirty windows on the Square. The walls were covered with huge canvases in massive gilt frames—historical battle-scenes. . . . "12 October 1812" and "6 November 1812" and "16/28 August 1813." . . . One had a gash across the upper right hand corner.

The place was all a huge barrack, and evidently had been for weeks, from the look of the floor and walls. Machine guns were mounted on window-sills, rifles stacked between the mattresses.

As we were looking at the pictures an alcoholic breath assailed me from the region of my left ear, and a voice said in thick but fluent French, "I see, by the way you admire the paintings, that you are foreigners." He was a short, puffy man with a baldish head as he removed his cap.

"Americans? Enchanted. I am Stabs-Capitan Vladimir

Artzibashev, absolutely at your service." It did not seem to occur to him that there was anything unusual in four strangers, one a woman, wandering through the defences of an army awaiting attack. He began to complain of the state of Russia.

"Not only these Bolsheviki," he said, "but the fine traditions of the Russian army are broken down. Look around you. These are all students in the officers' training schools. But are they gentlemen? Kerensky opened the officers' schools to the ranks, to any soldier who could pass an examination. Naturally there are many, many who are contaminated by the Revolution. . . ."

Without consequence he changed the subject. "I am very anxious to go away from Russia. I have made up my mind to join the American army. Will you please go to your Consul and make arrangements? I will give you my address." In spite of our protestations he wrote it on a piece of paper, and seemed to feel better at once. I have it still—*"Oranienbaumskaya Shkola Praporshchikov 2nd, Staraya Peterhof."*

"We had a review this morning early," he went on, as he guided us through the rooms and explained everything. "The Women's Battalion decided to remain loyal to the Government."

"Are the women soldiers in the Palace?"

"Yes, they are in the back rooms, where they won't be hurt if any trouble comes." He sighed. "It is a great responsibility," said he.

For a while we stood at the window, looking down on the Square before the Palace, where three companies of long-coated *yunkers* were drawn up under arms, being harangued by a tall, energetic-looking officer I recognised as Stankevich, chief Military Commissar of the Provisional Government. After a few minutes two of the com-

panies shouldered arms with a clash, barked three sharp
shouts, and went swinging off across the Square, disappear-
ing through the Red Arch into the quiet city.

"They are going to capture the Telephone Exchange,"
said some one. Three cadets stood by us, and we fell into
conversation. They said they had entered the schools
from the ranks, and gave their names—Robert Olev,
Alexei Vasilienko and Erni Sachs, an Esthonian. But now
they didn't want to be officers any more, because officers
were very unpopular. They didn't seem to know what to
do, as a matter of fact, and it was plain that they were not
happy.

But soon they began to boast. "If the Bolsheviki come
we shall show them how to fight. They do not dare to
fight, they are cowards. But if we should be overpowered,
well, every man keeps one bullet for himself. . . ."

At this point there was a burst of rifle-fire not far off.
Out on the Square all the people began to run, falling
flat on their faces, and the *izvoshchiki,* standing on the
corners, galloped in every direction. Inside all was uproar,
soldiers running here and there, grabbing up guns, rifle-
belts and shouting, "Here they come! Here they come!"
. . . But in a few minutes it quieted down again. The
izvoshchiki came back, the people lying down stood up.
Through the Red Arch appeared the *yunkers,* marching
a little out of step, one of them supported by two comrades.

It was getting late when we left the Palace. The sentries in the Square had all disappeared. The great semi-
circle of Government buildings seemed deserted. We went
into the Hotel France for dinner, and right in the middle
of soup the waiter, very pale in the face, came up and
insisted that we move to the main dining-room at the
back of the house, because they were going to put out the

lights in the café. "There will be much shooting," he said.

When we came out on the Morskaya again it was quite dark, except for one flickering street-light on the corner of the Nevsky. Under this stood a big armored automobile, with racing engine and oil-smoke pouring out of it. A small boy had climbed up the side of the thing and was looking down the barrel of a machine gun. Soldiers and sailors stood around, evidently waiting for something. We walked back up to the Red Arch, where a knot of soldiers was gathered staring at the brightly-lighted Winter Palace and talking in loud tones.

"No, comrades," one was saying. "How can we shoot at them? The Women's Battalion is in there—they will say we have fired on Russian women."

As we reached the Nevsky again another armoured car came around the corner, and a man poked his head out of the turret-top.

"Come on!" he yelled. "Let's go on through and attack!"

The driver of the other car came over, and shouted so as to be heard above the roaring engine. "The Committee says to wait. They have got artillery behind the wood-piles in there. . . ."

Here the street-cars had stopped running, few people passed, and there were no lights; but a few blocks away we could see the trams, the crowds, the lighted shop-windows and the electric signs of the moving-picture shows—life going on as usual. We had tickets to the Ballet at the Marinsky Theatre—all the theatres were open—but it was too exciting out of doors. . . .

In the darkness we stumbled over lumber-piles barricading the Police Bridge, and before the Stroganov Palace made out some soldiers wheeling into position a three-inch field-gun. Men in various uniforms were coming and going in an aimless way, and doing a great deal of talking. . . .

Up the Nevsky the whole city seemed to be out promenading. On every corner immense crowds were massed around a core of hot discussion. Pickets of a dozen soldiers with fixed bayonets lounged at the street-crossings, red-faced old men in rich fur coats shook their fists at them, smartly-dressed women screamed epithets; the soldiers argued feebly, with embarrassed grins. . . . Armoured cars went up and down the street, named after the first Tsars—Oleg, Rurik, Svetoslav—and daubed with huge red letters, "R. S. D. R. P." (*Rossiskaya Sotsial-Demokratitcheskaya Rabochaya Partia*).* At the Mikhailovsky a man appeared with an armful of newspapers, and was immediately stormed by frantic people, offering a rouble, five roubles, ten roubles, tearing at each other like animals. It was *Rabochi i Soldat,* announcing the victory of the Proletarian Revolution, the liberation of the Bolsheviki still in prison, calling upon the Army front and rear for support . . . a feverish little sheet of four pages, running to enormous type, containing no news. . . .

On the corner of the Sadovaya about two thousand citizens had gathered, staring up at the roof of a tall building, where a tiny red spark glowed and waned.

"See!" said a tall peasant, pointing to it. "It is a provocator. Presently he will fire on the people. . . ." Apparently no one thought of going to investigate.

*   *   *   *

The massive façade of Smolny blazed with lights as we drove up, and from every street converged upon it streams of hurrying shapes dim in the gloom. Automobiles and motorcycles came and went; an enormous elephant-col-

* Russian Social Democratic Labor Party.

oured armoured automobile, with two red flags flying from the turret, lumbered out with screaming siren. It was cold, and at the outer gate the Red Guards had built themselves a bonfire. At the inner gate, too, there was a blaze, by the light of which the sentries slowly spelled out our passes and looked us up and down. The canvas covers had been taken off the four rapid-fire guns on each side of the doorway, and the ammunition-belts hung snake-like from their breeches. A dun herd of armoured cars stood under the trees in the court-yard, engines going. The long, bare, dimly-illuminated halls roared with the thunder of feet, calling, shouting. . . . There was an atmosphere of recklessness. A crowd came pouring down the staircase, workers in black blouses and round black fur hats, many of them with guns slung over their shoulders, soldiers in rough dirt-coloured coats and grey fur *shapki** pinched flat, a leader or so—Lunacharsky, Kamenev—hurrying along in the centre of a group all talking at once, with harassed anxious faces, and bulging portfolios under their arms. The extraordinary meeting of the Petrograd Soviet was over. I stopped Kamenev—a quick-moving little man, with a wide, vivacious face set close to his shoulders. Without preface he read in rapid French a copy of the resolution just passed.

The Petrograd Soviet of Workers' and Soldiers' Deputies, saluting the victorious Revolution of the Petrograd proletariat and garrison, particularly emphasises the unity, organisation, discipline, and complete cooperation shown by the masses in this rising; rarely has less blood been spilled, and rarely has an insurrection succeeded so well.

The Soviet expresses its firm conviction that the Workers' and Peasants' Government which, as the government of the Soviets, will be created by the Revolution, and which will

* Caps.—*Ed.*

assure the industrial proletariat of the support of the entire mass of poor peasants, will march firmly toward Socialism, the only means by which the country can be spared the miseries and unheard-of horrors of war.

The new Workers' and Peasants' Government will propose immediately a just and democratic peace to all the belligerent countries.

It will suppress immediately the great landed property, and transfer the land to the peasants. It will establish workmen's control over production and distribution of manufactured products, and will set up a general control over the banks, which it will transform into a state monopoly.

The Petrograd Soviet of Workers' and Soldiers' Deputies calls upon the workers and the peasants of Russia to support with all their energy and all their devotion the Proletarian Revolution. The Soviet expresses its conviction that the city workers, allies of the poor peasants, will assure complete revolutionary order, indispensable to the victory of Socialism. The Soviet is convinced that the proletariat of the countries of Western Europe will aid us in conducting the cause of Socialism to a real and lasting victory.*

"You consider it won then?"

He lifted his shoulders. "There is much to do. Horribly much. It is just beginning. . . ."

On the landing I met Riazanov, vice-president of the Trade Unions, looking black and biting his grey beard. "It's insane! Insane!" he shouted. "The European working-class won't move! All Russia—" He waved his hand distractedly and ran off. Riazanov and Kamenev had both opposed the insurrection, and felt the lash of Lenin's terrible tongue. . . .

It had been a momentous session. In the name of the

---

* Drafted by Lenin, published in the form in which Reed quotes it in *Rabochii Put* of November 8, and now with minor emendations in Lenin's *Works*, Vol. XXVI, p. 210.—*Ed.*

Military Revolutionary Committee Trotsky had declared that the Provisional Government no longer existed.

"The characteristic of bourgeois governments," he said, "is to deceive the people. We, the Soviets of Workers', Soldiers' and Peasants' Deputies, are going to try an experiment unique in history; we are going to found a power which will have no other aim but to satisfy the needs of the soldiers, workers, and peasants."

Lenin had appeared, welcomed with a mighty ovation, prophesying world-wide Social Revolution. . . . And Zinoviev, crying, "This day we have paid our debt to the international proletariat, and struck a terrible blow at the war, a terrible body-blow at all the imperialists and particularly at Wilhelm the Executioner. . . ."

Then Trotsky, that telegrams had been sent to the front announcing the victorious insurrection, but no reply had come. Troops were said to be marching against Petrograd—a delegation must be sent to tell them the truth.

Cries, "You are anticipating the will of the All-Russian Congress of Soviets!"

Trotsky, coldly, "The will of the All-Russian Congress of Soviets has been anticipated by the rising of the Petrograd workers and soldiers!"

So we came into the great meeting-hall, pushing through the clamorous mob at the door. In the rows of seats, under the white chandeliers, packed immovably in the aisles and on the sides, perched on every window-sill, and even the edge of the platform, the representatives of the workers and soldiers of all Russia waited in anxious silence or wild exultation the ringing of the chairman's bell. There was no heat in the hall but the stifling heat of unwashed human bodies. A foul blue cloud of cigarette smoke rose from the mass and hung in the thick air. Occasionally some one in authority mounted the tribune and asked the comrades not to smoke; then everybody, smokers and all, took up the cry "Don't smoke, comrades!" and went on smoking. Petrovsky, Anarchist delegate from the Obukhov factory, made a seat for me beside him. Unshaven and filthy, he was reeling from three nights' sleepless work on the Military Revolutionary Committee.

On the platform sat the leaders of the old *Tsay-ee-kah* —for the last time dominating the turbulent Soviets, which they had ruled from the first days, and which were now risen against them. It was the end of the first period of the Russian revolution, which these men had attempted to guide in careful ways. . . . The three greatest of them were not there: Kerensky, flying to the front through country towns all doubtfully heaving up; Chkheidze, the old eagle, who had contemptuously retired to his own Georgian mountains, there to sicken with consumption; and the high-souled Tseretelli, also mortally striken, who, nevertheless, would return and pour out his beautiful eloquence for a lost cause. Gotz sat there, Dan, Lieber, Bogdanov, Broido, Filipovsky,—white-faced, hollow-eyed and indignant. Below them the second *siezd** of the All-Russian Soviets boiled and swirled, and over their heads the Military Revolutionary Committee functioned white-hot, holding in its hands the threads of insurrection and striking with a long arm. . . . It was 10.40 P. M.

Dan, a mild-faced, baldish figure in a shapeless military surgeon's uniform, was ringing the bell. Silence fell sharply intense, broken by the scuffling and disputing of the people at the door. . . .

"We have the power in our hands," he began sadly, stopped for a moment, and then went on in a low voice. "Comrades! The Congress of Soviets is meeting in such

* Congress.—*Ed.*

unusual circumstances and in such an extraordinary moment that you will understand why the *Tsay-ee-kah* considers it unnecessary to address you with a political speech.
This will become much clearer to you if you will recollect
that I am a member of the *Tsay-ee-kah,* and that at this
very moment our party comrades are in the Winter Palace under bombardment, sacrificing themselves to execute
the duty put on them by the *Tsay-ee-kah."* (Confused uproar.)

"I declare the first session of the Second Congress of
Soviets of Workers' and Soldiers' Deputies open!"

The election of the presidium took place amid stir and
moving about. Avanesov announced that by agreement
of the Bolsheviki, Left Socialist Revolutionaries and
Mensheviki Internationalists, it was decided to base the
presidium upon proportionality. Several Mensheviki leaped
to their feet protesting. A bearded soldier shouted at them,
"Remember what you did to us Bolsheviki when *we* were
the minority!" Result—14 Bolsheviki, 7 Socialist Revolutionaries, 3 Mensheviki and 1 Internationalist (Gorky's
group). Hendelmann, for the right and centre Socialist
Revolutionaries, said that they refused to take part in the
presidium; the same from Khinchuk,* for the Mensheviki;
and from the Mensheviki Internationalists, that until the
verification of certain circumstances, they too could not
enter the presidium. Scattering applause and hoots. One
voice, "Renegades, you call yourselves Socialists!" A representative of the Ukrainian delegates demanded, and received, a place. Then the old *Tsay-ee-kah* stepped down,
and in their places appeared Trotsky, Kamenev, Lunacharsky, Madame Kollentai, Nogin. . . . The hall rose,
thundering. How far they had soared, these Bolsheviki,

* Chairman of the Moscow Soviet, in 1920 joined the Communist Party
and became a Soviet functionary.—*Ed.*

from a despised and hunted sect less than four months ago, to this supreme place, the helm of great Russia in full tide of insurrection!

The order of the day, said Kamenev, was first, Organisation of Power; second, War and Peace; and third, the Constituent Assembly. Lozovsky, rising, announced that upon agreement of the bureau of all factions, it was proposed to hear and discuss the report of the Petrograd Soviet, then to give the floor to members of the *Tsay-ee-kah* and the different parties, and finally to pass to the order of the day.

But suddenly a new sound made itself heard, deeper than the tumult of the crowd, persistent, disquieting,—the dull shock of guns. People looked anxiously toward the clouded windows, and a sort of fever came over them. Martov, demanding the floor, croaked hoarsely, "The civil war is beginning, comrades! The first question must be a peaceful settlement of the crisis. On principle and from a political standpoint we must urgently discuss a means of averting civil war. Our brothers are being shot down in the streets! At this moment, when before the opening of the Congress of Soviets the question of Power is being settled by means of a military plot organised by one of the revolutionary parties—" for a moment he could not make himself heard above the noise, "All of the revolutionary parties must face the fact! The first *vopros* (question) before the Congress is the question of Power, and this question is already being settled by force of arms in the streets. . . . We must create a power which will be recognised by the whole democracy. If the Congress wishes to be the voice of the revolutionary democracy it must not sit with folded hands before the developing civil war, the result of which may be a dangerous outburst of counter-revolution. . . . The possibility of a peaceful outcome lies in the formation of a united democratic authority. . . . We must elect a delegation to negotiate with the other Socialist parties and organisations. . . ."

Always the methodical muffled boom of cannon through the windows, and the delegates, screaming at each other. . . . So, with the crash of artillery, in the dark, with hatred, and fear, and reckless daring, new Russia was being born.

The Left Socialist Revolutionaries and the United Social Democrats supported Martov's proposition. It was accepted.* A soldier announced that the All-Russian Peasants' Soviets had refused to send delegates to the Congress; he proposed that a committee be sent with a formal invitation. "Some delegates are present," he said. "I move that they be given votes." Accepted.

Kharash, wearing the epaulets of a captain, passionately demanded the floor. "The political hypocrites who control this Congress," he shouted, "told us we were to settle the question of Power—and it is being settled behind our backs, before the Congress opens! Blows are being struck against the Winter Palace, and it is by such blows that the nails are being driven into the coffin of the political party which has risked such an adventure!" Uproar. Followed him Gharra: "While we are here discussing propositions of peace, there is a battle on in the streets. . . . The Socialist Revolutionaries and the Mensheviki refuse to be involved in what is happening, and call upon all public forces to resist the attempt to capture the power. . . ." Kuchin, delegate of the 12th Army and representative of the Troudoviki: "I was sent here only for information,

* Lenin and Trotsky were both against it, but as a majority of the Congress, including its Bolshevik contingent, were manifestly for it, Lenin and Trotsky accepted the Martov resolution to gain time, divide their opponents, and in due course, see to it that the resolution would not be carried out.—*Ed.*

and I am returning at once to the Front, where all the Army Committees consider that the taking of power by the Soviets, only three weeks before the Constituent Assembly, is a stab in the back of the Army and a crime against the people—!" Shouts of "Lie! You lie!" . . . When he could be heard again, "Let's make an end of this adventure in Petrograd! I call upon all delegates to leave this hall in order to save the country and the Revolution!" As he went down the aisle in the midst of a deafening noise, people surged in upon him, threatening. . . . Then Khinchuk, an officer with a long brown goatee, speaking suavely and persuasively: "I speak for the delegates from the Front. The Army is perfectly represented in this Congress, and furthermore, the Army does not consider the Congress of Soviets necessary at this time, only three weeks before the opening of the Constituent—" shouts and stamping, always growing more violent. "The Army does not consider that the Congress of Soviets has the necessary authority—" Soldiers began to stand up all over the hall.

"Who are you speaking for? What do you represent?" they cried.

"The Central Executive Committee of the Soviet of the Fifth Army, the Second F— Regiment, the First N— Regiment, the Third S— Rifles. . . ."

"When were you elected? You represent the officers, not the soldiers! What do the soldiers say about it?" Jeers and hoots.

"We, the Front group, disclaim all responsibility for what has happened and is happening, and we consider it necessary to mobilise all self-conscious revolutionary forces for the salvation of the Revolution! The Front group will leave the Congress. . . . The place to fight is out on the streets!"

Immense bawling outcry. "You speak for the Staff—not for the Army!"

"I appeal to all reasonable soldiers to leave this Congress!"

"Kornilovets! Counter-revolutionist! Provocator!" were hurled at him.

On behalf of the Mensheviki, Khinchuk then announced that the only possibility of a peaceful solution was to begin negotiations with the Provisional Government for the formation of a new Cabinet, which would find support in all strata of society. He could not proceed for several minutes. Raising his voice to a shout he read the Menshevik declaration:

"Because the Bolsheviki have made a military conspiracy with the aid of the Petrograd Soviet, without consulting the other factions and parties, we find it impossible to remain in the Congress, and therefore withdraw, inviting the other groups to follow us and to meet for discussion of the situation!"

"Deserter!" At intervals in the almost continuous disturbance Hendelman, for the Socialist Revolutionaries, could be heard protesting against the bombardment of the Winter Palace. . . . "We are opposed to this kind of anarchy. . . ."

Scarcely had he stepped down than a young, lean-faced soldier, with flashing eyes, leaped to the platform, and dramatically lifted his hand:

"Comrades!" he cried and there was a hush. "My *familia* (name) is Peterson—I speak for the Second Lettish Rifles. You have heard the statements of two representatives of the Army committees; these statements would have some value *if their authors had been representatives of the Army*—" Wild applause. *"But they do not represent the soldiers!"* Shaking his fist. "The Twelfth

Army has been insisting for a long time upon the re-election of the Great Soviet and the Army Committee, but just as your own *Tsay-ee-kah,* our Committee refused to call a meeting of the representatives of the masses until the end of September, so that the reactionaries could elect their own false delegates to this Congress. I tell you now, the Lettish soldiers have many times said, 'No more resolutions! No more talk! We want deeds—the Power must be in our hands!' Let these impostor delegates leave the Congress! The Army is not with them!"

The hall rocked with cheering. In the first moments of the session, stunned by the rapidity of events, startled by the sound of cannon, the delegates had hesitated. For an hour hammer-blow after hammer-blow had fallen from that tribune, welding them together but beating them down. Did they stand then alone? Was Russia rising against them? Was it true that the Army was marching on Petrograd? Then this clear-eyed young soldier had spoken, and in a flash they knew it for the truth. . . . *This* was the voice of the soldiers—the stirring millions of uniformed workers and peasants were men like them, and their thoughts and feelings were the same. . . .

More soldiers . . . Gzhelshakh; for the Front delegates, announcing that they had only decided to leave the Congress by a small majority, and that *the Bolshevik members had not even taken part in the vote,* as they stood for division according to political parties, and not groups. "Hundreds of delegates from the Front," he said, "are being elected without the participation of the soldiers because the Army Committees are no longer the real representatives of the rank and file. . . ." Lukianov, crying that officers like Kharash and Khinchuk could not represent the Army in this congress,—but only the high command. "The real inhabitants of the trenches want with all their hearts the transfer of Power into the hands of the Soviets, and they expect very much from it!" . . . The tide was turning.

Then came Abramovich, for the *Bund,* the organ of the Jewish Social Democrats—his eyes snapping behind thick glasses, trembling with rage.*

"What is taking place now in Petrograd is a monstrous calamity! The *Bund* group joins with the declaration of the Mensheviki and Socialist Revolutionaries and will leave the Congress!" He raised his voice and hand. "Our duty to the Russian proletariat doesn't permit us to remain here and be responsible for these crimes. Because the firing on the Winter Palace doesn't cease, the Municipal Duma together with the Mensheviki and Socialist Revolutionaries, and the Executive Committee of the Peasants' Soviet, has decided to perish with the Provisional Government, and we are going with them! Unarmed we will expose our breasts to the machine guns of the Terrorists. . . . We invite all delegates to this Congress——" The rest was lost in a storm of hoots, menaces and curses which rose to a hellish pitch as fifty delegates got up and pushed their way out. . . .

Kamenev jangled the bell, shouting, "Keep your seats and we'll go on with our business!" And Trotsky, standing up with a pale, cruel face, letting out his rich voice in cool contempt, "All these so-called Socialist compromisers, these frightened Mensheviki, Socialist Revolutionaries, *Bund*—let them go! They are just so much refuse which will be swept into the garbage-heap of history!"

Riazanov, for the Bolsheviki, stated that at the request of the City Duma the Military Revolutionary Committee

* Reed is mistaken as to the speaker. He took the name from the Petrograd press, which made the same mistake. The speaker he is describing was Henrik Ehrlich, of the Bundist Right, an ardent defensist. Abramovich was of the Bund Left and a Menshevik-Internationalist. In 1917 he did not wear glasses, thick or otherwise.—*Ed.*

had sent a delegation to offer negotiations to the Winter Palace. "In this way we have done everything possible to avoid bloodshed. . . ."

We hurried from the place, stopping for a moment at the room where the Military Revolutionary Committee worked at furious speed, engulfing and spitting out panting couriers, despatching Commissars armed with power of life and death to all the corners of the city, amid the buzz of the telephonographs. The door opened, a blast of stale air and cigarette-smoke rushed out, we caught a glimpse of dishevelled men bending over a map under the glare of a shaded electric-light. . . . Comrade Josephov-Dukhvinski, a smiling youth with a mop of pale yellow hair, made out passes for us.

When we came into the chill night, all the front of Smolny was one huge park of arriving and departing automobiles, above the sound of which could be heard the far-off slow beat of the cannon. A great motor-truck stood there, shaking to the roar of its engine. Men were tossing bundles into it, and others receiving them, with guns beside them.

"Where are you going?" I shouted.

"Down-town—all over—everywhere!" answered a little workman, grinning, with a large exultant gesture.

We showed our passes. "Come along!" they invited. "But there'll probably be shooting——" We climbed in; the clutch slid home with a raking jar, the great car jerked forward, we all toppled backward on top of those who were climbing in; past the huge fire by the gate, and then the fire by the outer gate, glowing red on the faces of the workmen with rifles who squatted around it, and went bumping at top speed down the Suvorovsky Prospekt, swaying from side to side. . . . One man tore the wrapping from a bundle and began to hurl handfuls of paper into the air. We imitated him, plunging down through the dark street with a tail of white papers floating and eddying out behind. The late passerby stooped to pick them up; the patrols around bonfires on the corners ran out with uplifted arms to catch them. Sometimes armed men loomed up ahead, crying *"Stoi!"* and raising their guns, but our chauffeur only yelled something unintelligible and we hurtled on. . . .

I picked up a copy of the paper, and under a fleeting street-light read:

To the Citizens of Russia!*

The Provisional Government is deposed. The State Power has passed into the hands of the organ of the Petrograd Soviet of Workers' and Soldiers' Deputies, the Military Revolutionary Committee, which stands at the head of the Petrograd proletariat and garrison.

The cause for which the people were fighting: immediate proposal of a democratic peace, abolition of landlord property-rights over the land, labor control over production, creation of a Soviet Government—that cause is securely achieved.

LONG LIVE THE REVOLUTION OF WORKMEN, SOLDIERS AND PEASANTS!

Military Revolutionary Committee
Petrograd Soviet of Workers' and Soldiers' Deputies.

A slant-eyed, Mongolian-faced man who sat beside me, dressed in a goat-skin Caucasian cape, snapped, "Look out! Here the provocators always shoot from the windows!" We turned into Znamensky Square, dark and almost deserted, careened around Trubetskoy's brutal statue

* Personally drafted by Lenin.—*Ed.*

Отъ Военно - Революціоннаго Комитета при Петроградскомъ Совѣтѣ
Рабочихъ и Солдатскихъ Депутатовъ.

Къ Гражданамъ Россіи.

Временное Правительство низложено. Государ-
ственная власть перешла въ руки органа Петроградскаго Совѣта Рабочихъ и Солдатскихъ Депутатовъ Военно-Революціоннаго Комитета, стоящаго
во главѣ Петроградскаго пролетаріата и гарнизона.

Дѣло, за которое боролся народъ: немедленное пред-
ложеніе демократическаго мира, отмѣна помѣщичьей
собственности на землю, рабочій контроль надъ производствомъ, созданіе Совѣтскаго Правительства — это
дѣло обезпечено.

ДА ЗДРАВСТВУЕТЪ РЕВОЛЮЦІЯ РАБОЧИХЪ, СОЛДАТЪ И КРЕСТЬЯНЪ!

Военно-Революціонный Комитетъ
при Петроградскомъ Совѣтѣ
Рабочихъ и Солдатскихъ Депутатовъ

25 октября 1917 г. 10 ч. утра.

Proclamation of the Fall of the Provisional Government,
issued by the Military Revolutionary Committee on the night
of November 7th (our calendar), which we helped to distribute from a motor-truck just after the surrender of the
Winter Palace.

and swung down the wide Nevsky, three men standing up
with rifles ready, peering at the windows. Behind us the
street was alive with people running and stooping. We
could no longer hear the cannon, and the nearer we drew
to the Winter Palace end of the city the quieter and more
deserted were the streets. The City Duma was all brightly
lighted. Beyond that we made out a dark mass of people,
and a line of sailors, who yelled furiously at us to stop.
The machine slowed down, and we climbed out.

It was an astonishing scene. Just at the corner of the
Ekaterina Canal, under an arc-light, a cordon of armed
sailors was drawn across the Nevsky, blocking the way to
a crowd of people in column of fours. There were about
three or four hundred of them, men in frock coats, well-
dressed women, officers—all sorts and conditions of people. Among them we recognised many of the delegates
from the Congress, leaders of the Mensheviki and Socialist
Revolutionaries; Avksentiev, the lean, red-bearded
president of the Peasants' Soviets, Sarokin, Kerensky's
spokesman, Khinchuk, Abramovich; and at the head
white-bearded old Schreider, Mayor of Petrograd, and
Prokopovich, Minister of Supplies in the Provisional
Government, arrested that morning and released. I caught
sight of Malkin, reporter for the *Russian Daily News*.
"Going to die in the Winter Palace," he shouted cheerfully. The procession stood still, but from the front of it
came loud argument. Schreider and Prokopovich were
bellowing at the big sailor who seemed in command.

"We demand to pass!" they cried. "See, these comrades
come from the Congress of Soviets! Look at their tickets!
We are going to the Winter Palace!"

The sailor was plainly puzzled. He scratched his head
with an enormous hand, frowning. "I have orders from
the Committee not to let anybody go to the Winter Pal-

ace," he grumbled. "But I will send a comrade to telephone to Smolny. . . ."

"We insist upon passing! We are unarmed! We will march on whether you permit us or not!" cried old Schreider, very much excited.

"I have orders——" repeated the sailor sullenly.

"Shoot us if you want to! We will pass! Forward!" came from all sides. "We are ready to die, if you have the heart to fire on Russians and comrades! We bare our breasts to your guns!"

"No," said the sailor, looking stubborn, "I can't allow you to pass."

"What will you do if we go forward? Will you shoot?"

"No, I'm not going to shoot people who haven't any guns. We won't shoot unarmed Russian people. . . ."

"We will go forward! What can you do?"

"We will do something," replied the sailor, evidently at a loss. "We can't let you pass. We will do something."

"What will you do? What will you do?"

Another sailor came up, very much irritated. "We will spank you!" he cried, energetically. "And if necessary we will shoot you too. Go home now, and leave us in peace!"

At this there was a great clamour of anger and resentment, Prokopovich had mounted some sort of box, and, waving his umbrella, he made a speech:

"Comrades and citizens!" he said. "Force is being used against us! We cannot have our innocent blood upon the hands of these ignorant men! It is beneath our dignity to be shot down here in the street by switchmen—" (What he meant by "switchmen" I never discovered.) "Let us return to the Duma and discuss the best means of saving the country and the Revolution!"

Whereupon, in dignified silence, the procession marched

around and back up the Nevsky, always in column of fours. And taking advantage of the diversion we slipped past the guards and set off in the direction of the Winter Palace.

Here it was absolutely dark, and nothing moved but pickets of soldiers and Red Guards grimly intent. In front of the Kazan Cathedral a three-inch field-gun lay in the middle of the street, slewed sideways from the recoil of its last shot over the roofs. Soldiers were standing in every doorway talking in low tones and peering down toward the Police Bridge. I heard one voice saying: "It is possible that we have done wrong. . . ." At the corners patrols stopped all passersby—and the composition of these patrols was interesting, for in command of the regular troops was invariably a Red Guard. . . . The shooting had ceased.

Just as we came to the Morskaya somebody was shouting: "The *yunkers* have sent word they want us to go and get them out!" Voices began to give commands, and in the thick gloom we made out a dark mass moving forward, silent but for the shuffle of feet and the clinking of arms. We fell in with the first ranks.

Like a black river, filling all the street, without song or cheer we poured through the Red Arch, where the man just ahead of me said in a low voice: "Look out, comrades! Don't trust them. They will fire, surely!" In the open we began to run, stooping low and bunching together, and jammed up suddenly behind the pedestal of the Alexander Column.

"How many of you did they kill?" I asked.

"I don't know. About ten. . . ."

After a few minutes huddling there, some hundreds of men, the army seemed reassured and, without any orders, suddenly began again to flow forward. By this time, in the light that streamed out of all the Winter Palace windows, I could see that the first two or three hundred men were Red Guards, with only a few scattered soldiers. Over the barricade of firewood we clambered, and leaping down inside gave a triumphant shout as we stumbled on a heap of rifles thrown down by the *yunkers* who had stood there. On both sides of the main gateway the doors stood wide open, light streamed out, and from the huge pile came not the slightest sound.

Carried along by the eager wave of men we were swept into the right hand entrance, opening into a great bare vaulted room, the cellar of the East wing, from which issued a maze of corridors and stair-cases. A number of huge packing cases stood about, and upon these the Red Guards and soldiers fell furiously, battering them open with the butts of their rifles, and pulling out carpets, curtains, linen, porcelain plates, glassware. . . . One man went strutting around with a bronze clock perched on his shoulder; another found a plume of ostrich feathers, which he stuck in his hat. The looting was just beginning when somebody cried, "Comrades! Don't touch anything! Don't take anything! This is the property of the People!" Immediately twenty voices were crying, "Stop! Put everything back! Don't take anything! Property of the People!" Many hands dragged the spoilers down. Damask and tapestry were snatched from the arms of those who had them; two men took away the bronze clock. Roughly and hastily the things were crammed back in their cases, and self-appointed sentinels stood guard. It was all utterly spontaneous. Through corridors and up stair-cases the cry could be heard growing fainter and fainter in the distance, "Revolutionary discipline! Property of the People. . . ."

We crossed back over to the left entrance, in the West

wing. There order was also being established. "Clear the Palace!" bawled a Red Guard, sticking his head through an inner door. "Come, comrades, let's show that we're not thieves and bandits. Everybody out of the Palace except the Commissars, until we get sentries posted."

Two Red Guards, a soldier and an officer, stood with revolvers in their hands. Another soldier sat at a table behind them, with pen and paper. Shouts of "All out! All out!" were heard far and near within, and the Army began to pour through the door, jostling, expostulating, arguing. As each man appeared he was seized by the self-appointed committee, who went through his pockets and looked under his coat. Everything that was plainly not his property was taken away, the man at the table noted it on his paper, and it was carried into a little room. The most amazing assortment of objects were thus confiscated; statuettes, bottles of ink, bed-spreads worked with the Imperial monogram, candles, a small oil-painting, desk blotters, gold-handled swords, cakes of soap, clothes of every description, blankets. One Red Guard carried three rifles, two of which he had taken away from *yunkers;* another had four portfolios bulging with written documents. The culprits either sullenly surrendered or pleaded like children. All talking at once the committee explained that stealing was not worthy of the people's champions; often those who had been caught turned around and began to help go through the rest of the comrades.[3]

Yunkers came out, in bunches of three or four. The committee seized upon them with an excess of zeal, accompanying the search with remarks like, "Ah, Provocators! Kornilovists! Counter-revolutionists! Murderers of the People!" But there was no violence done, although the *yunkers* were terrified. They too had their pockets full of small plunder. It was carefully noted down by the scribe, and piled in the little room. . . . The *yunkers* were disarmed. "Now, will you take up arms against the People any more?" demanded clamouring voices.

"No," answered the *yunkers,* one by one. Whereupon they were allowed to go free.

We asked if we might go inside. The committee was doubtful, but the big Red Guard answered firmly that it was forbidden. "Who are you anyway?" he asked. "How do I know that you are not all Kerenskys? (There were five of us, two women.)*

"*Pazhal'st', tovarishchi!* Way, Comrades!" A soldier and a Red Guard appeared in the door, waving the crowd aside, and other guards with fixed bayonets. After them followed single file half a dozen men in civilian dress—the members of the Provisional Government. First came Kishkin, his face drawn and pale, then Rutenberg, looking sullenly at the floor; Tereshchenko was next, glancing sharply around; he stared at us with cold fixity. . . . They passed in silence; the victorious insurrectionists crowded to see, but there were only a few angry mutterings. It was only later that we learned how the people in the street wanted to lynch them, and shots were fired —but the sailors brought them safely to Peter-Paul. . . .

In the meanwhile unrebuked we walked into the Palace. There was still a great deal of coming and going, of exploring new-found apartments in the vast edifice, of searching for hidden garrisons of *yunkers* which did not exist. We went upstairs and wandered through room after room. This part of the Palace had been entered also by

* The five were John Reed, Albert Rhys Williams, Louise Bryant, Bessie Beatty and Alex Gomberg. The first four wrote about it, and the fifth, Gomberg, was interviewed concerning the adventure. Their accounts differ considerably, Reed's being the fullest, most vivid, and most imaginative. It is possible that Gomberg left before they finished their stay in the Winter Palace, otherwise we cannot explain why they were nearly shot because suspicious illiterate soldiers could not read their Russian passes, for Gomberg was Russian-born and spoke Russian fluently.—*Ed.*

other detachments from the side of the Neva. The paintings, statues, tapestries and rugs of the great state apartments were unharmed; in the offices, however, every desk
and cabinet had been ransacked, the papers scattered
over the floor, and in the living rooms beds had been
stripped of their coverings and ward-robes wrenched
open. The most highly prized loot was clothing, which the
working people needed. In a room where furniture was
stored we came upon two soldiers ripping the elaborate
Spanish leather upholstery from chairs. They explained it
was to make boots with. . . .

The old Palace servants in their blue and red and gold
uniforms stood nervously about, from force of habit re-
peating, "You can't go in there, *barin!* It is forbidden———" We penetrated at length to the gold and mala-
chite chamber with crimson brocade hangings where the
Ministers had been in session all that day and night, and
where the *shveitzari* had betrayed them to the Red Guards.
The long table covered with green baize was just as they
had left it, under arrest. Before each empty seat was pen
and ink and paper; the papers were scribbled over with
beginnings of plans of action, rough drafts of proclamations and manifestos. Most of these were scratched out,
as their futility became evident, and the rest of the sheet
covered with absent-minded geometrical designs, as the
writers sat despondently listening while Minister after
Minister proposed chimerical schemes. I took one of these
scribbled pages, in the hand writing of Konovalov, which
read, "The Provisional Government appeals to all classes
to support the Provisional Government—"

All this time, it must be remembered, although the Winter Palace was surrounded, the Government was in constant communication with the Front and with provincial
Russia. The Bolsheviki had captured the Ministry of

War early in the morning, but they did not know of the military telegraph office in the attic, nor of the private telephone line connecting it with the Winter Palace. In that attic a young officer sat all day, pouring out over the country a flood of appeals and proclamations; and when he heard that the Palace had fallen, put on his hat and walked calmly out of the building. . . .

Interested as we were, for a considerable time we didn't notice a change in the attitude of the soldiers and Red Guards around us. As we strolled from room to room a small group followed us, until by the time we reached the great picture-gallery where we had spent the afternoon with the *yunkers,* about a hundred men surged in after us. One giant of a soldier stood in our path, his face dark with sullen suspicion.

"Who are you?" he growled. "What are you doing here?" The others massed slowly around, staring and beginning to mutter. *"Provocatori!"* I heard somebody say. "Looters!" I produced our passes from the Military Revolutionary Committee. The soldier took them gingerly, turned them upside down and looked at them without comprehension. Evidently he could not read. He handed them back and spat on the floor. *"Bumagi!* Papers!" said he with contempt. The mass slowly began to close in, like wild cattle around a cow-puncher on foot. Over their heads I caught sight of an officer, looking helpless, and shouted to him. He made for us, shouldering his way through.

"I'm the Commissar," he said to me. "Who are you? What is it?" The others held back, waiting. I produced the papers.

"You are foreigners?" he rapidly asked in French. "It is very dangerous. . . ." Then he turned to the mob,

Facsimile of the beginning of a proclamation, written in pencil by A. I. Konovalov, Minister of Commerce and Industry in the Provisional Government, and then scratched out as the hopelessness of the situation became more and more evident. The geometrical figure beneath was probably idly drawn while the Ministers were waiting for the end.

holding up our documents. "Comrades!" he cried. "These people are foreign comrades—from America. They have come here to be able to tell their countrymen about the bravery and the revolutionary discipline of the proletarian army!"

"How do you know that?" replied the big soldier. "I tell you they are provocators! They say they came here to observe the revolutionary discipline of the proletarian army, but they have been wandering freely through the Palace, and how do we know they haven't got their pockets full of loot?"

"Pravilno!" snarled the others, pressing forward.

"Comrades! Comrades!" appealed the officer, sweat standing out on his forehead. "I am Commissar of the Military Revolutionary Committee. Do you trust me? Well, I tell you that these passes are signed with the same names that are signed to my pass!"

He led us down through the Palace and out through a door opening onto the Neva quay, before which stood the usual committee going through pockets. . . . "You have narrowly escaped," he kept muttering, wiping his face.

"What happened to the Women's Battalion?" we asked.

"Oh—the women!" He laughed. "They were all huddled up in a back room. We had a terrible time deciding what to do with them—many were in hysterics, and so on. So finally we marched them up to the Finland Station and put them on a train for Levashovo, where they have a camp.[4] . . ."

We came out into the cold, nervous night, murmurous with obscure armies on the move, electric with patrols. From across the river, where loomed the darker mass of Peter-Paul, came a hoarse shout. . . . Underfoot the sidewalk was littered with broken stucco, from the cornice of the Palace where two shells from the battleship *Avrora* had struck; that was the only damage done by the bombardment. . . .

It was now after three in the morning. On the Nevsky all the street-lights were again shining, the cannon gone, and the only signs of war were Red Guards and soldiers squatting around fires. The city was quiet—probably never so quiet in its history; on that night not a single hold-up occurred, not a single robbery.

But the City Duma Building was all illuminated. We mounted to the galleried Alexander Hall, hung with its great, gold-framed, red-shrouded Imperial portraits. About a hundred people were grouped around the platform, where Skobelev was speaking. He urged that the Committee of Public Safety be expanded, so as to unite all the anti-Bolshevik elements in one huge organisation, to be called the Committee for Salvation of Country and Revolution. And as we looked on, the Committee for Salvation was formed—that Committee which was to develop into the most powerful enemy of the Bolsheviki, appearing, in the next week, sometimes under its own partisan name, and sometimes as the strictly non-partisan Committee of Public Safety. . . .

Dan, Gotz, Avksentiev were there, some of the insurgent Soviet delegates, members of the Executive Committee of the Peasants' Soviets, old Prokopovich, and even members of the Council of the Republic—among whom Vinaver and other Cadets. Lieber cried that the convention of Soviets was not a legal convention, that the old *Tsay-ee-kah* was still in office. . . . An appeal to the country was drafted.

We hailed a cab. "Where to?" But when we said "Smolny," the *izvoshchik* shook his head. *"Niet!"* said he, "there are devils. . . ." It was only after weary wandering that we found a driver willing to take us—and he wanted thirty rubles, and stopped two blocks away.

The windows of Smolny were still ablaze, motors came and went, and around the still-leaping fires the sentries huddled close, eagerly asking everybody the latest news. The corridors were full of hurrying men, hollow-eyed and dirty. In some of the committee-rooms people lay sleeping on the floor, their guns beside them. In spite of the seceding delegates, the hall of meetings was crowded with people, roaring like the sea. As we came in, Kamenev was reading the list of arrested Ministers. The name of Tereshchenko was greeted with thunderous applause, shouts of satisfaction, laughter; Rutenburg came in for less; and at the mention of Palchinsky, a storm of hoots, angry cries, cheers burst forth. . . . It was announced that Chudnovsky had been appointed Commissar of the Winter Palace.

Now occurred a dramatic interruption. A big peasant, his bearded face convulsed with rage, mounted the platform and pounded with his fist on the presidium table.

"We, Socialist Revolutionaries, insist upon the immediate release of the Socialist Ministers arrested in the Winter Palace! Comrades! Do you know that four comrades who risked their lives and their freedom fighting against tyranny of the Tsar, have been flung into Peter-Paul prison—the historical tomb of Liberty?" In the uproar he pounded and yelled. Another delegate climbed up beside him, and pointed at the presidium.

"Are the representatives of the revolutionary masses going to sit quietly here while the *Okhrana* of the Bolsheviki tortures their leaders?"

Trotsky was gesturing for silence. "These 'comrades' who are now caught plotting the crushing of the Soviets with the adventurer Kerensky—is there any reason to handle them with gloves? After July 16th and 18th they didn't use much ceremony with us!" With a triumphant ring in his voice he cried, "Now that the *oborontsi* and the faint-hearted have gone, and the whole task of defending and saving the Revolution rests on our shoulders, it is particularly necessary to work—work—work! We have decided to die rather than give up!"

Followed him a Commissar from Tsarskoye Selo, panting and covered with the mud of his ride. "The garrison of Tsarskoye Selo is on guard at the gates of Petrograd, ready to defend the Soviets and the Military Revolutionary Committee!" Wild cheers. "The Cycle Corps sent from the front has arrived at Tsarskoye, and the soldiers are now with us; they recognise the power of the Soviets, the necessity of immediate transfer of land to the peasants and industrial control to the workers. The Fifth Battalion of Cyclists, stationed at Tsarskoye, is ours. . . ."

Then the delegate of the Third Cycle Battalion. In the midst of delirious enthusiasm he told how the cycle corps had been ordered *three days before* from the South-west front to the "defence of Petrograd." They suspected, however, the meaning of the order; and at the station of Peredolsk were met by representatives of the Fifth Battalion from Tsarskoye. A joint meeting was held, and it was discovered that "among the cyclists not a single man was found willing to shed the blood of his brothers, or to support a Government of bourgeois and land-owners!"

Kapelinski, for the Mensheviki Internationalists, proposed to elect a special committee to find a peaceful solution to the civil war. "There isn't any peaceful solution!" bellowed the crowd. "Victory is the only solution!" The vote was overwhelmingly against, and the Mensheviki Internationalists left the Congress in a whirlwind of jocular insults. There was no longer any panic fear. . . .

Kamenev from the platform shouted after them, "The Mensheviki Internationalists claimed 'emergency' for the question of a 'peaceful solution,' but they always voted for suspension of the order of the day in favour of declarations of factions which wanted to leave the Congress. It is evident," finished Kamenev, "that the withdrawal of all these renegades was decided upon beforehand!"

The assembly decided to ignore the withdrawal of the factions, and proceed to the appeal to the workers, soldiers and peasants of all Russia:

To Workers, Soldiers and Peasants*

The Second All-Russian Congress of Soviets of Workers' and Soldiers' Deputies has opened. It represents the great majority of the Soviets. There are also a number of Peasant deputies. Based upon the will of the great majority of the workers', soldiers and peasants, based upon the triumphant uprising of the Petrograd workmen and soldiers, the Congress assumes the Power.

The Provisional Government is deposed. Most of the members of the Provisional Government are already arrested.

The Soviet authority will at once propose an immediate democratic peace to all nations, and an immediate truce on all fronts. It will assure the free transfer of landlord, crown and monastery lands to the Land Committees, defend the soldiers' rights, enforcing a complete democratisation of the Army, establish workers' control over production, ensure the convocation of the Constituent Assembly at the proper date, take means to supply bread to the cities and articles of first necessity to the villages, and secure to all nationalities living in Russia a real right to independent existence.

The Congress resolves: that all local power shall be transferred to the Soviets of Workers', Soldiers' and Peasants' Deputies, which must enforce revolutionary order.

* Drafted by Lenin personally, this appeal occupied the entire first page of *Rabochii i Soldat* on November 8.

The Congress calls upon the soldiers in the trenches to be watchful and steadfast. The Congress of Soviets is sure that the revolutionary Army will know how to defend the Revolution against all attacks of Imperialism, until the new Government shall have brought about the conclusion of the democratic peace which it will directly propose to all nations. The new Government will take all necessary steps to secure everything needful to the revolutionary Army, by means of a determined policy of requisition and taxation of the propertied classes, and also to improve the situation of soldiers' families.

The Kornilovets—Kerensky, Kaledin and others, are endeavouring to lead troops against Petrograd. Several regiments, deceived by Kerensky, have sided with the insurgent People.

Soldiers! Make active resistance to the Kornilovets—Kerensky! Be on guard!

Railway men! Stop all troop-trains being sent by Kerensky against Petrograd!

Soldiers, Workers, Clerical employees! The destiny of the Revolution and democratic peace is in your hands!

Long live the Revolution!

> *The All-Russian Congress of Soviets of Workers' and Soldiers' Deputies.*
> *Delegates from the Peasants' Soviets.*

It was exactly 5:17 A. M. when Krylenko, staggering with fatigue, climbed to the tribune with a telegram in his hand.

"Comrades! From the Northern Front. The Twelfth Army sends greetings to the Congress of Soviets, announcing the formation of a Military Revolutionary Committee which has taken over the command of the Northern Front!" Pandemonium, men weeping, embracing each other. "General Chermisov has recognised the Committee —Commissar of the Provisional Government Voitinsky has resigned!"

So, Lenin and the Petrograd workers had decided on insurrection, the Petrograd Soviet had overthrown the Provisional Government, and thrust the *coup d'etat* upon the Congress of Soviets. Now there was all great Russia to win—and then the world! Would Russia follow and rise? And the world—what of it? Would the peoples answer and rise, a red world-tide?

Although it was six in the morning, night was yet heavy and chill. There was only a faint unearthly pallor stealing over the silent streets, dimming the watch-fires, the shadow of a terrible dawn grey-rising over Russia. . . .

NOTES TO CHAPTER IV

1 Events of November 7th

From 4 A. M. until dawn Kerensky remained at the Petrograd Staff Headquarters, sending orders to the Cossacks and to the *yunkers* in the Officers' Schools in and around Petrograd—all of whom answered that they were unable to move.

Colonel Polkovnikov, Commandant of the City, hurried between the Staff and the Winter Palace, evidently without any plan. Kerensky gave an order to open the bridges; three hours passed without any action, and then an officer and five men went out on their own initiative, and putting to flight a picket of Red Guards, opened the Nicolai Bridge. Immediately after they left, however, some sailors closed it again.

Kerensky ordered the print-shop of *Rabochi Put* to be occupied. The officer detailed to the work was promised a squad of soldiers; two hours later he was promised some *yunkers;* then the order was forgotten.

An attempt was made to recapture the Post Office and the Telegraph Agency; a few shots were fired, and the Government troops announced that they would no longer oppose the Soviets.

To a delegation of *yunkers* Kerensky said, "As chief of the Provisional Government and as Supreme Commander I know nothing, I cannot advise you; but as a veteran revolutionist, I appeal to you, young revolutionists, to remain at your posts and defend the conquests of the Revolution."

Orders of Kishkin, November 7th:

"By decree of the Provisional Government . . . I am invested with extraordinary powers for the reestablishment of order in Petrograd, in complete command of all civil and military authorities. . . ."

*　　*　　*　　*

"In accordance with the powers conferred upon me by the Provisional Government, I herewith relieve from his functions as Commandant of the Petrograd Military District Colonel George Polkovnikov. . . ."

*　　*　　*　　*

Appeal to the Population signed by Vice-Premier Konovalov, November 7th:

"Citizens! Save the fatherland, the republic and your freedom. Maniacs have raised a revolt against the only governmental power chosen by the people, the Provisional Government. . . .

"The members of the Provisional Government fulfil their duty, remain at their post, and continue to work for the good of the fatherland, the reestablishment of order, and the convocation of the Constituent Assembly, future sovereign of Russia and of all the Russian peoples. . . .

"Citizens, you must support the Provisional Government. You must strengthen its authority. You must oppose these maniacs, with whom are joined all enemies of liberty and order, and the followers of the Tsarist régime, in order to wreck the Constituent Assembly, destroy the conquests of the Revolution, and the future of our dear fatherland. . . .

"Citizens! Organise around the Provisional Government for the defence of its temporary authority, in the name of order and the happiness of all peoples. . . ."

*　　*　　*　　*

Proclamation of the Provisional Government.

"The Petrograd Soviet . . . has declared the Provisional Government overthrown, and has demanded that the Governmental power be turned over to it, under threat of bombarding the Winter Palace with the cannon of Peter-Paul Fortress, and of the cruiser *Avrora,* anchored in the Neva.

"The Government can surrender its authority only to the Constituent Assembly; for that reason it has decided not to submit, and to demand aid from the population and the Army. A telegram has been sent to the *Stavka;* and an answer received says that a strong detachment of troops is being sent. . . .

"Let the Army and the People reject the irresponsible attempts of the Bolsheviki to create a revolt in the rear. . . ."

About 9 A. M. Kerensky left for the Front. . . .

Toward evening two soldiers on bicycles presented themselves at the Staff Headquarters, as delegates of the garrison of Peter-Paul Fortress. Entering the meeting-room of the Staff, where Kishkin, Rutenburg, Paltchinski, General Bagratouni, Colonel Paradielov and Count Tolstoy were gathered, they demanded the immediate surrender of the Staff; threatening, in case of refusal, to bombard headquarters. . . . After two panicky conferences the Staff retreated to the Winter Palace, and the headquarters were occupied by Red Guards. . . .

Late in the afternoon several Bolshevik armoured cars cruised around the Palace Square, and Soviet soldiers tried unsuccessfully to parley with the *yunkers.* . . .

Firing on the Palace began about 7 o'clock in the evening. . . .

At 10 P. M. began an artillery bombardment from three sides, in which most of the shells were blanks, only three small shrapnels striking the façade of the Palace. . . .

2   Kerensky in Flight

Leaving Petrograd in the morning of November 7th, Kerensky arrived by automobile at Gatchina, where he demanded a special train. Toward evening he was in Ostrov, Province of Pskov. The next morning, extraordinary session of the local Soviet of Workers' and Soldiers' Deputies, with participation of Cossack delegates —there being 6,000 Cossacks at Ostrov.

Kerensky spoke to the assembly, appealing for aid against the Bolsheviki, and addressed himself almost exclusively to the Cossacks. The soldier delegates protested.

"Why did you come here?" shouted voices. Kerensky answered, "To ask the Cossacks' assistance in crushing the Bolshevik insurrection!" At this there were violent protestations, which increased when he continued, "I broke the Kornilov attempt, and I will break the Bolsheviki!" The noise became so great that he had to leave the platform. . . .

The soldier deputies and the Ussuri Cossacks decided to arrest Kerensky, but the Don Cossacks prevented them, and got him away by train. . . . A Military Revolutionary Committee, set up during the day, tried to inform the garrison of Pskov; but the telephone and telegraph lines were cut. . . .

Kerensky did not arrive at Pskov. Revolutionary soldiers had cut the railway line, to prevent troops being sent against the capital. On the night of November 8th he arrived by automobile at Luga, where he was well received by the Death Battalions stationed there.

Next day he took train for the South-West Front, and visited the Army Committee at headquarters. The Fifth Army, however, was wild with enthusiasm over the news of the Bolshevik success, and the Army Committee was unable to promise Kerensky any support.

From there he went to the *Stavka,* at Moghilev, where he ordered ten regiments from different parts of the Front to move against Petrograd. The soldiers almost unanimously refused; and those regiments which did start halted on the way. About five thousand Cossacks finally followed him. . . .

3   Looting of the Winter Palace

I do not mean to maintain that there was no looting in the Winter Palace. Both after and *before* the Winter Palace fell, there was considerable pilfering. The statement of the Socialist Revolutionary paper *Narod,* and of members of the City Duma, to the effect that precious objects to the value of 500,000,000 rubles had been stolen, was, however, a gross exaggeration.

The most important art treasures of the Palace—paintings, statues, tapestries, rare porcelains and armories,—had been transferred to Moscow during the month of September; and they were still in good order in the basement of the Imperial Palace there ten days after the capture of the Kremlin by Bolshevik troops. I can personally testify to this. . . .

Individuals, however, especially the general public, which was allowed to circulate freely through the Winter Palace for several days after its capture, made away with table silver, clocks, bedding, mirrors and some odd vases of valuable porcelain and semi-precious stone, to the value of about $50,000.

The Soviet Government immediately created a special commission, composed of artists and archaeologists, to recover the stolen objects. On November 1st* two proclamations were issued:

"CITIZENS OF PETROGRAD!

"We urgently ask all citizens to exert every effort to find whatever possible of the objects stolen from the Winter Palace in the night of November 7-8,* and to forward them to the Commandant of the Winter Palace.

"Receivers of stolen goods, antiquarians, and all who are proved to be hiding such objects will be held legally responsible and punished with all severity.

"*Commissars for the Protection of Museums*
and Artistic Collections,

"G. YATMANOV, B. MANDELBAUM."

*   *   *

"TO REGIMENTAL AND FLEET COMMITTEES

"In the night of November 7-8, in the Winter Palace, which is the inalienable property of the Russian people, valuable objects of art were stolen.

"We urgently appeal to all to exert every effort, so that the stolen objects are returned to the Winter Palace.

"*Commissars . . .*

"G. YATMANOV, B. MANDELBAUM."

About half the loot was recovered, some of it in the baggage of foreigners leaving Russia.

A conference of artists and archaeologists, held at the suggestion of Smolny, appointed a commission to make an inventory of the Winter Palace treasures, which was given complete charge of the Palace and of all artistic collections and State museums in

---

* Apparently Reed has updated the Old Style calendar by adding 13 days in the second of these statements, but failed to do so in the first. "November 7-8" originally read "October 25-26," i.e., the night of the capture of the Winter Palace as dated by the Old Style calendar. "November 1" should by the same procedure read "November 14." This proclamation is not reproduced in the most recent Soviet compilation of "The Decrees of the Soviet Power" nor the documents of the Military Revolutionary Committee, but a number of decrees on the looting of the Winter Palace are in those compilations. One of the most important of these is an order of the Military Revolutionary Committee dated November 10 (November 3, Old Style) to make a search and seizure of objects looted from the Winter Palace in "pawnshops, markets, shops of dealers in antiques, and private homes."—*Ed.*

Petrograd. On November 16th the Winter Palace was closed to the public while the inventory was being made. . . .

During the last week in November a decree was issued by the Council of People's Commissars, changing the name of the Winter Palace to "People's Museum," entrusting it to the complete charge of the artistic-archæological commission, and declaring that henceforth all Governmental activities within its walls were prohibited. . . .*

4   Rape of the Women's Battalion

Immediately following the taking of the Winter Palace all sorts of sensational stories were published in the anti-Bolshevik press, and told in the City Duma, about the fate of the Women's Battalion defending the Palace. It was said that some of the girl-soldiers had been thrown from the windows into the street, most of the rest had been violated, and many had committed suicide as a result of the horrors they had gone through.

The City Duma appointed a commission to investigate the matter. On November 16th the commission returned from Levashovo, headquarters of the Women's Battalion. Madame Tyrkova** reported that the girls had been at first taken to the barracks of the Pavlovsky Regiment, and that there some of them had been badly treated; but that at present most of them were at Levashovo, and the rest scattered about the city in private houses. Dr. Mandelbaum, another of the commission, testified drily that *none* of the women had been thrown out of the windows of the Winter Palace, that *none* were wounded, that three had been violated, and that one had committed suicide, leaving a note which said that she had been "disappointed in her ideals."

On November 21st the Military Revolutionary Committee officially dissolved the Women's Battalion, at the request of the girls themselves, who returned to civilian clothes.

In Louise Bryant's book, "Six Red Months in Russia," there is an interesting description of the girl-soldiers during this time.

---

* This decree is not in the published collection of decrees. The Winter Palace is now called as before "Winter Palace" and alternatively "State Hermitage Museum." The looting of the Palace was more extensive than Reed suggests, but that the physical damage was light is confirmed by other sources.—*Ed*.

** Ariadna Tyrkova-Williams, Member of the Central Executive Committee of the Cadet Party. There is no mention of this matter in her memoirs but there is no reason to doubt the accuracy of Reed's report.—*Ed*.

CHAPTER V

PLUNGING AHEAD

Thursday, November 8th. Day broke on a city in the wildest excitement and confusion, a whole nation heaving up in long hissing swells of storm. Superficially all was quiet; hundreds of thousands of people retired at a prudent hour, got up early, and went to work. In Petrograd the street-cars were running, the stores and restaurants open, theatres going, an exhibition of paintings advertised. . . . All the complex routine of common life—humdrum even in war-time—proceeded as usual. Nothing is so astounding as the vitality of the social organism—how it persists, feeding itself, clothing itself, amusing itself, in the face of the worst calamities. . . .

The air was full of rumours about Kerensky, who was said to have raised the Front, and to be leading a great army against the capital. *Volia Naroda* published a *prikaz* launched by him at Pskov:

The disorders caused by the insane attempt of the Bolsheviki place the country on the verge of a precipice, and demand the effort of our entire will, our courage and the devotion of every one of us, to win through the terrible trial which the fatherland is undergoing. . . .

Until the declaration of the composition of the new Government—if one is formed—every one ought to remain at his

post and fulfil his duty toward bleeding Russia. It must be
remembered that the least interference with existing Army
organisations can bring on irreparable misfortunes, by opening the Front to the enemy. Therefore it is indispensable to
preserve at any price the morale of the troops, by assuring
complete order and the preservation of the Army from new
shocks, and by maintaining absolute confidence between
officers and their subordinates. I order all the chiefs and
Commissars, in the name of the safety of the country, to
stay at their posts, as I myself retain the post of Supreme
Commander, until the Provisional Government of the Republic shall declare its will. . . .

In answer, this placard on all the walls:

From the All-Russian Congress of Soviets

"The ex-Ministers Konovalov, Kishkin, Tereshchenko, Mali-
antovitch, Nikitin and others have been arrested by the
Military Revolutionary Committee. Kerensky has fled. All
Army organisations are ordered to take every measure for
the immediate arrest of Kerensky and his conveyance to
Petrograd.

"All assistance given to Kerensky will be punished as a
serious crime against the state."

With brakes released the Military Revolutionary Committee whirled, throwing off orders, appeals, decrees, like
sparks.[1] . . . Kornilov was ordered brought to Petrograd. Members of the Peasant Land Committees imprisoned by the Provisional Government were declared free.
Capital punishment in the army was abolished. Government employees were ordered to continue their work, and
threatened with severe penalties if they refused. All pillage,
disorder and speculation were forbidden under pain of
death. Temporary Commissars were appointed to the var-

ious Ministries: Foreign Affairs, Vuritsky* and Trotsky; Interior and Justice, Rykov; Labor, Shliapnikov; Finance, Menzhinsky; Public Welfare, Madame Kollontai; Commerce, Ways and Communications, Riazanov; Navy, the sailor Korbir; Posts and Telegraphs, Spiro; Theatres, Muraviov; State Printing Office, Gherbychev; for the City of Petrograd, Lieutenant Nesterov; for the Northern Front, Pozern. . . .

To the Army, appeal to set up Military Revolutionary Committees. To the railway workers, to maintain order, especially not to delay the transport of food to the cities and the front. . . . In return, they were promised representation in the Ministry of Ways and Communications.

Cossack brothers! (said one proclamation). You are being led against Petrograd. They want to force you into battle with the revolutionary workers and soldiers of the capital. Do not believe a word that is said by our common enemies, the land-owners and the capitalists.

At our Congress are represented all the conscious organisations of workers, soldiers and peasants of Russia. The Congress wishes also to welcome into its midst the worker-Cossacks. The Generals of the Black Band, henchmen of the land-owners, of Nicolai the Cruel, are our enemies.

They tell you that the Soviets wish to confiscate the lands of the Cossacks. This is a lie. It is only from the great Cossack landlords that the Revolution will confiscate the land to give it to the people.

Organise Soviets of Cossacks' Deputies! Join with the Soviets of Workers' and Soldiers' Deputies!

Show the Black Band that you are not traitors to the People, and that you do not wish to be cursed by the whole of revolutionary Russia! . . .

Cossack brothers, execute no orders of the enemies of the people. Send your delegates to Petrograd to talk it over with

* No doubt should be Uritsky.—*Ed*.

us. . . . The Cossacks of the Petrograd garrison, to their honour, have not justified the hope of the People's enemies. . . .

Cossack brothers! The All-Russian Congress of Soviets extends to you a fraternal hand. Long live the brotherhood of the Cossacks with the soldiers, workers and peasants of all Russia!

On the other side, what a storm of proclamations posted up, hand-bills scattered everywhere, newspapers—screaming and cursing and prophesying evil. Now raged the battle of the printing press—all other weapons being in the hands of the Soviets.

First, the appeal of the Committee for Salvation of Country and Revolution, flung broadcast over Russia and Europe.[2]

To the Citizens of the Russian Republic!

Contrary to the will of the revolutionary masses, on November 7th the Bolsheviki of Petrograd criminally arrested part of the Provisional Government, dispersed the Council of the Republic, and proclaimed an illegal power. Such violence committed against the Government of revolutionary Russia at the moment of its greatest external danger, is an indescribable crime against the fatherland.

The insurrection of the Bolsheviki deals a mortal blow to the cause of national defence, and postpones immeasurably the moment of peace so greatly desired.

Civil war, begun by the Bolsheviki, threatens to deliver the country to the horrors of anarchy and counter-revolution, and cause the failure of the Constituent Assembly, which must affirm the republican régime and transmit to the People forever their right to the land.

Preserving the continuity of the only legal Governmental power, the Committee for Salvation of Country and Revolution, established on the night of November 7th, takes the initiative in forming a new Provisional Government; which, basing itself on the forces of democracy, will conduct the country to the Constituent Assembly and save it from anarchy and counter-revolution. The Committee for Salvation summons you, citizens, to refuse to recognise the power of violence. Do not obey its orders!

Rise for the defence of the country and Revolution!

Support the Committee for Salvation!

Signed by the Council of the Russian Republic, the Municipal Duma of Petrograd, the *Tsay-ee-kah* (*First Congress*), the Executive Committee of the Peasants' Soviets, and from the Congress itself the Front group, the factions of Socialist Revolutionaries, Mensheviki, Populist Socialists, Unified Social Democrats, and the group "Yedinstvo."

Then posters from the Socialist Revolutionary party, the Mensheviki *oborontsi,* Peasants' Soviets again; from the Central Army Committee, the *Tsentroflot.* . . .

. . . Famine will crush Petrograd! (they cried). The German armies will trample on our liberty. Black Hundred *pogroms* will spread over Russia, if we all—conscious workers, soldiers, citizens—do not unite. . . .

Do not trust the promises of the Bolsheviki! The promise of immediate peace—is a lie! The promise of bread—a hoax! The promise of land—a fairy tale! . . .

They were all in this manner.

Comrades! You have been basely and cruelly deceived! The seizure of power has been accomplished by the Bolsheviki alone. . . . They concealed their plot from the other Socialist parties composing the Soviet. . . .

You have been promised land and freedom, but the

counter-revolution will profit by the anarchy called forth by the Bolsheviki, and will deprive you of land and freedom. . . .

The newspapers were as violent.

Our duty (said the *Dielo Naroda*) is to unmask these traitors to the working-class. Our duty is to mobilise all our forces and mount guard over the cause of the Revolution! . . .

Izvestia, for the last time speaking in the name of the old *Tsay-ee-kah*, threatened awful retribution.

As for the Congress of Soviets, we affirm that there has been no Congress of Soviets! We affirm that it was merely a private conference of the Bolshevik faction! And in that case, they have no right to cancel the powers of the *Tsay-ee-kah*. . . .

Novaya Zhizn, while pleading for a new Government that should unite all the Socialist parties, criticised severely the action of the Socialist Revolutionaries and the Mensheviki in quitting the Congress, and pointed out that the Bolshevik insurrection meant one thing very clearly: that all illusions about coalition with the bourgeoisie were henceforth demonstrated vain. . . .

Rabochi Put blossomed out as *Pravda*, Lenin's newspaper which had been suppressed in July. It crowed, bristling:

Workers, soldiers, peasants! In March you struck down the tyranny of the clique of nobles. Yesterday you struck down the tyranny of the bourgeois gang. . . .

The first task now is to guard the approaches to Petrograd.

The second is definitely to disarm the counter-revolution-ary elements of Petrograd.

The third is definitely to organise the revolutionary power and assure the realisation of the popular programme. . . .

What few Cadet organs appeared, and the bourgeoisie generally, adopted a detached, ironical attitude toward the whole business, a sort of contemptuous "I-told-you-so" to the other parties. Influential Cadets were to be seen hovering around the Municipal Duma, and on the out-skirts of the Committee for Salvation. Other than that, the bourgoisie lay low, biding its hour—which could not be far off. That the Bolsheviki would remain in power longer than three days never occurred to anybody—except perhaps to Lenin, Trotsky, the Petrograd workers and the simpler soldiers. . . .

In the high, amphitheatrical Nicolai Hall that after-noon I saw the Duma sitting in *permanence,* tempestuous, grouping around it all the forces of opposition. The old Mayor, Schreider, majestic with his white hair and beard, was describing his visit to Smolny the night before, to protest in the name of the Municipal Self-Government. "The Duma, being the only existing legal Government in the city, elected by equal, direct and secret suffrage, would not recognise the new power," he had told Trotsky. And Trotsky had answered, "There is a constitutional remedy for that. The Duma can be dissolved and re-elected. . . ." At this report there was a furious outcry.

"If one recognises a Government by bayonet," con-tinued the old man, addressing the Duma, "well, we have one; but I consider legitimate only a Government recog-nised by the people, by the majority, and not one created by the usurpation of a minority!" Wild applause on all benches except those of the Bolsheviki. Amid renewed tumult the Mayor announced that the Bolsheviki already were violating Municipal autonomy by appointing Commissars in many departments.

The Bolshevik speaker shouted, trying to make himself heard, that the decision of the Congress of Soviets meant that all Russia backed up the action of the Bolsheviki.

"You!" he cried. "You are not the real representative of the people of Petrograd!" Shrieks of "Insult! Insult!" The old Mayor, with dignity, reminded him that the Duma was elected by the freest possible popular vote. "Yes," he answered, "but that was a long time ago—like the *Tsay-ee-kah*—like the Army Committee."

"There has been no new Congress of Soviets!" they yelled at him.

"The Bolshevik faction refuses to remain any longer in this nest of counter-revolution—" Uproar. "—and we demand a re-election of the Duma. . . ." Whereupon the Bolsheviki left the chamber, followed by cries of "German agents! Down with the traitors!"

Shingariov, Cadet, then demanded that all Municipal functionaries who had consented to be Commissars of the Military Revolutionary Committee be discharged from their position and indicted. Schreider was on his feet, putting a motion to the effect that the Duma protested against the menace of the Bolsheviki to dissolve it, and as the legal representative of the population, it would refuse to leave its post.

Outside, the Alexander Hall was crowded for the meeting of the Committee for Salvation, and Skobelev was again speaking. "Never yet," he said, "was the fate of the Revolution so acute, never yet did the question of the existence of the Russian state excite so much anxiety, never yet did history put so harshly and categorically the question—is Russia to be or not to be! The great hour for

the salvation of the Revolution has arrived, and in consciousness thereof we observe the close union of the live
forces of the revolutionary democracy, by whose organised will a centre for the salvation of the country and
the Revolution has already been created. . . ." And much
of the same sort. "We shall die sooner than surrender our
post!"

Amid violent applause it was announced that the
Union of Railway Workers had joined the Committee for
Salvation. A few moments later the Post and Telegraph
Employees came in; then some Mensheviki Internationalists entered the hall, to cheers. The Railway men said they
did not recognise the Bolsheviki and had taken the entire
railroad apparatus into their own hands, refusing to en-
trust it to any usurpatory power. The Telegraphers' delegate declared that the operators had flatly refused to work
their instruments as long as the Bolshevik Commissar was
in the office. The Postmen would not deliver or accept
mail at Smolny. . . . All the Smolny telephones were cut
off. With great glee it was reported how Uritsky had gone
to the Ministry of Foreign Affairs to demand the secret
treaties, and how Neratov had put him out. The Government employees were all stopping work. . . .

It was war—war deliberately planned, Russian fashion;
war by strike and sabotage. As we sat there the chairman
read a list of names and assignments; so-and-so was to
make the round of the Ministries; another was to visit the
banks; some ten or twelve were to work the barracks and
persuade the soldiers to remain neutral—"Russian
soldiers, do not shed the blood of your brothers!"; a committee was to go and confer with Kerensky; still others
were despatched to provincial cities, to form branches of
the Committee for Salvation, and link together the anti-
Bolshevik elements.

The crowd was in high spirits. "These Bolsheviki *will* try to dictate to the *intelligentsia?* We'll show them!" . . . Nothing could be more striking than the contrast between this assemblage and the Congress of Soviets. There, great masses of shabby soldiers, grimy workmen, peasants— poor men, bent and scarred in the brute struggle for existence; here the Menshevik and Social Revolutionary leaders—Avksentievs, Dans, Liebers,—the former Socialist Ministers—Skobelevs, Chernovs,—rubbed shoulders with Cadets like oily Shatsky, sleek Vinaver; with journalists, students, intellectuals of almost all camps. This Duma crowd was well-fed, well-dressed; I did not see more than three proletarians among them all. . . .

News came. Kornilov's faithful *Tekhintsi** had slaughtered his guards at Bykhov, and he had escaped. Kaledin was marching north. . . . The Soviet of Moscow had set up a Military Revolutionary Committee, and was negotiating with the commandant of the city for possession of the arsenal, so that the workers might be armed.

With these facts was mixed an astounding jumble of rumours, distortions, and plain lies. For instance, an intelligent young Cadet, formerly private secretary to Miliukov and then to Tereshchenko, drew us aside and told us all about the taking of the Winter Palace.

"The Bolsheviki were led by German and Austrian officers," he affirmed.

"Is that so?" we replied, politely. "How do you know?"

"A friend of mine was there and saw them."

"How could he tell they were German officers?"

"Oh, because they wore German uniforms!"

There were hundreds of such absurd tales, and they were not only solemnly published by the anti-Bolshevik press, but believed by the most unlikely persons—Social-

* See Notes and Explanations.

ist Revolutionaries and Mensheviki who had always been distinguished by their sober devotion to facts. . . .

But more serious were the stories of Bolshevik violence and terrorism. For example, it was said and printed that the Red Guards had not only thoroughly looted the Winter Palace, but that they had massacred the *yunkers* after disarming them, had killed some of the Ministers in cold blood; and as for the woman soldiers, most of them had been violated, and many had committed suicide because of the tortures they had gone through. . . . All these stories were swallowed whole by the crowd in the Duma. And worse still, the mothers and fathers of the students and of the women read these frightful details, *often accompanied by lists of names,* and toward nightfall the Duma began to be besieged by frantic citizens. . . .

A typical case is that of Prince Tumanov, whose body, it was announced in many newspapers, had been found floating in the Moika Canal. A few hours later this was denied by the Prince's family, who added that the Prince was under arrest, so the press identified the dead man as General Demissov. The General having also come to life, we investigated, and could find no trace of any body having been found whatever. . . .

As we left the Duma building two boy scouts were distributing hand-bills[2] to the enormous crowd which blocked the Nevsky in front of the door—a crowd composed almost entirely of business men, shop-keepers, *chinovniki,* clerks. One read:

From the Municipal Duma

The Municipal Duma in its meeting of October 26th, in view of the events of the day decrees: To announce the inviolability of private dwellings. Through the House Committees it calls upon the population of the town of Petrograd to meet with decisive repulse all attempts to enter by force private apartments, not stopping at the use of arms, in the interests of the self-defence of citizens.

Up on the corner of the Liteiny, five or six Red Guards and a couple of sailors had surrounded a news-dealer and were demanding that he hand over his copies of the Menshevik *Rabochaya Gazeta* (Workers' Gazette). Angrily he shouted at them, shaking his first, as one of the sailors tore the papers from his stand. An ugly crowd had gathered around, abusing the patrol. One little workman kept explaining doggedly to the people and the newsdealer, over and over again, "It has Kerensky's proclamation in it. It says we killed Russian people. It will make bloodshed. . . ."

Smolny was tenser than ever, if that were possible. The same running men in the dark corridors, squads of workers with rifles, leaders with bulging portfolios arguing, explaining, giving orders as they hurried anxiously along, surrounded by friends and lieutenants. Men literally out of themselves, living prodigies of sleeplessness and work —men unshaven, filthy, with burning eyes, who drove upon their fixed purpose full speed on engines of exaltation. So much they had to do, so much! Take over the Government, organise the City, keep the garrison loyal, fight the Duma and the Committee for Salvation, keep out the Germans, prepare to do battle with Kerensky, inform the provinces what had happened, propagandise from Archangel to Vladivostok. . . . Government and Municipal employees refusing to obey their Commissars, post and telegraph refusing them communication, railroads stonily ignoring their appeals for trains, Kerensky coming, the garrison not altogether to be trusted, the

Cossacks waiting to come out. . . . Against them not only the organised bourgeoisie, but all the other Socialist parties except the Left Socialist Revolutionaries, a few Mensheviki Internationalists and the Social Democrat Internationalists, and even they undecided whether to stand by or not. With them, it is true, the workers and the soldier-masses—the peasants an unknown quantity—but after all the Bolsheviki were a political faction not rich in trained and educated men. . . .

Riazanov was coming up the front steps, explaining in a sort of humorous panic that he, Commissar of Commerce, knew nothing whatever of business. In the up-stairs café sat a man all by himself in the corner, in a goat-skin cape and clothes which had been—I was going to say "slept in," but of course he hadn't slept—and a three days' growth of beard. He was anxiously figuring on a dirty envelope, and biting his pencil meanwhile. This was Menzhinsky, Commissar of Finance, whose qualifications were that he had once been clerk in a French bank. . . . And these four half-running down the hall from the office of the Military Revolutionary Committee, and scribbling on bits of paper as they run—these were Commissars despatched to the four corners of Russia to carry the news, argue, or fight—with whatever arguments or weapons came to hand. . . .

The Congress was to meet at one o'clock, and long since the great meeting-hall had filled, but by seven there was yet no sign of the presidium. . . . The Bolshevik and Left Social Revolutionary factions were in session in their own rooms. All the livelong afternoon Lenin and Trotsky had fought against compromise. A considerable part of the Bolsheviki were in favour of giving way so far as to create a joint all-Socialist government. "We can't hold on!" they cried. "Too much is against us. We haven't got the men. We will be isolated, and the whole thing will fall." So Kamenev, Riazanov and others.

But Lenin, with Trotsky beside him, stood firm as a rock. "Let the compromisers accept our programme and they can come in! We won't give way an inch. If there are comrades here who haven't the courage and the will to dare what we dare, let them leave with the rest of the cowards and conciliators! Backed by the workers and soldiers we shall go on."

At five minutes past seven came word from the left Socialist Revolutionaries to say that they would remain in the Military Revolutionary Committee.

"See!" said Lenin. "They are following!"

A little later, as we sat at the press table in the big hall, an Anarchist who was writing for the bourgeois papers proposed to me that we go and find out what had become of the presidium. There was nobody in the *Tsay-ee-kah* office, nor in the bureau of the Petrograd Soviet. From room to room we wandered, through vast Smolny. Nobody seemed to have the slightest idea where to find the governing body of the Congress. As we went my companion described his ancient revolutionary activities, his long and pleasant exile in France. . . . As for the Bolsheviki, he confided to me that they were common, rude, ignorant persons, without æsthetic sensibilities. He was a real specimen of the Russian *intelligentsia*. . . . So he came at last to Room 17, office of the Military Revolutionary Committee, and stood there in the midst of all the furious coming and going. The door opened, and out shot a squat, flat-faced man in a uniform without insignia, who seemed to be smiling—which smile, after a minute, one saw to be the fixed grin of extreme fatigue. It was Krylenko.

My friend, who was a dapper, civilized-looking young man, gave a cry of pleasure and stepped forward.

"Nicolai Vasilievitch!" he said, holding out his hand. "Don't you remember me, comrade? We were in prison together."

Krylenko made an effort and concentrated his mind and sight. "Why yes," he answered finally, looking the other up and down with an expression of great friendliness. "You are S——. *Zdra'stvuitye!*" They kissed. "What are you doing in all this?" He waved his arm around.

"Oh, I'm just looking on. . . . You seem very successful."

"Yes," replied Krylenko, with a sort of doggedness, "The proletarian Revolution is a great success." He laughed. "Perhaps—perhaps, however, we'll meet in prison again!"

When we got out into the corridor again my friend went on with his explanations. "You see, I'm a follower of Kropotkin. To us the Revolution is a great failure; it has not aroused the patriotism of the masses. Of course that only proves that the people are not ready for Revolution. . . ."

It was just 8.40 when a thundering wave of cheers announced the entrance of the presidium, with Lenin—great Lenin—among them. A short, stocky figure, with a big head set down in his shoulders, bald and bulging. Little eyes, a snubbish nose, wide, generous mouth, and heavy chin; clean-shaven now, but already beginning to bristle with the well-known beard of his past and future. Dressed in shabby clothes, his trousers much too long for him. Unimpressive, to be the idol of a mob, loved and revered as perhaps few leaders in history have been. A strange popular leader—a leader purely by virtue of intellect; colourless, humourless, uncompromising and detached, without picturesque idiosyncrasies—but with the power of explaining profound ideas in simple terms, of analysing a concrete situation. And combined with shrewdness, the greatest intellectual audacity.

Kamenev was reading the report of the actions of the Military Revolutionary Committee; abolition of capital punishment in the Army, restoration of the free right of propaganda, release of officers and soldiers arrested for political crimes, orders to arrest Kerensky and confiscation of food supplies in private store-houses. . . . Tremendous applause.

Again the representative of the *Bund*. The uncompromising attitude of the Bolsheviki would mean the crushing of the Revolution; therefore, the *Bund* delegates must refuse any longer to sit in the Congress. Cries from the audience, "We thought you walked out last night! How many more times are you going to walk out?"

Then the representative of the Mensheviki Internationalists. Shouts, "What! You here still?" The speaker explained that only part of the Mensheviki Internationalists left the Congress; the rest were going to stay——

"We consider it dangerous and perhaps even mortal for the Revolution to transfer the power to the Soviets"—Interruptions—"but we feel it our duty to remain in the Congress and vote against the transfer here!"

Other speakers followed, apparently without any order. A delegate of the coal-miners of the Don Basin called upon the Congress to take measures against Kaledin, who might cut off coal and food from the capital. Several soldiers just arrived from the Front brought the enthusiastic greetings of their regiments. . . . Now Lenin, gripping the edge of the reading stand, letting his little

winking eyes travel over the crowd as he stood there waiting, apparently oblivious to the long-rolling ovation, which
lasted several minutes. When it finished, he said simply,
"We shall now proceed to construct the Socialist order!"
Again that overwhelming human roar.

"The first thing is the adoption of practical measures to
realise peace. . . . We shall offer peace to the peoples of
all the belligerent countries upon the basis of the Soviet
terms—no annexations, no indemnities, and the right of
self-determination of peoples. At the same time, according
to our promise, we shall publish and repudiate the secret
treaties. . . . The question of War and Peace is so clear
that I think that I may, without preamble, read the project
of a Proclamation to the Peoples of All the Belligerent
Countries. . . ."

His great mouth, seeming to smile, opened wide as he
spoke; his voice was hoarse—not unpleasantly so, but as
if it had hardened that way after years and years of
speaking—and went on monotonously, with the effect of
being able to go on forever. . . . For emphasis he bent
forward slightly. No gestures. And before him, a thousand simple faces looking up in intent adoration.

Proclamation to the Peoples and Governments of All the Belligerent Nations.*

The Workers' and Peasants' Government, created by the
revolution of November 6th and 7th and based on the
Soviets of Workers', Soldiers' and Peasants' Deputies, proposes to all the belligerent peoples and to their Governments
to begin immediately negotiations for a just and democratic
peace.

The Government means by a just and democratic peace,

* This proclamation was drafted by Lenin, as was the decree on peace
which followed it.—*Ed.*

which is desired by the immense majority of the workers and the labouring classes, exhausted and depleted by the war—that peace which the Russian workers and peasants, after having struck down the Tsarist monarchy, have not ceased to demand categorically—immediate peace without annexations (that is to say, without conquest of foreign territory, without forcible annexation of other nationalities), and without indemnities.

The Government of Russia proposes to all the belligerent peoples immediately to conclude such a peace, by showing themselves willing to enter upon the decisive steps of negotiations aiming at such a peace, at once, without the slightest delay, before the definitive ratification of all the conditions of such a peace by the authorised assemblies of the people of all countries and of all nationalities.

By annexation or conquest of foreign territory, the Government means—conformably to the conception of democratic rights in general, and the rights of the working-class in particular—all union to a great and strong State of a small or weak nationality, without the voluntary, clear and precise expression of its consent and desire; whatever be the moment when such an annexation by force was accomplished, whatever be the degree of civilisation of the nation annexed by force or maintained outside the frontiers of another State, no matter if that nation be in Europe or in the far countries across the sea.

If any nation is retained by force within the limits of another State; if, in spite of the desire expressed by it, (it matters little if that desire be expressed by the press, by popular meetings, decisions of political parties, or by disorders and riots against national oppression), that nation is not given the right of deciding by free vote—without the slightest constraint, after the complete departure of the armed forces of the nation which has annexed it or wishes to annex it or is stronger in general—the form of its national and political organisation, such a union constitutes an annexation—that is to say, conquest and an act of violence.

To continue this war in order to permit the strong and rich nations to divide among themselves the weak and conquered nationalities is considered by the Government the greatest possible crime against humanity; and the Government solemnly proclaims its decision to sign a treaty of peace which will put an end to this war upon the above conditions, equally fair for all nationalities without exception.

The Government abolishes secret diplomacy, expressing before the whole country its firm decision to conduct all the negotiations in the light of day before the people, and will proceed immediately to the full publication of all secret treaties confirmed or concluded by the Government of landowners and capitalists, from March until November 7th, 1917. All the clauses of the secret treaties which, as occur in a majority of cases, have for their object to procure advantages and privileges for Russian capitalists, to maintain or augment the annexations of the Russian imperialists, are denounced by the Government immediately and without discussion.

In proposing to all Governments and all peoples to engage in public negotiations for peace, the Government declares itself ready to carry on these negotiations by telegraph, by post, or by pourparlers between the representatives of the different countries, or at a conference of these representatives. To facilitate these pourparlers, the Government appoints its authorised representatives in the neutral countries.

The Government proposes to all the governments and to the peoples of all the belligerent countries to conclude an immediate armistice, at the same time suggesting that the armistice ought to last three months, during which time it is perfectly possible, not only to hold the necessary pourparlers between the representatives of all the nations and nationalities without exception drawn into the war or forced to take part in it, but also to convoke authorised assemblies of representatives of the people of all countries, for the purpose of the definite acceptance of the conditions of peace.

In addressing this offer of peace to the Governments and to the peoples of all the belligerent countries, the Provisional

Workers' and Peasants' Government of Russia addresses equally and in particular the conscious workers of the three nations most devoted to humanity and the three most important nations among those taking part in the present war— England, France, and Germany. The workers of these countries have rendered the greatest services to the cause of progress and of Socialism. The splendid examples of the Chartist movement in England, the series of revolutions, of world-wide historical significance, accomplished by the French proletariat—and finally, in Germany, the historic struggle against the Laws of Exception, an example for the workers of the whole world of prolonged and stubborn action, and the creation of the formidable organisations of German proletarians—all these models of proletarian heroism, these monuments of history, are for us a sure guarantee that the workers of these countries will understand the duty imposed upon them to liberate humanity from the horrors and consequences of war; and that these workers, by decisive, energetic and continued action, will help us to bring to a successful conclusion the cause of peace—and at the same time, the cause of the liberation of the exploited working masses from all slavery and all exploitation.

When the grave thunder of applause had died away, Lenin spoke again:

"We propose to the Congress to ratify this declaration. We address ourselves to the Governments as well as to the peoples, for a declaration which would be addressed only to the peoples of the belligerent countries might delay the conclusion of peace. The conditions of peace, drawn up during the armistice, will be ratified by the Constituent Assembly. In fixing the duration of the armistice at three months, we desire to give to the peoples as long a rest as possible after this bloody extermination, and ample time for them to elect their representatives. This proposal of peace will meet with resistance on the

part of the imperialist governments—we don't fool ourselves on that score. But we hope that revolution will
soon break out in all the belligerent countries; that is why
we address ourselves especially to the workers of France,
England and Germany. . . .

"The revolution of November 6th and 7th," he ended,
"has opened the era of the Social Revolution. . . . The
labour movement, in the name of peace and Socialism,
shall win, and fulfil its destiny. . . ."

There was something quiet and powerful in all this,
which stirred the souls of men. It was understandable
why people believed when Lenin spoke. . . .

By crowd vote it was quickly decided that only representatives of political factions should be allowed to speak
on the motion and that speakers should be limited to
fifteen minutes.

First Karelin for the Left Socialist Revolutionaries.
"Our faction had no opportunity to propose amendments
to the text of the proclamation; it is a private document
of the Bolsheviki. But we will vote for it because we agree
with its spirit. . . ."

For the Social Democrats Internationalists, Kramarov,
long, stoop-shouldered and near-sighted—destined to
achieve some notoriety as the Clown of the Opposition.
Only a Government composed of all the Socialist parties,
he said, could possess the authority to take such important
action. If a Socialist coalition were formed, his faction
would support the entire programme; if not, only part of
it. As for the proclamation, the Internationalists were in
thorough accord with its main points. . . .

Then one after another, amid rising enthusiasm;
Ukrainian Social Democracy, support; Lithuanian Social
Democracy, support; Populist Socialists, support; Polish
Social Democracy, support; Polish Socialists, support—

but would prefer a Socialist coalition; Lettish Social Democracy, support.* . . . Something was kindled in these men. One spoke of the "coming World-Revolution, of which we are the advance-guard"; another of "the new age of brotherhood, when all the peoples will become one great family. . . ." An individual member claimed the floor. "There is contradiction here," he said. "First you offer peace without annexations and indemnities, and then you say you will consider all peace offers. To consider means to accept. . . ."

Lenin was on his feet. "We want a just peace, but we are not afraid of a revolutionary war. . . . Probably the imperialist Governments will not answer our appeal—but we shall not issue an ultimatum to which it will be easy to say no. . . . If the German proletariat realises that we are ready to consider all offers of peace, that will perhaps be the last drop which overflows the bowl—revolution will break out in Germany. . . .

"We consent to examine all conditions of peace, but that doesn't mean that we shall accept them. . . . For some of our terms we shall fight to the end—but possibly for others will find it impossible to continue the war. . . . Above all, we want to finish the war. . . ."

It was exactly 10:35 when Kamenev asked all in favour of the proclamation to hold up their cards. One delegate dared to raise his hand against, but the sudden sharp outburst around him brought it swiftly down. . . . Unanimous.

Suddenly, by common impulse, we found ourselves on our feet, mumbling together into the smooth lifting unison of the *Internationale*. A grizzled old soldier was sobbing like a child. Alexandra Kollontai rapidly winked the tears

* These were not official spokesmen of their parties, but pro-Bolshevik members. In the case of the Letts, however, the leading committee was pro-Bolshevik.—*Ed.*

back. The immense sound rolled through the hall, burst windows and doors and seared into the quiet sky. "The war is ended! The war is ended!" said a young workman near me, his face shining. And when it was over, as we stood there in a kind of awkward hush, some one in the back of the room shouted, "Comrades! Let us remember those who have died for liberty!" So we began to sing the Funeral March, that slow, melancholy and yet triumphant chant, so Russian and so moving. The *Internationale* is an alien air, after all. The Funeral March seemed the very soul of those dark masses whose delegates sat in this hall, building from their obscure visions a new Russia—and perhaps more.

You fell in the fatal fight
For the liberty of the people, for the honour of the people . . .
You gave up your lives and everything dear to you,
You suffered in horrible prisons,
You went to exile in chains. . . .

Without a word you carried your chains because you could not ignore your suffering brothers,
Because you believed that justice is stronger than the sword. . . .
The time will come when your surrendered life will count.
That time is near; when tyranny falls the people will rise, great and free!

Farewell, brothers, you chose a noble path,
You are followed by the new and fresh army ready to die and to suffer. . . .

Farewell, brothers, you chose a noble path,
At your grave we swear to fight, to work for freedom and the people's happiness. . . .

For this did they lie there, the martyrs of March, in
their cold Brotherhood Grave on Mars Field; for this
thousands and tens of thousands had died in the prisons,
in exile, in Siberian mines. It had not come as they expected it would come, nor as the *intelligentsia* desired it;
but it had come—rough, strong, impatient of formulas,
contemptuous of sentimentalism; *real*. . . .

Lenin was reading the Decree on Land:*

(1.) All private ownership of land is abolished immediately
without compensation.

(2.) All land-owners' estates, and all lands belonging to the
Crown, to monasteries, church lands with all their live stock
and inventoried property, buildings and all appurtenances,
are transferred to the disposition of the township Land
Committees and the district Soviets of Peasants' Deputies
until the Constituent Assembly meets.

(3.) Any damage whatever done to the confiscated property which from now on belongs to the whole People, is
regarded as a serious crime, punishable by the revolutionary
tribunals. The district Soviets of Peasants' Deputies shall
take all necessary measures for the observance of the strictest
order during the taking over of the land-owners' estates, for
the determination of the dimensions of the plots of land and
which of them are subject to confiscation, for the drawing up
of an inventory of the entire confiscated property, and for
the strictest revolutionary protection of all the farming
property on the land, with all buildings, implements, cattle,
supplies of products, etc., passing into the hands of the
People.

* Drafted by Lenin. This was the decree which he acknowledged solved the
land problem in a way not desired by the Bolsheviks and contrary to their
program, but lifted verbatim from the program prepared by the Socialist
Revolutionary Party for adoption by the Peasant Unions and Peasant Soviets.
—Ed.

(4.) For guidance during the realisation of the great land reforms until their final resolution by the Constituent Assembly, shall serve the following peasant *nakaz*[3] (instructions), drawn up on the basis of 242 local peasant *nakazi* by the editorial board of the *"Izvestia* of the All-Russian Soviet of Peasants' Deputies," and published in No. 88 of said *"Izvestia"* (Petrograd, No. 88, August 19th, 1917).

The lands of peasants and of Cossacks serving in the Army shall not be confiscated.

"This is not," explained Lenin, "the project of former Minister Chernov, who spoke of 'erecting a frame-work' and tried to realise reforms from above. From below, on the spot, will be decided the questions of division of the land. The amount of land received by each peasant will vary according to the locality. . . .

"Under the Provisional Government, the *pomieshchiki* flatly refused to obey the orders of the Land Committees —those Land Committees projected by Lvov, brought into existence by Shingariov, and administered by Kerensky!" [4]

Before the debates could begin a man forced his way violently through the crowd in the aisle and climbed upon the platform. It was Pianikh, member of the Executive Committee of the Peasants' Soviets, and he was mad clean through.

"The Executive Committee of the All-Russian Soviets of Peasants' Deputies protests against the arrest of our comrades, the Ministers Salazkin and Mazlov!" * he flung

* Sergei Sergeievich Salazkin, active in the zemstvo movement, Minister of Education from September to November, 1917; Semyon Leontovich Maslov, right SR, factional opponent of Chernov, who succeeded him as Minister of Agriculture and replaced his draft law on the redistribution of the land by a somewhat more conservative and limited one, applying only to lands rented by the peasants and not to the entire land of the country. Both drafts provided for instructions to the local land committees and the granting of corresponding powers to those committees.—*Ed.*

harshly in the faces of the crowd, "We demand their
instant release! They are now in Peter-Paul fortress. We
must have immediate action! There is not a moment to
lose!"

Another followed him, a soldier with disordered beard
and flaming eyes. "You sit here and talk about giving the
land to the peasants, and you commit an act of tyrants and
usurpers against the peasants' chosen representatives! I
tell you—" he raised his fist, "if one hair of their heads is
harmed, you'll have a revolt on your hands!" The crowd
stirred confusedly.

Then up rose Trotsky, calm and venomous, conscious
of power, greeted with a roar. "Yesterday the Military
Revolutionary Committee decided to release the Socialist
Revolutionary and Menshevik Ministers, Mazlov, Salazkin, Gvozdov and Maliantovich—on principle. That they
are still in Peter-Paul is only because we have had so
much to do. . . . They will, however, be detained at their
homes under arrest until we have investigated their complicity in the treacherous acts of Kerensky during the
Kornilov affair!"

"Never," shouted Pianikh, "in any revolution have such
things been seen as go on here!"

"You are mistaken," responded Trotsky. "Such things
have been seen even in this revolution. Hundreds of our
comrades were arrested in the July days. . . . When
Comrade Kollontai was released from prison by the doc-
tor's orders, Avksentiev placed at her door two former
agents of the Tsar's secret police!" The peasants withdrew, muttering, followed by ironical hoots.

The representative of the Left Socialist Revolutionaries
spoke on the Land Decree. While agreeing in principle,
his faction could not vote on the question until after discussion. The Peasants' Soviets should be consulted. . . .

The Mensheviki Internationalists, too, insisted on a party caucus.

Then the leader of the Maximalists, the Anarchist wing of the peasants: "We must do honour to a political party which puts such an act into effect the first day, without jawing about it!"

A typical peasant was in the tribune, long hair, boots and sheep-skin coat, bowing to all corners of the hall. "I wish you well, comrades and citizens," he said. "There are some Cadets walking around outside. You arrested our Socialist peasants—why not arrest them?"

This was the signal for a debate of excited peasants. It was precisely like the debate of soldiers of the night before. Here were the real proletarians of the land. . . .

"Those members of our Executive Committee, Avksentiev and the rest, whom we thought were the peasants' protectors—they are only Cadets too! Arrest them! Arrest them!"

Another, "Who are these Pianikhs, these Avksentievs? They are not peasants at all! They only wag their tails!"

How the crowd rose to them, recognising brothers!

The Left Socialist Revolutionaries proposed a half-hour intermission. As the delegates streamed out, Lenin stood up in his place.

"We must not lose time, comrades! News all-important to Russia must be on the press to-morrow morning. No delay!"

And above the hot discussion, argument, shuffling of feet could be heard the voice of an emissary of the Military Revolutionary Committee, crying, "Fifteen agitators wanted in room 17 at once! To go to the Front!" . . .

It was almost two hours and a half later that the delegates came straggling back, the presidium mounted the platform, and the session recommenced by the reading of telegrams from regiment after regiment, announcing their adhesion to the Military Revolutionary Committee.

In leisurely manner the meeting gathered momentum. A delegate from the Russian troops on the Macedonian front spoke bitterly of their situation. "We suffer there more from the friendship of our 'Allies' than from the enemy," he said. Representatives of the Tenth and Twelfth Armies, just arrived in hot haste, reported, "We support you with all our strength!" A peasant-soldier protested against the release of "the traitor Socialists, Mazlov and Salazkin"; as for the Executive Committee of the Peasants' Soviets, it should be arrested *en masse!* Here was real revolutionary talk. . . . A deputy from the Russian Army in Persia declared he was instructed to demand all power to the Soviets. . . . A Ukrainian officer, speaking in his native tongue: "There is no nationalism in this crisis. . . . *Da zdravstvuyet* the proletarian dictatorship of all lands!" Such a deluge of high and hot thoughts that surely Russia would never again be dumb!

Kamenev remarked that the anti-Bolshevik forces were trying to stir up disorders everywhere, and read an appeal of the Congress to all the Soviets of Russia:

The All-Russian Congress of Soviets of Workers' and Soldiers' Deputies, including some Peasants' Deputies, calls upon the local Soviets to take immediate energetic measures to oppose all counter-revolutionary anti-Jewish action and all *pogroms,* whatever they may be. The honour of the Workers', Peasants' and Soldiers' Revolution demands that no *pogrom* be tolerated.

The Red Guard of Petrograd, the revolutionary garrison and the sailors have maintained complete order in the capital.

Workers, soldiers and peasants, you should follow everywhere the example of the workers and soldiers of Petrograd.

Comrade soldiers and Cossacks, on us falls the duty of assuring real revolutionary order.

All revolutionary Russia and the entire world have their eyes on us. . . .

At two o'clock the Land Decree was put to vote, with only one against and the peasant delegates wild with joy. . . . So plunged the Bolsheviki ahead, irresistible, over-riding hesitation and opposition—the only people in Russia who had a definite programme of action while the others talked for eight long months.

Now arose a soldier, gaunt, ragged and eloquent, to protest against the clause of the *nakaz* tending to deprive military deserters from a share in village land allotments. Bawled at and hissed at first, his simple, moving speech finally made silence. "Forced against his will into the butchery of the trenches," he cried, "which you your-selves, in the Peace decree, have voted senseless as well as horrible, he greeted the Revolution with hope of peace and freedom. Peace? The Government of Kerensky forced him again to go forward into Galicia to slaughter and be slaughtered; to his pleas for peace, Tereshchenko simply laughed. . . . Freedom? Under Kerensky he found his Committees suppressed, his newspapers cut off, his party speakers put in prison. . . . At home in his village, the landlords were defying his Land Committees, jailing his comrades. . . . In Petrograd the bourgeoisie, in alli-ance with the Germans, were sabotaging the food and ammunition for the Army. . . . He was without boots, or clothes. . . . Who forced him to desert? The Gov-ernment of Kerensky, which you have overthrown!" At the end there was applause.

But another soldier hotly denounced it: "The Government of Kerensky is not a screen behind which can be hidden dirty work like desertion! Deserters are scoundrels, who run away home and leave their comrades to die in the trenches alone! Every deserter is a traitor, and should be punished. . . ." Uproar, shouts of *"Dovolno! Teesche!"* Kamenev hastily proposed to leave the matter to the Government for decision.[5]

At 2.30 A. M. fell a tense hush. Kamenev was reading the decree of the Constitution of Power:*

Until the meeting of the Constituent Assembly, a provisional Workers' and Peasants' Government is formed, which shall be named the Council of People's Commissars.[6]

The administration of the different branches of state activity shall be intrusted to commissions, whose composition shall be regulated to ensure the carrying out of the programme of the Congress, in close union with the mass-organisations of working-men, working-women, sailors, soldiers, peasants and clerical employees. The governmental power is vested in a *collegium* made up of the chairmen of these commissions, that is to say, the Council of People's Commissars.

Control over the activities of the People's Commissars, and the right to replace them, shall belong to the All-Russian Congress of Soviets of Workers', Peasants' and Soldiers' Deputies, and its Central Executive Committee.

Still silence; as he read the list of Commissars, bursts of applause after each name, Lenin's and Trotsky's especially.**

President of the Council: Vladimir Ulianov (*Lenin*)
Interior: A. I. Rykov

* Drafted by Lenin.—*Ed.*
** For some reason Reed's list was unusually inaccurate. He gave wrong initials to Rykov, Dybenko, Stepanov-Skvortsov, Antonov-Ovseenko, Oppokov-Lomov, and Teodorovich, all of which errors have been corrected here.—*Ed.*

Agriculture: V. P. Miliutin

Labour: A. G. Shliapnikov

Military and Naval Affairs—a committee composed of V. A. Ovseenko (*Antonov*), N. V. Krylenko, and P. E. Dybenko.

Commerce and Industry: V. P. Nogin

Popular Education: A. V. Lunacharsky

Finance: I. I. Skvortsov (*Stepanov*)

Foreign Affairs: L. D. Bronstein (*Trotsky*)

Justice: G. I. Oppokov (*Lomov*)

Supplies: I. A. Teodorovich

Post and Telegraph: N. P. Avilov (*Glebov*)

Chairman for Nationalities: I. V. Djugashvili (*Stalin*)

Railroads: To be filled later.

There were bayonets at the edges of the room, bayonets pricking up among the delegates; the Military Revolutionary Committee was arming everybody, Bolshevism was arming for the decisive battle with Kerensky, the sound of whose trumpets came up the south-west wind. . . . In the meanwhile nobody went home; on the contrary hundreds of newcomers filtered in, filling the great room solid with stern-faced soldiers and workmen who stood for hours and hours, indefatigably intent. The air was thick with cigarette smoke, and human breathing, and the smell of coarse clothes and sweat.

Avilov of the staff of *Novaya Zhizn* was speaking in the name of the Social Democrat Internationalists and the remnant of the Mensheviki Internationalists; Avilov, with his young, intelligent face, looking out of place in his smart frock-coat.

"We must ask ourselves where we are going. . . . The ease with which the Coalition Government was upset cannot be explained by the strength of the left wing of the democracy, but only by the incapacity of the Government to give the people peace and bread. And the left wing cannot maintain itself in power unless it can solve these questions. . . .

"Can it give bread to the people? Grain is scarce. The majority of the peasants will not be with you, for you cannot give them the machinery they need. Fuel and other primary necessities are almost impossible to procure. . . .

"As for peace, that will be even more difficult. The Allies refused to talk with Skobelev. They will never accept the proposition of a peace conference from *you.* You will not be recognised either in London and Paris, or in Berlin. . . .

"You cannot count on the effective help of the proletariat of the Allied countries, because in most countries it is very far from the revolutionary struggle; remember, the Allied democracy was unable even to convoke the Stockholm Conference. Concerning the German Social Democrats, I have just talked with Comrade Goldenberg, one of our delegates to Stockholm; he was told by the representatives of the Extreme Left that revolution in Germany was impossible during the war. . . ." Here interruptions began to come thick and fast, but Avilov kept on.

"The isolation of Russia will fatally result either in the defeat of the Russian Army by the Germans, and the patching up of a peace between the Austro-German coalition and the Franco-British coalition *at the expense of Russia*—or in a separate peace with Germany.

"I have just learned that the Allied ambassadors are preparing to leave, and that Committees for Salvation

of Country and Revolution are forming in all the cities of
Russia. . . .

"No one party can conquer these enormous difficulties.
The majority of the people, supporting a government of
Socialist coalition, can alone accomplish the Revolu-
tion. . . ."

He then read the resolution of the two factions:

Recognising that for the salvation of the conquests of the
Revolution it is indispensable immediately to constitute a
government based on the revolutionary democracy organised
in the Soviets of Workers', Soldiers' and Peasants' Deputies,
recognising moreover that the task of this government is the
quickest possible attainment of peace, the transfer of the land
into the hands of the agrarian committees, the organisation of
control over industrial production, and the convocation of
the Constituent Assembly on the date decided, the Congress
appoints an executive committee to constitute such a government after an agreement with the groups of the democracy
which are taking part in the Congress.

In spite of the revolutionary exaltation of the triumphant crowd, Avilov's cool tolerant reasoning had
shaken them. Toward the end, the cries and hisses died
away, and when he finished there was even some clapping.

Karelin followed him—also young, fearless, whose
sincerity no one doubted—for the Left Socialist Revolutionaries, the party of Maria Spiridonova, the party which
almost alone followed the Bolsheviki, and which represented the revolutionary peasants.

"Our party has refused to enter the Council of People's
Commissars because we do not wish forever to separate
ourselves from the part of the revolutionary army which
left the Congress, a separation which would make it

impossible for us to serve as intermediaries between the Bolsheviki and the other groups of the democracy. . . . And that is our principal duty at this moment. We cannot sustain any government except a government of Socialist coalition. . . .

"We protest, moreover, against the tyrannical conduct of the Bolsheviki. Our Commissars have been driven from their posts. Our only organ, *Znamia Truda* (Banner of Labour), was forbidden to appear yesterday. . . .

"The Central Duma is forming a powerful Committee for Salvation of Country and Revolution, to fight you. Already you are isolated, and your Government is without the support of a single other democratic group. . . ."

And now Trotsky stood upon the raised tribune, confident and dominating, with that sarcastic expression about his mouth which was almost a sneer. He spoke, in a ringing voice, and the great crowd rose to him.

"These considerations on the dangers of isolation of our party are not new. On the eve of insurrection our fatal defeat was also predicted. Everybody was against us; only a faction of the Socialist Revolutionaries of the left was with us in the Military Revolutionary Committee. How is it that we were able to overturn the Government almost without bloodshed? . . . That fact is the most striking proof that we *were not isolated*. In reality the Provisional Government was isolated; the democratic parties which march against us were isolated, are isolated, and forever cut off from the proletariat!

"They speak of the necessity for a coalition. There is only one coalition possible—the coalition of the workers, soldiers and poorest peasants; and it is our party's honour to have realised that coalition. . . . What sort of coalition did Avilov mean? A coalition with those who supported the Government of Treason to the People? Coalition doesn't always add to strength. For example, could we have organised the insurrection with Dan and Avksentiev in our ranks?" Roars of laughter.

"Avksentiev gave little bread. Will a coalition with the *oborontsi* furnish more? Between the peasants and Avksentiev, who ordered the arrest of the Land Committees, we choose the peasants! Our Revolution will remain the classic revolution of history. . . .

"They accuse us of repelling an agreement with the other democratic parties. But is it we who are to blame? Or must we, as Karelin put it, blame it on a 'misunderstanding'? No, comrades. When a party in full tide of revolution, still wreathed in powder-smoke, comes to say, 'Here is the Power—take it!'—and when those to whom it is offered go over to the enemy, that is not a misunderstanding . . . that is a declaration of pitiless war. And it isn't we who have declared war. . . .

"Avilov menaces us with failure of our peace efforts—if we remain 'isolated.' I repeat, I don't see how a coalition with Skobelev, or even Tereshchenko, can help us to get peace! Avilov tries to frighten us by the threat of a peace at our expense. And I answer that in any case, if Europe continues to be ruled by the imperialist bourgeoisie, revolutionary Russia will inevitably be lost. . . .

"There are only two alternatives; either the Russian Revolution will create a revolutionary movement in Europe, or the European powers will destroy the Russian Revolution!"

They greeted him with an immense crusading acclaim, kindling to the daring of it, with the thought of championing mankind. And from that moment there was something conscious and decided about the insurrectionary masses, in all their actions, which never left them.

But on the other side, too, battle was taking form.

Kamenev recognised a delegate from the Union of Railway Workers, a hardfaced, stocky man with an attitude of implacable hostility. He threw a bombshell.

"In the name of the strongest organisation in Russia I demand the right to speak, and I say to you: the *Vikzhel* charges me to make known the decision of the Union concerning the constitution of Power. The Central Committee refuses absolutely to support the Bolsheviki if they persist in isolating themselves from the whole democracy of Russia!" Immense tumult all over the hall.

"In 1905, and in the Kornilov days, the Railway Workers were the best defenders of the Revolution. But you did not invite us to your Congress—" Cries, "It was the old *Tsay-ee-kah* which did not invite you!" The orator paid no attention. "We do not recognise the legality of this Congress; since the departure of the Mensheviki and Socialist Revolutionaries there is not a legal quorum. . . . The Union supports the old *Tsay-ee-kah,* and declares that the Congress has no right to elect a new Committee. . . .

"The Power should be a Socialist and revolutionary Power, responsible before the authorised organs of the entire revolutionary democracy. Until the constitution of such a power, the Union of Railway Workers, which refuses to transport counter-revolutionary troops to Petrograd, at the same time forbids the execution of any order whatever without the consent of the *Vikzhel*. The *Vikzhel* also takes into its hands the entire administration of the railroads of Russia."

At the end he could hardly be heard for the furious storm of abuse which beat upon him. But it was a heavy blow—that could be seen in the concern on the faces of the presidium. Kamenev, however, merely answered that there could be no doubt of the legality of the Congress, as even the quorum established by the old *Tsay-ee-kah* was

exceeded—in spite of the secession of the Mensheviki and
Socialist Revolutionaries. . . .

Then came the vote on the Constitution of Power, which
carried the Council of People's Commissars into office by
an enormous majority. . . .

The election of the new *Tsay-ee-kah,* the new parliament
of the Russian Republic, took barely fifteen minutes. Trotsky announced its composition: 100 members, of which
70 Bolsheviki. . . . As for the peasants, and the seceding
factions, places were to be reserved for them. "We welcome
into the Government all parties and groups which will
adopt our programme," ended Trotsky.

And thereupon the Second All-Russian Congress of
Soviets was dissolved, so that the members might hurry to
their homes in the four corners of Russia and tell of the
great happenings. . . .

It was almost seven when we woke the sleeping conduc-
tors and motor-men of the street-cars which the Street-
Railway Workers' Union always kept waiting at Smolny
to take the Soviet delegates to their homes. In the crowded
car there was less happy hilarity than the night before, I
thought. Many looked anxious; perhaps they were saying
to themselves, "Now we are masters, how can we do our
will?"

At our apartment-house we were held up in the dark
by an armed patrol of citizens and carefully examined.
The Duma's proclamation was doing its work. . . .

The landlady heard us come in, and stumbled out in a
pink silk wrapper.

"The House Committee has again asked that you take
your turn on guard-duty with the rest of the men," she
said.

"What's the reason for this guard-duty?"

"To protect the house and the women and children."

"Who from?"

"Robbers and murderers."

"But suppose there came a Commissar from the Military Revolutionary Committee to search for arms?"

"Oh, that's what they'll *say* they are. . . . And besides, what's the difference?"

I solemnly affirmed that the Consul had forbidden all American citizens to carry arms—especially in the neighbourhood of the Russian *intelligentsia*. . . .

NOTES TO CHAPTER V

1 Appeals and Proclamations

From the Military Revolutionary Committee, November 8:

"To All Army Committees and All Soviets of Soldiers' Deputies.

"The Petrograd garrison has overturned the Government of Kerensky, which had risen against the Revolution and the People. . . . In sending this news to the Front and the country, the Military Revolutionary Committee requests all soldiers to keep vigilant watch on the conduct of officers. Officers who do not frankly and openly declare for the Revolution should be immediately arrested as enemies.

"The Petrograd Soviet interprets the programme of the new Government as: immediate proposals of a general democratic peace, the immediate transfer of great landed estates to the peasants, and the honest convocation of the Constituent Assembly. The people's revolutionary Army must not permit troops of doubtful morale to be sent to Petrograd. Act by means of arguments, by means of moral suasion—but if that fails, halt the movement of troops by implacable force.

"The present order must be immediately read to all military units of every branch of the service. Whoever keeps the knowledge of this order from the soldier-masses . . . commits a serious crime against the Revolution, and will be punished with all the rigour of revolutionary law.

"Soldiers! For peace, bread, land, and popular government!"

*　　*　　*　　*

"To All Front and Rear Army, Corps, Divisional, Regimental and Company Committees, and All Soviets of Workers', Soldiers' and Peasants' Deputies.

"Soldiers and Revolutionary Officers!

"The Military Revolutionary Committee, by agreement with the majority of the workers, soldiers, and peasants, has decreed that General Kornilov and all the accomplices of his conspiracy shall be brought immediately to Petrograd, for incarceration in Peter-Paul Fortress and arraignment before a military revolutionary court-martial. . . .

"All who resist the execution of this decree are declared by the Committee to be traitors to the Revolution, and their orders are herewith declared null and void."

The Military Revolutionary Committee Attached to the Petrograd Soviet of Workers' and Soldiers' Deputies.

*　　*　　*　　*

"To all Provincial and District Soviets of Workers', Soldiers' and Peasants' Deputies.

"By resolution of the All-Russian Congress of Soviets, all arrested members of Land Committees are immediately set free. The Commissars who arrested them are to be arrested.

"From this moment all power belongs to the Soviets. The Commissars of the Provisional Government are removed. The presidents of the various local Soviets are invited to enter into direct relations with the revolutionary Government."

Military Revolutionary Committee.

2 Protest of the Municipal Duma

"The Central City Duma, elected on the most democratic principles, has undertaken the burden of managing Municipal affairs and food supplies at the time of the greatest disorganisation. At the present moment the Bolshevik party, three weeks before the elections to the Constituent Assembly, and in spite of the menace of the external enemy, having removed by armed force the only legal revolutionary authority, is making an attempt against the rights and independence of the Municipal Self-Government, demanding submission to its Commissars and its illegal authority.

"In this terrible and tragic moment the Petrograd City Duma, in the face of its constituents, and of all Russia, declares loudly that it will not submit to any encroachments on its rights and its independence, and will remain at the post of responsibility to which it has been called by the will of the population of the capital.

"The Central City Duma of Petrograd appeals to all Dumas and Zemstvos of the Russian Republic to rally to the defence of one of the greatest conquests of the Russian Revolution—the independence and inviolability of popular self-government."

3 Land Decree—Peasants' "Nakaz"

The Land question can only be permanently settled by the general Constituent Assembly.

The most equitable solution of the Land question should be as follows:

1. The right of private ownership of land is abolished forever; land cannot be sold, nor leased, nor mortgaged, nor alienated in any way. All dominical lands, lands attached to titles, lands belonging to the Emperor's cabinet, to monasteries, churches, possession lands, entailed lands, private estates, communal lands, peasant free-holds, and others, are confiscated without compensation, and become national property, and are placed at the disposition of the workers who cultivate them.

Those who are damaged because of this social transformation of the rights of property are entitled to public aid during the time necessary for them to adapt themselves to the new conditions of existence.

2. All the riches beneath the earth—ores, oil, coal, salt, etc.—as well as forests and waters having a national importance, become the exclusive property of the State. All minor streams, lakes and forests are placed in the hands of the communities, on condition of being managed by the local organs of government.

3. All plots of land scientifically cultivated—gardens, plantations, nurseries, seed-plots, green-houses, and others—shall not be

divided, but transformed into model farms, and pass into the hands of the State or of the community, according to their size and importance.

Buildings, communal lands and villages with their private gardens and their orchards remain in the hands of their present owners; the dimensions of these plots and the rate of taxes for their use shall be fixed by law.

4. All studs, governmental and private cattle-breeding and bird-breeding establishments, and others, are confiscated and become national property, and are transferred either to the State or to the community, according to their size and importance.

All questions of compensation for the above are within the competence of the Constituent Assembly.

5. All inventoried agricultural property of the confiscated lands, machinery and live-stock, are transferred without compensation to the State or the community, according to their quantity and importance.

The confiscation of such machinery or live-stock shall not apply to the small properties of peasants.

6. The right to use the land is granted to all citizens, without distinction of sex, who wish to work the land themselves, with the help of their families, or in partnership, and only so long as they are able to work. No hired labour is permitted.

In the event of the incapacity for work of a member of the commune for a period of two years, the commune shall be bound to render him assistance during this time by working his land in common.

Farmers who through old age or sickness have permanently lost the capacity to work the land themselves, shall surrender their land and receive instead a Government pension.

7. The use of the land should be equalised—that is to say, the land shall be divided among the workers according to local conditions, the unit of labour and the needs of the individual.

The way in which land is to be used may be individually determined upon: as homesteads, as farms, by communes, by partnerships, as will be decided by the villages and settlements.

8. All land upon its confiscation is pooled in the general People's Land Fund. Its distribution among the workers is carried out by the local and central organs of administration, beginning with the village democratic organisations and ending with the

central provincial institutions—with the exception of urban and rural cooperative societies.

The Land Fund is subject to periodical redistribution according to the increase of population and the development of productivity and rural economy.

In case of modification of the boundaries of allotments, the original centre of the allotment remains intact.

The lands of persons retiring from the community return to the Land Fund; providing that near relatives of the persons retiring, or friends designated by them, shall have preference in the re-distribution of these lands.

When lands are returned to the Land Fund, the money expended for manuring or improving the land, which has not been exhausted, shall be reimbursed.

If in some localities the Land Fund is insufficient to satisfy the local population, the surplus population should emigrate.

The organisation of the emigration, also the costs thereof, and the providing of emigrants with the necessary machinery and live-stock, shall be the business of the State.

The emigration shall be carried out in the following order: first, the peasants without land who express their wish to emigrate; then the undesirable members of the community, deserters, etc., and finally, by drawing lots on agreement.

All which is contained in this *nakaz*, being the expression of the indisputable will of the great majority of conscious peasants of Russia, is declared to be a temporary law, and until the convocation of the Constituent Assembly, becomes effective immediately so far as is possible, and in some parts of it gradually, as will be determined by the District Soviets of Peasants' Deputies.

4

There is no such remark against Chernov in Lenin's speech as published next day in *Pravda* and *Izvestia* or as reproduced in his *Works,* Vol. XXVI, pp. 225-29. Reed is correct, however, in saying that Chernov wanted a uniform planned distribution of the land rather than chaotic decision by whoever happened to be on the spot in each village. He feared, too, that the soldiers would all rush home if they knew that only those on the spot would get land according to the noise they could make or the following they could gather. Chernov wanted uniform decisions to be given to the local land committees to guide them. Lenin actually said a kind word for Chernov when he was forced out as Minister of Agriculture. In the speech here summarized by Reed, as it was reported in *Pravda* are these interesting passages:

"Voices are raised here to declare that the decree itself and the *nakaz* were drawn up by the Socialist Revolutionaries. Let us admit that it is so. Isn't it all the same who has drawn it up? But as a democratic government, we cannot evade the decisions of the popular depths, even if we are not in agreement with them. And even if the peasantry should continue to follow the Socialist Revolutionaries in the future and even if they give that party a majority in the Constituent Assembly, then there too we will say: 'So be it.' " (Vol. XXVI, p. 228). The peasants did give the Socialist Revolutionary Party an overwhelming majority in the country as a whole (Reed reports only the vote in Petrograd where the SR's were not so strong), and Chernov was overwhelmingly elected the Chairman of the Constituent Assembly. Lenin's answer then was to dissolve the Constituent Assembly by force of arms after its very first session.—*Ed.*

5   The Land and Deserters

The Government was not forced to make any decision concerning the rights of deserters to the land. The end of the war and the demobilisation of the army automatically removed the deserter problem. . . .

6   The Council of People's Commissars

The Council of People's Commissars was at first composed entirely of Bolsheviki. This was not entirely the fault of the Bolsheviki, however. On November 8th they offered portfolios to members of the Left Socialist Revolutionaries, who declined.

CHAPTER VI

THE COMMITTEE
FOR SALVATION

Friday, November 9th. . . .

Novocherkask, November 8th.

In view of the revolt of the Bolsheviki, and their attempt to depose the Provisional Government and to seize the power in Petrograd . . . the Cossack Government declares that it considers these acts criminal and absolutely inadmissible. In consequence, the Cossacks will lend all their support to the Provisional Government, which is a government of coalition. Because of these circumstances, and until the return of the Provisional Government to power, and the restoration of order in Russia, I take upon myself, beginning November 7th, all the power in that which concerns the region of the Don.

Signed: ATAMAN KALEDIN

President of the Government of the Cossack Troops.

Prikaz of the Minister-President Kerensky, dated at Gatchina:

I, Minister-President of the Provisional Government, and Supreme Commander of all the armed forces of the Russian

Republic, declare that I am at the head of regiments from the Front who have remained faithful to the fatherland.

I order all the troops of the Military District of Petrograd, who through mistake or folly have answered the appeal of the traitors to the country and the Revolution, to return to their duty without delay.

This order shall be read in all regiments, battalions and squadrons.

Signed: *Minister-President of the Provisional Government and Supreme Commander* A. F. KERENSKY.

Telegram from Kerensky to the General in Command of the Northern Front:

The town of Gatchina has been taken by the loyal regiments without bloodshed. Detachments of Cronstadt sailors, and of the Semionovsky and Ismailovsky regiments, gave up their arms without resistance and joined the Government troops.

I order all the designated units to advance as quickly as possible. The Military Revolutionary Committee has ordered its troops to retreat. . . .

Gatchina, about thirty kilometers south-west, had fallen during the night. Detachments of the two regiments mentioned—not the sailors—while wandering captainless in the neighbourhood, had indeed been surrounded by Cossacks and given up their arms; but it was not true that they had joined the Government troops. At this very moment crowds of them, bewildered and ashamed, were up at Smolny trying to explain. They did not think the Cossacks were so near. . . . They had tried to argue with the Cossacks. . . .

Apparently the greatest confusion prevailed along the revolutionary front. The garrisons of all the little towns

southward had split hopelessly, bitterly into two factions—
or three: the high command being on the side of Kerensky,
in default of anything stronger, the majority of the rank
and file with the Soviets, and the rest unhappily wavering.

Hastily the Military Revolutionary Committee appointed to command the defence of Petrograd an ambitious
regular Army captain, Muraviov; the same Muraviov who
had organised the Death Battalions during the summer,
and had once been heard to advise the Government that "it
was too lenient with the Bolsheviki; they must be wiped
out." A man of military mind, who admired power and
audacity, perhaps sincerely. . . .

Beside my door when I came down in the morning were
posted two new orders of the Military Revolutionary Committee, directing that all shops and stores should open as
usual, and that all empty rooms and apartments should be
put at the disposal of the Committee. . . .

For thirty-six hours now the Bolsheviki had been cut
off from provincial Russia and the outside world. The
railway men and telegraphers refused to transmit their
despatches, the postmen would not handle their mail. Only
the Government wireless at Tsarskoye Selo launched
half-hourly bulletins and manifestoes to the four corners
of heaven; the Commissars of Smolny raced the Commissars of the City Duma on speeding trains half across the
earth; and two aeroplanes, laden with propaganda, fled
high up toward the Front. . . .

But the eddies of insurrection were spreading through
Russia with a swiftness surpassing any human agency. Helsingfors Soviet passed resolutions of support; Kiev Bolsheviki captured the arsenal and the telegraph station,
only to be driven out by delegates to the Congress of
Cossacks, which happened to be meeting there; in Kazan, a
Military Revolutionary Committee arrested the local garri-

son staff and the Commissar of the Provisional Government; from far Krasnoyarsk, in Siberia, came news that the Soviets were in control of the Municipal institutions; at Moscow, where the situation was aggravated by a great strike of leather-workers on one side, and a threat of general lock-out on the other, the Soviets had voted overwhelmingly to support the action of the Bolsheviki in Petrograd. . . . Already a Military Revolutionary Committee was functioning.

Everywhere the same thing happened. The common soldiers and the industrial workers supported the Soviets by a vast majority; the officers, *yunkers* and middle class generally were on the side of the Government—as were the bourgeois Cadets and the "moderate" Socialist parties. In all these towns sprang up Committees for Salvation of Country and Revolution, arming for civil war. . . .

Vast Russia was in a state of solution. As long ago as 1905 the process had begun; the March Revolution had merely hastened it, and giving birth to a sort of forecast of the new order, had ended by merely perpetuating the hollow structure of the old régime. Now, however, the Bolsheviki, in one night, had dissipated it, as one blows away smoke. Old Russia was no more; human society flowed molten in primal heat, and from the tossing sea of flame was emerging the class struggle, stark and pitiless —and the fragile, slowly-cooling crust of new planets. . . .

In Petrograd sixteen Ministries were on strike, led by the Ministries of Labour and of Supplies—the only two created by the all-Socialist Government of August.

If ever men stood alone the "handful of Bolsheviki" apparently stood alone that grey chill morning, with all storms towering over them.[1] Back against the wall, the Military Revolutionary Committee struck—for its life. *"De l'audace, encore de l'audace, et toujours de l'audace. . . ."*

At five in the morning the Red Guards entered the printing office of the City Government, confiscated thousands
of copies of the Appeal-Protest of the Duma, and suppressed the official Municipal organ—the *Viestnik Gorod-
skovo Samoupravleniya* (Bulletin of the Municipal Self-
Government). All the bourgeois newspapers were torn
from the presses, even the *Golos Soldata,* journal of the
old *Tsay-ee-kah*—which, however, changing its name to
Soldatski Golos, appeared in an edition of a hundred thousand copies, bellowing rage and defiance:

The men who began their stroke of treachery in the
night, who have suppressed the newspapers, will not keep the
country in ignorance long. The country will know the truth!
It will appreciate you, Messrs. the Bolsheviki! We shall
see! . . .

As we came down the Nevsky a little after midday the
whole street before the Duma building was crowded with
people. Here and there stood Red Guards and sailors,
with bayonetted rifles, each one surrounded by about a
hundred men and women—clerks, students, shopkeepers,
chinovniki—shaking their fists and bawling insults and
menaces. On the steps stood boy-scouts and officers, distributing copies of the *Soldatski Golos*. A workman with a
red band around his arm and a revolver in his hand stood
trembling with rage and nervousness in the middle of a
hostile throng at the foot of the stairs, demanding the
surrender of the papers. . . . Nothing like this, I imagine,
ever occurred in history. On one side a handful of workmen and common soldiers, with arms in their hands, representing a victorious insurrection—and perfectly miserable;
on the other a frantic mob made up of the kind of people
that crown the sidewalks of Fifth Avenue at noon-time,

sneering, abusing, shouting, "Traitors! Provocators! *Oprichniki!**"

The doors were guarded by students and officers with white arm-bands lettered in red, "Militia of the Committee of Public Safety," and half a dozen boy-scouts came and went. Upstairs the place was all commotion. Captain Gomberg was coming down the stairs. "They're going to dissolve the Duma," he said. "The Bolshevik Commissar is with the Mayor now." As we reached the top Riazanov came hurrying out. He had been to demand that the Duma recognise the Council of Peoples' Commissars, and the Mayor had given him a flat refusal.

In the offices a great babbling crowd, hurrying, shouting, gesticulating—Government officials, intellectuals, journalists, foreign correspondents, French and British officers. . . . The City Engineer pointed to them triumphantly. "The Embassies recognise the Duma as the only power now," he explained. "For these Bolshevik murderers and robbers it is only a question of hours. All Russia is rallying to us. . . ."

In the Alexander Hall a monster meeting of the Committee for Salvation. Fillipovsky in the chair and Skobelev again in the tribune, reporting, to immense applause, new adhesions to the Committee; Executive Committee of Peasants' Soviets, old *Tsay-ee-kah,* Central Army Committee, *Tsentroflot,* Menshevik, Socialist Revolutionary and Front group delegates from the Congress of Soviets, Central Committees of the Menshevik, Socialist Revolutionary, Populist Socialist parties, "Yedinstvo" group, Peasants' Union, Cooperatives, Zemstvos, Municipalities, Post and Telegraph Unions, *Vikzhel,* Council of the Russian Republic, Union of Unions,** Merchants' and Manufacturers' Association. . . .

---

* Savage body-guards of Ivan the Terrible, 17th century.
** See Notes and Explanations.

". . . The power of the Soviets is not a democratic power, but a dictatorship—and not the dictatorship of the proletariat, but *against* the proletariat. All those who have felt or know how to feel revolutionary enthusiasm must join now for the defence of the Revolution. . . .

"The problem of the day is not only to render harmless irresponsible demagogues, but to fight against the counter-revolution. . . . If rumours are true that certain generals in the provinces are attempting to profit by events in order to march on Petrograd with other designs, it is only one more proof that we must establish a solid base of democratic government. Otherwise, troubles with the Right will follow troubles from the Left. . . .

"The garrison of Petrograd cannot remain indifferent when citizens buying the *Golos Soldata* and newsboys selling the *Rabochaya Gazeta* are arrested in the streets. . . .

"The hour of resolutions has passed. . . . Let those who have no longer faith in the Revolution retire. . . . To establish a united power, we must again restore the prestige of the Revolution. . . .

"Let us swear that either the Revolution shall be saved —or we shall perish!"

The hall rose, cheering, with kindling eyes. There was not a single proletarian anywhere in sight. . . .

Then Weinstein:

"We must remain calm, and not act until public opinion is firmly grouped in support of the Committee for Salvation—then we can pass from the defensive to action!"

The *Vikzhel* representative announced that his organisation was taking the initiative in forming the new Government, and its delegates were now discussing the matter with Smolny. . . . Followed a hot discussion: were the Bolsheviki to be admitted to the new Government? Martov pleaded for their admission; after all, he said, they represented an important political party. Opinions were very much divided upon this, the right wing Mensheviki and Socialist Revolutionaries, as well as the Populist Socialists, the Cooperatives and the bourgeois elements being bitterly against. . . .

"They have betrayed Russia," one speaker said. "They have started civil war and opened the front to the Germans. The Bolsheviki must be mercilessly crushed. . . ."

Skobelev was in favor of excluding both the Bolsheviki and the Cadets.

We got into conversation with a young Socialist Revolutionary, who had walked out of the Democratic Conference together with the Bolsheviki, that night when Tseretelli and the "compromisers" forced Coalition upon the democracy of Russia.

"You here?" I asked him.

His eyes flashed fire. "Yes!" he cried. "I left the Congress with my party Wednesday night. I have not risked my life for twenty years and more to submit now to the tyranny of the Dark People. Their methods are intolerable. But they have not counted on the peasants. . . . When the peasants begin to act, then it is a question of minutes before they are done for."

"But the peasants—will they act? Doesn't the Land decree settle the peasants? What more do they want?"

"Ah, the Land decree!" he said furiously. "Yes, do you know what that Land decree is? It is *our* decree—it is the Socialist Revolutionary programme, intact! My party framed that policy, after the most careful compilation of the wishes of the peasants themselves. It is an outrage. . . ."

"But if it is your own policy, why do you object? If it is the peasants' wishes, why will they oppose it?"

"You don't understand! Don't you see that the peasants will immediately realise that it is all a trick—that these usurpers have stolen the Socialist Revolutionary programme?"

I asked if it were true that Kaledin was marching north.

He nodded, and rubbed his hands with a sort of bitter satisfaction. "Yes. Now you see what these Bolsheviki have done. They have raised the counter-revolution against us. The Revolution is lost. The Revolution is lost."

"But won't you defend the Revolution?"

"Of course we will defend it—to the last drop of our blood. But we won't cooperate with the Bolsheviki in any way. . . ."

"But if Kaledin comes to Petrograd, and the Bolsheviki defend the city. Won't you join with them?"

"Of course not. We will defend the city also, but we won't support the Bolsheviki. Kaledin is the enemy of the Revolution, but the Bolsheviki are equally enemies of the Revolution."

"Which do you prefer—Kaledin or the Bolsheviki?"

"It is not a question to be discussed!" he burst out impatiently. "I tell you, the Revolution is lost. And it is the Bolsheviki who are to blame. But listen—why should we talk of such things? Kerensky is coming. . . . Day after tomorrow we shall pass to the offensive. . . . Already Smolny has sent delegates inviting us to form a new Government. But we have them now—they are absolutely impotent. . . . We shall not cooperate. . . ."

Outside there was a shot. We ran to the windows. A Red Guard, finally exasperated by the taunts of the crowd, had shot into it, wounding a young girl in the arm. We could see her being lifted into a cab, surrounded by an excited throng, the clamour of whose voices floated up to us. As we looked, suddenly an armoured automobile appeared around the corner of the Mikhailovsky, its guns sluing this way and that. Immediately the crowd began to run, as Petrograd crowds do, falling down and lying still in the street, piled in the gutters, heaped up behind telephone-poles. The car lumbered up to the steps of the Duma and a man stuck his head out of the turret, demanding the surrender of the *Soldatski Golos*. The boy-scouts jeered and scuttled into the building. After a moment the automobile wheeled undecidedly around and went off up the Nevsky, while some hundreds of men and women picked themselves up and began to dust their clothes. . . .

Inside was a prodigious running-about of people with armfuls of *Soldatski Golos,* looking for places to hide them. . . .

A journalist came running into the room, waving a paper.

"Here's a proclamation from Krasnov!" he cried. Everybody crowded around. "Get it printed—get it printed quick, and around to the barracks!"

By the order of the Supreme Commander I am appointed commandant of the troops concentrated under Petrograd.

Citizens, soldiers, valorous Cossacks of the Don, of the Kuban, of the Transbaikal, of the Amur, of the Yenissei, to all you who have remained faithful to your oath I appeal; to you who have sworn to guard inviolable your oath of Cossack—I call upon you to save Petrograd from anarchy, from famine, from tyranny, and to save Russia from the indelible shame to which a handful of ignorant men, bought by the gold of Wilhelm, are trying to submit her.

The Provisional Government, to which you swore fidelity in the great days of March, is not overthrown, but by violence expelled from the edifice in which it held its meetings. However the Government, with the help of the Front armies, faithful to their duty, with the help of the Council of Cossacks, which has united under its command all the Cossacks and which, strong with the morale which reigns in its ranks, and acting in accordance with the will of the Russian people, has sworn to serve the country as its ancestors served it in the Troublous Times of 1612, when the Cossacks of the Don delivered Moscow, menaced by the Swedes, the Poles, and the Lithuanians. Your Government still exists. . . .

The active army considers these criminals with horror and contempt. Their acts of vandalism and pillage, their crimes, the German mentality with which they regard Russia—stricken down but not yet surrendered—have alienated from them the entire people.

Citizens, soldiers, valorous Cossacks of the garrison of Petrograd; send me your delegates so that I may know who are traitors to their country and who are not, that there may be avoided an effusion of innocent blood.

Almost the same moment word ran from group to group that the building was surrounded by Red Guards. An officer strode in, a red band around his arm, demanding the Mayor. A few minutes later he left and old Schreider came out of his office, red and pale by turns.

"A special meeting of the Duma!" he cried. "Immediately!"

In the big hall proceedings were halted. "All members of the Duma for a special meeting!"

"What's the matter?"

"I don't know—going to arrest us—going to dissolve the Duma—arresting members at the door—" so ran the excited comments.

In the Nicolai Hall there was barely room to stand. The Mayor announced that troops were stationed at all the doors, prohibiting all exit and entrance, and that a Commissar had threatened arrest and the dispersal of the Municipal Duma. A flood of impassioned speeches from members, and even from the galleries, responded. The freely-elected City Government could not be dissolved by *any* power; the Mayor's person and that of all the members were inviolable; the tyrants, the provocators, the German agents should never be recognised; as for these threats to dissolve us, let them try—only over our dead bodies shall they seize this chamber, where like the Roman senators of old we await with dignity the coming of the Goths. . . .

Resolution, to inform the Dumas and Zemstvos of all Russia by telegraph. Resolution, that it was impossible for the Mayor or the Chairman of the Duma to enter into any relations whatever with representatives of the Military Revolutionary Committee or with the so-called Council of People's Commissars. Resolution, to address another appeal to the population of Petrograd to stand up for the defence of their elected town government. Resolution, to remain in permanent session. . . .

In the meanwhile one member arrived with the information that he had telephoned to Smolny, and that the Military Revolutionary Committee said that no orders had been given to surround the Duma, and that the troops would be withdrawn. . . .

As we went downstairs Riazanov burst in through the front door, very agitated.

"Are you going to dissolve the Duma?" I asked.

"My God, no!" he answered. "It is all a mistake. I told the Mayor this morning that the Duma would be left alone. . . ." *

---

* The Duma was dissolved nevertheless by a decree of November 29. The Mayor, G. I. Shreider, of whom, as the reader must have noticed, Reed speaks always with respect despite his hostility to the Bolshevik seizure of power, was a Socialist Revolutionary of the moderate left. He was arrested at the end of November but released again because the Military Revolutionary Committee could not think of any charge to make against him. Contrary to the doctrinaire belief that the big towns were "Marxist," i.e., Social Demo-

Out on the Nevsky, in the deepening dusk, a long double file of cyclists came riding, guns slung on their shoulders. They halted, and the crowd pressed in and deluged them with questions.

"Who are you? Where do you come from?" asked a fat old man with a cigar in his mouth.

"Twelfth Army. From the front. We came to support the Soviets against the damn' bourgeoisie!"

"Ah!" were furious cries. "Bolshevik gendarmes! Bolshevik Cossacks!"

A little officer in a leather coat came running down the steps. "The garrison is turning!" he muttered in my ear. "It's the beginning of the end of the Bolsheviki. Do you want to see the turn of the tide? Come on!" He started at a half-trot up the Mikhailovsky, and we followed.

"What regiment is it?"

"The *bronoviki.* . . ." Here was indeed serious trouble. The *bronoviki* were the Armoured Car troops, the key to the situation; whoever controlled the *bronoviki* controlled the city. "The Commissars of the Committee for Salvation and the Duma have been talking to them. There's a meeting on to decide. . . ."

"Decide what? Which side they'll fight on?"

"Oh, no. That's not the way to do it. They'll never fight against the Bolsheviki. They will vote to remain neutral —and then the *yunkers* and Cossacks——"

The door of the great Mikhailovsky Riding-School yawned blackly. Two sentinels tried to stop us, but we brushed by hurriedly, deaf to their indignant expostula-

cratic, or Liberal, many of the larger cities in 1917 elected Socialist Revolutionaries as mayors: G. I. Shreider in Petrograd, V. V. Rudnev in Moscow, E. P. Riabtsev in Kiev, I. N. Lordkipanidze in Odessa, A. A. Nikolaev in Rostov-on-Don, Mukoseev in Saratov, S. A. Nikonov in Sevastopol, etc. O. S. Minor, leading SR, became president of the City Duma of Moscow and V. A. Karelin of the City Duma of Karkhov. In the villages the SR had no serious opposition.—*Ed.*

tions. Inside only a single arc-light burned dimly, high up near the roof of the enormous hall, whose lofty pilasters and rows of windows vanished in the gloom. Around dimly squatted the monstrous shapes of the armoured cars. One stood alone in the centre of the place, under the light, and round it were gathered some two thousand dun-colored soldiers, almost lost in the immensity of that imperial building. A dozen men, officers, chairmen of the Soldiers' Committees and speakers, were perched on top of the car, and from the central turret a soldier was speaking. This was Khanjunov, who had been president of last summer's all-Russian Congress of *Bronoviki*. A lithe, handsome figure in his leather coat with lieutenant's shoulder-straps, he stood pleading eloquently for neutrality.

"It is an awful thing," he said, "for Russians to kill their Russian brothers. There must not be civil war between soldiers who stood shoulder to shoulder against the Tsar, and conquered the foreign enemy in battles which will go down in history! What have we, soldiers, got to do with these squabbles of political parties? I will not say to you that the Provisional Government was a democratic Government; we want no coalition with the bourgeoisie—no. But we must have a Government of the united democracy,* or Russia is lost! With such a Government there will be no need for civil war, and the killing of brother by brother!"

This sounded reasonable—the great hall echoed to the crash of hands and voices.

A soldier climbed up, his face white and strained. "Comrades!" he cried, "I came from the Rumanian front, to urgently tell you all: there must be peace! Peace at

---

* "The democracy" was a term that the Soviet parties generally applied to themselves. A "united democracy" would therefore be a coalition government of all the socialist parties represented in the Soviets.—*Ed.*

once! Whoever can give us peace, whether it be the Bol-sheviki or this new Government, we will follow. Peace! We at the front cannot fight any longer. We cannot fight either Germans or Russians——" With that he leaped down, and a sort of confused agonised sound rose up from all that surging mass, which burst into something like anger when the next speaker, a Menshevik *oboronets* tried to say that the war must go on until the Allies were vic-torious.

"You talk like Kerensky!" shouted a rough voice.

A Duma delegate, pleading for neutrality. Him they listened to, muttering uneasily, feeling him not one of them. Never have I seen men trying so hard to under-stand, to decide. They never moved, stood staring with a sort of terrible intentness at the speaker, their brows wrinkled with the effort of thought, sweat standing out on their foreheads; great giants of men with the innocent clear eyes of children and the faces of epic warriors. . . .

Now a Bolshevik was speaking, one of their own men, violently, full of hate. They liked him no more than the other. It was not their mood. For the moment they were lifted out of the ordinary run of common thoughts, think-ing in terms of Russia, of Socialism, the world, as if it depended on them whether the Revolution were to live or die. . . .

Speaker succeeded speaker, debating amid tense silence, roars of approval, or anger: should we come out or not? Khanjunov returned, persuasive and sympathetic. But wasn't he an officer, and an *oboronets,* however much he talked of peace? Then a workman from Vasili Ostrov, but him they greeted with, "And are *you* going to give us peace, workingman?" Near us some men, many of them officers, formed a sort of *claque* to cheer the advocates of Neutrality. They kept shouting, "Khanjunov! Khanjunov!"

and whistled insultingly when the Bolsheviki tried to speak.

Suddenly the committeemen and officers on top of the automobile began to discuss something with great heat and much gesticulation. The audience shouted to know what was the matter, and all the great mass tossed and stirred. A soldier, held back by one of the officers, wrenched himself loose and held up his hand.

"Comrades!" he cried, "Comrade Krylenko is here and wants to speak to us." An outburst of cheers, whistlings, yells of *"Prosim! Prosim! Doloi!* Go ahead! Go ahead! Down with him!" in the midst of which the People's Commissar for Military Affairs clambered up the side of the car, helped by hands before and behind, pushed and pulled from below and above. Rising he stood for a moment, and then walked out on the radiator, put his hands on his hips and looked around smiling, a squat, short-legged figure, bare-headed, without insignia on his uniform.

The *claque* near me kept up a fearful shouting, "Khanjunov! We want Khanjunov! Down with him! Shut up! Down with the traitor!" The whole place seethed and roared. Then it began to move, like an avalanche bearing down upon us, great black-browed men forcing their way through.

"Who is breaking up our meeting?" they shouted. "Who is whistling here?" The *claque,* rudely burst asunder, went flying—nor did it gather again. . . .

"Comrade soldiers!" began Krylenko, in a voice husky with fatigue. "I cannot speak well to you; I am sorry; but I have not had any sleep for four nights. . . .

"I don't need to tell you that I am a soldier. I don't need to tell you that I want peace. What I must say is that the Bolshevik party, successful in the Workers' and Soldiers' Revolution, by the help of you and of all the rest

of the brave comrades who have hurled down forever
the power of the blood-thirsty bourgeoisie, promised to
offer peace to all the peoples, and that has already been
done—to-day!" Tumultuous applause.

"You are asked to remain neutral—to remain neutral
while the *yunkers* and the Death Battalions, who are *never*
neutral, shoot us down in the streets and bring back to
Petrograd Kerensky—or perhaps some other of the gang.
Kaledin is marching from the Don. Kerensky is coming
from the front. Kornilov is raising the *Tekhintsi* to repeat
his attempt of August. All these Mensheviki and Socialist
Revolutionaries who call upon you now to prevent civil
war—how have they retained the power except by civil
war, that civil war which has endured ever since last July,
and in which they constantly stood on the side of the
bourgeoisie, as they do now?

"How can I persuade you, if you have made up your
minds? The question is very plain. On one side are
Kerensky, Kaledin, Kornilov, the Mensheviki, Socialist
Revolutionaries, Cadets, Dumas, officers. . . . They tell
us that their objects are good. On the other side are the
workers, the soldiers and sailors, the poorest peasants.
The Government is in your hands. You are the masters.
Great Russia belongs to you. Will you give it back?"

While he spoke, he kept himself up by sheer evident
effort of will, and as he went on the deep sincere feeling
back of his words broke through the tired voice. At the
end he tottered, almost falling; a hundred hands reached
up to help him down, and the great dim spaces of the hall
gave back the surf of sound that beat upon him.

Khanjunov tried to speak again, but "Vote! Vote!
Vote!" they cried. At length, giving in, he read the resolution: that the *bronoviki* withdraw their representative from
the Military Revolutionary Committee, and declare their

neutrality in the present civil war. All those in favour should go to the right; those opposed, to the left. There was a moment of hesitation, a still expectancy, and then the crowd began to surge faster and faster, stumbling over one another, to the left, hundreds of big soldiers in a solid mass rushing across the dirt floor in the faint light. . . . Near us about fifty men were left stranded, stubbornly in favour, and even as the high roof shook under the shock of victorious roaring, they turned and rapidly walked out of the building—and, some of them, out of the Revolution. . . .

Imagine this struggle being repeated in every barracks of the city, the district, the whole front, all Russia. Imagine the sleepless Krylenkos, watching the regiments, hurrying from place to place, arguing, threatening, entreating. And then imagine the same in all the locals of every labour union, in the factories, the villages, on the battle-ships of the far-flung Russian fleets; think of the hundreds of thousands of Russian men staring up at speakers all over the vast country, workmen, peasants, soldiers, sailors, trying so hard to understand and to choose, thinking so intensely—and deciding so unanimously at the end. So was the Russian Revolution. . . .

Up at Smolny the new Council of People's Commissars was not idle. Already the first decree was on the presses, to be circulated in thousands through the city streets that night, and shipped in bales by every train southward and east:

In the name of the Government of the Russian Republic, chosen by the All-Russian Congress of Soviets of Workers' and Soldiers' Deputies with participation of peasant deputies, the Council of People's Commissars decrees:

1. The elections for the Constituent Assembly shall take place at the date determined upon—November 12.*

2. All electoral commissions, organs of local self-government, Soviets of Workers', Soldiers' and Peasants' Deputies, and soldiers' organisations on the front should make every effort to assure free and regular elections at the date determined upon.

In the name of the Government of the Russian Republic, *The President of the Council of People's Commissars,*
VLADIMIR ULIANOV—LENIN.

In the Municipal building the Duma was in full blast. A member of the Council of the Republic was talking as we came in. The Council, he said, did not consider itself dissolved at all, but merely unable to continue its labours until it secured a new meeting-place. In the meanwhile, its Committee of Elders had determined to enter *en masse* the Committee for Salvation. . . . This, I may remark parenthetically, is the last time history mentions the Council of the Russian Republic. . . .

Then followed the customary string of delegates from the Ministries, the *Vikzhel,* the Union of Posts and Telegraphs, for the hundredth time reiterating their determination not to work for the Bolshevik usurpers. A *yunker* who had been in the Winter Palace told a highly-coloured tale of the heroism of himself and his comrades, and disgraceful conduct of the Red Guards—all of which was devoutly believed. Somebody read aloud an account in the Socialist Revolutionary paper *Narod,* which stated that five hundred million rubles' worth of damage had been done in the Winter Palace, and describing in great detail the loot and breakage.

From time to time couriers came from the telephone

---

* November 25 on the New Style calendar that Reed has been using throughout the book.—*Ed.*

with news. The four Socialist Ministers had been released from prison. Krylenko had gone to Peter-Paul to tell Admiral Verderevsky that the Ministry of Marine was deserted, and to beg him, for the sake of Russia, to take charge under the authority of the Council of People's Commissars; and the old seaman had consented. . . . Kerensky was advancing north from Gatchina, the Bolshevik garrisons falling back before him. Smolny had issued another decree, enlarging the powers of the City Dumas to deal with food supplies.

This last piece of insolence caused an outburst of fury. He, Lenin, the usurper, the tyrant, whose Commissars had seized the Municipal garage, entered the Municipal warehouses, were interfering with the Supply Committees and the distribution of food—he presumed to define the limits of power of the free, independent, autonomous City Government! One member, shaking his fist, moved to cut off the food of the city if the Bolsheviki dared to interfere with the Supply Committees. . . . Another, representative of the Special Supply Committee, reported that the food situation was very grave, and asked that emissaries be sent out to hasten food trains.

Diedonenko announced dramatically that the garrison was wavering. The Semionovsky regiment had already decided to submit to the orders of the Socialist Revolutionary party; the crews of the torpedo-boats on the Neva were shaky. Seven members were at once appointed to continue the propaganda. . . .

Then the old Mayor stepped into the tribune: "Comrades and citizens! I have just learned that the prisoners in Peter-Paul are in danger. Fourteen *yunkers* of the Pavlovsk school have been stripped and tortured by the Bolshevik guards. One has gone mad. They are threatening to lynch the Ministers!" There was a whirlwind of indignation and horror, which only grew more violent when a stocky little woman dressed in grey demanded the floor, and lifted up her hard, metallic voice. This was Vera Slutskaya, veteran revolutionist and Bolshevik member of the Duma.

"That is a lie and a provocation!" she said, unmoved at the torrent of abuse. "The Workers' and Peasants' Government, which has abolished the death penalty, cannot permit such deeds. We demand that this story be investigated, at once; if there is any truth in it, the Government will take energetic measures!"

A commission composed of members of all parties was immediately appointed, and with the Mayor, sent to Peter-Paul to investigate. As we followed them out, the Duma was appointing another commission to meet Kerensky—to try and avoid bloodshed when he entered the capital. . . .

It was midnight when we bluffed our way past the guards at the gate of the fortress, and went forward under the faint glimmer of rare electric lights along the side of the church where lie the tombs of the Tsars, beneath the slender golden spire and the chimes, which, for months, continued to play *Bozhe Tsaria Khrani** every day at noon. . . . The place was deserted; in most of the windows there were not even lights. Occasionally we bumped into a burly figure stumbling along in the dark, who answered questions with the usual, *"Ya nié znayu."*

On the left loomed the low dark outline of Trubetskoi Bastion, that living grave in which so many martyrs of liberty had lost their lives or their reason in the days of the Tsar, where the Provisional Government had in turn shut up the Ministers of the Tsar, and now the Bolsheviki

* "God save the Tsar."

Коммссаръ

Главнаго Управленія до-

мовъ заключенія

.6. . Коя/1917 г..

№. 213...

Петроградъ, Смольный

Институтъ, комн. № 56.-

ПРОПУСКЪ

Представителю Американскихъ Соціалистическихъ

газетъ Д К О Н У   Р И Д У , во всѣ мѣста заклю-

ченія тг. Петрограда и Кронштата, для общаго зона'

комбенія положенія заключенныхъ и широкаго общес-

твеннаго освѣдомленія въ цѣляхъ прекращенія газетѓ

й травли противъ демократіи.-

ный К о м и с с а р ъ

С е к р е т а р ъ

Pass from the the Department of Prisons of the Soviet
Government to visit freely all prisons of Petrograd and
Cronstadt.

TRANSLATION:

          Commissar
Chief Bureau of Prisons
6th of November, 1917.
      No. 213
Petrograd, Smolny
Institute, room No. 56—

PASS

    To the representative of the American Socialist press, JOHN
REED, to visit all places of confinement in the cities of Petrograd and Cronstadt, for the purpose of generally investigating
the condition of the prisoners, and for thorough social information for the purpose of stopping the flood of newspaper
lies against democracy.

               Chief Commissar
               Secretary

had shut up the Ministers of the Provisional Government.

    A friendly sailor led us to the office of the commandant,
in a little house near the Mint. Half a dozen Red Guards,
sailors and soldiers were sitting around a hot room full of
smoke, in which a samovar steamed cheerfully. They wel-

comed us with great cordiality, offering tea. The commandant was not in; he was escorting a commission of "*sabotazhniki*" (sabotageurs) from the City Duma, who insisted that the *yunkers* were all being murdered. This seemed to amuse them very much. At one side of the room sat a bald-headed, dissipated-looking little man in a frock-coat and a rich fur coat, biting his moustache and staring around him like a cornered rat. He had just been arrested. Somebody said, glancing carelessly at him, that he was a Minister or something. . . . The little man didn't seem to hear it; he was evidently terrified, although the occupants of the room showed no animosity whatever toward him.

I went across and spoke to him in French. "Count Tolstoy," he answered, bowing stiffly. "I do not understand why I was arrested. I was crossing the Troitsky Bridge on my way home when two of these—of these—persons held me up. I was a Commissar of the Provisional Government attached to the General Staff, but in no sense a member of the Government. . . ."

"Let him go," said a sailor. "He's harmless. . . ."

"No," responded the soldier who had brought the prisoner. "We must ask the commandant."

"Oh, the commandant!" sneered the sailor. "What did you make a revolution for? To go on obeying officers?"

A *praporshchik** of the Pavlovsky regiment was telling us how the insurrection started. "The *polk* (regiment) was on duty at the General Staff the night of the 6th. Some of my comrades and I were standing guard; Ivan Pavlovich and another man—I don't remember his name—well, they hid behind the window-curtains in the room where the Staff was having a meeting, and they heard a great many things. For example, they heard orders to bring the

---

* Ensign, corresponding to our second lieutenant.—*Ed.*

Gatchina *yunkers* to Petrograd by night, and an order for the Cossacks to be ready to march in the morning. . . . The principal points in the city were to be occupied before dawn. Then there was the business of opening the bridges. But when they began to talk about surrounding Smolny, then Ivan Pavlovitch couldn't stand it any longer. That minute there was a good deal of coming and going, so he slipped out and came down to the guard-room, leaving the other comrade to pick up what he could.

"I was already suspicious that something was going on. Automobiles full of officers kept coming, and all the Ministers were there. Ivan Pavlovich told me what he had heard. It was half-past two in the morning. The secretary of the regimental Committee was there, so we told him and asked what to do.

" 'Arrest everybody coming and going!' he says. So we began to do it. In an hour we had some officers and a couple of Ministers, whom we sent up to Smolny right away. But the Military Revolutionary Committee wasn't ready; they didn't know what to do; and pretty soon back came the order to let everybody go and not arrest anybody else. Well, we ran all the way to Smolny, and I guess we talked for an hour before they finally saw that it was war. It was five o'clock when we got back to the Staff, and by that time most of them were gone. But we got a few, and the garrison was all on the march. . . ."

A Red Guard from Vasili Ostrov described in great detail what had happened in his district on the great day of the rising. "We didn't have any machine-guns over there," he said, laughing, "and we couldn't get any from Smolny. Comrade Zalkind, who was a member of the *Uprava* (Central Bureau) of the Ward Duma, remembered all at once that there was lying in the meeting-room of the *Uprava* a machine-gun which had been captured from the Germans. So he and I and another comrade went there. The Mensheviki and Socialist Revolutionaries were having a meeting. Well, we opened the door and walked right in on them, as they sat around the table—twelve or fifteen of them, three of us. When they saw us they stopped talking and just stared. We walked right across the room, uncoupled the machine-gun; Comrade Zalkind picked up one part, I the other, we put them on our shoulders and walked out—and not a single man said a word!"

"Do you know how the Winter Palace was captured?" asked a third man, a sailor. "Along about eleven o'clock we found out there weren't any more *yunkers* on the Neva side. So we broke in the doors and filtered up the different stairways one by one, or in little bunches. When we got to the top of the stairs the *yunkers* held us up and took away our guns. Still our fellows kept coming up, little by little, until we had a majority. Then we turned around and took away the *yunkers'* guns. . . ."

Just then the commandant entered—a merry-looking young non-commissioned officer with his arm in a sling, and deep circles of sleeplessness under his eyes. His eye fell first on the prisoner, who at once began to explain.

"Oh, yes," interrupted the other. "You were one of the committee who refused to surrender the Staff Wednesday afternoon. However, we don't want you, citizen. Apologies—" He opened the door and waved his arm for Count Tolstoy to leave. Several of the others, especially the Red Guards, grumbled protests, and the sailor remarked triumphantly, "*Vot!* There! Didn't I say so?"

Two soldiers now engaged his attention. They had been elected a committee of the fortress garrison to protest. The prisoners, they said, were getting the same food as the guards, when there wasn't even enough to keep a man from being hungry. "Why should the counter-revolutionists be treated so well?"

"We are revolutionists, comrades, not bandits," answered the commandant. He turned to us. We explained that rumours were going about that the *yunkers* were being tortured, and the lives of the Ministers threatened. Could we perhaps see the prisoners, so as to be able to prove to the world——?"

"No," said the young soldier, irritably. "I am not going to disturb the prisoners again. I have just been compelled to wake them up—they were sure we were going to massacre them. . . . Most of the *yunkers* have been released anyway, and the rest will go out to-morrow." He turned abruptly away.

"Could we talk to the Duma commission, then?"

The commandant, who was pouring himself a glass of tea, nodded. "They are still out in the hall," he said carelessly.

Indeed they stood there just outside the door, in the feeble light of an oil lamp, grouped around the Mayor and talking excitedly.

"Mr. Mayor," I said, "we are American correspondents. Will you please tell us officially the result of your investigations?"

He turned to us his face of venerable dignity.

"There is no truth in the reports," he said slowly. "Except for the incidents which occurred as the Ministers were being brought here, they have been treated with every consideration. As for the *yunkers,* not one has received the slightest injury. . . ."

Up the Nevsky, in the empty after-midnight gloom, an interminable column of soldiers shuffled in silence—to battle with Kerensky. In dim back streets automobiles without lights flitted to and fro, and there was furtive activity in Fontanka 6, headquarters of the Peasants' Soviet, in a certain apartment of a huge building on the Nevsky, and in the *Inzhnierny Zamok* (School of Engineers); the Duma was illuminated. . . .

In Smolny Institute the Military Revolutionary Committee flashed baleful fire, pounding like an over-loaded dynamo. . . .

NOTES TO CHAPTER VI

1 Appeals and Denunciations

Appeal to all Citizens and to the Military Organisations of the Socialist Revolutionary Party.

"The senseless attempt of the Bolsheviki is on the eve of complete failure. The garrison is disaffected. . . . The Ministries are idle, bread is lacking. All factions except a handful of Bolsheviki have left the Congress of Soviets. The Bolsheviki are alone! Abuses of all sorts, acts of vandalism and pillage, the bombardment of the Winter Palace, arbitrary arrests—all these crimes committed by the Bolsheviki have aroused against them the resentment of the majority of the sailors and soldiers. The *Tsentroflot* refuses to submit to the orders of the Bolsheviki. . . .

"We call upon all sane elements to gather around the Committee for Salvation of Country and Revolution; to take serious measures to be ready, at the first call of the Central Committee of the Party, to act against the counter-revolutionists, who will doubtless attempt to profit by these troubles provoked by the Bolshevik adventure, and to watch closely the external enemy, who also would like to take advantage of this opportune moment when the Front is weakened. . . ."

> *The Military Section of the Central Committee of
> the Socialist Revolutionary Party.*

* * * *

From *Pravda:*

"What is Kerensky?

"A usurper, whose place is in Peter-Paul prison, with Kornilov and Kishkin.

"A criminal and a traitor to the workers, soldiers and peasants, who believed in him.

"Kerensky? A murderer of soldiers!

"Kerensky? A public executioner of peasants!

"Kerensky? A strangler of workers!

"Such is the second Kornilov who now wants to butcher Liberty!"

CHAPTER VII

THE REVOLUTIONARY
FRONT

Saturday, November 10th. . . .

> Citizens!
> The Military Revolutionary Committee declares that it will
> not tolerate any violation of revolutionary order. . . .
> Theft, brigandage, assaults and attempts at massacre will
> be severely punished. . . .
> Following the example of the Paris Commune, the Com-
> mittee will destroy without mercy any looter or instigator of
> disorder. . . .

Quiet lay the city. Not a hold-up, not a robbery, not
even a drunken fight. By night armed patrols went through
the silent streets, and on the corners soldiers and Red
Guards squatted around little fires, laughing and singing.
In the daytime great crowds gathered on the sidewalks listening to interminable hot debates between students and
soldiers, business men and workmen.

Citizens stopped each other on the street.

"The Cossacks are coming?"

"No. . . ."

"What's the latest?"

"I don't know anything. Where's Kerensky?"

"They say only eight versts from Petrograd. . . . Is it true that the Bolsheviki have fled to the battleship *Avrora*?"

"They say so. . . ."

Only the walls screamed, and the few newspapers; denunciation, appeal, decree. . . .

An enormous poster carried the hysterical manifesto of the Executive Committee of the Peasants' Soviets:

. . . They (the Bolsheviki) dare to say that they are supported by the Soviets of Peasants' Deputies, and that they are speaking on behalf of the Soviets of Peasants' Deputies. . . .

Let all working-class Russia know that this is a LIE, AND THAT ALL THE WORKING PEASANTS—in the person of—the EXECUTIVE COMMITTEE OF ALL-RUSSIAN SOVIETS OF PEASANTS' DEPUTIES—refutes with indignation all participation of the organised peasantry in this criminal violation of the will of the working-classes. . . .

From the Soldier Section of the Socialist Revolutionary party:

The insane attempt of the Bolsheviki is on the eve of collapse. The garrison is divided. . . . The Ministries are on strike and bread is getting scarcer. All factions except the few Bolsheviki have left the Congress. The Bolsheviki are alone. . . .

We call upon all sane elements to group themselves around the Committee for Salvation of Country and Revolution, and to prepare themselves seriously to be ready at the first call of the Central Committee. . . .

In a hand-bill the Council of the Republic recited its wrongs:

Ceding to the force of bayonets, the Council of the Republic has been obliged to separate, and temporarily to interrupt its meetings.

The usurpers, with the words "Liberty and Socialism" on their lips, have set up a rule of arbitrary violence. They have arrested the members of the Provisional Government, closed the newspapers, seized the printing-shops. . . . This power must be considered the enemy of the people and the Revolution; it is necessary to do battle with it, and to pull it down. . . .

The Council of the Republic, until the resumption of its labours, invites the citizens of the Russian Republic, to group themselves around the . . . local Committees for Salvation of Country and Revolution, which are organising the overthrow of the Bolsheviki and the creation of a Government capable of leading the country to the Constituent Assembly.

Dielo Naroda said:

A revolution is a rising of all the people. . . . But here what have we? Nothing but a handful of poor fools deceived by Lenin and Trotsky. . . . Their decrees and their appeals will simply add to the museum of historical curiosities. . . .

And *Narodnoye Slovo* (People's Word—Populist Socialist):

"Workers' and Peasants' Government?" That is only a pipe-dream; nobody, either in Russia or in the countries of our Allies, will recognise this "Government"—or even in the enemy countries. . . .

The bourgeois press had temporarily disappeared. . . .*
Pravda had an account of the first meeting of the new

---

* For the fate of the press, "bourgeois," and socialist, see note 1, at the end of this chapter.—*Ed.*

Tsay-ee-kah, now the parliament of the Russian Soviet Republic. Miliutin, Commissar of Agriculture, remarked that the Peasants' Executive Committee had called an All-Russian Peasant Congress for December 13th.

"But we cannot wait," he said. "We must have the backing of the peasants. I propose that *we* call the Congress of Peasants, and do it immediately. . . ." The Left Socialist Revolutionaries agreed. An Appeal to the Peasants of Russia was hastily drafted, and a committee of five elected to carry out the project.

The question of detailed plans for distributing the land, and the question of Workers' Control of Industry, were postponed until the experts working on them should submit a report.

Three decrees were read and approved: first, Lenin's "General Rules for the Press," ordering the suppression of all newspapers inciting to resistance and disobedience to the new Government, inciting to criminal acts, or deliberately perverting the news;[1] the Decree of Moratorium for House-rents; and the Decree Establishing a Workers' Militia.[2] Also orders, one giving the Municipal Duma power to requisition empty apartments and houses, the other directing the unloading of freightcars in the railroad terminals, to hasten the distribution of necessities and to free the badly-needed rolling-stock. . . .

Two hours later the Executive Committee of the Peasants' Soviets was sending broadcast over Russia the following telegram:

The arbitrary organisation of the Bolsheviki, which is called "Bureau of Organisation for the National Congress of Peasants," is inviting all the Peasants' Soviets to send delegates to the Congress at Petrograd. . . .

The Executive Committee of the Soviets of Peasants'

Deputies declares that it considers, now as well as before, that it would be dangerous to take away from the provinces at this moment the forces necessary to prepare for elections to the Constituent Assembly, which is the only salvation of the working-class and the country. We confirm the date of the Congress of Peasants, *December 13th.*

At the Duma all was excitement, officers coming and going, the Mayor in conference with the leaders of the Committee for Salvation. A Councillor ran in with a copy of Kerensky's proclamation, dropped by hundreds from an aeroplane low-flying down the Nevsky, which threatened terrible vengeance on all who did not submit, and ordered soldiers to lay down their arms and assemble immediately in Mars Field.

The Minister-President had taken Tsarskoye Selo, we were told, and was already in the Petrograd campagna, five miles away. He would enter the city to-morrow—in a few hours. The Soviet troops in contact with his Cossacks were said to be going over to the Provisional Government. Chernov was somewhere in between, trying to organise the "neutral" troops into a force to halt the civil war.

In the city the garrison regiments were leaving the Bolsheviki, they said. Smolny was already abandoned. . . . All the Governmental machinery had stopped functioning. The employees of the State Bank had refused to work under Commissars from Smolny, refused to pay out money to them. All the private banks were closed. The Ministries were on strike. Even now a committee from the Duma was making the rounds of business houses, collecting a fund [3] to pay the salaries of the strikers. . . .

Trotsky had gone to the Ministry of Foreign Affairs and ordered the clerks to translate the Decree on Peace into foreign languages; six hundred functionaries had hurled their resignations in his face. . . . Shliapnikov, Commissar of Labour, had commanded all the employees of his Ministry to return to their places within twenty-four hours, or lose their places and their pension-rights; only the door-servants had responded. . . . Some of the branches of the Special Food Supply Committee had suspended work rather than submit to the Bolsheviki. . . . In spite of lavish promises of high wages and better conditions, the operators at the Telephone Exchange would not connect Soviet headquarters. . . .

The Socialist Revolutionary Party had voted to expel all members who had remained in the Congress of Soviets, and all who were taking part in the insurrection. . . .

News from the provinces. Moghilev had declared against the Bolsheviki. At Kiev the Cossacks had overthrown the Soviets and arrested all the insurrectionary leaders. The Soviet and garrison of Luga, thirty thousand strong, affirmed its loyalty to the Provisional Government, and appealed to all Russia to rally around it. Kaledin had dispersed all Soviets and Unions in the Don Basin, and his forces were moving north. . . .

Said a representative of the Railway Workers: "Yesterday we sent a telegram all over Russia demanding that war between the political parties cease at once, and insisting on the formation of a coalition Socialist Government. Otherwise we shall call a strike to-morrow night. . . . In the morning there will be a meeting of all factions to consider the question. The Bolsheviki seem anxious for an agreement. . . ."

"If they last that long!" laughed the City Engineer, a stout, ruddy man. . . .

As we came up to Smolny—not abandoned, but busier than ever, throngs of workers and soldiers running in and out, and doubled guards everywhere—we met the reporters for the bourgeois and "moderate" Socialist papers.

"Threw us out!" cried one, from *Volia Naroda*. "Bonch-Bruevich came down to the Press Bureau and told us to leave! Said we were spies!" They all began to talk at once: "Insult! Outrage! Freedom of the press!"

In the lobby were great tables heaped with stacks of appeals, proclamations and orders of the Military Revolutionary Committee. Workmen and soldiers staggered past, carrying them to waiting automobiles.

One began:

To the Pillory!

In this tragic moment through which the Russian masses are living, the Mensheviki and their followers and the Right Socialist Revolutionaries have betrayed the working-class. They have enlisted on the side of Kornilov, Kerensky and Savinkov. . . .

They are printing orders of the traitor Kerensky and creating a panic in the city, spreading the most ridiculous rumours of mythical victories by that renegade. . . .

Citizens! Don't believe these false rumours. No power can defeat the People's Revolution. . . . Premier Kerensky and his followers await speedy and well-deserved punishment. . . .

We are putting them in the Pillory. We are abandoning them to the enmity of all workers, soldiers, sailors and peasants, on whom they are trying to rivet the ancient chains. They will never be able to wash from their bodies the stain of the people's hatred and contempt.

Shame and curses to the traitors of the People! . . .

The Military Revolutionary Committee had moved into larger quarters, room 17 on the top floor. Red Guards were at the door. Inside, the narrow space in front of the railing was crowded with well-dressed persons, outwardly respectful but inwardly full of murder—bourgeois who wanted permits for their automobiles, or passports to leave the city, among them many foreigners. . . . Bill Shatov and Peters were on duty. They suspended all other business to read us the latest bulletins.

The One Hundred Seventy-ninth Reserve Regiment offers its unanimous support. Five thousand stevedores at the Putilov wharves greet the new Government. Central Committee of the Trade Unions—enthusiastic support. The garrison and squadron at Reval elect Military Revolutionary Committees to cooperate, and despatch troops. Military Revolutionary Committees control in Pskov and Minsk. Greetings from the Soviets of Tsaritsin, Rovensky-on-Don, Chernogorsk, Sevastopol. . . . The Finland Division, the new Committees of the Fifth and Twelfth Armies, offer allegiance. . . .

From Moscow the news is uncertain. Troops of the Military Revolutionary Committee occupy the strategic points of the city; two companies on duty in the Kremlin have gone over to the Soviets, but the Arsenal is in the hands of Colonel Riabtsev and his *yunkers*. The Military Revolutionary Committee demanded arms for the workers, and Riabtsev parleyed with them until this morning, when suddenly he sent an ultimatum to the Committee, ordering Soviet troops to surrender and the Committee to disband. Fighting has begun. . . .

In Petrograd the Staff submitted to Smolny's Commissars at once. The *Tsentroflot,* refusing, was stormed by Dybenko and a company of Cronstadt sailors, and a new *Tsentroflot* set up, supported by the Baltic and the Black Sea battleships. . . .

But beneath all the breezy assurance there was a chill

premonition, a feeling of uneasiness in the air. Kerensky's Cossacks were coming fast; they had artillery. Skrypnik, Secretary of the Factory-Shop Committees, his face drawn and yellow, assured me that there was a whole army corps of them, but he added, fiercely, "They'll never take us alive!" Petrovsky laughed weariedly, "To-morrow maybe we'll get a sleep—a long one. . . ." Lozovsky, with his emaciated, red-bearded face, said, "What chance have we? All alone. . . . A mob against trained soldiers!"

South and south-west the Soviets had fled before Kerensky, and the garrisons of Gatchina, Pavlovsk, Tsarskoye Selo were divided—half voting to remain neutral, the rest, without officers, falling back on the capital in the wildest disorder.

In the halls they were pasting up bulletins:

From Krasnoye Selo, November 10th, 8 A.M.

To be communicated to all Commanders of Staffs, Commanders in Chief, Commanders, everywhere and to all, all, all.

The ex-Minister Kerensky has sent a deliberately false telegram to every one everywhere to the effect that the troops of revolutionary Petrograd have voluntarily surrendered their arms and joined the armies of the former Government, the Government of Treason, and that the soldiers have been ordered by the Military Revolutionary Committee to retreat. The troops of a free people do not retreat nor do they surrender.

Our troops have left Gatchina in order to avoid bloodshed between themselves and their mistaken brother Cossacks, and in order to take a more convenient position, which is at present so strong that if Kerensky and his companions in arms should even increase their forces ten times, still there would be no cause for anxiety. The spirit of our troops is excellent.

In Petrograd all is quiet.

Chief of the Defence of Petrograd and the Petrograd District,

Lieutenant-Colonel MURAVIOV.

As we left the Military Revolutionary Committee, Antonov entered, a paper in his hand, looking like a corpse. "Send this," said he.

To All District Soviets of Workers' Deputies and Factory-Shop Committees

ORDER

The Kornilovist bands of Kerensky are threatening the approaches to the capital. All the necessary orders have been given to crush mercilessly the counter-revolutionary attempt against the people and its conquests.

The Army and the Red Guard of the Revolution are in need of the immediate support of the workers.

WE ORDER THE WARD SOVIETS AND FACTORY-SHOP COMMITTEES:

1. To move out the greatest possible number of workers for the digging of trenches, the erection of barricades and reinforcing of wire entanglements.

2. Wherever it shall be necessary for this purpose to stop work at the factories this shall be done immediately.

3. All common and barbed wire available must be assembled, and also all implements for the digging of trenches and the erection of barricades.

4. All available arms must be taken.

5. THE STRICTEST DISCIPLINE IS TO BE OBSERVED, AND EVERY ONE MUST BE READY TO SUPPORT THE ARMY OF THE REVOLUTION BY ALL MEANS.

Chairman of the Petrograd Soviet of Workers' and Soldiers' Deputies,
People's Commissar LEON TROTSKY.

Chairman of the Military Revolutionary Committee,
Commander in Chief PODVOISKY.

As we came out into the dark and gloomy day all around the grey horizon factory whistles were blowing, a hoarse and nervous sound, full of foreboding. By tens of thousands the working-people poured out, men and women; by tens of thousands the humming slums belched out their dun and miserable hordes. Red Petrograd was in danger! Cossacks! South and southwest they poured through the shabby streets toward the Moskovsky Gate, men, women and children, with rifles, picks, spades, rolls of wire, cartridge-belts over their working clothes. . . . Such an immense, spontaneous outpouring of a city never was seen! They rolled along torrent-like, companies of soldiers borne with them, guns, motor-trucks, wagons— the revolutionary proletariat defending with its breast the capital of the Workers' and Peasants' Republic!

Before the door of Smolny was an automobile. A slight man with thick glasses magnifying his red-rimmed eyes, his speech a painful effort, stood leaning against a mud-guard with his hands in the pockets of a shabby raglan. A great bearded sailor, with the clear eyes of youth, prowled restlessly about, absently toying with an enormous blue-steel revolver, which never left his hand. These were Antonov and Dybenko.

Some soldiers were trying to fasten two military bicycles on the running-board. The chauffeur violently protested; the enamel would get scratched, he said. True, he was a Bolshevik, and the automobile was commandeered from

a bourgeois; true the bicycles were for the use of orderlies.
But the chauffeur's professional pride was revolted. . . .
So the bicycles were abandoned. . . .

The People's Commissars for War and Marine were
going to inspect the revolutionary front—wherever that
was. Could we go with them? Certainly not. The automobile only held five—the two Commissars, two orderlies
and the chauffeur. However, a Russian acquaintance of
mine, whom I will call Trusishka, calmly got in and sat
down, nor could any argument dislodge him. . . .

I see no reason to doubt Trusishka's story of the
journey. As they went down the Suvorovsky Prospekt
some one mentioned food. They might be out three or
four days, in a country indifferently well provisioned. They
stopped the car. Money? The Commissar of War looked
through his pockets—he hadn't a kopek. The Commissar
of Marine was broke. So was the chauffeur. Trusishka
bought the provisions. . . .

Just as they turned into the Nevsky a tire blew out.

"What shall we do?" asked Antonov.

"Commandeer another machine!" suggested Dybenko,
waving his revolver. Antonov stood in the middle of the
street and signalled a passing machine, driven by a
soldier.

"I want that machine," said Antonov.

"You won't get it," responded the soldier.

"Do you know who I am?" Antonov produced a paper
upon which was written that he had been appointed Commander-in-Chief of all the armies of the Russian Republic,
and that every one should obey him without question.

"I don't care if you're the devil himself," said the
soldier, hotly. "This machine belongs to the First Machine-
Gun Regiment, and we're carrying ammunition in it, and
you can't have it. . . ."

The difficulty, however, was solved by the appearance of an old battered taxi-cab, flying the Italian flag. (In time of trouble private cars were registered in the name of foreign consulates, so as to be safe from requisition.) From the interior of this was dislodged a fat citizen in an expensive fur coat, and the party continued on its way.

Arrived at Narvskaya Zastava, about ten miles out, Antonov called for the commandant of the Red Guard. He was led to the edge of the town, where some few hundred workmen had dug trenches and were waiting for the Cossacks.

"Everything all right here, comrade?" asked Antonov.

"Everything perfect, comrade," answered the commandant. "The troops are in excellent spirits. . . . Only one thing—we have no ammunition. . . ."

"In Smolny there are two billion rounds," Antonov told him. "I will give you an order." He felt in his pockets. "Has any one a piece of paper?"

Dybenko had none—nor the couriers. Trusishka had to offer his note-book. . . .

"Devil! I have no pencil!" cried Antonov. "Who's got a pencil?" Needless to say, Trusishka had the only pencil in the crowd. . . .

We who were left behind made for the Tsarskoye Selo station. Up the Nevsky, as we passed, Red Guards were marching, all armed, some with bayonets and some without. The early twilight of winter was falling. Heads up they tramped in the chill mud, irregular lines of four, without music, without drums. A red flag crudely lettered in gold, "Peace! Land!" floated over them. They were very young. The expression on their faces was that of men who know they are going to die. . . . Half-fearful, half-con-

Исполнительный Комитет
Петроградскаго Сов.
Рабочихъ и Солдатскихъ
Депутатовъ

Военный Отдѣлъ

28 Октября 191.

26/435

УДОСТОВѢРЕНIЕ.

Настоящее удостовѣренiе дано представите.
Американской Соцiалъ – демократiи Интернацiона-
листъ товарищу ДЖОНУ ГИДЪ въ томъ,
Военно – Революцiонный Комитетъ Петербургскаго
Совѣта Рабочихъ и Солдатскихъ Депутатомъ пред-
ставляетъ имъ право свободнаго проѣзда по всѣмъ.
Сѣверному фронту въ цѣляхъ освѣдомленiя нашихъ
Американскихъ товарищей интернацiоналистовъ съ
событiями въ Россiи.

Предсѣдатель:

Секретарь:

This pass was issued upon the recommendation of Trotsky
three days after the Bolshevik Revolution. It gives me the
right of free travel to the Northern front—and an added note
on the back extends the permission to all fronts. It will be
noticed that the text speaks of the *Petersburg,* instead of the
Petrograd Soviet; *it* was the fashion among thorough-going
internationalists to abolish all names which smacked of
"patriotism"; but at the same time, it would not do to restore
the "Saint." . . .

TRANSLATION:

Executive Committee/Petrograd Soviet of
Workers' and Soldiers' Deputies
   Military Section
    28th October, 1917
       No. 1435

CERTIFICATE

The present certificate is given to the representative of the American Social Democracy, the internationalist comrade JOHN REED. The Military Revolutionary Committee of the Petersburg Soviet of Workers' and Soldiers' Deputies gives him the right of free travel through the entire Northern front, for the purpose of reporting to our American comrades-internationalists concerning events in Russia.

For the President
For the Secretary

---

temptuous, the crowds on the sidewalk watched them pass, in hateful silence. . . .

At the railroad station nobody knew just where Kerensky was, or where the front lay. Trains went no further, however, than Tsarskoye. . . .

Our car was full of commuters and country people going home, laden with bundles and evening papers. The talk was all of the Bolshevik rising. Outside of that, however, one would never have realised that civil war was rending mighty Russia in two, and that the train was headed into the zone of battle. Through the window we could see, in the swiftly-deepening darkness, masses of soldiers going along the muddy road toward the city, flinging out their arms in argument. A freight-train, swarming with troops and lit up by huge bonfires, was halted on a siding. That was all. Back along the flat horizon the glow of the city's lights faded down the night. A street-car crawled distantly along a far-flung suburb. . . .

Tsarskoye Selo station was quiet, but knots of soldiers stood here and there talking in low tones and looking uneasily down the empty track in the direction of Gatchina. I asked some of them which side they were on. "Well," said one, "we don't exactly know the rights of the matter. . . . There is no doubt that Kerensky is a provocator, but we do not consider it right for Russian men to be shooting Russian men."

In the station commandant's office was a big, jovial,

bearded common soldier, wearing the red arm-band of a regimental committee. Our credentials from Smolny commanded immediate respect. He was plainly for the Soviets, but bewildered.

"The Red Guards were here two hours ago, but they went away again. A Commissar came this morning, but he returned to Petrograd when the Cossacks arrived."

"The Cossacks are here then?"

He nodded, gloomily. "There has been a battle. The Cossacks came early in the morning. They captured two or three hundred of our men, and killed about twenty-five."

"Where are the Cossacks?"

"Well, they didn't get this far. I don't know just where they are. Off that way. . . ." He waved his arm vaguely westward.

We had dinner—an excellent dinner, better and cheaper than could be got in Petrograd—in the station restaurant. Nearby sat a French officer who had just come on foot from Gatchina. All was quiet there, he said. Kerensky held the town. "Ah, these Russians," he went on, "they are original! What a civil war! Everything except the fighting!"

We sallied out into the town. Just at the door of the station stood two soldiers with rifles and bayonets fixed. They were surrounded by about a hundred business men, Government officials and students, who attacked them with passionate argument and epithet. The soldiers were uncomfortable and hurt, like children unjustly scolded.

A tall young man with a supercilious expression, dressed in the uniform of a student, was leading the attack.

"You realise, I presume," he said insolently, "that by taking up arms against your brothers you are making yourselves the tools of murderers and traitors?"

"Now brother," answered the soldier earnestly, "you don't understand. There are two classes, don't you see, the proletariat and the bourgeoisie. We——"

"Oh, I know that silly talk!" broke in the student rudely. "A bunch of ignorant peasants like you hear somebody bawling a few catch-words. You don't understand what they mean. You just echo them like a lot of parrots." The crowd laughed. "I'm a Marxian student. And I tell you that this isn't Socialism you are fighting for. It's just plain pro-German anarchy!"

"Oh, yes, I know," answered the soldier, with sweat dripping from his brow. "You are an educated man, that is easy to see, and I am only a simple man. But it seems to me——"

"I suppose," interrupted the other contemptuously, "that you believe Lenin is a real friend of the proletariat?"

"Yes, I do," answered the soldier, suffering.

"Well, my friend, do you know that Lenin was sent through Germany in a closed car? Do you know that Lenin took money from the Germans?"

"Well, I don't know much about that," answered the soldier stubbornly, "but it seems to me that what he says is what I want to hear, and all the simple men like me. Now there are two classes, the bourgeoise and the proletariat——"

"You are a fool! Why, my friend, I spent two years in Schlüsselburg for revolutionary activity, when you were still shooting down revolutionists and singing 'God Save the Tsar!' My name is Vasili Keorgevich Panyin. Didn't you ever hear of me?"

"I'm sorry to say I never did," answered the soldier with humility. "But then, I am not an educated man. You are probably a great hero."

"I am," said the student with conviction. "And I am

opposed to the Bolsheviki, who are destroying our Russia, our free Revolution. Now how do you account for that?"

The soldier scratched his head. "I can't account for it at all," he said, grimacing with the pain of his intellectual processes. "To me it seems perfectly simple—but then, I'm not well educated. It seems like there are only two classes, the proletariat and the bourgeoisie———"

"There you go again with your silly formula!" cried the student.

"———only two classes," went on the soldier, doggedly. "And whoever isn't on one side is on the other . . ."

We wandered on up the street, where the lights were few and far between, and where people rarely passed. A threatening silence hung over the place—as of a sort of purgatory between heaven and hell, a political No Man's Land. Only the barber shops were all brilliantly lighted and crowded, and a line formed at the doors of the public bath; for it was Saturday night, when all Russia bathes and perfumes itself. I haven't the slightest doubt that Soviet troops and Cossacks mingled in the places where these ceremonies were performed.

The nearer we came to the Imperial Park, the more deserted were the streets. A frightened priest pointed out the headquarters of the Soviet, and hurried on. It was in the wing of one of the Grand Ducal palaces, fronting the Park. The windows were dark, the door locked. A soldier, lounging about with his hands in the top of his trousers, looked us up and down with gloomy suspicion. "The Soviet went away two days ago," said he. "Where?" A shrug. "*Nié znayu*. I don't know."

A little further along was a large building, brightly illuminated. From within came a sound of hammering. While we were hesitating, a soldier and a sailor came down the street, hand in hand. I showed them my pass from Smolny. "Are you for the Soviets?" I asked. They did not answer, but looked at each other in a frightened way.

"What is going on in there?" asked the sailor, pointing to the building.

"I don't know."

Timidly the soldier put out his hand and opened the door a crack. Inside a great hall hung with bunting and evergreens, rows of chairs, a stage being built.

A stout woman with a hammer in her hand and her mouth full of tacks came out. "What do you want?" she asked.

"Is there a performance to-night?" said the sailor, nervously.

"There will be private theatricals Sunday night," she answered severely. "Go away."

We tried to engage the soldier and sailor in conversation, but they seemed frightened and unhappy, and drew off into the darkness.

We strolled toward the Imperial Palaces, along the edge of the vast, dark gardens, their fantastic pavilions and ornamental bridges looming uncertainly in the night, and soft water splashing from the fountains. At one place, where a ridiculous iron swan spat unceasingly from an artificial grotto, we were suddenly aware of observation, and looked up to encounter the sullen, suspicious gaze of half a dozen gigantic armed soldiers, who stared moodily down from a grassy terrace. I climbed up to them. "Who are you?" I asked.

"We are the guard," answered one. They all looked very depressed, as undoubtedly they were, from weeks and weeks of all-day all-night argument and debate.

"Are you Kerensky's troops, or the Soviets'?"

There was silence for a moment, as they looked uneasily at each other. Then, "We are neutral," said he.

We went on through the arch of the huge Ekaterina Palace, into the Palace enclosure itself, asking for headquarters. A sentry outside a door in a curving white wing of the Palace said that the commandant was inside.

In a graceful, white, Georgian room, divided into unequal parts by a two-sided fire-place, a group of officers stood anxiously talking. They were pale and distracted, and evidently hadn't slept. To one, an oldish man with a white beard, his uniform studded with decorations, who was pointed out as the Colonel, we showed our Bolshevik papers.

He seemed surprised. "How did you get here without being killed?" he asked politely. "It is very dangerous in the streets just now. Political passion is running very high in Tsarskoye Selo. There was a battle this morning, and there will be another to-morrow morning. Kerensky is to enter the town at eight o'clock."

"Where are the Cossacks?"

"About a mile over that way." He waved his arm.

"And you will defend the city against them?"

"Oh dear no." He smiled. "We are holding the city for Kerensky." Our hearts sank, for our passes stated that we were revolutionary to the core. The Colonel cleared his throat. "About those passes of yours," he went on. "Your lives will be in danger if you are captured. Therefore, if you want to see the battle, I will give you an order for rooms in the officers' hotel, and if you will come back here at seven o'clock in the morning, I will give you new passes."

"So you are for Kerensky?" we said.

"Well, not exactly *for* Kerensky." The Colonel hesitated.

"You see, most of the soldiers in the garrison are Bolsheviki, and to-day, after the battle, they all went away in the direction of Petrograd, taking the artillery with them. You might say that none of the *soldiers* are for Kerensky; but some of them just don't want to fight at all. The *officers* have almost all gone over to Kerensky's forces, or simply gone away. We are—ahem—in a most difficult position, as you see. . . ."

We did not believe that there would be any battle. . . . The Colonel courteously sent his orderly to escort us to the railroad station. He was from the South, born of French immigrant parents in Bessarabia. "Ah," he kept saying, "it is not the danger or the hardships I mind, but being so long, three years, away from my mother. . . ."

Looking out of the window of the train as we sped through the cold dark toward Petrograd, I caught glimpses of clumps of soldiers gesticulating in the light of fires, and of clusters of armoured cars halted together at cross-roads, the chauffeurs hanging out of the turrets and shouting to each other. . . .

All the troubled night over the bleak flats leaderless bands of soldiers and Red Guards wandered, clashing and confused, and the Commissars of the Military Revolutionary Committee hurried from one group to another, trying to organise a defence. . . .

Back in town excited throngs were moving in tides up and down the Nevsky. Something was in the air. From the Warsaw Railway station could be heard far-off cannonade. In the *yunker* schools there was feverish activity. Duma members went from barracks to barracks, arguing and pleading, narrating fearful stories of Bolshevik violence —massacre of the *yunkers* in the Winter Palace, rape of the women soldiers, the shooting of the girl before the

Duma, the murder of Prince Tumanov. . . . In the Alexander Hall of the Duma building the Committee for Salvation was in special session; Commissars came and went, running. . . . All the journalists expelled from Smolny were there, in high spirits. They did not believe our report of conditions in Tsarskoye. Why, everybody knew that Tsarskoye was in Kerensky's hands, and that the Cossacks were now at Pulkovo. A committee was being elected to meet Kerensky at the railway station in the morning. . . .

One confided to me, in strictest secrecy, that the counter-revolution would begin at midnight. He showed me two proclamations, one signed by Gotz and Polkovnikov, ordering the *yunker* schools, soldier convalescents in the hospitals, and the Knights of St. George to mobilise on a war footing and wait for orders from the Committee for Salvation; the other from the Committee for Salvation itself, which read as follows:

To the Population of Petrograd!

Comrades, workers, soldiers and citizens of revolutionary Petrograd!

The Bolsheviki, while appealing for peace at the front, are inciting to civil war in the rear.

Do not listen to their provocatory appeals!

Do not dig trenches!

Down with the traitorous barricades!

Lay down your arms!

Soldiers, return to your barracks!

The war begun in Petrograd—is the death of the Revolution.

In the name of liberty, land, and peace, unite around the Committee for Salvation of Country and Revolution!

As we left the Duma a company of Red Guards, stern-faced and desperate, came marching down the dark, deserted street with a dozen prisoners—members of the local branch of the Council of Cossacks, caught red-handed plotting counter-revolution in their headquarters. . . .

A soldier, accompanied by a small boy with a pail of paste, was sticking up great flaring notices:

By virtue of the present, the city of Petrograd and its suburbs are declared in a state of siege. All assemblies or meetings in the streets, and generally in the open air, are forbidden until further orders.

N. PODVOISKY, President of the Military Revolutionary Committee.

As we went home the air was full of confused sound—automobile horns, shouts, distant shots. The city stirred uneasily, wakeful.

In the small hours of the morning a company of *yunkers,* disguised as soldiers of the Semionovsky Regiment, presented themselves at the Telephone Exchange just before the hour of changing guard. They had the Bolshevik password, and took charge without arousing suspicion. A few minutes later Antonov appeared, making a round of inspection. Him they captured and locked in a small room. When the relief came it was met by a blast of rifle-fire, several being killed.

Counter-revolution had begun. . . .

NOTES TO CHAPTER VII

1 On the Press

In the serious decisive hour of the Revolution and the days immediately following it, the Provisional Revolutionary Committee is compelled to adopt a series of measures against the counter-revolutionary press of all shades.

Immediately on all sides there are cries that the new Socialist authority is in this violating the essential principles of its own programme by an attempt against the freedom of the press.

The Workers' and Peasants' Government calls the attention of the population to the fact that in our country, behind this liberal shield, is hidden the opportunity for the wealthier classes to seize the lion's share of the whole press, and by this means to poison the popular mind and bring confusion into the consciousness of the masses.

Every one knows that the bourgeois press is one of the most powerful weapons of the bourgeoisie. Especially in this critical moment, when the new authority of the workers and peasants is in process of consolidation, it is impossible to leave it in the hands of the enemy, at a time when it is not less dangerous than bombs and machine-guns. This is why temporary and extraordinary measures have been adopted for the purpose of stopping the flow of filth and calumny in which the yellow and green press would be glad to drown the young victory of the people.

As soon as the new order is consolidated, all administrative measures against the press will be suspended; full liberty will be given it within the limits of responsibility before the law, in accordance with the broadest and most progressive regulations. . . .

Bearing in mind, however, the fact that any restrictions of the freedom of the press, even in critical moments, are admissible only within the bounds of necessity, the Council of People's Commissars decrees as follows:

1. The following classes of newspapers shall be subject to closure: (a) Those inciting to open resistance or disobedience to the Workers' and Peasants' Government; (b) Those creating confusion by obviously and deliberately perverting the news; (c) Those inciting to acts of a criminal character punishable by the laws.

2. The temporary or permanent closing of any organ of the press shall be carried out only by virtue of a resolution of the Council of People's Commissars.

3. The present decree is of a temporary nature, and will be revoked by a special *ukaz* when normal conditions of public life are re-established.

President of the Council of People's Commissars,
VLADIMIR ULIANOV (LENIN).

Supplementary Note on the Fate of the Press. Lenin softened his first attack on the freedom of the press by emphasizing that the decree was "of a temporary nature" and to be "revoked when normal conditions of public life are re-established." The French have a proverb which says, *"Ce n'est que le provisoire qui dure."* Since "normal conditions of public life" have never been re-established, there is today a one-party press in the Soviet Union. But the Bolsheviks had so long been advocates of freedom of the press while they were an opposition, that Lenin met at first much resistance even from many of his closest associates when he attempted to shut down the other socialist journals. It is even doubtful that Lenin himself intended to close them down permanently. The first step was the seizure of printing plants and stocks of paper "for the needs of the revolution." Sometimes this was on the orders of the Military-Revolutionary Committee, and sometimes by simple acts of groups of sailors, Red Guardsmen, or Anarchists. On November 8, *Russkaya Volya* was seized on the order of the Military-Revolutionary Committee and put under "the honorary guard of the splendid soldiers" of two regiments. The same day *Den* (*Dien,* according to Reed's spelling), a liberal daily ("bourgeois"), was closed "for starting a campaign of baiting of the Soviets." On November 9, the printing plants of *Birzhevaya Vedomost* and *Ogonka* were seized by Anarchists with the approval of the Committee. But various papers, particularly those of the socialist parties, continued to appear or to reappear. On November 19, the Printers' Union sent a delegation to the Military-Revolutionary Committee to demand that the attacks on the freedom of the workers' press should cease. They declared that the Bolsheviks were using violence to "force the people to read journals of a single tendency" thereby "undermining the Constituent Assembly." They were willing to fight the bourgeois press themselves, but thought that if the workers' press were free and strong it would not have to fear the bourgeois press either. On December 1, all non-Bolshevik papers except *Delo Naroda* and Gorky's *Novaya Zhizn* were closed for printing an appeal of the Provisional Government, which still claimed to be the legitimate one. Once more the papers reappeared within a few days. On November 20, Lenin drafted a decree declaring advertising a monopoly of the government and its official organ. Thereupon a number of workers' papers for the first time printed advertisements in the name of freedom of the press. These were closed down, but reappeared upon agreeing not to print ads. On November 17, Lenin introduced a resolution pledging that after the government had seized all stocks of paper and all printing plants and made them a government monopoly, it would permit their use by "political parties and groups in proportion . . . to the number of their adherents." But when the Constituent Assembly elections proved that the Socialist Revolutionaries had the most adherents, and should therefore have more newspapers than the Bolsheviks, Lenin decided to forget his promise. Socialist papers continued to play hide and seek with the government for some time. Gorky's *Novaya Zhizn* was not suppressed until the summer of 1918. Some socialist journals, particularly that of the Mensheviks, managed to continue to appear underground at infrequent intervals in sparse editions until early in the twenties.—*Ed.*

2   On Workers' Militia

1. All Soviets of Workers' and Soldiers' Deputies shall form a Workers' Militia.

2. This Workers' Militia shall be entirely at the orders of the Soviets of Workers' and Soldiers' Deputies.

3. Military and civil authorities must render every assistance in arming the workers and in supplying them with technical equipment, even to the extent of requisitioning arms belonging to the War Department of the Government.

4. This decree shall be promulgated by telegraph.

Petrograd, November 10, 1917.

People's Commissar of the Interior.

A. I. RYKOV.

This decree encouraged the formation of companies of Red Guards all over Russia, which became the most valuable arm of the Soviet Government in the ensuing civil war.

3   The Strike Fund

The fund for the striking Government employees and bank clerks was subscribed by banks and business houses of Petrograd and other cities, and also by foreign corporations doing business in Russia. All who consented to strike against the Bolsheviki were paid full wages, and in some cases their pay was increased. It was the realisation of the strike fund contributors that the Bolsheviki were firmly in power, followed by their refusal to pay strike benefits, which finally broke the strike.

CHAPTER VIII

COUNTER-REVOLUTION

Next morning, Sunday the 11th, the Cossacks entered Tsarskoye Selo, Kerensky[1] himself riding a white horse and all the church-bells clamouring. From the top of a little hill outside the town could be seen the golden spires and many-coloured cupolas, the sprawling grey immensity of the capital spread along the dreary plain, and beyond, the steely Gulf of Finland.

There was no battle. But Kerensky made a fatal blunder. At seven in the morning he sent word to the Second Tsarskoye Selo Rifles to lay down their arms. The soldiers replied that they would remain neutral, but would not disarm. Kerensky gave them ten minutes in which to obey. This angered the soldiers; for eight months they had been governing themselves by committee, and this smacked of the old régime. . . . A few minutes later Cossack artillery opened fire on the barracks, killing eight men. From that moment there were no more "neutral" soldiers in Tsarskoye. . . .

Petrograd woke to bursts of rifle-fire, and the tramping thunder of men marching. Under the high dark sky a cold wind smelt of snow. At dawn the Military Hotel and the Telegraph Agency had been taken by larger forces of *yunkers,* and bloodily recaptured. The Telephone Station was besieged by sailors, who lay behind barricades of barrels, boxes and tin sheets in the middle of the Morskaya, or sheltered themselves at the corner of the Gorokhovaya and of St. Isaac's Square, shooting at anything that moved. Occasionally an automobile passed in and out, flying the Red Cross flag. The sailors let it pass. . . .

Albert Rhys Williams was in the Telephone Exchange. He went out with the Red Cross automobile, which was ostensibly full of wounded. After circulating about the city, the car went by devious ways to the Mikhailovsky *yunker* school, headquarters of the counter-revolution. A French officer, in the court-yard, seemed to be in command. . . . By this means ammunition and supplies were conveyed to the Telephone Exchange. Scores of these pretended ambulances acted as couriers and ammunition trains for the *yunkers.*

Five or six armoured cars, belonging to the disbanded British Armoured Car Division, were in their hands. As Louise Bryant was going along St. Isaac's Square one came rolling up from the Admiralty, on its way to the Telephone Exchange. At the corner of the Gogolia, right in front of her, the engine stalled. Some sailors ambushed behind wood-piles began shooting. The machine-gun in the turret of the thing slewed around and spat a hail of bullets indiscriminately into the wood-piles and the crowd. In the archway where Miss Bryant stood seven people were shot dead, among them two little boys. Suddenly, with a shout, the sailors leaped up and rushed into the flaming open; closing around the monster, they thrust their bayonets into the loop-holes, again and again, yelling. . . . The chauffeur pretended to be wounded, and they let him go free—to run to the Duma and swell the tale

of Bolshevik atrocities. . . . Among the dead was a
British officer. . . .*

Later the newspapers told of another French officer,
captured in a *yunker* armoured car and sent to Peter-Paul.
The French Embassy promptly denied this, but one of
the City Councillors told me that he himself had procured
the officer's release from prison. . . .

Whatever the official attitude of the Allied Embassies,
individual French and British officers were active these
days, even to the extent of giving advice at executive
sessions of the Committee for Salvation.

All day long in every quarter of the city there were
skirmishes between *yunkers* and Red Guards, battles between armoured cars. . . . Volleys, single shots and the
shrill chatter of machine-guns could be heard, far and
near. The iron shutters of the shops were drawn, but
business still went on. Even the moving-picture shows, all
outside lights dark, played to crowded houses. The street-
cars ran. The telephones were all working; when you
called Central, shooting could be plainly heard over the
wire. . . . Smolny was cut off, but the Duma and the
Committee for Salvation were in constant communication
with all the *yunker* schools and with Kerensky at Tsarskoye.

At seven in the morning the Vladimir *yunker* school
was visited by a patrol of soldiers, sailors and Red Guards,
who gave the *yunkers* twenty minutes to lay down their
arms. The ultimatum was rejected. An hour later the
yunkers got ready to march, but were driven back by a
violent fusillade from the corner of the Grebetskaya and
the Bolshoy Prospekt. Soviet troops surrounded the build-

* This story of French and British officers directing the military cadets in
their attack on the telephone exchange presumably has no more truth in it
than the story that German officers led the Red Guard attack on the Winter
Palace. Louise Bryant, whom Reed cites as an eyewitness, does not tell it in
her account of the episode.—*Ed.*

ing and opened fire, two armoured cars cruising back and forth with machine guns raking it. The *yunkers* telephoned for help. The Cossacks replied that they dare not come, because a large body of sailors with two cannon commanded their barracks. The Pavlovsk school was surrounded. Most of the Mikhailov *yunkers* were fighting in the streets. . . .

At half-past eleven three field-pieces arrived. Another demand to surrender was met by the *yunkers* shooting down two of the Soviet delegates under the white flag. Now began a real bombardment. Great holes were torn in the walls of the school. The *yunkers* defended themselves desperately; shouting waves of Red Guards, assaulting, crumpled under the withering blast. . . . Kerensky telephoned from Tsarskoye to refuse all parley with the Military Revolutionary Committee.

Frenzied by defeat and their heaps of dead, the Soviet troops opened a tornado of steel and flame against the battered building. Their own officers could not stop the terrible bombardment. A Commissar from Smolny named Kirilov tried to halt it; he was threatened with lynching. The Red Guards' blood was up.

At half-past two the *yunkers* hoisted a white flag; they would surrender if they were guaranteed protection. This was promised. With a rush and a shout thousands of soldiers and Red Guards poured through windows, doors and holes in the wall. Before it could be stopped five *yunkers* were beaten and stabbed to death. The rest, about two hundred, were taken to Peter-Paul under escort, in small groups so as to avoid notice. On the way a mob set upon one party, killing eight more *yunkers*. . . . More than a hundred Red Guards and soldiers had fallen. . . .

Two hours later the Duma got a telephone message that the victors were marching toward the *Inzhnierny Zamok*

—the Engineers' school. A dozen members immediately set out to distribute among them armfuls of the latest proclamation of the Committee for Salvation. Several did not come back. . . . All the other schools surrendered without resistance, and the *yunkers* were sent unharmed to Peter-Paul and Cronstadt. . . .

The Telephone Exchange held out until afternoon, when a Bolshevik armoured car appeared, and the sailors stormed the place. Shrieking, the frightened telephone girls ran to and fro; the *yunkers* tore from their uniforms all distinguishing marks, and one offered Williams *anything* for the loan of his overcoat, as a disguise. . . . "They will massacre us! They will massacre us!" they cried, for many of them had given their word at the Winter Palace not to take up arms against the People. Williams offered to mediate if Antonov were released. This was immediately done; Antonov and Williams made speeches to the victorious sailors, inflamed by their many dead—and once more the *yunkers* went free. . . . All but a few, who in their panic tried to flee over the roofs, or to hide in the attic, and were found and hurled into the street.

Tired, bloody, triumphant, the sailors and workers swarmed into the switchboard room, and finding so many pretty girls, fell back in an embarrassed way and fumbled with awkward feet. Not a girl was injured, not one insulted. Frightened, they huddled in the corners, and then, finding themselves safe, gave vent to their spite. "Ugh! The dirty, ignorant people! The fools!" . . . The sailors and Red Guards were embarrassed. "Brutes! Pigs!" shrilled the girls, indignantly putting on their coats and hats. Romantic had been their experience passing up cartridges and dressing the wounds of their dashing defenders, the *yunkers,* many of them members of noble families, fighting to restore their beloved Tsar! These were just common workmen, peasants, "Dark People." . . .

The Commissar of the Military Revolutionary Committee, little Vishniak, tried to persuade the girls to remain. He was effusively polite. "You have been badly treated," he said. "The telephone system is controlled by the Municipal Duma. You are paid sixty rubles a month, and have to work ten hours and more. . . . From now on all that will be changed. The Government intends to put the telephones under control of the Ministry of Posts and Telegraphs. Your wages will be immediately raised to one hundred and fifty rubles, and your working-hours reduced. As members of the working-class you should be happy——"

Members of the *working-class* indeed! Did he mean to infer that there was anything in common between these —these animals—and *us?* Remain? Not if they offered a thousand rubles! . . . Haughty and spiteful the girls left the place. . . .

The employees of the building, the line-men and labourers—they stayed. But the switch-boards must be operated—the telephone was vital. . . . Only half a dozen trained operators were available. Volunteers were called for; a hundred responded, sailors, soldiers, workers. The six girls scurried backward and forward, instructing, helping, scolding. . . . So, crippled, halting, but *going,* the wires slowly began to hum. The first thing was to connect Smolny with the barracks and the factories; the second, to cut off the Duma and the *yunker* schools. . . . Late in the afternoon word of it spread through the city, and hundreds of bourgeois called up to scream, "Fools! Devils! How long do you think you will last? Wait till the Cossacks come!"

Dusk was already falling. On the almost deserted Nevsky, swept by a bitter wind, a crowd had gathered before the Kazan Cathedral, continuing the endless debate; a few workmen, some soldiers and the rest shopkeepers, clerks and the like.

"But Lenin won't get Germany to make peace!" cried one.

A violent young soldier replied. "And whose fault is it? Your damn Kerensky, dirty bourgeois! To hell with Kerensky! We don't want him! We want Lenin. . . ."

Outside the Duma an officer with a white arm-band was tearing down posters from the wall, swearing loudly. One read:

To the Population of Petrograd!

At this dangerous hour, when the Municipal Duma ought to use every means to calm the population, to assure it bread and other necessities, the Right Socialist Revolutionaries and the Cadets, forgetting their duty, have turned the Duma into a counter-revolutionary meeting, trying to raise part of the population against the rest, so as to facilitate the victory of Kornilov-Kerensky. Instead of doing their duty, the Right Socialist Revolutionaries and the Cadets have transformed the Duma into an arena of political attack upon the Soviets of Workers', Soldiers' and Peasants' Deputies, against the revolutionary Government of peace, bread and liberty.

Citizens of Petrograd, we, the Bolshevik Municipal Councillors elected by you—we want you to know that the Right Socialist Revolutionaries and the Cadets are engaged in counter-revolutionary action, have forgotten their duty, and are leading the population to famine, to civil war. We, elected by 183,000 votes, consider it our duty to bring to the attention of our constituents what is going on in the Duma, and declare that we disclaim all responsibility for the terrible but inevitable consequences. . . .

Far away still sounded occasional shots, but the city lay quiet, cold, as if exhausted by the violent spasms which had torn it.

In the Nicolai Hall the Duma session was coming to
an end. Even the truculent Duma seemed a little stunned.
One after another the Commissars reported—capture of
the Telephone Exchange, street-fighting, the taking of the
Vladimir school. . . . "The Duma," said Trupp, "is on
the side of the democracy in its struggle against arbitrary
violence; but in any case, whichever side wins, the Duma
will always be against lynchings and torture. . . ."

Konovski, Cadet, a tall old man with a cruel face:
"When the troops of the legal Government arrive in Petrograd, they will shoot down these insurgents, and that will
not be lynching!" Protests all over the hall, even from his
own party.

Here there was doubt and depression. The counter-
revolution was being put down. The Central Committee
of the Socialist Revolutionary party had voted lack of
confidence in its officers; the left wing was in control;
Avksentiev had resigned. A courier reported that the
Committee of Welcome sent to meet Kerensky at the railway station had been arrested. In the streets could be
heard the dull rumble of distant cannonading, south and
southwest. Still Kerensky did not come. . . .

Only three newspapers were out—*Pravda, Dielo Naroda*
and *Novaya Zhizn.* All of them devoted much space to the
new "coalition" Government. The Socialist Revolutionary
paper demanded a Cabinet without either Cadets or Bolsheviki. Gorky was hopeful; Smolny had made concessions. A purely Socialist Government was taking shape—
all elements except the bourgeoisie. As for *Pravda,* it
sneered:

We ridicule these coalitions with political parties whose
most prominent members are petty journalists of doubtful
reputation; our "coalition" is that of the proletariat and the
revolutionary Army with the poor peasants. . . .

On the walls a vainglorious announcement of the *Vikzhel*, threatening to strike if both sides did not compromise:

The conquerors of these riots, the saviours of the wreck of our country, these will be neither the Bolsheviki, nor the Committee for Salvation, nor the troops of Kerensky—but we, the Union of Railwaymen. . . .

Red Guards are incapable of handling a complicated business like the railways; as for the Provisional Government, it has shown itself incapable of holding the power. . . .

We refuse to lend our services to any party which does not act by authority of . . . a Government based on the confidence of all the democracy. . . .

Smolny thrilled with the boundless vitality of inexhaustible humanity in action.

In Trade Union headquarters Lozovsky introduced me to a delegate of the Railway Workers of the Nicolai line, who said that the men were holding huge mass-meetings, condemning the action of their leaders.

"All power to the Soviets!" he cried, pounding on the table. "The *oborontsi* in the Central Committee are playing Kornilov's game. They tried to send a mission to the Stavka, but we arrested them at Minsk. . . . Our branch has demanded an All-Russian Convention, and they refuse to call it. . . ."

The same situation as in the Soviets, the Army Committees. One after another the various democratic organisations, all over Russia, were cracking and changing. The Cooperatives were torn by internal struggles; the meetings of the Peasants' Executive broke up in stormy wrangling; even among the Cossacks there was trouble. . . .

On the top floor the Military Revolutionary Committee was in full blast, striking and slacking not. Men went in, fresh and vigorous; night and day and night and day they threw themselves into the terrible machine; and came out limp, blind with fatigue, hoarse and filthy, to fall on the floor and sleep. . . . The Committee for Salvation had been outlawed. Great piles of new proclamations[2] littered the floor:

. . . The conspirators, who have no support among the garrison or the working-class, above all counted on the suddenness of their attack. Their plan was discovered in time by Sub-Lieutenant Blagonravov, thanks to the revolutionary vigilance of a soldier of the Red Guard, whose name shall be made public. At the centre of the plot was the Committee for Salvation. Colonel Polkovnikov was in command of their forces, and the orders were signed by Gotz, former member of the Provisional Government, allowed at liberty on his word of honour. . . .

Bringing these facts to the attention of the Petrograd population, the Military Revolutionary Committee orders the arrest of all concerned in the conspiracy, who shall be tried before the Revolutionary Tribunal. . . .

From Moscow, word that the *yunkers* and Cossacks had surrounded the Kremlin and ordered the Soviet to lay down their arms. The Soviet forces complied, and as they were leaving the Kremlin, were set upon and shot down. Small forces of Bolsheviki had been driven from the Telephone and Telegraph offices; the *yunkers* now held the centre of the city. . . . But all around them the Soviet troops were mustering. Street-fighting was slowly gathering way; all attempts at compromise had failed. . . . On

the side of the Soviet, ten thousand garrison soldiers and a
few Red Guards; on the side of the Government, six
thousand *yunkers,* twenty-five hundred Cossacks and two
thousand White Guards.

The Petrograd Soviet was meeting, and next door the
new *Tsay-ee-kah,* acting on the decrees and orders[3] which
came down in a steady stream from the Council of People's Commissars in session upstairs; on the Order in
Which Laws Are to be Ratified and Published, Establishing an Eight-hour Day for Workers, and Lunacharsky's
"Basis for a System of Popular Education." Only a few
hundred people were present at the two meetings, most
of them armed. Smolny was almost deserted, except for
the guards, who were busy at the hall windows, setting up
machine-guns to command the flanks of the building.

In the *Tsay-ee-kah* a delegate of the *Vikzhel* was speaking:

"We refuse to transport the troops of either party. . . .
We have sent a committee to Kerensky to say that if he
continues to march on Petrograd we will break his lines
of communication. . . ."

He made the usual plea for a conference of all the
Socialist parties to form a new Government. . . .

Kamenev answered discreetly. The Bolsheviki would
be very glad to attend the conference. The centre of
gravity, however, lay not in composition of such a Government, but in its acceptance of the programme of the
Congress of Soviets. . . . The *Tsay-ee-kah* had deliberated on the declaration made by the Left Socialist Revolutionaries and the Social Democrats Internationalists, and
had accepted the proposition of proportional representation at the conference, even including delegates from the
Army Committees and the Peasants' Soviets. . . .

In the great hall, Trotsky recounted the events of the day.

"We offered the Vladimir *yunkers* a chance to surrender," he said. "We wanted to settle matters without bloodshed. But now that blood has been spilled there is only one way—pitiless struggle. It would be childish to think we can win by any other means. . . . The moment is decisive. Everybody must cooperate with the Military Revolutionary Committee, report where there are stores of barbed wire, benzine,* guns. . . . We've won the power; now we must keep it!"

The Menshevik Yoffe tried to read his party's declaration, but Trotsky refused to allow "a debate about principle."

"Our debates are now in the streets," he cried. "The decisive step has been taken. We all, and I in particular, take the responsibility for what is happening. . . ."

Soldiers from the front, from Gatchina, told their stories. One from the Death Battalion, Four Hundred Eighty-first Artillery: "When the trenches hear of this, they will cry, 'This is *our* Government!'" A *yunker* from Peterhof said that he and two others had refused to march against the Soviets; and when his comrades had returned from the defence of the Winter Palace they appointed him their Commissar, to go to Smolny and offer their services to the *real* Revolution. . . .

Then Trotsky again, fiery, indefatigable, giving orders, answering questions.

"The petty bourgeoisie, in order to defeat the workers, soldiers and peasants, would combine with the devil himself!" he said once. Many cases of drunkenness had been remarked the last two days. "No drinking, comrades! No

---

* What the English call *petrol* and the Americans *gasoline.—Ed.*

one must be on the streets after eight in the evening, except the regular guards. All places suspected of having
stores of liquor should be searched, and the liquor destroyed.[4] No mercy to the sellers of liquor. . . ."

The Military Revolutionary Committee sent for the
delegation from the Viborg section; then for the members
from Putilov. They clumped out hurriedly.

"For each revolutionist killed," said Trotsky, "we shall
kill five counter-revolutionists!"

Down-town again. The Duma brilliantly illuminated
and great crowds pouring in. In the lower hall wailing and
cries of grief; the throng surged back and forth before the
bulletinboard, where was posted a list of *yunkers* killed in
the day's fighting—or supposed to be killed, for most of
the dead afterward turned up safe and sound. . . . Up
in the Alexander Hall the Committee for Salvation held
forth. The gold and red epaulettes of officers were conspicuous, the familiar faces of the Menshevik and Socialist
Revolutionary intellectuals, the hard eyes and bulky
magnificence of bankers and diplomats, officials of the
old régime, and well-dressed women. . . .

The telephone girls were testifying. Girl after girl came
to the tribune—over-dressed, fashion-aping little girls,
with pinched faces and leaky shoes. Girl after girl, flush-
ing with pleasure at the applause of the "nice" people of
Petrograd, of the officers, the rich, the great names of
politics—girl after girl, to narrate her sufferings at the
hands of the proletariat, and proclaim her loyalty to all
that was old, established and powerful. . . .

The Duma was again in session in the Nicolai Hall.
The Mayor said hopefully that the Petrograd regiments
were ashamed of their actions; propaganda was making
headway. . . . Emissaries came and went, reporting hor-

ПРИКАЗЪ № 2.

Отъ Комитета гв. Финляндскаго рез. полка всѣмъ домовымъ Комитетамъ и гражданамъ Васильевскаго Острова.

Буржуазія избрала подлый способъ борьбы съ пролетаріатомъ, она въ разныхъ частяхъ города устроила огромные винные склады и наталкиваетъ на нихъ солдатъ, стараясь виномъ внести расколъ въ ряды Революціонной арміи.

Приказывается всѣмъ домовымъ Комитетамъ въ 3-хъ час. срокъ по расклейкѣ этого приказа сообщить лично и секретно объ имѣющихся у нихъ ЗАПАСАХЪ ВИНА Предсѣдат. Полк. Ком. гв. Финляндск. полка.

Лица, не исполнившія этого приказа, будутъ арестованы и преданы самому БЕЗПОЩАДНОМУ СУДУ, а ИМУЩЕСТВО ИХЪ будетъ КОНФИСКО-ВАНО, обнаруженные же запасы вина будутъ ВЗРЫВАТЬСЯ ДИНАМИТОМЪ черезъ 2 часа послѣ предупрежденія, ибо менѣе рѣшительныя мѣры, какъ намъ показалъ опытъ, не приводятъ къ желанной цѣли.

Объявляемъ, что особыхъ предупрежденій передъ началомъ взрыва не будетъ.

Полковой Комитетъ гв. Финляндскаго полка.

Revolutionary law and order. A proclamation of the Finland Regiment, in December, 1917, announcing desperate remedies for "wine pogroms." For translation see Note 5.

rible deeds by the Bolsheviki, interceding to save the
yunkers, busily investigating. . . .

"The Bolsheviki," said Trupp, "will be conquered by
moral force, and not by bayonets. . . ."

Meanwhile all was not well on the revolutionary front.
The enemy had brought up armoured trains, mounted
with cannon. The Soviet forces, mostly raw Red Guards,
were without officers and without a definite plan. Only
five thousand regular soldiers had joined them; the rest
of the garrison was either busy suppressing the *yunker*
revolt, guarding the city, or undecided what to do. At
ten in the evening Lenin addressed a meeting of delegates
from the city regiments, who voted overwhelmingly to
fight. A Committee of five soldiers was elected to serve as
General Staff, and in the small hours of the morning the
regiments left their barracks in full battle array. . . . Going home I saw them pass, swinging along with the regular tread of veterans, bayonets in perfect alignment,
through the deserted streets of the conquered city. . . .

At the same time, in the headquarters of the *Vikzhel*
down on the Sadovaya, the conference of all the Socialist
parties to form a new Government was under way.
Abramovich, for the centre Mensheviki, said that there
should be neither conquerors nor conquered—that bygones should be bygones. . . . In this were agreed all the
left wing parties. Dan, speaking in the name of the right
Mensheviki, proposed to the Bolsheviki the following conditions for a truce: The Red Guard to be disarmed, and
the Petrograd garrison to be placed at the orders of the
Duma; the troops of Kerensky not to fire a single shot or
arrest a single man; a Ministry of all the Socialist parties
except the Bolsheviki. For Smolny Riazanov and Kamenev
declared that a coalition ministry of all parties was acceptable, but protested at Dan's proposals. The Socialist Revo-

lutionaries were divided; but the Executive Committee of the Peasants' Soviets and the Populist Socialists flatly refused to admit the Bolsheviki. . . . After bitter quarrelling a commission was elected to draw up a workable plan. . . .

All that night the commission wrangled, and all the next day, and the next night. Once before, on the 9th of November, there had been a similar effort at conciliation, led by Martov and Gorky; but at the approach of Kerensky and the activity of the Committee for Salvation, the right wing of the Mensheviki, Socialist Revolutionaries and Populist Socialists suddenly withdrew. Now they were awed by the crushing of the *yunker* rebellion. . . .

Monday the 12th was a day of suspense. The eyes of all Russia were fixed on the grey plain beyond the gates of Petrograd, where all the available strength of the old order faced the unorganised power of the new, the unknown. In Moscow a truce had been declared; both sides parleyed, awaiting the result in the capital. Now the delegates to the Congress of Soviets, hurrying on speeding trains to the farthest reaches of Asia, were coming to their homes, carrying the fiery cross. In wide-spreading ripples news of the miracle spread over the face of the land, and in its wake towns, cities and far villages stirred and broke, Soviets and Military Revolutionary Committees against Dumas, Zemstvos and Government Commissars—Red Guards against White—street fighting and passionate speech. . . . The results waited on the word from Petrograd. . . .

Smolny was almost empty, but the Duma was thronged and noisy. The old Mayor, in his dignified way, was protesting against the Appeal of the Bolshevik Councillors. "The Duma is not a centre of counter-revolution," he said, warmly. "The Duma takes no part in the present struggle between the parties. But at a time when there is no legal power in the land, the only centre of order is the Municipal Self-Government. The peaceful population recognises this fact; the foreign Embassies recognise only such documents as are signed by the Mayor of the town. The mind of a European does not admit of any other situation, as the Municipal Self-Government is the only organ which is capable of protecting the interests of the citizens. The City is bound to show hospitality to all organisations which desire to profit by such hospitality, and therefore the Duma cannot prevent the distribution of any newspapers whatever within the Duma building. The sphere of our work is increasing, and we must be given full liberty of action, and our rights must be respected by both parties. . . .

"We are perfectly neutral. When the Telephone Exchange was occupied by the *yunkers* Colonel Polkovnikov ordered the telephones to Smolny disconnected, but I protested, and the telephones were kept going. . . ."

At this there was ironic laughter from the Bolshevik benches, and imprecations from the right.

"And yet," went on Schreider, "they look upon us as counter-revolutionaries and report us to the population. They deprive us of our means of transport by taking away our last motor-cars. It will not be our fault if there is famine in the town. Protests are of no use. . . ."

Kobozev, Bolshevik member of the Town Board, was doubtful whether the Military Revolutionary Committee had requisitioned the Municipal automobiles. Even granting the fact, it was probably done by some unauthorised individual, in the emergency.

"The Mayor," he continued, "tells us that we must not

make political meetings out of the Duma. But every Menshevik and Socialist Revolutionary here talks nothing but party propaganda, and at the door they distribute their illegal newspapers, *Iskri* (Sparks), *Slodatski Golos* and *Rabochaya Gazeta,* inciting to insurrection. What if we Bolsheviki should also begin to distribute our papers here? But this shall not be, for we respect the Duma. We have not attacked the Municipal Self-Government, and we shall not do so. But you have addressed an Appeal to the population, and we are entitled also to do so. . . ."

Followed him Shingariov, Cadet, who said that there could be no common language with those who were liable to be brought before the Attorney General for indictment, and who must be tried on the charge of treason. . . . He proposed again that all Bolshevik members should be expelled from the Duma. This was tabled, however, for there were no personal charges against the members, and they were active in the Municipal administration.

Then two Mensheviki Internationalists, declaring that the Appeal of the Bolshevik Councillors was a direct incitement to massacre. "If everything that is against the Bolsheviki is counter-revolutionary," said Pinkevich, "then I do not know the difference between revolution and anarchy. . . . The Bolsheviki are depending upon the passions of the unbridled masses; we have nothing but moral force. We will protest against massacres and violence from both sides, as our task is to find a peaceful issue."

"The notice posted in the streets under the heading 'To the Pillory,' which calls upon the people to destroy the Mensheviki and Socialist Revolutionaries," said Nazarev, "is a crime which you, Bolsheviki, will not be able to wash away. Yesterday's horrors are but a preface to what you are preparing by such a proclamation. . . . I have always tried to reconcile you with the other parties, but at present I feel for you nothing but contempt!"

The Bolshevik Councillors were on their feet, shouting angrily, assailed by hoarse, hateful voices and waving arms. . . .

Outside the hall I ran into the City Engineer, the Menshevik Gomberg and three or four reporters. They were all in high spirits.

"See!" they said. "The cowards are afraid of us. They don't dare arrest the Duma! Their Military Revolutionary Committee doesn't dare to send a Commissar into this building. Why, on the corner of the Sadovaya to-day, I saw a Red Guard try to stop a boy selling *Soldatski Golos*. . . . The boy just laughed at him, and a crowd of people wanted to lynch the bandit. It's only a few hours more, now. Even if Kerensky wouldn't come they haven't the men to run a Government. Absurd! I understand they're even fighting among themselves at Smolny!"

A Socialist Revolutionary friend of mine drew me aside. "I know where the Committee for Salvation is hiding," he said. "Do you want to go and talk with them?"

By this time it was dusk. The city had again settled down to normal—shop-shutters up, lights shining, and on the streets great crowds of people slowly moving up and down and arguing. . . .

At Number 86 Nevsky we went through a passage into a courtyard, surrounded by tall apartment buildings. At the door of apartment 229 my friend knocked in a peculiar way. There was a sound of scuffling; an inside door slammed; then the front door opened a crack and a woman's face appeared. After a minute's observation she led us in—a placid-looking, middle-aged lady who at once cried, "Kyril, it's all right!" In the dining-room, where a

samovar steamed on the table and there were plates full
of bread and raw fish, a man in uniform emerged from
behind the window-curtains, and another, dressed like a
workman, from a closet. They were delighted to meet an
American reporter. With a certain amount of gusto both
said that they would certainly be shot if the Bolsheviki
caught them. They would not give me their names, but
both were Socialist Revolutionaries. . . .

"Why," I asked, "do you publish such lies in your
newspapers?"

Without taking offence the officer replied, "Yes, I
know; but what can we do?" He shrugged. "You must
admit that it is necessary for us to create a certain frame
of mind in the people. . . ."

The other man interrupted. "This is merely an adventure on the part of the Bolsheviki. They have no intellectuals. . . . The Ministries won't work. . . . Russia is
not a city, but a whole country. . . . Realising that they
can only last a few days, we have decided to come to
the aid of the strongest force opposed to them—Kerensky
—and help to restore order."

"That is all very well," I said. "But why do you combine with the Cadets?"

The pseudo-workman smiled frankly. "To tell you the
truth, at this moment the masses of the people are following the Bolsheviki. We have no following—now. We
can't mobilise a handful of soldiers. There are no arms
available. . . . The Bolsheviki are right to a certain extent; there are at this moment in Russia only two parties
with any force—the Bolsheviki and the reactionaries, who
are all hiding under the coat-tails of the Cadets. The
Cadets think they are using us; but it is really we who are
using the Cadets. When we smash the Bolsheviki we shall
turn against the Cadets. . . ."

"Will the Bolsheviki be admitted into the new Government?"

He scratched his head. "That's a problem," he admitted. "Of course if they are not admitted, they'll probably do this all over again. At any rate, they will have a chance to hold the balance of power in the Constituent—that is, if there is a Constituent."

"And then, too," said the officer, "that brings up the question of admitting the Cadets into the new Government—and for the same reasons. You know the Cadets do not really want the Constituent Assembly—not if the Bolsheviki can be destroyed now." He shook his head. "It is not easy for us Russians, politics. You Americans are born politicians; you have had politics all your lives. But for us—well, it has only been a year, you know!"

"What do you think of Kerensky?" I asked.

"Oh, Kerensky is guilty of the sins of the Provisional Government," answered the other man. "Kerensky himself forced us to accept coalition with the bourgeoisie. If he had resigned, as he threatened, it would have meant a new Cabinet crisis only sixteen weeks before the Constituent Assembly, and that we wanted to avoid."

"But didn't it amount to that anyway?"

"Yes, but how were we to know? They tricked us—the Kerenskys and Avksentievs. Gotz is a little more radical. I stand with Chernov, who is a real revolutionist. . . . Why, only to-day Lenin sent word that he would not object to Chernov entering the Government.

"We wanted to get rid of the Kerensky Government too, but we thought it better to wait for the Constituent. . . . At the beginning of this affair I was with the Bolsheviki, but the Central Committee of my party voted unanimously against it—and what could I do? It was a matter of party discipline. . . .

"In a week the Bolshevik Government will go to pieces; if the Socialist Revolutionaries could only stand aside and wait, the Government would fall into their hands. But if we wait a week the country will be so disorganised that the German imperialists will be victorious. That is why we began our revolt with only two regiments of soldiers promising to support us—and they turned against us. . . . That left only the *yunkers*. . . ."

"How about the Cossacks?"

The officer sighed. "They did not move. At first they said they would come out if they had infantry support. They said moreover that they had their men with Kerensky, and that they were doing their part. . . . Then, too, they said that the Cossacks were always accused of being the hereditary enemies of democracy. . . . And finally, 'The Bolsheviki promise that they will not take away our land. There is no danger to us. We remain neutral.' "

During this talk people were constantly entering and leaving—most of them officers, their shoulder-straps torn off. We could see them in the hall, and hear their low, vehement voices. Occasionally, through the half-drawn portières, we caught a glimpse of a door opening into a bath-room, where a heavily-built officer in a colonel's uniform sat on the toilet, writing something on a pad held in his lap. I recognised Colonel Polkovnikov, former commandant of Petrograd, for whose arrest the Military Revolutionary Committee would have paid a fortune.

"Our programme?" said the officer. "This is it. Land to be turned over to the Land Committees. Workmen to have full representation in the control of industry. An energetic peace programme, but not an ultimatum to the world such as the Bolsheviki issued. The Bolsheviki cannot keep their promises to the masses, even to the country itself. We won't let them. . . . They stole our land programme in order to get the support of the peasants. That is dishonest. If they had waited for the Constituent Assembly——"

"It doesn't matter about the Constituent Assembly!" broke in the officer. "If the Bolsheviki want to establish a Socialist state here, we cannot work with them in any event! Kerensky made the great mistake. He let the Bolsheviki know what he was going to do by announcing in the Council of the Republic that he had ordered their arrest. . . ."

"But what," I said, "do you intend to do now?"

The two men looked at one another. "You will see in a few days. If there are enough troops from the front on our side, we shall not compromise with the Bolsheviki. If not, perhaps we shall be forced to. . . ."

Out again on the Nevsky we swung on the step of a streetcar bulging with people, its platforms bent down from the weight and scraping along the ground, which crawled with agonising slowness the long miles to Smolny.

Meshkovsky, a neat, frail little man, was coming down the hall, looking worried. The strikes in the Ministries, he told us, were having their effect. For instance, the Council of People's Commissars had promised to publish the Secret Treaties; but Neratov, the functionary in charge, had disappeared, taking the documents with him. They were supposed to be hidden in the British Embassy. . . .

Worst of all, however, was the strike in the banks. "Without money," said Menshinsky, "we are helpless. The wages of the railroad men, of the postal and telegraph employees, must be paid. . . . The banks are closed; and the key to the situation, the State Bank, is also shut. All the bank-clerks in Russia have been bribed to stop work. . . .

"But Lenin has issued an order to dynamite the State

Bank vaults, and there is a Decree just out, ordering the private banks to open to-morrow, or we will open them ourselves!"

The Petrograd Soviet was in full swing, thronged with armed men. Trotsky reporting:

"The Cossacks are falling back from Krasnoye Selo." (Sharp, exultant cheering.) "But the battle is only beginning. At Pulkovo heavy fighting is going on. All available forces must be hurried there. . . .

"From Moscow, bad news. The Kremlin is in the hands of the *yunkers*, and the workers have only a few arms. The result depends upon Petrograd.

"At the front, the decrees on Peace and Land are provoking great enthusiasm. Kerensky is flooding the trenches with tales of Petrograd burning and bloody, of women and children massacred by the Bolsheviki. But no one believes him. . . .

"The crusers *Oleg, Avrora* and *Respublica* are anchored in the Neva, their guns trained on the approaches to the city. . . ."

"Why aren't you out there with the Red Guards?" shouted a rough voice.

"I'm going now!" answered Trotsky, and left the platform. His face a little paler than usual, he passed down the side of the room, surrounded by eager friends, and hurried out to the waiting automobile.

Kamenev now spoke, describing the proceedings of the reconciliation conference. The armistice conditions proposed by the Mensheviki, he said, had been contemptuously rejected. Even the branches of the Railwaymen's Union had voted against such a proposition. . . .

"Now that we've won the power and are sweeping all Russia," he declared, "all they ask of us are three little things: 1. To surrender the power. 2. To make the soldiers continue the war. 3. To make the peasants forget about the land. . . .

Lenin appeared for a moment, to answer the accusations of the Socialist Revolutionaries:

"They charge us with stealing their land programme. . . . If that is so, we bow to them. It is good enough for us. . . ."

So the meeting roared on, leader after leader explaining, exhorting, arguing, soldier after soldier, workman after workman, standing up to speak his mind and his heart. . . . The audience flowed, changing and renewed continually. From time to time men came in, yelling for the members of such and such a detachment, to go to the front; others, relieved, wounded, or coming to Smolny for arms and equipment, poured in. . . .

It was almost three o'clock in the morning when, as we left the hall, Holtzman, of the Military Revolutionary Committee, came running down the hall with a transfigured face.

"It's all right!" he shouted, grabbing my hands. "Telegram from the front. Kerensky is smashed! Look at this!"

He held out a sheet of paper, scribbled hurriedly in pencil, and then, seeing we couldn't read it, he declaimed aloud:

Pulkovo. Staff. 2.10 A.M.
The night of October 30th to 31st will go down in history. The attempt of Kerensky to move counter-revolutionary troops against the capital of the Revolution has been decisively repulsed. Kerensky is retreating, we are advancing. The soldiers, sailors and workers of Petrograd have shown that they can and will with arms in their hands enforce the will and authority of the democracy. The bourgeoisie tried to isolate the revolutionary army. Kerensky attempted to break

it by the force of the Cossacks. Both plans met a pitiful defeat.

The grand idea of the domination of the worker and peasant democracy closed the ranks of the army and hardened its will. All the country from now on will be convinced that the Power of the Soviets is no ephemeral thing, but an invincible fact. . . . The repulse of Kerensky is the repulse of the land owners, the bourgeoisie and the Kornilovists in general. The repulse of Kerensky is the confirmation of the right of the people to a peaceful free life, to land, bread and power. The Pulkovo detachment by its valorous blow has strengthened the cause of the Workers' and Peasants' Revolution. There is no return to the past. Before us are struggles, obstacles and sacrifices. But the road is clear and victory is certain.

Revolutionary Russia and the Soviet Power can be proud of their Pulkovo detachment, acting under the command of Colonel Walden. Eternal memory to those who fell! Glory to the warriors of the Revolution, the soldiers and the officers who were faithful to the People!

Long live revolutionary, popular, Socialist Russia!

In the name of the Council,

L. TROTSKY, People's Commissar. . . .

Driving home across Znamensky Square, we made out an unusual crowd in front of the Nicolai Railway Station. Several thousand sailors were massed there, bristling with rifles.

Standing on the steps, a member of the *Vikzhel* was pleading with them.

"Comrades, we cannot carry you to Moscow. We are neutral. We do not carry troops for either side. We cannot take you to Moscow, where already there is terrible civil war. . . ."

All the seething Square roared at him; the sailors began

to surge forward. Suddenly another door was flung wide; in it stood two or three brakemen, a fireman or so.

"This way, comrades!" cried one. "We will take you to Moscow—or Vladivostok, if you like! Long live the Revolution!"

NOTES TO CHAPTER VIII

1 Kerensky's Advance

On November 9th Kerensky and his Cossacks arrived at Gatchina, where the garrison, hopelessly split into two factions, immediately surrendered. The members of the Gatchina Soviet were arrested, and at first threatened with death; later they were released on good behaviour.

The Cossack advance-guards, practically unopposed, occupied Pavlovsk, Alexandrovsk and other stations, and reached the outskirts of Tsarskoye Selo next morning November 10th. At once the garrison divided into three groups—the officers, loyal to Kerensky; part of the soldiers and non-commissioned officers, who declared themselves "neutral"; and most of the rank and file, who were for the Bolsheviki. The Bolshevik soldiers, who were without leaders or organisation, fell back toward the capital. The local Soviet also withdrew to the village of Pulkovo.

From Pulkovo six members of the Tsarskoye Selo Soviet went with an automobile-load of proclamations to Gatchina, to propagandise the Cossacks. They spent most of the day going around Gatchina from one Cossack barracks to another, pleading, arguing and explaining. Toward evening some officers discovered their presence and they were arrested and brought before General Krasnov, who said, "You fought against Kornilov: now you are opposing Kerensky. I'll have you all shot!"

After reading aloud to them the order appointing him commander-in-chief of the Petrograd District, Krasnov asked if they were Bolsheviki. They replied in the affirmative—upon which Krasnov went away; a short time later an officer came and set them free, saying that it was by order of General Krasnov. . . .

In the meanwhile delegations continued to arrive from Petrograd; from the Duma, the Commitee for Salvation, and, last of all, from the *Vikzhel*. The Union of Railway Workers insisted that some agreement be reached to halt the civil war, and demanded that Kerensky treat with the Bolsheviki, and that he stop the advance on Petrograd. In case of refusal, the *Vikzhel* threatened a general strike at midnight of November 11th.

Kerensky asked to be allowed to discuss the matter with the Socialist Ministers and with the Committee for Salvation. He was plainly undecided.

On the 11th Cossack outposts reached Krasnoye Selo, from which the local Soviet and the heterogeneous forces of the Military Revolutionary Committee precipitately retired, some of them surrendering. . . . That night they also touched Pulkovo, where the first real resistance was encountered. . . .

Cossacks deserters began to dribble into Petrograd, declaring that Kerensky had lied to them, that he had spread broadcast over the front proclamations which said that Petrograd was burning, that the Bolsheviki had invited the Germans to come in, and that they were murdering women and children and looting indiscriminately. . . .

The Military Revolutionary Committee immediately sent out some dozens of "agitators," with thousands of printed appeals, to inform the Cossacks of the real situation. . . .

2 Proclamations of the Military Revolutionary Committee

"To All Soviets of Workers', Soldiers' and Peasants' Deputies.

"The All-Russian Congress of Soviets of Workers', Soldiers' and Peasants' Deputies charges the local Soviets immediately to take the most energetic measures to oppose all counter-revolutionary anti-Semitic disturbances, and all *pogroms* of whatever nature. The honour of the workers', peasants' and soldiers' Revolution cannot tolerate any disorders. . . .

"The Red Guard of Petrograd, the revolutionary garrison and the sailors have maintained complete order in the capital.

"Workers, soldiers, and peasants, everywhere you should follow the example of the workers and soldiers of Petrograd.

"Comrades soldiers and Cossacks, on us falls the duty of keeping real revolutionary order.

"All revolutionary Russia and the whole world have their eyes on you. . . ."

*   *   *   *

"The All-Russian Congress of Soviets decrees:

"To abolish capital punishment at the Front, which was reintroduced by Kerensky.

"Complete freedom of propaganda is to be re-established in the country. All soldiers and revolutionary officers now under arrest for so-called political 'crimes' are at once to be set free."

*   *   *   *

"The ex-Premier Kerensky, overthrown by the people, refuses to submit to the Congress of Soviets and attempts to struggle against the legal Government elected by the All-Russian Congress —the Council of People's Commissars. The Front has refused to aid Kerensky. Moscow has rallied to the new Government. In many cities (Minsk, Moghilev, Kharkov) the power is in the hands of the Soviets. No infantry detachment consents to march against the Workers' and Peasants' Government, which, in accord with the firm will of the Army and the people, has begun peace negotiations and has given the land to the peasants. . . .

"We give public warning that if the Cossacks do not halt Kerensky, who has deceived them and is leading them against Petrograd, the revolutionary forces will rise with all their might for the defence of the precious conquests of the Revolution—Peace and Land.

"Citizens of Petrograd! Kerensky fled from the city, abandoning the authority to Kishkin, who wanted to surrender the capital to the Germans; Rutenburg, of the Black Band, who sabotaged the Municipal Food Supply; and Paltchinsky, hated by the whole democracy. Kerensky has fled, abandoning you to the Germans, to famine, to bloody massacres. The revolting people have arrested Kerensky's Ministers, and you have seen how the order and supplying of Petrograd at once improved. Kerensky, at the demand of the aristocrat proprietors, the capitalists, speculators, marches against you for the purpose of giving back the land to the landowners, and continuing the hated and ruinous war.

"Citizens of Petrograd! We know that the great majority of you are in favour of the people's revolutionary authority, against the Kornilovtsi led by Kerensky. Do not be deceived by the lying declarations of the impotent bourgeois conspirators, who will be pitilessly crushed.

"Workers, soldiers, peasants! We call upon you for revolutionary devotion and discipline.

"Millions of peasants and soldiers are with us.

"The victory of the people's Revolution is assured!"

3   Acts of the Council of People's Commissars

In this book I am giving only such decrees as are in my opinion pertinent to the Bolshevik conquest of power. The rest belong to a detailed account of the Structure of the Soviet State, for which I have no place in this work. This will be dealt with very fully in the second volume, now in preparation, "Kornilov to Brest-Litovsk."

Concerning Dwelling-Places

1. The independent Municipal Self-Governments have the right to sequestrate all unoccupied or uninhabited dwelling-places.

2. The Municipalities may, according to laws and arrangements established by them, install in all available lodgings citizens who have no place to live, or who live in congested or unhealthy lodgings.

3. The Municipalities may establish a service of inspection of dwelling places, organise it and define its powers.

4. The Municipalities may issue orders on the institution of House Committees, define their organisation, their powers and give them juridical authority.

5. The Municipalities may create Housing Tribunals, define their powers and their authority.

6. This decree is promulgated by telegraph.

People's Commissar of the Interior,

A. I. RYKOV.

*   *   *   *

On Social Insurance

The Russian proletariat has inscribed on its banners the promise of complete Social Insurance of wage-workers, as well as of the town and village poor. The Government of the Tsar, the proprietors and the capitalists, as well as the Government of coalition

and conciliation, failed to realise the desires of the workers with
regard to Social Insurance.

The Workers' and Peasants' Government, relying upon the
support of the Soviets of Workers', Soldiers' and Peasants' Deputies, announces to the working-class of Russia and to the town and
village poor, that it will immediately prepare laws on Social Insurance based on the formulas proposed by the Labour organisations:

1. Insurance for all wage-workers without exception, as well as
for all urban and rural poor.

2. Insurance to cover all categories of loss of working capacity,
such as illness, infirmities, old age, childbirth, widowhood, orphan-
age, and unemployment.

3. All the costs of insurance to be charged to employers.

4. Compensation of at least full wages in all loss of working
capacity and unemployment.

5 Complete workers' self-government of all Insurance institutions.

In the name of the Government of the Russian Republic,

The People's Commissar of Labour,

ALEXANDER SHLIAPNIKOV.

On Popular Education

Citizens of Russia!

With the insurrection of November 7th the working masses
have won for the first time the real power.

The All-Russian Congress of Soviets has temporarily transferred
this power both to its Executive Committee and to the Council of
People's Commissars.

By the will of the revolutionary people, I have been appointed
People's Commissar of Education.

The work of guiding in general the people's education, inasmuch
as it remains with the central government, is, until the Constituent
Assembly meets, entrusted to a Commission on the People's Education, whose chairman and executive is the People's Commissar.

Upon what fundamental propositions will rest this State Commission? How is its sphere of competence determined?

The General Line of Educational Activity: Every genuinely
democratic power must, in the domain of education, in a country
where illiteracy and ignorance reign supreme, make its first aim

the struggle against this darkness. It must acquire in the shortest time *universal literacy*, by organising a network of schools answering to the demands of modern pedagogics; it must introduce universal, obligatory and free tuition for all, and establish at the same time a series of such teachers' institutes and seminaries as will in the shortest time furnish a powerful army of people's teachers so necessary for the universal instruction of the population of our boundless Russia.

Decentralisation: The State Commission on People's Education is by no means a central power governing the institutions of instruction and education. On the contrary, the entire school work ought to be transferred to the organs of local self-government. The independent work of the workers, soldiers and peasants, establishing on their own initiative cultural educational organisations, must be given full autonomy, both by the State centre and the Municipal centres.

The work of the State Commission serves as a link and helpmate to organise resources of material and moral support to the Municipal and private institutions, particularly to those with a class-character established by the workers.

The State Committee on People's Education: A whole series of invaluable law projects was elaborated from the beginning of the Revolution by the State Committee for People's Education, a tolerably democratic body as to its composition, and rich in experts. The State Commission sincerely desires the collaboration of this Committee.

It has addressed itself to the bureau of the Committee, with the request at once to convoke an extraordinary session of the Committee for the fulfilment of the following programme:

1. The revision of rules of representation in the Committee, in the sense of greater democratisation.

2. The revision of the Committee's rights in the sense of widening them, and of converting the Committee into a fundamental State institute for the elaboration of law projects calculated to reorganise public instruction and education in Russia upon democratic principles.

3. The revision, jointly with the new State Commission, of the laws already created by the Committee, a revision required by the fact that in editing them the Committee had to take into account the bourgeois spirit of previous Ministries, which obstructed it even in this its narrowed form.

After this revision these laws will be put into effect without any bureaucratic red tape, in the revolutionary order.

The Pedagogues and the Societists: The State Commission welcomes the pedagogues to the bright and honourable work of educating the people—the masters of the country.

No one measure in the domain of the people's education ought to be adopted by any power without the attentive deliberation of those who represent the pedagogues.

On the other hand, a decision cannot by any means be reached exclusively through the cooperation of specialists. This refers as well to reforms of the institutes of general education.

The cooperation of the pedagogues with the social forces—this is how the Commission will work both in its own constitution, in the State Committee, and in all its activities.

As its first task the Commission considers the improvement of the teachers' status, and first of all of those very poor though almost most important contributors to the work of culture—the elementary school teachers. Their just demands ought to be satisfied at once and at any cost. The proletariat of the schools has in vain demanded an increase of salary to one hundred rubles per month. It would be a disgrace any longer to keep in poverty the teachers of the overwhelming majority of the Russian people.

But a real democracy cannot stop at mere literacy, at universal elementary instruction. It must endeavour to organise a uniform secular school of several grades. The ideal is, equal and if possible higher education for all the citizens. So long as this idea has not been realised for all, the natural transition through all the schooling grades up to the university—a transition to a higher stage—must depend entirely upon the pupil's aptitude, and not upon the resources of his family.

The problem of a genuinely democratic organisation of instruction is particularly difficult in a country impoverished by a long, criminal, imperialistic war; but the workers who have taken the power must remember that education will serve them as the greatest instrument in their struggle for a better lot and for a spiritual growth. However needful it may be to curtail other articles of the people's budget, the expenses on education must stand high. A large educational budget is the pride and glory of a nation. The free and enfranchised peoples of Russia will not forget this.

The fight against illiteracy and ignorance cannot be confined to a thorough establishment of school education for children and youths. Adults, too, will be anxious to save themselves from the debasing position of a man who cannot read and write. The school for adults must occupy a conspicuous place in the general plan of popular instruction.

Instruction and Education: One must emphasise the difference between instruction and education.

Instruction is the transmission of ready knowledge by the teacher to his pupil. Education is a creative process. The personality of the individual is being "educated" throughout life, is being formed, grows richer in content, stronger and more perfect.

The toiling masses of the people—the workmen, the peasants, the soldiers—are thirsting for elementary and advanced instruction. But they are also thirsting for education. Neither the government nor the intellectuals nor any other power outside of themselves can give it to them. The school, the book, the theatre, the museum, etc., may here be only aids. They have their own ideas, formed by their social position, so different from the position of those ruling classes and intellectuals who have hitherto created culture. They have their own ideas, their own emotions, their own ways of approaching the problems of personality and society. The city labourer, according to his own fashion, the rural toiler according to his, will each build his clear world-conception permeated with the class-idea of the workers. There is no more superb or beautiful phenomenon than the one of which our nearest descendants will be both witnesses and participants: The building by collective Labour of its own general, rich and free soul.

Instruction will surely be an important but not a decisive element. What is more important here is the criticism, the creativeness of the masses themselves; for science and art have only in some of their parts a general human importance. They suffer radical changes with every far-reaching class upheaval.

Throughout Russia, particularly among the city labourers, but also among the peasants, a powerful wave of cultural educational movement has arisen, workers' and soldiers' organisations of this kind are multiplying rapidly. To meet them, to lend them support, to clear the road before them, is the first task of a revolutionary and popular government in the domain of democratic education.

The Constituent Assembly will doubtless soon begin its work. It alone can permanently establish the order of national and social life in our country, and at the same time the general character of the organisation of popular education.

Now, however, with the passage of power to the Soviets, the really democratic character of the Constituent Assembly is assured. The line which the State Commission, relying upon the State Committee, will follow, will hardly suffer any modification under the influence of the Constituent Assembly. Without pre-determining it, the new People's Government considers itself within its rights in enacting in this domain a series of measures which aim at enriching and enlightening as soon as possible the spiritual life of the country.

The Ministry: The present work must in the interim proceed through the Ministry of the People's Education. Of all the necessary alterations in its composition and construction the State Commission will have charge, elected by the Executive Committee of the Soviets and the State Committee. Of course the order of State authority in the domain of the people's education will be established by the Constituent Assembly. Until then, the Ministry must play the part of the executive apparatus for both the State Committee and the State Commission for People's Education.

The pledge of the country's safety lies in the cooperation of all its vital and genuinely democratic forces.

We believe that the energetic effort of the working people and of the honest enlightened intellectuals will lead the country out of its painful crisis, and through complete democracy to the reign of Socialism and the brotherhood of nations.

People's Commissar on Education,
A. V. LUNACHARSKY.

*   *   *

On the Order in Which the Laws Are to be Ratified and Published

1. Until the convocation of the Constituent Assembly, the enacting and publishing of laws shall be carried out in the order decreed by the present Provisional Workmen's and Peasants' Government, elected by the All-Russian Congress of Workers', Peasants' and Soldiers' Deputies.

2. Every bill is presented for consideration of the Government by the respective Ministry, signed by the duly authorised People's Commissar; or it is presented by the legislative section attached to the Government, signed by the chief of the section.

3. After its ratification by the Government, the decree in its final

edition, in the name of the Russian Republic, is signed by the president of the Council of People's Commissars, or for him by the People's Commissar who presented it for the consideration of the Government, and is then published.

4. The date of publishing it in the official "Gazette of the Provisional Workmen's and Peasants' Government," is the date of its becoming law.

5. In the decree there may be appointed a date, other than the date of publication, on which it shall become law, or it may be promulgated by telegraph; in which case it is to be regarded in every locality as becoming law upon the publication of the telegram.

6. The promulgation of legislative acts of the government by the State Senate is abolished. The Legislative Section attached to the Council of People's Commissars issues periodically a collection of regulations and orders of the government which possess the force of law.

7. The Central Executive Committee of the Soviets of Workers', Peasants', and Soldiers' Deputies (*Tsay-ee-kah*) has at all times the right to cancel, alter or annul any of the Government decrees.

In the name of the Russian Republic, the President of the Council of People's Commissars,

V. ULIANOV-LENIN.

4   The Liquor Problem*

Order Issued by the Military Revolutionary Committee

1. Until further order the production of alcohol and alcoholic drinks is prohibited.

2. It is ordered to all producers of alcohol and alcoholic drinks to inform not later than on the 27th inst. of the exact site of their stores.

3. All culprits against this order will be tried by a Military Revolutionary Court.

THE MILITARY REVOLUTIONARY COMMITTEE.

* Other anxious discussions and orders on the liquor problem are shown in the Minutes and Resolutions of the Military Revolutionary Committee for November 19, November 27, December 2, 7, 8, 11, and 12. Reports on the matter were delivered to the Committee by Dzerzhinski, Lunacharsky, and Galkin. How many times the matter was discussed in the VTsik and the Council of Cimmissars cannot now be established, but Trotsky's works show that he addressed the Soviet on this problem on November 11 (four days after the uprising) and again on December 2.—*Ed.*

5   Order No. 2

From the Committee of the Finland Guard Reserve Regiment to all House Committees and to the citizens of Vasili Ostrov.

The bourgeoisie has chosen a very sinister method of fighting the proletariat; it has established in various parts of the city huge wine depots, and distributes liquor among the soldiers, in this manner attempting to sow dissatisfaction in the ranks of the Revolutionary army.

It is herewith ordered to all house committees, that at 3 o'clock, the time set for posting this order, they shall in person and secretly notify the President of the Committee of the Finland Guard Regiment, concerning the amount of wine in their premises.

Those who violate this order will be arrested and given trial before a merciless court, and their property will be confiscated, and the stock of wine discovered will be

BLOWN UP WITH DYNAMITE

2 hours after this warning,

because more lenient measures, as experience has shown, do not bring the desired results.

REMEMBER, THERE WILL BE NO OTHER WARNING BEFORE THE EXPLOSIONS.

Regimental Committee of the Finland Guard Regiment.

CHAPTER IX

VICTORY

Order Number 1

To the Troops of the Pulkovo Detachment.

November 13, 1917. 38 minutes past 9 a.m.

After a cruel fight the troops of the Pulkovo detachment completely routed the counter-revolutionary forces, who retreated from their positions in disorder, and under cover of Tsarskoye Selo fell back toward Pavlovsk II and Gatchina.

Our advanced units occupied the northeastern extremity of Tsarskoye Selo and the station Alexandrovskaya. The Colpino detachment was on our left, the Krasnoye Selo detachment to our right.

I ordered the Pulkovo forces to occupy Tsarskoye Selo, to fortify its approaches, especially on the side of Gatchina.

Also to pass and occupy Pavlocskoye, fortifying its southern side, and to take up the railroad as far as Dno.

The troops must take all measures to strengthen the positions occupied by them, arranging trenches and other defensive works.

They must enter into close liaison with the detachments of Colpino and Krasnoye Selo, and also with the Staff of the Commander in Chief for the Defence of Petrograd.

Signed,

*Commander in Chief over all Forces acting against
the Counter-revolutionary Troops of Kerensky,*

Lieutenant-Colonel MURAVIOV.

Tuesday morning. But how is this? Only two days ago the Petrograd campagna was full of leaderless bands, wandering aimlessly; without food, without artillery, without a plan. What had fused that disorganised mass of undisciplined Red Guards, and soldiers without officers, into an army obedient to its own elected high command, tempered to meet and break the assault of cannon and Cossack cavalry? [1]

People in revolt have a way of defying military precedent. The ragged armies of the French Revolution are not forgotten—Valmy and the Lines of Weissembourg. Massed against the Soviet forces were *yunkers,* Cossacks, landowners, nobility Black Hundreds—the Tsar come again, *Okhrana* and Siberian chains; and the vast and terrible menace of the Germans. . . . Victory, in the words of Carlyle, meant "Apotheosis and Millennium without end!"

Sunday night, the Commissars of the Military Revolutionary Committee returning desperately from the field, the garrison of Petrograd elected its Committee of five, its Battle Staff, three soldiers and two officers, all certified free from counter-revolutionary taint. Colonel Muraviov, ex-patriot, was in command—an efficient man, but to be carefully watched. At Colpino, at Obukhovo, at Pulkovo and Krasnoye Selo were formed provisional detachments, increased in size as the stragglers came in from the surrounding country—mixed soldiers, sailors and Red Guards, parts of regiments, infantry, cavalry and artillery all together, and a few armoured cars.

Day broke, and the pickets of Kerensky's Cossacks came in touch. Scattered rifle-fire, summons to surrender. Over the bleak plain on the cold quiet air spread the sound of battle, falling upon the ears of roving bands as they gathered about their little fires, waiting. . . . So it

was beginning! They made toward the battle; and the
worker hordes pouring out along the straight roads
quickened their pace. . . . Thus upon all the points of
attack automatically converged angry human swarms, to
be met by Commissars and assigned positions, or work to
do. This was *their* battle, for *their* world; the officers in
command were elected by *them*. For the moment that
incoherent multiple will was one will. . . .

Those who participated in the fighting described to me
how the sailors fought until they ran out of cartridges, and
then stormed; how the untrained workmen rushed the
charging Cossacks and tore them from their horses; how
the anonymous hordes of the people, gathering in the darkness around the battle, rose like a tide and poured over
the enemy. . . . Before midnight of Monday the Cossacks
broke and were fleeing, leaving their artillery behind them,
and the army of the proletariat, on a long ragged front,
moved forward and rolled into Tsarskoye, before the enemy
had a chance to destroy the great Government wireless
station, from which now the Commissars of Smolny were
hurling out to the world paeans of triumph. . . .[2]

To all Soviets of Workers' and Soldiers' Deputies

The 12th of November, in a bloody combat near Tsarskoye
Selo, the revolutionary army defeated the counter-revolutionary troops of Kerensky and Kornilov. In the name of
the Revolutionary Government I order all regiments to take
the offensive against the enemies of the revolutionary democracy, and to take all measures to arrest Kerensky, and
also to oppose any adventure which might menace the conquests of the Revolution and the victory of the proletariat.
Long live the Revolutionary Army!

MURAVIOV.

News from the provinces. . . .

At Sevastopol the local Soviet had assumed the power; a huge meeting of the sailors on the battleships in the harbour had forced their officers to line up and swear allegiance to the new Government. At Nizhni Novgorod the Soviet was in control. From Kazan came reports of a battle in the streets, *yunkers* and a brigade of artillery against the Bolshevik garrison. . . .

Desperate fighting had broken out again in Moscow. The *yunkers* and White Guards held the Kremlin and the centre of the town, beaten upon from all sides by the troops of the Military Revolutionary Committee. The Soviet artillery was stationed in Skobelev Square, bombarding the City Duma building, the Prefecture and the Hotel Metropole. The cobblestones of the Tverskaya and Nikitskaya had been torn up for trenches and barricades. A hail of machine-gun fire swept the quarters of the great banks and commercial houses. There were no lights, no telephones; the bourgeois population lived in the cellars. . . . The last bulletin said that the Military Revolutionary Committee had delivered an ultimatum to the Committee of Public Safety, demanding the immediate surrender of the Kremlin, or bombardment would follow.

"Bombard the Kremlin?" cried the ordinary citizen. "They dare not!"

From Vologda to Chita in far Siberia, from Pskov to Sevastopol on the Black Sea, in great cities and little villages, civil war burst into flame. From thousands of factories, peasant communes, regiments and armies, ships on the wide sea, greetings poured into Petrograd—greetings to the Government of the People.

The Cossack Government at Novocherkask telegraphed to Kerensky, *"The Government of the Cossack troops invites the Provisional Government and the members of the*

*Council of the Republic to come, if possible, to Novocher-
kask, where we can organise in common the struggle
against the Bolsheviki."*

In Finland, also, things were stirring. The Soviet of
Helsingfors and the *Tsentrobalt* (Central Committee of the
Baltic Fleet), jointly proclaimed a state of siege, and
declared that all attempts to interfere with the Bolshevik
forces, and all armed resistance to its orders, would be
severely repressed. At the same time the Finnish Railway
Union called a country-wide general strike, to put into
operation the laws passed by the Socialist Diet of June,
1917, dissolved by Kerensky. . . .

Early in the morning I went out to Smolny. Going up
the long wooden sidewalk from the outer gate I saw the
first thin, hesitating snow-flakes fluttering down from the
grey, windless sky. "Snow!" cried the soldier at the door,
grinning with delight. "Good for the health!" Inside, the
long, gloomy halls and bleak rooms seemed deserted. No
one moved in all the enormous pile. A deep, uneasy sound
came to my ears, and looking around, I noticed that
everywhere on the floor, along the walls, men were sleeping. Rough, dirty men, workers and soldiers, spattered
and caked with mud, sprawled alone or in heaps, in the
careless attitudes of death. Some wore ragged bandages
marked with blood. Guns and cartridge-belts were scattered about. . . . The victorious proletarian army!

In the upstairs buffet so thick they lay that one could
hardly walk. The air was foul. Through the clouded
windows a pale light streamed. A battered samovar, cold,
stood on the counter, and many glasses holding dregs of
tea. Beside them lay a copy of the Military Revolutionary
Committee's last bulletin, upside down, scrawled with
painful hand-writing. It was a memorial written by some

soldier to his comrades fallen in the fight against Kerensky, just as he had set it down before falling on the floor to sleep. The writing was blurred with what looked like tears. . . .

> Alexei Vinogradov
> D. Maskvin
> S. Stolbikov
> A. Voskresensky
> D. Leonsky
> D. Preobrazhensky
> V. Laidansky
> M. Berchikov

These men were drafted into the Army on November 15th, 1916. Only three are left of the above.

> Mikhail Berchikov
> Alexei Voskresensky
> Dmitri Leonsky

*   *   *

Sleep, warrior eagles, sleep with peaceful soul.
You have deserved, our own ones, happiness and
Eternal peace. Under the earth of the grave
You have straitly closed your ranks. Sleep, Citizens!

Only the Military Revolutionary Committee still functioned, unsleeping. Skrypnik, emerging from the inner room, said that Gotz had been arrested, but had flatly denied signing the proclamation of the Committee for Salvation, as had Avksentiev; and the Committee for Salvation itself had repudiated the Appeal to the garrison. There was still disaffection among the city regiments, Skrypnik reported; the Volhynsky Regiment had refused to fight against Kerensky.

Several detachments of "neutral" troops, with Chernov

at their head, were at Gatchina, trying to persuade Kerensky to halt his attack on Petrograd.

Skrypnik laughed. "There can be no 'neutrals' now," he said. "We've won!" His sharp, bearded face glowed with an almost religious exaltation. "More than sixty delegates have arrived from the Front, with assurances of support by all the armies except the troops on the Rumanian front, who have not been heard from. The Army Committees have suppressed all news from Petrograd, but we now have a regular system of couriers. . . ."

Down in the front hall Kamenev was just entering, worn out by the all-night session of the Conference to Form a New Government, but happy. "Already the Socialist Revolutionaries are inclined to admit us into the new Government," he told me. "The right wing groups are frightened by the Revolutionary Tribunals; they demand, in a sort of panic, that we dissolve them before going any further. . . . We have accepted the proposition of the *Vikzhel* to form a homogeneous Socialist Ministry, and they're working on that now. You see, it all springs from our victory. When we were down, they wouldn't have us at any price; now everybody's in favour of some agreement with the Soviets. . . . What we need is a really decisive victory. Kerensky wants an armistice, but he'll have to surrender.[2] . . ."

That was the temper of the Bolshevik leaders. To a foreign journalist who asked Trotsky what statement he had to make to the world, Trotsky replied: "At this moment the only statement possible is the one we are making through the mouths of our cannon!"

But there was an undercurrent of real anxiety in the tide of victory; the question of finances. Instead of opening the banks, as had been ordered by the Military Revolutionary Committee, the Union of Bank Employees had

ШТАБЪ

Военно-Револю-
ціоннаго Коми-
тета.

Совѣта Р. и С. д.   УДОСТОВѢРЕНІЕ.

2 ноября 1917 г.

№ 1860

Дано сіе журналистамъ Нью-Іоркской соціалистической прессы Джану РИТѢ въ томъ, что текстъ телеграм-
мы просмотрѣнъ Правительствомъ Народныхъ Комиссаровъ
и препятствій къ отправленію не имѣется, а также
предлагается всячески содѣйствовать ея отправленію
по назначенію.

За Главнокомандующаго   *Avonov*

Начальникъ Штаба   *Влад. Бончъ-Бруевичъ*

Order given me at Staff headquarters by command of the
Council of People's Commissars, to transmit the first despatch
out of Petrograd after the November Revolution, over the
Government wires to America.

TRANSLATION:

STAFF
Military Revolutionary
Committee
Sov. W. & S. D.
2 November, 1917
No. 1860

CERTIFICATE

Is given by the present to the journalist of the New York
Socialist press JOHN REED, that the text of the telegram (herewith) has been examined by the Government of People's
Commissars, and there is no objection to its transmission,
and also it is recommended that all cooperate in every way
to transmit same to its destination.

For the Commander in Chief. ANTONOV.
Chief of Staff, VLAD. BONCH-BRUEVITCH.

held a meeting and declared a formal strike. Smolny had demanded some thirty-five millions of rubles from the State Bank, and the cashier had locked the vaults, only paying out money to the representatives of the Provisional Government. The reactionaries were using the State Bank as a political weapon; for instance, when the *Vikzhel* demanded money to pay the salaries of the employees of the Government railroads, it was told to apply to Smolny. . . .

I went to the State Bank to see the new Commissar, a red-haired Ukrainian Bolshevik named Petrovich. He was trying to bring order out of the chaos in which affairs had been left by the striking clerks. In all the offices of the huge place perspiring volunteer workers, soldiers and sailors, their tongues sticking out of their mouths in the intensity of their effort, were poring over the great ledgers with a bewildered air. . . .

The Duma building was crowded. There were still isolated cases of defiance toward the new Government, but they were rare. The Central Land Committee had appealed to the Peasants, ordering them not to recognise the Land Decree passed by the Congress of the Soviets, because it would cause confusion and civil war. Mayor Schreider announced that because of the Bolshevik insurrection, the elections to the Constituent Assembly would have to be indefinitely postponed.

Two questions seemed to be uppermost in all minds, shocked by the ferocity of the civil war; first, a truce to the bloodshed[3]—second, the creation of a new Government. There was no longer any talk of "destroying the Bolsheviki"—and very little about excluding them from the Government, except from the Populist Socialists and the Peasants' Soviets. Even the Central Army Committee at the *Stavka,* the most determined enemy of Smolny, telephoned from Moghilev: "If, to constitute the new Ministry, it is necessary to come to an understanding with the Bolsheviki, we agree to admit them *in a minority* to the Cabinet."

Pravda, ironically calling attention to Kerensky's "humanitarian sentiments," published his despatch to the Committee for Salvation:

In accord with the proposals of the Committee for Salvation and all the democratic organisations united around it, I have halted all military action against the rebels. A delegate of the Committee has been sent to enter into negotiations. Take all measures to stop the useless shedding of blood.

The *Vikzhel* sent a telegram to all Russia:

The Conference of the Union of Railway Workers with the representatives of both the belligerent parties, who admit the necessity of an agreement, protest energetically against the use of political terrorism in the civil war, especially when it is carried on between different factions of the revolutionary democracy, and declare that political terrorism, in whatever form, is in contradiction to the very idea of the negotiations for a new Government. . . .

Delegations from the Conference were sent to the Front, to Gatchina. In the Conference itself everything seemed on the point of final settlement. It had even been decided to elect a provisional People's Council, composed of about four hundred members—seventy-five representing Smolny, seventy-five the old *Tsay-ee-kah,* and the rest split up among the Town Dumas, the Trade Unions, Land Committees and political parties. Chernov was mentioned as

Веселый выпускъ. Цѣна 20 коп.

КАКЪ БУРЖУИ власть ПОТЕРЯЛИ

Акафистъ Сашкѣ—Болтуну.

Сказочки и пѣсенки для дѣтей призывнаго возраста.

Какъ они царствовали. — Что они распѣвали. — Что теперь поютъ.

Popular leaflet sold in the streets just after the Bolshevik insurrection, containing rhymes and jokes about the defeated bourgeoisie and the "moderate" Socialist leaders. Called, "HOW THE BOORZHUI (BOURGEOISIE) LOST THE POWER."

the new Premier. Lenin and Trotsky, rumour said, were to be excluded. . . .

About noon I was again in front of Smolny, talking with the driver of an ambulance bound for the revolutionary front. Could I go with him? Certainly! He was a volunteer, a University student, and as we rolled down the street shouted over his shoulder to me phrases of execrable German: *"Also, gut! Wir nach die Kasernen zu essen gehen!"* I made out that there would be lunch at some barracks.

On the Kirochnaya we turned into an immense courtyard surrounded by military buildings, and mounted a dark stairway to a low room lit by one window. At a long wooden table were seated some twenty soldiers, eating *shchi* (cabbage soup) from a great tin wash-tub with wooden spoons, and talking loudly with much laughter.

"Welcome to the Battalion Committee of the Sixth Reserve Engineers' Battalion!" cried my friend, and introduced me as an American Socialist. Whereat every one rose to shake my hand, and one old soldier put his arms around me and gave me a hearty kiss. A wooden spoon was produced and I took my place at the table. Another tub, full of *kasha,* was brought in, a huge loaf of black bread, and of course the inevitable tea-pots. At once every one began asking me questions about America: Was it true that people in a free country sold their votes for *money?* If so, how did they get what they wanted? How about this "Tammany"? Was it true that in a free country a little group of people could control a whole city, and exploited it for their personal benefit? Why did the people stand it? Even under the Tsar such things could not happen in Russia; true, here there was always graft, but to buy and sell a whole city full of people! And in a free

country! Had the people no revolutionary feeling? I tried
to explain that in my country people tried to change things
by law.

"Of course," nodded a young sergeant, named Baklanov,
who spoke French. "But you have a highly developed
capitalist class? Then the capitalist class must control the
legislatures and the courts. How then can the people
change things? I am open to conviction, for I do not
know your country; but to me it is incredible. . . ."

I said that I was going to Tsarskoye Selo. "I, too," said
Baklanov, suddenly. "And I—and I——" The whole
roomful decided on the spot to go to Tsarskoye Selo.

Just then came a knock on the door. It opened, and
in it stood the figure of the Colonel. No one rose, but all
shouted a greeting. "May I come in?" asked the Colonel.
"Prosim! Prosim!" they answered heartily. He entered,
smiling, a tall, distinguished figure in a goat-skin cape
embroidered with gold. "I think I heard you say that you
were going to Tsarskoye Selo, comrades," he said. "Could
I go with you?"

Baklanov considered. "I do not think there is anything
to be done here to-day," he answered. "Yes, comrade, we
shall be very glad to have you." The Colonel thanked
him and sat down, filling a glass with tea.

In a low voice, for fear of wounding the Colonel's pride,
Baklonov explained to me. "You see, I am chairman of
the Committee. We control the Battalion absolutely,
except in action, when the Colonel is delegated by us to
command. In action his orders must be obeyed, but he is
strictly responsible to us. In barracks he must ask our
permission before taking any action. . . . You might
call him our Executive Officer. . . ."

Arms were distributed to us, revolvers and rifles—"we
might meet some Cossacks, you know"—and we all piled

into the ambulance, together with three great bundles of
newspapers for the front. Straight down the Liteiny we
rattled, and along the Zagorodny Prospekt. Next to me sat
a youth with the Shoulder-straps of a Lieutenant, who
seemed to speak all European languages with equal flu-
ency. He was a member of the Battalion Committee.

"I am not a Bolshevik," he assured me, emphatically.
"My family is a very ancient and noble one. I, myself, am,
you might say, a Cadet. . . ."

"But how——?" I began, bewildered.

"Oh, yes, I am a member of the Committee. I make no
secret of my political opinions, but the others do not
mind, because they know I do not believe in opposing the
will of the majority. . . . I have refused to take any
action in the present civil war, however, for I do not
believe in taking up arms against my brother Russians. . . ."

"Provocator! Kornilovets!" the others cried at him
gaily, slapping him on the shoulder. . . .

Passing under the huge grey stone archway of the Moskovsky Gate, covered with golden hieroglyphics, ponder-
ous Imperial eagles and the names of Tsars, we sped
out on the wide straight highway, grey with the first light
fall of snow. It was thronged with Red Guards, stumbling
along on foot toward the revolutionary front, shouting
and singing; and others, grey-faced and muddy, coming
back. Most of them seemed to be mere boys. Women
with spades, some with rifles and bandoleers, others wearing the Red Cross on their arm-bands—the bowed, toil-
worn women of the slums. Squads of soldiers marching out
of step, with an affectionate jeer for the Red Guards;
sailors, grim-looking; children with bundles of food for
their fathers and mothers; all these, coming and going,
trudged through the whitened mud that covered the

cobbles of the highway inches deep. We passed cannon, jingling southward with their caissons; trucks bound both ways, bristling with armed men; ambulances full of wounded from the direction of the battle, and once a peasant cart, creaking along, in which sat a white-faced boy bent over his shattered stomach and screaming monotonously. In the fields on either side women and old men were digging trenches and stringing barbed wire entanglements.

Back northward the clouds rolled away dramatically, and the pale sun came out. Across the flat, marshy plain Petrograd glittered. To the right, white and gilded and coloured bulbs and pinnacles; to the left, tall chimneys, some pouring out black smoke; and beyond, a lowering sky over Finland. On each side of us were churches, monasteries. . . . Occasionally a monk was visible, silently watching the pulse of the proletarian army throbbing on the road.

At Pulkovo the road divided, and there we halted in the midst of a great crowd, where the human streams poured from three directions, friends meeting, excited and congratulatory, describing the battle to one another. A row of houses facing the cross-roads was marked with bullets, and the earth was trampled into mud half a mile around. The fighting had been furious here. . . . In the near distance riderless Cossack horses circled hungrily, for the grass of the plain had died long ago. Right in front of us an awkward Red Guard was trying to ride one, falling off again and again, to the childlike delight of a thousand rough men.

The left road, along which the remnants of the Cossacks had retreated, led up a little hill to a hamlet, where there was a glorious view of the immense plain, grey as a wind-less sea, tumultuous clouds towering over, and the im-

perial city disgorging its thousands along all the roads. Far
over to the left lay the little hill of Krasnoye Selo, the
parade-ground of the Imperial Guards' summer camp,
and the Imperial Dairy. In the middle distance nothing
broke the monotony but a few walled monasteries and
convents, some isolated factories, and several large buildings with unkempt grounds that were asylums and orphan-
ages. . . .

"Here," said the driver, as we went on over a barren
hill, "here was where Vera Slutskaya died. Yes, the Bolshevik member of the Duma. It happened early this morning. She was in an automobile, with Zalkind and another
man. There was a truce, and they started for the front
trenches. They were talking and laughing, when all of a
sudden, from the armoured train in which Kerensky himself was riding, somebody saw the automobile and fired
a cannon. The shell struck Vera Slutskaya and killed
her. . . ."

And so we came into Tsarskoye, all bustling with the
swaggering heroes of the proletarian horde. Now the
palace where the Soviet had met was a busy place. Red
Guards and sailors filled the court-yard, sentries stood at
the doors, and a stream of couriers and Commissars
pushed in and out. In the Soviet room a samovar had been
set up, and fifty or more workers, soldiers, sailors and
officers stood around, drinking tea and talking at the
top of their voices. In one corner two clumsy-handed
workingmen were trying to make a multigraphing machine
go. At the centre table, the huge Dybenko bent over a
map, marking out positions for the troops with red and
blue pencils. In his free hand he carried, as always, the
enormous blue-steel revolver. Anon he sat himself down
at a typewriter and pounded away with one finger; every

little while he would pause, pick up the revolver, and lovingly spin the chamber.

A couch lay along the wall, and on this was stretched a young workman. Two Red Guards were bending over him, but the rest of the company did not pay any attention. In his breast was a hole; through his clothes fresh blood came welling up with every heart-beat. His eyes were closed, and his young, bearded face was greenish-white. Faintly and slowly he still breathed, with every breath sighing, *"Mir budit! Mir budit!* (Peace is coming! Peace is coming!)"

Dybenko looked up as we came in. "Ah," he said to Baklanov. "Comrade, will you go up to the Commandant's headquarters and take charge? Wait; I will write you credentials." He went to the typewriter and slowly picked out the letters.

The new Commandant of Tsarskoye Selo and I went toward the Ekaterina Palace, Baklanov very excited and important. In the same ornate, white room some Red Guards were rummaging curiously around, while my old friend, the Colonel, stood by the window biting his moustache. He greeted me like a long-lost brother. At a table near the door sat the French Bessarabian. The Bolsheviki had ordered him to remain, and continue his work.

"What could I do?" he muttered. "People like myself cannot fight on either side in such a war as this, no matter how much we may instinctively dislike the dictatorship of the mob. . . . I only regret that I am so far from my mother in Bessarabia!"

Baklanov was formally taking over the office from the Commandant. "Here," said the Colonel nervously, "are the keys to the desk."

A Red Guard interrupted. "Where's the money?" he

asked rudely. The Colonel seemed surprised. "Money? Money? Ah, you mean the chest. There it is," said the Colonel, "just as I found it when I took possession three days ago. Keys?" The Colonel shrugged. "I have no keys."

The Red Guard sneered knowingly. "Very convenient," he said.

"Let us open the chest," said Baklanov. "Bring an axe. Here is an American comrade. Let him smash the chest open, and write down what he finds there."

I swung the axe. The wooden chest was empty.

"Let's arrest him," said the Red Guard, venomously. "He is Kerensky's man. He has stolen the money and given it to Kerensky."

Baklanov did not want to. "Oh, no," he said. "It was the Kornilovets before him. He is not to blame."

"The devil!" cried the Red Guard. "He is Kerensky's man, I tell you. If *you* won't arrest him, then *we* will, and we'll take him to Petrograd and put him in Peter-Paul, where he belongs!" At this the other Red Guards growled assent. With a piteous glance at us the Colonel was led away. . . .

Down in front of the Soviet palace an auto-truck was going to the front. Half a dozen Red Guards, some sailors, and a soldier or two, under command of a huge workman, clambered in, and shouted to me to come along. Red Guards issued from headquarters, each of them staggering under an arm-load of small, corrugated-iron bundles, filled with *grubit*—which, they say, is ten times as strong, and five times as sensitive as dynamite; these they threw into the truck. A three-inch cannon was loaded and then tied onto the tail of the truck with bits of rope and wire.

We started away with a shout, at top speed of course;

the heavy truck swaying from side to side. The cannon leaped from one wheel to the other, and the *grubit* bombs went rolling back and forth over our feet, fetching up against the sides of the car with a crash.

The big Red Guard, whose name was Vladimir Nicolaievich, plied me with questions about America. "Why did America come into the war? Are the American workers ready to throw over the capitalists? What is the situation in the Mooney case now? Will they extradite Berkman to San Francisco?" and others, very difficult to answer, all delivered in a shout above the roaring of the truck, while we held on to each other and danced amid the caroming bombs.

Occasionally a patrol tried to stop us. Soldiers ran out into the road before us, shouted *"Stoi!"* and threw up their guns.

We paid no attention. "The devil take you!" cried the Red Guards. "We don't stop for anybody! We're Red Guards!" And we thundered imperiously on, while Vladimir Nicolaievich bellowed to me about the internationalisation of the Panama Canal, and such matters. . . .

About five miles out we saw a squad of sailors marching back, and slowed down.

"Where's the front, brothers?"

The foremost sailor halted and scratched his head. "This morning," he said, "it was about half a kilometer down the road. But the damn thing isn't anywhere now. We walked and walked and walked, but we couldn't find it."

They climbed into the truck, and we proceeded. It must have been about a mile further that Vladimir Nicolaievich cocked his ear and shouted to the chauffeur to stop.

"Firing!" he said. "Do you hear it?" For a moment dead silence, and then, a little ahead and to the left, three shots in rapid succession. Along here the side of the road was heavily wooded. Very much excited now, we crept along, speaking in whispers, until the truck was nearly opposite the place where the firing had come from. Descending, we spread out, and every man carrying his rifle, went stealthily into the forest.

Two comrades, meanwhile, detached the cannon and slewed it around until it aimed as nearly as possible at our backs.

It was silent in the woods. The leaves were gone, and the tree-trunks were a pale wan colour in the low, sickly autumn sun. Not a thing moved, except the ice of little woodland pools shivering under our feet. Was it an ambush?

We went uneventfully forward until the trees began to thin, and paused. Beyond, in a little clearing, three soldiers sat around a small fire, perfectly oblivious.

Vladimir Nicolaievich stepped forward. *"Zra'zvuitye,* comrades!" he greeted, while behind him one cannon, twenty rifles and a truck-load of *grubit* bombs hung by a hair. The soldiers scrambled to their feet.

"What was the shooting going on around here?"

One of the soldiers answered, looking relieved, "Why we were just shooting a rabbit or two, comrade. . . ."

The truck hurtled on toward Romanov, through the bright, empty day. At the first cross-roads two soldiers ran out in front of us, waving their rifles. We slowed down, and stopped.

"Passes, comrades!"

The Red Guards raised a great clamour. "We are Red Guards. We don't need any passes. . . . Go on, never mind them!"

But a sailor objected. "This is wrong, comrades. We must have revolutionary discipline. Suppose some counter-revolutionaries came along in a truck and said: 'We don't need any passes?' The comrades don't know you."

At this there was a debate. One by one, however, the sailors and soldiers joined with the first. Grumbling, each Red Guard produced his dirty *bumaga* (paper). All were alike except mine, which had been issued by the Revolutionary Staff at Smolny. The sentries declared that I must go with them. The Red Guards objected strenuously, but the sailor who had spoken first insisted. "This comrade we know to be a true comrade," he said. "But there are orders of the Committee, and these orders must be obeyed. That is revolutionary discipline. . . ."

In order not to make any trouble, I got down from the truck, and watched it disappear careening down the road, all the company waving farewell. The soldiers consulted in low tones for a moment, and then led me to a wall, against which they placed me. It flashed upon me suddenly; they were going to shoot me!

In all three directions not a human being was in sight. The only sign of life was smoke from the chimney of a *dacha,* a rambling wooden house a quarter of a mile up the side road. The two soldiers were walking out into the road. Desperately I ran after them.

"But comrades! See! Here is the seal of the Military Revolutionary Committee!"

They stared stupidly at my pass, then at each other.

"It is different from the others," said one, sullenly. "We cannot read, brother."

I took him by the arm. "Come!" I said. "Let's go to that house. Some one there can surely read." They hesitated. "No," said one. The other looked me over. "Why not?" he muttered. "After all, it is a serious crime to kill an innocent man."

We walked up to the front door of the house and

knocked. A short, stout woman opened it, and shrank back in alarm, babbling, "I don't know anything about them! I don't know anything about them!" One of my guards held out the pass. She screamed. "Just to read it, comrade." Hesitatingly she took the paper and read aloud, swiftly:

The bearer of this pass, John Reed, is a representative of the American Social-Democracy, an internationalist. . . .

Out on the road again the two soldiers held another consultation. "We must take you to the Regimental Committee," they said. In the fast-deepening twilight we trudged along the muddy road. Occasionally we met squads of soldiers, who stopped and surrounded me with looks of menace, handing my pass around and arguing violently as to whether or not I should be killed. . . .

It was dark when we came to the barracks of the Second Tsarskoye Selo Rifles, low sprawling buildings huddled along the post-road. A number of soldiers slouching at the entrance asked eager questions. A spy? A provocator? We mounted a winding stair and emerged into a great, bare room with a huge stove in the centre, and rows of cots on the floor, where about a thousand soldiers were playing cards, talking, singing, and asleep. In the roof was a jagged hole made by Kerensky's cannon. . . .

I stood in the doorway, and a sudden silence ran among the groups, who turned and stared at me. Of a sudden they began to move, slowly and then with a rush, thundering, with faces full of hate. "Comrades! Comrades!" yelled one of my guards. "Committee! Committee!" The throng halted, banked around me, muttering. Out of them shouldered a lean youth, wearing a red arm-band.

"Who is this?" he asked roughly. The guards explained.

"Give me the paper!" He read it carefully, glancing at me with keen eyes. Then he smiled and handed me the pass. "Comrades, this is an American comrade. I am Chairman of the Committee, and I welcome you to the Regiment. . . ." A sudden general buzz grew into a roar of greeting, and they pressed forward to shake my hand.

"You have not dined? Here we have had our dinner. You shall go to the Officers' Club, where there are some who speak your language. . . ."

He led me across the court-yard to the door of another building. An aristocratic-looking youth, with the shoulder-straps of a Lieutenant, was entering. The Chairman presented me, and shaking hands, went back.

"I am Stepan Georgevich Morovsky, at your service," said the Lieutenant, in perfect French. From the ornate entrance-hall a ceremonial staircase led upward, lighted by glittering lustres. On the second floor billiard-rooms, card-rooms, a library opened from the hall. We entered the dining-room, at a long table in the centre of which sat about twenty officers in full uniform, wearing their gold- and silver-handled swords, the ribbons and crosses of Imperial decorations. All rose politely as I entered, and made a place for me beside the Colonel, a large, impressive man with a grizzled beard. Orderlies were deftly serving dinner. The atmosphere was that of any officers' mess in Europe. Where was the Revolution?

"You are not Bolsheviki?" I asked Morovsky.

A smile went around the table, but I caught one or two glancing furtively at the orderly.

"No," answered my friend. "There is only one Bolshevik officer in this regiment. He is in Petrograd to-night. The Colonel is a Menshevik. Captain Kherlov there is a Cadet. I myself am a Socialist Revolutionary of the right wing. . . . I should say that most of the officers in the

Army are not Bolsheviki, but like me they believe in
democracy; they believe that they must follow the soldier-
masses. . . ."

Dinner over, maps were brought, and the Colonel spread
them out on the table. The rest crowded around to see.

"Here," said the Colonel, pointing to pencil marks,
"were our positions this morning. Vladimir Kyrilovich,
where is your company?"

Captain Kherlov pointed. "According to orders, we
occupied the position along this road. Karsavin relieved me
at five o'clock."

Just then the door of the room opened, and there
entered the Chairman of the Regimental Committee, with
another soldier. They joined the group behind the Colonel,
peering at the map.

"Good," said the Colonel. "Now the Cossacks have
fallen back ten kilometres in our sector. I do not think
it is necessary to take up advanced positions. Gentlemen,
for to-night you will hold the present line, strengthening
the positions by——"

"If you please," interrupted the Chairman of the Regimental Committee. "The orders are to advance with all
speed, and prepare to engage the Cossacks north of
Gatchina in the morning. A crushing defeat is necessary.
Kindly make the proper dispositions."

There was a short silence. The Colonel again turned to
the map. "Very well," he said, in a different voice. "Stepan
Georgevich, you will please——" Rapidly tracing lines
with a blue pencil, he gave his orders, while a sergeant
made shorthand notes. The sergeant then withdrew, and
ten minutes later returned with the orders typewritten,
and one carbon copy. The Chairman of the Committee
studied the map with a copy of the orders before him.

"All right," he said, rising. Folding the carbon copy,

he put it in his pocket. Then he signed the other, stamped it with a round seal taken from his pocket, and presented it to the Colonel. . . .

Here was the Revolution!

I returned to the Soviet palace in Tsarskoye in the Regimental Staff automobile. Still the crowds of workers, soldiers and sailors pouring in and out, still the choking press of trucks, armoured cars, cannon before the door, and the shouting, the laughter of unwonted victory. Half a dozen Red Guards forced their way through, a priest in the middle. This was Father Ivan, they said, who had blessed the Cossacks when they entered the town. I heard afterward that he was shot. . . .[4]

Dybenko was just coming out, giving rapid orders right and left. In his hand he carried the big revolver. An automobile stood with racing engine at the kerb. Alone, he climbed in the rear seat, and was off—off to Gatchina, to conquer Kerensky.

Toward nightfall he arrived at the outskirts of the town, and went on afoot. What Dybenko told the Cossacks nobody knows, but the fact is that General Krasnov and his staff and several thousand Cossacks surrendered, and advised Kerensky to do the same.[5]

As for Kerensky—I reprint here the deposition made by General Krasnov on the morning of November 14th:

"Gatchina, November 14, 1917. To-day, about three o'clock (A. M.), I was summoned by the Supreme Commander (Kerensky). He was very agitated, and very nervous.

" 'General,' he said to me, 'you have betrayed me. Your Cossacks declare categorically that they will arrest me and deliver me to the sailors.'

" 'Yes,' I answered, 'there is talk of it, and I know that you have no sympathy anywhere.'

" 'But the officers say the same thing.'

" 'Yes, most of all it is the officers who are discontented with you.'

" 'What shall I do? I ought to commit suicide!'

" 'If you are an honourable man, you will go immediately to Petrograd with a white flag, you will present yourself to the Military Revolutionary Committee, and enter into negotiations as Chief of the Provisional Government.'

" 'All right. I will do that, General.'

" 'I will give you a guard and ask that a sailor go with you.'

" 'No, no, not a sailor. Do you know whether it is true that Dybenko is here?'

" 'I don't know who Dybenko is.'

" 'He is my enemy.'

" 'There is nothing to do. If you play for high stakes you must know how to take a chance.'

" 'Yes. I'll leave to-night!'

" 'Why? That would be a flight. Leave calmly and openly, so that every one can see that you are not running away.'

" 'Very well. But you must give me a guard on which I can count.'

" 'Good.'

"I went out and called the Cossack Russkov, of the Tenth Regiment of the Don, and ordered him to pick out ten Cossacks to accompany the Supreme Commander. Half an hour later the Cossacks came to tell me that Kerensky was not in his quarters, that he had run away.

"I gave the alarm and ordered that he be searched for, supposing that he could not have left Gatchina, but he could not be found. . . ."

And so Kerensky fled, alone, "disguised in the uniform of a sailor," and by that act lost whatever popularity he had retained among the Russian masses. . . .

I went back to Petrograd riding on the front seat of an auto truck, driven by a workman and filled with Red Guards. We had no kerosene, so our lights were not burning. The road was crowded with the proletarian army going home, and new reserves pouring out to take their places. Immense trucks like ours, columns of artillery, wagons, loomed up in the night, without lights, as we were. We hurtled furiously on, wrenched right and left to avoid collisions that seemed inevitable, scraping wheels, followed by the epithets of pedestrians.

Across the horizon spread the glittering lights of the capital, immeasurably more splendid by night than by day, like a dike of jewels heaped on the barren plain.

The old workman who drove held the wheel in one hand, while with the other he swept the far-gleaming capital in an exultant gesture.

"Mine!" he cried, his face all alight. "All mine now! My Petrograd!"

NOTES TO CHAPTER IX

1   Military Revolutionary Committee. Bulletin No. 2

November 12th, in the evening, Kerensky sent a proposition to the revolutionary troops—"to lay down their arms." Kerensky's men opened artillery fire. Our artillery answered and compelled the enemy to be silent. The Cossacks assumed the offensive. The deadly fire of the sailors, the Red Guards and the soldiers forced the Cossacks to retreat. Our armoured cars rushed in among the ranks of the enemy. The enemy is fleeing. Our troops are in pursuit. The order has been given to arrest Kerensky. Tsarskoye Selo has been taken by the revolutionary troops.

The Lettish Riflemen: The Military Revolutionary Committee

has received precise information that the valiant Lettish Riflemen
have arrived from the Front and taken up a position in the rear
of Kerensky's bands.

From the Staff of the Military Revolutionary Committee

The seizure of Gatchina and Tsarskoye Selo by Kerensky's
detachments is to be explained by the complete absence of artillery
and machine-guns in these places, whereas Kerensky's cavalry was
provided with artillery from the beginning. The last two days were
days of enforced work for our Staff, to provide the necessary
quantity of guns, machine-guns, field telephones, etc., for the
revolutionary troops. When this work—with the energetic assistance of the District Soviets and the factories (the Putilov
Works, Obukhov and others)—was accomplished, the issue of the
expected encounter left no place for doubt: on the side of the
revolutionary troops there was not only a surplus in quantity and
such a powerful material base as Petrograd, but also an enormous
moral advantage. All the Petrograd regiments moved out to the
positions with tremendous enthusiasm. The Garrison Conference
elected a Control Commission of five soldiers, thus securing a
complete unity between the commander in chief and the garrison.
At the Garrison Conference it was unanimously decided to begin
decisive action.

The artillery fire on the 12th of November developed with
extraordinary force by 3 P.M. The Cossacks were completely demoralised. A parliamentarian came from them to the staff of the
detachment at Krasnoye Selo, and proposed to stop the firing,
threatening otherwise to take "decisive" measures. He was answered that the firing would cease when Kerensky laid down his
arms.

In the developing encounter all sections of the troops—the
sailors, soldiers and the Red Guards—showed unlimited courage.
The sailors continued to advance until they had fired all their
cartridges. The number of casualties has not been established yet,
but it is larger on the part of the counter-revolutionary troops,
who experienced great losses through one of our armoured cars.

Kerensky's staff, fearing that they would be surrounded, gave
the order to retreat, which retreat speedily assumed a disorderly
character. By 11-12 P.M., Tsarskoye Selo, including the wireless
station, was entirely occupied by the troops of the Soviets. The
Cossacks retreated towards Gatchina and Colpino.

The morale of the troops is beyond all praise. The order has been given to pursue the retreating Cossacks. From the Tsarskoye Selo station a radio-telegram was sent immediately to the Front and to all local Soviets throughout Russia. Further details will be communicated . . .

2.

There is little resemblance between the accounts given to Reed by heroes-after-the battle organized with his romantic narrative skill, and the actual battle around Gatchina, Pulkovo and Tsarskoye Selo. The picture which emerges from both Soviet official documents and the accounts of Kerensky, Krasnov, Stankevich, Woytinsky, etc., is one of little fighting and many cross currents of intrigue and propaganda. Workers could not be turned into soldiers overnight. Their ranks broke each time they were under fire; many landed in the hospital with broken jaws because they did not know that a gun will kick when fired. The Petrograd regiments each followed their own plan and whim, most of them refusing to leave Petrograd. Only the Kronstadt sailors fought well and held tenaciously under fire. Krasnov wavered as to whether he should support Kerensky or let the Provisional Government fall and then join with other generals in "dealing with the Bolsheviks later." The Cossacks broke, not under a hail of bullets, but under a hail of cross currents of propaganda. From the Cossack Soviet came pressure upon them and their commander to refuse to defend Kerensky who had "betrayed Kornilov." From Bolshevik agitators came arguments that Kerensky was supported only by officers. No organized unit of infantry was with him in the field, only volunteer officers and the small contingent of six or seven hundred Cossacks. Many generals promised Kerensky reinforcements in response to his urgent calls, but some would not and some could not supply them. Cheremissov deliberately ordered the troops not to advance to his aid, while Krasnov delayed his attack for a fatal day, ordered a retreat when only an advance might have given a possibility of victory, then he and the Cossacks tried to hand over Kerensky to the Bolsheviks in return for an honorable safe-conduct with all their officers, horses and arms, to the Cossack lands. Kerensky managed to learn of the terms and escaped in disguise as a sailor. Woytinsky, the Commissar with the troops marching towards Petrograd was surrendered to the

Bolsheviks after an argument that "as he was not a Cossack nor a Cossack officer" the agreement for honorable safe-conduct did not apply to him.—*Ed.*

3   Events of the 13th in Petrograd

Three regiments of the Petrograd garrison refused to take any part in the battle against Kerensky. On the morning of the 13th they summoned to a joint conference sixty delegates from the Front, in order to find some way to stop the civil war. This conference appointed a committee to go and persuade Kerensky's troops to lay down their arms. They proposed to ask the Government soldiers the following questions: (1) Will the soldiers and Cossacks of Kerensky recognise the *Tsay-ee-kah* as the repository of Governmental power, responsible to the Congress of Soviets? (2) Will the soldiers and Cossacks accept the decrees of the second Congress of Soviets? (3) Will they accept the Land and Peace decrees? (4) Will they agree to cease hostilities and return to their units? (5) Will they consent to the arrest of Kerensky, Krasnov and Savinkov?

At the meeting of the Petrograd Soviet, Zinoviev said, "It would be foolish to think that this committee could finish the affair. The enemy can only be broken by force. However, it would be a crime for us not to try every peaceful means to bring the Cossacks over to us. . . . What we need is a military victory. . . . The news of an armistice is premature. Our staff will be ready to conclude an armistice when the enemy can no longer do any harm. . . .

"At present, the influence of our victory is creating new political conditions. . . . To-day the Socialist Revolutionaries are inclined to admit the Bolsheviki into the new Government. . . . A decisive victory is indispensable, so that those who hesitate will have no further hesitation. . . ."

At the City Duma all attention was concentrated on the formation of the new Government. In many factories and barracks already Revolutionary Tribunals were operating, and the Bolsheviki were threatening to set up more of these, and try Gotz and Avksentiev before them. Dan proposed that an ultimatum be sent demanding the abolition of these Revolutionary Tribunals, or the other members of the Conference would immediately break off all negotiations with the Bolsheviki.

Shingariov, Cadet, declared that the Municipality ought not to take part in any agreement with the Bolsheviki. . . . "Any agreement with the maniacs is impossible until they lay down their arms and recognise the authority of independent courts of law. . . ."

Yartsev, for the *Yedinstvo* group, declared that any agreement with the Bolsheviki would be equivalent to a Bolshevik victory. . . .

Mayor Schreider, for the Socialist Revolutionaries, stated that he was opposed to all agreement with the Bolsheviki. . . . "As for a Government, that ought to spring from the popular will; and since the popular will has been expressed in the municipal elections, the popular will which can create a Government is actually concentrated in the Duma. . . ."

After other speakers, of which only the representative of the Mensheviki Internationalists was in favour of considering the admission of the Bolsheviki into the new Government, the Duma voted to continue its representatives in the *Vikzhel's* conference, but to insist upon the restoration of the Provisional Government before everything, and to exclude the Bolsheviki from the new power. . . .

4   Truce. Krasnov's Answer to the Committee for Salvation

"In answer to your telegram proposing an immediate armistice, the Supreme Commander, not wishing further futile bloodshed, consents to enter into negotiations and to establish relations between the armies of the Government and the insurrectionists. He proposes to the General Staff of the insurrectionists to recall its regiments to Petrograd, to declare the line Ligovo-Pulkovo-Colpino neutral, and to allow the advance-guards of the Government cavalry to enter Tsarskoye Selo, for the purpose of establishing order. The answer to this proposal must be placed in the hands of our envoys before eight o'clock to-morrow morning.

KRASNOV."

5   Events at Tsarskoye Selo

On the evening that Kerensky's troops retreated from Tsarskoye Selo, some priests organised a religious procession through the streets of the town, making speeches to the citizens in which they asked the people to support the rightful authority, the Provisional Government. When the Cossacks had retreated, and the first Red Guards entered the town, witnesses reported that the priests had incited the people against the Soviets, and had said prayers at the grave of Rasputin, which lies behind the Imperial Palace. One of the priests, Father Ivan Kuchurov, was arrested and shot by the infuriated Red Guards. . . .

Just as the Red Guards entered the town the electric lights were shut off, plunging the streets in complete darkness. The director of the electric light plant, Lubovich, was arrested by the Soviet troops and asked why he had shut off the lights. He was found some time later in the room where he had been imprisoned with a revolver in his hand and a bullethole in his temple.

The Petrograd anti-Bolshevik papers came out next day with headlines, "Plekhanov's temperature 39 degrees!" Plekhanov lived at Tsarskoye Selo, where he was lying ill in bed. Red Guards arrived at the house and searched it for arms, questioning the old man.

"What class of society do you belong to?" they asked him.

"I am a revolutionist," answered Plekhanov, "who for forty years has devoted his life to the struggle for liberty!"

"Anyway," said a workman, "you have now sold yourself to the bourgeoisie!"

The workers no longer knew Plekhanov, pioneer of the Russian Social Democracy! *

6 Appeal of the Soviet Government

"The detachments at Gatchina, deceived by Kerensky, have laid down their arms and decided to arrest Kerensky. The chief of the counter-revolutionary campaign has fled. The Army, by an enormous majority, has pronounced in favour of the second All-Russian Congress of Soviets, and of the Government which it has created. Scores of delegates from the Front have hastened to Petrograd to assure the Soviet Government of the Army's fidelity. No twisting of the facts, no calumny against the revolutionary

---

* On the night of November 15, the Military Revolutionary Committee sent the following radiogram to Tsarskoe Selo's Soviet:

"The Military Revolutionary Committee of the Central and Petrograd Soviets of Workers' and Soldiers' Deputies directs the Tsarskoe Selo Soviet . . . immediately to undertake extraordinary measures for the complete security of the comfort and safety of citizen Gerogii Valentinovich Plekhanov."—*Ed.*

workers, soldiers, and peasants, has been able to defeat the People. The Workers' and Soldiers' Revolution is victorious. . . .

"The *Tsay-ee-kah* appeals to the troops which march under the flag of the counter-revolution, and invites them immediately to lay down their arms—to shed no longer the blood of their brothers in the interests of a handful of land-owners and capitalists. The Workers', Soldiers' and Peasants' Revolution curses those who remain even for a moment under the flag of the People's enemies. . . .

"Cossacks! Come over to the rank of the victorious People! Railwaymen, postmen, telegraphers—all, **all** support the new Government of the People!"

CHAPTER X

MOSCOW

The Military Revolutionary Committee, with a fierce intensity, followed up its victory:

> November 14th.
>
> To all Army, corps, divisional and regimental Committees, to all Soviets of Workers', Soldiers' and Peasants' Deputies, to all, all, all.
>
> Conforming to the agreement between the Cossacks, *yunkers*, soldiers, sailors and workers, it has been decided to arraign Alexander Feodorvich Kerensky before a tribunal of the people. We demand that Kerensky be arrested, and that he be ordered, in the name of the organisations hereinafter mentioned, to come immediately to Petrograd and present himself to the tribunal.
>
> Signed,
>> *The Cossacks of the First Division of Ussuri Cavalry; the Committee of Yunkers of the Petrograd detachment of Franc-Tireurs; the delegate of the Fifth Army.*
>>
>> People's Commissar Dybenko.

The Committee for Salvation, the Duma, the Central Committee of the Socialist Revolutionary party—proudly claiming Kerensky as a member—all passionately protested that he could only be held responsible to the Constituent Assembly.

On the evening of November 16th I watched two thousand Red Guards swing down the Zagorodny Prospekt behind a military band playing the *Marseillaise*—and how appropriate it sounded—with blood-red flags over the dark ranks of workmen, to welcome home again their brothers who had defended "Red Petrograd." In the bitter dusk they tramped, men and women, their tall bayonets swaying; through streets faintly lighted and slippery with mud, between silent crowds of bourgeois, contemptuous but fearful. . . .

All were against them—business men, speculators, investors, land-owners, army officers, politicians, teachers, students, professional men, shop-keepers, clerks, agents. The other Socialist parties hated the Bolsheviki with an implacable hatred. On the side of the Soviets were the rank and file of the workers, the sailors, all the undemoralised soldiers, the landless peasants, and a few—a very few—intellectuals. . . .

From the farthest corners of great Russia, whereupon desperate street-fighting burst like a wave, news of Kerensky's defeat came echoing back—the immense roar of proletarian victory. Kazan, Saratov, Novgorod, Vinnitza —where the streets had run with blood; Moscow, where the Bolsheviki had turned their artillery against the last strong-hold of the bourgeoisie—the Kremlin.

"They are bombarding the Kremlin!" The news passed from mouth to mouth in the streets of Petrograd, almost with a sense of terror. Travellers from "white and shining little mother Moscow" told fearful tales. Thousands killed; the Tverskaya and the Kuznetsky Most in flames; the church of Vasili Blazhenny a smoking ruin; Uspensky

Cathedral crumbling down; the Spasskaya Gate of the Kremlin tottering; the Duma burned to the ground.[1]

Nothing that the Bolsheviki had done could compare with this fearful blasphemy in the heart of Holy Russia. To the ears of the devout sounded the shock of guns crashing in the face of the Holy Orthodox Church, and pounding to dust the sanctuary of the Russian nation. . . .

On November 15th, Lunacharsky, Commissar of Education, broke into tears at the session of the Council of People's Commissars, and rushed from the room, crying, "I cannot stand it! I cannot bear the monstrous destruction of beauty and tradition. . . ."

That afternoon his letter of resignation was published in the newspapers:

I have just been informed, by people arriving from Moscow, what has happened there.

The Cathedral of St. Basil the Blessed, the Cathedral of the Assumption, are being bombarded. The Kremlin, where are now gathered the most important art treasures of Petrograd and of Moscow, is under artillery fire. There are thousands of victims.

The fearful struggle there has reached a pitch of bestial ferocity.

What is left? What more can happen?

I cannot bear this. My cup is full. I am unable to endure these horrors. It is impossible to work under the pressure of thoughts which drive me mad!

That is why I am leaving the Council of People's Commissars.

I fully realise the gravity of this decision. But I can bear no more. . . .[2]

That same day the White Guards and *yunkers* in the Kremlin surrendered, and were allowed to march out unharmed. The treaty of peace follows:

1. The Committee of Public Safety ceases to exist.

2. The White Guard gives up its arms and dissolves. The officers retain their swords and regulations side-arms. In the Military Schools are retained only the arms necessary for instruction; all others are surrendered by the *yunkers*. The Military Revolutionary Committee guarantees the liberty and inviolability of the person.

3. To settle the question of disarmament, as set forth in section 2, a special commission is appointed, consisting of representatives from all organisations which took part in the peace negotiations.

4. From the moment of the signature of this peace treaty, both parties shall immediately give order to cease firing and halt all military operations, taking measures to ensure punctual obedience to this order.

5. At the signature of the treaty, all prisoners made by the two parties shall be released. . . .

For two days now the Bolsheviki had been in control of the city. The frightened citizens were creeping out of their cellars to seek their dead; the barricades in the streets were being removed. Instead of diminishing, however, the stories of destruction in Moscow continued to grow. . . . And it was under the influence of these fearful reports that we decided to go there.

Petrograd, after all, in spite of being for a century the seat of Government, is still an artificial city. Moscow is real Russia, Russia as it was and will be; in Moscow we would get the true feeling of the Russian people about the Revolution. Life was more intense there.

For the past week the Petrograd Military Revolutionary Committee, aided by the rank and file of the Railway Workers, had seized control of the Nicolai Railroad, and hurled trainload after trainload of sailors and Red Guards southwest. . . . We were provided with passes from Smolny, without which no one could leave the capital.

. . . When the train backed into the station, a mob of shabby soldiers, all carrying huge sacks of eatables, stormed the doors, smashed the windows, and poured into all the compartments, filling up the aisles and even climbing onto the roof. Three of us managed to wedge our way into a compartment, but almost immediately about twenty soldiers entered. . . . There was room for only four people; we argued, expostulated, and the conductor joined us—but the soldiers merely laughed. Were they to bother about the comfort of a lot of *boorzhui* (bourgeois)? We produced the passes from Smolny; instantly the soldiers changed their attitude.

"Come, comrades," cried one, "these are American *tovarishchi*. They have come thirty thousand versts to see our Revolution, and they are naturally tired. . . ."

With polite and friendly apologies the soldiers began to leave. Shortly afterward we heard them breaking into a compartment occupied by two stout, well-dressed Russians, who had bribed the conductor and locked their door. . . .

About seven o'clock in the evening we drew out of the station, an immense long train drawn by a weak little locomotive burning wood, and stumbled along slowly, with many stops. The soldiers on the roof kicked with their heels and sang whining peasant songs; and in the corridor, so jammed that it was impossible to pass, violent political debates raged all night long. Occasionally the conductor came through, as a matter of habit, looking for tickets. He found very few except ours, and after a half-hour of futile wrangling, lifted his arms despairingly and withdrew. The atmosphere was stifling, full of smoke and foul odours; if it hadn't been for the broken windows we would doubtless have smothered during the night.

In the morning, hours late, we looked out upon a snowy world. It was bitter cold. About noon a peasant woman got on with a basket-full of bread-chunks and a great can of luke warm coffee-substitute. From then on until dark there was nothing but the packed train, jolting and stopping, and occasional stations where a ravenous mob swooped down on the scantily-furnished buffet and swept it clean. . . . At one of these halts I ran into Nogin and Rykov, the seceding Commissars, who were returning to Moscow to put their grievances before their own Soviet;* and further along was Bukharin, a short, red-bearded man with the eyes of a fanatic—"more Left than Lenin," they said of him. . . .

Then the three strokes of the bell and we made a rush for the train, worming our way through the packed and noisy aisle. . . . A good-natured crowd, bearing the discomfort with humourous patience, interminably arguing about everything from the situation in Petrograd to the British Trade-Union system, and disputing loudly with the few *boorzhui* who were on board. Before we reached Moscow almost every car had organised a Committee to secure and distribute food, and these Committees became divided into political factions, who wrangled over fundamental principles. . . .

The station at Moscow was deserted. We went to the office of the Commissar, in order to arrange for our return tickets. He was a sullen youth with the shoulder-straps of a Lieutenant; when we showed him our papers from Smolny, he lost his temper and declared that he was no Bolshevik, that he represented the Committee of Public Safety. . . . It was characteristic—in the general turmoil attending the conquest of the city, the chief railway station had been forgotten by the victors. . . .

Not a cab in sight. A few blocks down the street, however, we woke up a grotesquely-padded *izvoschik* asleep

* See Chapter XI.

upright on the box of his little sleigh. "How much to the centre of the town?"

He scratched his head. "The *barini* won't be able to find a room in any hotel," he said. "But I'll take you around for a hundred rubles. . . ." Before the Revolution it cost *two!* We objected, but he simply shrugged his shoulders. "It takes a good deal of courage to drive a sleigh now-adays," he went on. We could not beat him down below fifty. . . . As we sped along the silent, snowy half-lighted streets, he recounted his adventures during the six days' fighting. "Driving along, or waiting for a fare on the corner," he said, "all of a sudden *pooff!* a cannon ball ex-ploding here, *pooff!* a cannon ball there, *ratt-ratt!* a ma-chine-gun. . . . I gallop, the devils shooting all around. I get to a nice quiet street and stop, doze a little, *pooff!* another cannon ball, *ratt-ratt.* . . . Devils! Devils! Devils! Brrr!"

In the centre of the town the snow-piled streets were quiet with the stillness of convalescence. Only a few arc-lights were burning, only a few pedestrians hurried along the side-walks. An icy wind blew from the great plain, cutting to the bone. At the first hotel we entered an office illuminated by two candles.

"Yes, we have some very comfortable rooms, but all the windows are shot out. If the *gospodin* does not mind a little fresh air. . . ."

Down the Tverskaya the shop-windows were broken, and there were shell-holes and torn-up paving stones in the street. Hotel after hotel, all full, or the proprietors still so frightened that all they could say was, "No, no, there is no room! There is no room!" On the main streets, where the great banking-houses and mercantile houses lay, the Bolshevik artillery had been indiscriminately effective. As one Soviet official told me, "Whenever we didn't know just where the *yunkers* and White Guards were, we bombarded their pocketbooks. . . ."

At the big Hotel National they finally took us in; for we were foreigners, and the Military Revolutionary Committee had promised to protect the dwellings of foreigners. . . . On the top floor the manager showed us where shrapnel had shattered several windows. "The animals!" said he, shaking his fist at imaginary Bolsheviki. "But wait! Their time will come; in just a few days now their ridiculous Government will fall, and then we shall make them suffer!"

We dined at a vegetarian restaurant with the enticing name, "I Eat Nobody," and Tolstoy's picture prominent on the walls, and then sallied out into the streets.

The headquarters of the Moscow Soviet was in the palace of the former Governor-General, an imposing white building fronting Skobelev Square. Red Guards stood sentry at the door. At the head of the wide, formal stairway, whose walls were plastered with announcements of committee-meetings and addresses of political parties, we passed through a series of lofty ante-rooms, hung with red-shrouded pictures in gold frames, to the splendid state salon, with its magnificent crystal lustres and gilded cornices. A low-voiced hum of talk, underlaid with the whirring bass of a score of sewing machines, filled the place. Huge bolts of red and black cotton cloth were unrolled, serpentining across the parqueted floor and over tables, at which sat half a hundred women, cutting and sewing streamers and banners for the Funeral of the Revolutionary Dead. The faces of these women were roughened and scarred with life at its most difficult; they worked now sternly, many of them with eyes red from weeping. . . . The losses of the Red Army had been heavy.

At a desk in one corner was Rogov, an intelligent,

bearded man with glasses, wearing the black blouse of a worker. He invited us to march with the Central Executive Committee in the funeral procession next morning. . . .

"It is impossible to teach the Socialist Revolutionaries and the Mensheviki anything!" he exclaimed. "They compromise from sheer habit. Imagine! They proposed that we hold a joint funeral with the *yunkers!*"

Across the hall came a man in a ragged soldier-coat and *shapka,* whose face was familiar; I recognised Melnichansky, whom I had known as the watch-maker George Melcher in Bayonne, New Jersey, during the great Standard Oil strike. Now, he told me, he was secretary of the Moscow Metal-Workers' Union, and a Commissar of the Military Revolutionary Committee during the fighting. . . .

"You see me!" he cried, showing his decrepit clothing. "I was with the boys in the Kremlin when the *yunkers* came the first time. They shut me up in the cellar and swiped my overcoat, my money, watch and even the ring on my finger. This is all I've got to wear!"

From him I learned many details of the bloody six-day battle which had rent Moscow in two. Unlike in Petrograd, in Moscow the City Duma had taken command of the *yunkers* and White Guards. Rudnev, the Mayor, and Minor, president of the Duma,* had directed the activities of the Committee of Public Safety and the troops. Riabtsev, Commandant of the city, a man of democratic in-

---

QUESTIONNAIRE FOR THE BOURGEOISIE

Distributed to all bourgeois households in Moscow by the Moscow Military Revolutionary Committee, so as to provide a basis for the requisition of clothing for the Army and the poor workers. For translation see Note 3, p. 343.

* Both were leaders of the Socialist-Revolutionary Party.—*Ed.*

Районъ	Фамилія		Денежный К-тъ.
№	Имя.	Отчество.	№

Адресъ .... _уличе или переулок_ .... д. № .... кв. № ....

ИМѢЮТСЯ ЗАПАСЫ.

Полъ.	Возрастъ.	Тканей.	Арш.	Готовыхъ вещей.	Шт.
		Бѣльевыхъ		Пальто { зимнихъ, лѣтнихъ и осеннихъ. }	
Средній мѣсячный		Легк. платьевыхъ (для костюмовъ) .			
Доходъ.	Расходъ.			Платьевъ и костюм. . .	
		Тяж. платьевыхъ (для пальто) . .		Смѣнъ бѣлья	
Мѣсяч. плата.				Паръ обуви	
За квартиру.	За комнату.	Прочихъ сортовъ .		Паръ галошъ	

Даю подписку въ томъ, что показанныя свѣдѣнія правильны и что карточекъ въ другомъ мѣстѣ не получалъ. Москва, ... дня 191 г.

Подпись ....

Подпись квартиронанимателя

Печать домового комитета.

stincts, had hesitated about opposing the Military Revolutionary Committee; but the Duma had forced him. . . . It was the Mayor, who had urged the occupation of the Kremlin; "They will never dare fire on you there," he said. . . .

One garrison regiment, badly demoralised by long inactivity, had been approached by both sides. The regiment held a meeting to decide what action to take. Resolved, that the regiment remain neutral, and continue its present activities—which consisted in peddling rubbers and sunflower seeds!

"But worst of all," said Melnichansky, "we had to organise while we were fighting. The other side knew just what it wanted; but here the soldiers had their Soviet and the workers theirs. . . . There was a fearful wrangle over who should be Commander-in-chief; some regiments talked for days before they decided what to do; and when the officers suddenly deserted us, we had no battle-staff to give orders. . . ."

Vivid little pictures he gave me. On a cold grey day he had stood at a corner of the Nikitskaya, which was swept by blasts of machine-gun fire. A throng of little boys were gathered there—street waifs who used to be newsboys. Shrill, excited as if with a new game, they waited until the firing slackened, and then tried to run across the street. . . . Many were killed, but the rest dashed backward and forward, laughing, daring each other. . . .

Late in the evening I went to the *Dvorianskoye Sobranie* —the Nobles' Club—where the Moscow Bolsheviki were to meet and consider the report of Nogin, Rykov and the others who had left the Council of People's Commissars.

The meeting-place was a theatre, in which, under the old régime, to audiences of officers and glittering ladies, amateur presentations of the latest French comedy had once taken place.

At first the place filled with the intellectuals—those who lived near the centre of the town. Nogin spoke, and most of his listeners were plainly with him. It was very late before the workers arrived; the working-class quarters were on the outskirts of the town, and no street-cars were running. But about midnight they began to clump up the stairs, in groups of ten or twenty—big, rough men, in coarse clothes, fresh from the battle-line, where they had fought like devils for a week, seeing their comrades fall all about them.

Scarcely had the meeting formally opened before Nogin was assailed with a tempest of jeers and angry shouts. In vain he tried to argue, to explain; they would not listen. He had left the Council of People's Commissars; he had deserted his post while the battle was raging. As for the bourgeois press, here in Moscow there was no more bourgeois press; even the City Duma had been dissolved.[4] Bukharin stood up, savage, logical, with a voice which plunged and struck, plunged and struck. . . . Him they listened to with shining eyes. Resolution, to support the action of the Council of People's Commissars, passed by overwhelming majority. So spoke Moscow. . . .

Late in the night we went through the empty streets and under the Iberian Gate to the great Red Square in front of the Kremlin. The church of Vasili Blazheny loomed fantastic, its bright-coloured, convoluted and blasoned cupolas vague in the darkness. There was no sign of any damage. . . . Along one side of the square the dark towers and walls of the Kremlin stood up. On the high walls flickered redly the light of hidden flames; voices reached us across the immense place, and the sound of picks and shovels. We crossed over.

ВОЕННО-РЕВОЛЮЦІОННЫЙ КОМИТЕТЪ
ПРИ
МОСКОВСКОМЪ СОВѢТѢ
Рабочихъ и Солдатскихъ
Депутатовъ.   КОМЕНДАНТУ ГОРОДА МОСКВЫ

МОСКВА, Тверская.
д. бывш. Генералъ Губернатора
оцо

Ноября 10 дня 191 7
№ 2092

    Настоящимъ Военно-революціонный
Комитетъ проситъ выдатьпропускъ для
осмотра Кремля представителямъ Амери-
канской Соціалистической партіи при
Соціалистической прессѣ тов. Ридъ и
Брайантъ.

Pass to the Kremlin, issued by the Moscow Military Revolutionary Committee just after the capture of the Kremlin by
the Bolsheviki.

TRANSLATION:

Military-Revolutionary Committee
attached to the
Moscow Soviet of
Workers' and Soldiers'
Deputies
Moscow, Tverskaya,
House of the former
Governor General
November 10, 1917
No. 2092

Mountains of dirt and rock were piled high near the base of the wall. Climbing these we looked down into two massive pits, ten or fifteen feet deep and fifty yards long, where hundreds of soldiers and workers were digging in the light of huge fires.

A young student spoke to us in German. "The Brotherhood Grave," he explained. "To-morrow we shall bury here five hundred proletarians who died for the Revolution."

He took us down into the pit. In frantic haste swung the picks and shovels, and the earth-mountains grew. No one spoke. Overhead the night was thick with stars, and the ancient Imperial Kremlin wall towered up immeasurably.

"Here in this holy place," said the student, "holiest of all Russia, we shall bury our most holy. Here where are the tombs of the Tsars, our Tsar—the People—shall sleep. . . ." His arm was in a sling, from a bullet-wound gained in the fighting. He looked at it. "You foreigners look down on us Russians because so long we tolerated a mediæval monarchy," said he. "But we saw that the Tsar was not the only tyrant in the world; capitalism was worse, and in all the countries of the world capitalism was Emperor. . . . Russian revolutionary tactics are best. . . ."

As we left, the workers in the pit, exhausted and running with sweat in spite of the cold, began to climb

---

TO THE COMMANDANT OF THE CITY OF MOSCOW

By this the Military Revolutionary Committee requests to give a pass for the purpose of investigating the Kremlin, to the representatives of the American Socialist party attached to the Socialist press, comrades Reed and Bryant.

Chief of the Military Revolutionary Committee
For the Secretary

wearily out. Across the Red Square a dark knot of men came hurrying. They swarmed into the pits, picked up the tools and began digging, digging, without a word. . . .

So, all the long night volunteers of the People relieved each other, never halting in their driving speed, and the cold light of the dawn laid bare the great Square, white with snow, and the yawning brown pits of the Brotherhood Grave, quite finished.

We rose before sunrise, and hurried through the dark streets to Skobelev Square. In all the great city not a human being could be seen; but there was a faint sound of stirring, far and near, like a deep wind coming. In the pale half-light a little group of men and women were gathered before the Soviet headquarters, with a sheaf of gold-lettered red banners—the Central Executive Committee of the Moscow Soviets. It grew light. From afar the vague stirring sound deepened and became louder, a steady and tremendous bass. The city was rising. We set out down the Tverskaya, the banners flapping overhead. The little street chapels along our way were locked and dark, as was the Chapel of the Iberian Virgin, which each new Tsar used to visit before he went to the Kremlin to crown himself, and which, day or night, was always open and crowded, and brilliant with the candles of the devout gleaming on the gold and silver and jewels of the ikons. Now, for the first time since Napoleon was in Moscow, they say, the candles were out.

The Holy Orthodox Church had withdrawn the light of its countenance from Moscow, the nest of irreverent vipers who had bombarded the Kremlin. Dark and silent and cold were the churches; the priests had disappeared. There were no popes to officiate at the Red Burial, there had been no sacrament for the dead, nor were any prayers to be said over the grave of the blasphemers. Tikhon, Metropolitan of Moscow, was soon to excommunicate the Soviets. . . .

Also the shops were closed, and the propertied classes stayed at home—but for other reasons. This was the Day of the People, the rumour of whose coming was thunderous as surf. . . .

Already through the Iberian Gate a human river was flowing, and the vast Red Square was spotted with people, thousands of them. I remarked that as the throng passed the Iberian Chapel, where always before the passerby had crossed himself, they did not seem to notice it. . . .

We forced our way through the dense mass packed near the Kremlin wall, and stood upon one of the dirt-mountains. Already several men were there, among them Muranov, the soldier who had been elected Commandant of Moscow—a tall, simple-looking, bearded man with a gentle face.

Through all the streets to the Red Square the torrents of people poured, thousands upon thousands of them, all with the look of the poor and the toiling. A military band came marching up, playing the *Internationale,* and spontaneously the song caught and spread like wind-ripples on a sea, slow and solemn. From the top of the Kremlin wall gigantic banners unrolled to the ground; red, with great letters in gold and in white, saying, "Martyrs of the Beginning of World Social Revolution," and "Long Live the Brotherhood of Workers of the World."

A bitter wind swept the Square, lifting the banners. Now from the far quarters of the city the workers of the different factories were arriving, with their dead. They could be seen coming through the Gate, the blare of their banners, and the dull red—like blood—of the coffins they carried. These were rude boxes, made of unplaned wood and daubed with crimson, borne high on the shoulders of rough men who marched with tears streaming down their faces, and followed by women who sobbed and screamed, or walked stiffly, with white, dead faces. Some of the coffins were open, the lid carried behind them; others were covered with gilded or silvered cloth, or had a soldier's hat nailed on the top. There were many wreaths of hideous artificial flowers. . . .

Through an irregular lane that opened and closed again the procession slowly moved toward us. Now through the Gate was flowing an endless stream of banners, all shades of red, with silver and gold lettering, knots of crepe hanging from the top—and some Anarchist flags, black with white letters. The band was playing the Revolutionary Funeral March, and against the immense singing of the mass of people, standing uncovered, the paraders sang hoarsely, choked with sobs. . . .

Between the factory-workers came companies of soldiers with their coffins, too, and squadrons of cavalry, riding at salute, and artillery batteries, the cannon wound with red and black—forever, it seemed. Their banners said, "Long live the Third International!" or "We Want an Honest, General, Democratic Peace!"

Slowly the marchers came with their coffins to the entrance of the grave, and the bearers clambered up with their burdens and went down into the pit. Many of them were women—squat, strong proletarian women. Behind the dead came other women—women young and broken, or old, wrinkled women making noises like hurt animals, who tried to follow their sons and husbands into the Brotherhood Grave, and shrieked when compassionate hands restrained them. The poor love each other so!

All the long day the funeral procession passed, coming in by the Iberian Gate and leaving the Square by way of the Nikolskaya, a river of red banners. bearing words of hope and brotherhood and stupendous prophecies, against a back-ground of fifty thousand people,—under the eyes of the world's workers and their descendants forever. . . .

One by one the five hundred coffins were laid in the pits. Dusk fell, and still the banners came drooping and fluttering, the band played the Funeral March, and the huge assemblage chanted. In the leafless branches of the trees above the grave the wreaths were hung, like strange, multi-coloured blossoms. Two hundred men began to shovel in the dirt. It rained dully down upon the coffins with a thudding sound, audible beneath the singing. . . .

The lights came out. The last banners passed, and the last moaning women, looking back with awful intensity as they went. Slowly from the great Square ebbed the proletarian tide. . . .

I suddenly realised that the devout Russian people no longer needed priests to pray them into heaven. On earth they were building a kingdom more bright than any heaven had to offer, and for which it was a glory to die. . . .

NOTES TO CHAPTER X

1 Damage to the Kremlin

I myself verified the damage to the Kremlin, which I visited immediately after the bombardment. The Little Nicolai Palace, a building of no particular importance, which was occupied occasionally by receptions of one of the Grand Duchesses, had served as barracks for the *yunkers*. It was not only bombarded, but pretty well sacked; fortunately there was nothing in it of particular historical value.

Uspensky Cathedral had a shell-hole in one of the cupolas, but except for a few feet of mosaic in the ceiling, was undamaged. The frescoes on the porch of Blagoveschensky Cathedral were badly damaged by a shell. Another shell hit the corner of Ivan Veliki. Tchudovsky Monastery was hit about thirty times, but only one shell went through a window into the interior, the others breaking the brick window-moulding and the roof-cornices.

The clock over the Spasskaya Gate was smashed. Troitsky Gate was battered, but easily reparable. One of the lower towers had lost its brick spire.

The church of St. Basil was untouched, as was the great Imperial Palace, with all the treasures of Moscow and Petrograd in its cellar, and the crown jewels in the Treasury. These places were not even entered.

2   Lunacharsky's Declaration

"Comrades! You are the young masters of the country, and although now you have much to do and think about, you must know how to defend your artistic and scientific treasures.

"Comrades! That which is happening at Moscow is a horrible, irreparable misfortune. . . . The People in its struggle for the power has mutilated our glorious capital.

"It is particularly terrible in these days of violent struggle, of destructive warfare, to be Commissar of Public Education. Only the hope of the victory of Socialism, the source of a new and superior culture, brings me comfort. On me weighs the responsibility of protecting the artistic wealth of the people. . . . Not being able to remain at my post, where I had no influence, I resigned. My comrades, the other Commissars, considered this resignation inadmissible. I shall therefore remain at my post. . . . And moreover, I understand that the damage done to the Kremlin is not as serious as has been reported. . . .

"But I beg you, comrades, to give me your support. . . . Preserve for yourselves and your descendants the beauty of our land; be the guardians of the property of the People.

"Soon, very soon, even the most ignorant, who have been held in ignorance so long, will awake and understand what a source of joy, strength and wisdom is art. . . ."

3 Questionnaire for the Bourgeoisie

Ward.........	Family Name..............................	House Committee
No...........		
Address......	Christian Name.......... Profession.........	No..............

Sex	Age	Supplies on Hand				
		Textiles	*Arshins*	Ready Made Clothes		Pieces
Monthly Average		For Underwear....	....	Overcoats: Winter..............	....	
Income	Expenditures	For Suits.........	....	Summer...........	....	
		For Overcoats.....	....	Fall................	....	
Monthly Rent				Dresses and Suits...	....	
				Underwear........	....	
Apt.	Room			Shoes..............	....	
		Other Kinds......	....	Rubbers...........	....	

I the undersigned declare that the data given above is true, and that I have not received this card elsewhere.

Signature........................

(Signature of leaseholder)

Moscow,................191 .

(Seal of the House Committee.)

4 Revolutionary Financial Measure

Order

In virtue of the powers vested in me by the Military Revolutionary Committee attached to the Moscow Soviet of Workers' and Soldiers' Deputies, I decree:

1. All banks with branches, the Central State Savings Bank with branches, and the savings banks at the Post and Telegraph offices are to be opened beginning November 22nd, from 11 A.M. to 1 P.M. until further order.

2. On current accounts and on the books of the savings banks, payments will be made by the above mentioned institutions, of not more than 150 rubles for each depositor during the course of the next week.

3. Payments of amounts exceeding 150 rubles a week on cur-

rent accounts and savings banks books, also payments on other
accounts of all kinds will be allowed during the next three days
—November 22nd, 23d, and 24th, only in the following cases:

(a) On the accounts of military organisations for the satisfaction of their needs;

(b) For the payment of salaries of employees and the earnings
of workers according to the tables and lists certified by the Factory Committees or Soviets of Employees, and attested by the
signatures of the Commissars, or the representatives of the Military Revolutionary Committee, and the district Military Revolutionary Committees.

4. Not more than 150 rubles are to be paid against drafts;
the remaining sums are to be entered on current account, payments on which are to be made in the order established by the
present decree.

5. All other banking operations are prohibited during these
three days.

6. The receipt of money on all accounts is allowed for any
amount.

7. The representatives of the Finance Council for the certifica-
tion of the authorisations indicated in clause 3 will hold their
office in the building of the Stock Exchange, Ilyinka Street, from
10 A.M. to 2 P.M.

8. The Banks and Savings Banks shall send the totals of daily
cash operations by 5 P.M. to the headquarters of the Soviet,
Skobelev Square, to the Military Revolutionary Committee, for
the Finance Council.

9. All employees and managers of credit institutions of all
kinds who refuse to comply with this decree shall be responsible
as enemies of the Revolution and of the mass of the population,
before the Revolutionary Tribunals. Their names shall be published
for general information.

10. For the control of the operations of Branches of the Savings
Banks and Banks within the limits of this decree, the district
Military Revolutionary Committees shall elect three representa-
tives and appoint their place of business.

Fully-authorised Commissar of the Military Revolutionary
Committee,
S. SHEVERDIN-MAKSIMENKO.

CHAPTER XI

THE CONQUEST OF POWER[1]

Declaration of the Rights of the Peoples of Russia[2]

. . . The first Congress of Soviets, in June of this year, proclaimed the right of the peoples of Russia to self-determination.

The second Congress of Soviets, in November last, confirmed this inalienable right of the peoples of Russia more decisively and definitely.

Executing the will of these Congresses, the Council of People's Commissars has resolved to establish as a basis for its activity in the question of Nationalities, the following principles:

(1) The equality and sovereignty of the peoples of Russia.

(2) The right of the peoples of Russia to free self-determination, even to the point of separation and the formation of an independent state.

(3) The abolition of any and all national and national-religious privileges and disabilities.

(4) The free development of national minorities and ethnographic groups inhabiting the territory of Russia.

Decrees will be prepared immediately upon the formation of a Commission on Nationalities.

In the name of the Russian Republic,
People's Commissar for Nationalities
YUSSOV DJUGASHVILI-STALIN
President of the Council of People's Commissars
V. ULIANOV (LENIN)

The Central Rada at Kiev immediately declared Ukraine an independent Republic, as did the Government of Finland, through the Senate at Helsingfors. Independent "Governments" spring up in Siberia and the Caucasus. The Polish Chief Military Committee swiftly gathered together the Polish troops in the Russian army, abolished their Committees and established an iron discipline. . . .

All these "Governments" and "movements" had two characteristics in common; they were controlled by the propertied classes, and they feared and detested Bolshevism. . . .

Steadily, amid the chaos of shocking change, the Council of People's Commissars hammered at the scaffolding of the Socialist order. Decree on Social Insurance, on Workers' Control, Regulations for Volost Land Committees, Abolition of Ranks and Titles, Abolition of Courts and the Creation of People's Tribunals. . . .[3]

Army after army, fleet after fleet, sent deputations, "joyfully to greet the new Government of the People."

In front of Smolny, one day, I saw a ragged regiment just come from the trenches. The soldiers were drawn up before the great gates, thin and grey-faced, looking up at the building as if God were in it. Some pointed out the Imperial eagles over the door, laughing. . . . Red Guards came to mount guard. All the soldiers turned to look, curiously, as if they had heard of them but never seen them. They laughed good-naturedly and pressed out of line to slap the Red Guards on the back, with half-joking, half-admiring remarks. . . .

The Provisional Government was no more. On November 15th, in all the churches of the capital, the priests stopped praying for it. But as Lenin himself told the *Tsay-ee-kah,* that was "only the beginning of the conquest of power." Deprived of arms, the opposition, which still controlled the economic life of the country, settled down to organise disorganisation, with all the Russian genius for cooperative action—to obstruct, cripple and discredit the Soviets.

The strike of Government employees was well organised, financed by the banks and commercial establishments. Every move of the Bolsheviki to take over the Government apparatus was resisted.

Trotsky went to the Ministry of Foreign Affairs; the functionaries refused to recognise him, locked themselves in, and when the doors were forced, resigned. He demanded the keys of the archives; only when he brought workmen to force the locks were they given up. Then it was discovered that Neratov, former assistant Foreign Minister, had disappeared with the Secret Treaties. . . .

Shliapnikov tried to take possession of the Ministry of Labour. It was bitterly cold, and there was no one to light the fires. Of all the hundreds of employees, not one would show him where the office of the Minister was. . . .

Alexandra Kollontai, appointed the 13th of November Commissar of Public Welfare—the department of charities and public institutions—was welcomed with a strike of all but forty of the functionaries in the Ministry. Immediately the poor of the great cities, the inmates of institutions, were plunged in miserable want: delegations of starving cripples, of orphans with blue, pinched faces, besieged the building. With tears streaming down her face, Kollontai arrested the strikers until they should deliver the keys of the office and the safe; when she got the keys, however, it was discovered that the former Minister, Countess Panina, had gone off with all the funds, which she refused to surrender except on the order of the Constituent Assembly.[4]

In the Ministry of Agriculture, the Ministry of Supplies, the Ministry of Finance, similar incidents occurred. And the employees, summoned to return or forfeit their positions and their pensions, either stayed away or returned to sabotage. . . . Almost all the *intelligentsia* being anti-Bolshevik, there was nowhere for the Soviet Government to recruit new staffs. . . .

The private banks remained stubbornly closed, with a back door open for speculators. When Bolshevik Commissars entered, the clerks left, secreting the books and removing the funds. All the employees of the State Bank struck except the clerks in charge of the vaults and the manufacture of money, who refused all demands from Smolny and privately paid out huge sums to the Committee for Salvation and the City Duma.

Twice a Commissar, with a company of Red Guards, came formally to insist upon the delivery of large sums for Government expenses. The first time, the City Duma members and the Menshevik and Socialist Revolutionary leaders were present in imposing numbers, and spoke so gravely of the consequences that the Commissar was frightened. The second time he arrived with a warrant, which he proceeded to read aloud in due form; but some one called his attention to the fact that it had no date and no seal, and the traditional Russian respect for "documents" forced him again to withdraw. . . .

The officials of the Credit Chancery destroyed their books, so that all record of the financial relations of Russia with foreign countries was lost.

The Supply Committees, the administrations of the Municipal-owned public utilities, either did not work at all, or sabotaged. And when the Bolsheviki, compelled by the desperate needs of the city population, attempted to help or to control the public service, all the employees went on strike immediately, and the Duma flooded Russia with telegrams about Bolshevik "violation of Municipal autonomy."

At Military headquarters, and in the offices of the Ministries of War and Marine, where the old officials had consented to work, the Army Committees and the high command blocked the Soviets in every way possible, even to the extent of neglecting the troops at the front. The *Vikzhel* was hostile, refusing to transport Soviet troops; every troop-train that left Petrograd was taken out by force, and railway officials had to be arrested each time— whereupon the *Vikzhel* threatened an immediate general strike unless they were released. . . .

Smolny was plainly powerless. The newspapers said that all the factories of Petrograd must shut down for lack of fuel in three weeks; the *Vikzhel* announced that trains must cease running by December first; there was food for three days only in Petrograd, and no more coming in; and the Army on the Front was starving. . . . The Committee for Salvation, the various Central Committees, sent word all over the country, exhorting the population to ignore the Government decrees. And the Allied Embassies were either coldly indifferent, or openly hostile. . . .

The opposition newspapers, suppressed one day and reappearing next morning under new names, heaped bitter sarcasm on the new regime.[5] Even *Novaya Zhizn* characterised it as "a combination of demagoguery and impotence."

From day to day (it said) the Government of the People's Commissars sinks deeper and deeper into the mire of superficial haste. Having easily conquered the power . . . the Bolsheviki can not make use of it.

Powerless to direct the existing mechanism of Government, they are unable at the same time to create a new one which might work easily and freely according to the theories of social experimenters.

Just a little while ago the Bolsheviki hadn't enough men to run their growing party—a work above all of speakers and writers; where then are they going to find trained men to execute the diverse and complicated functions of government?

The new Government acts and threatens, it sprays the country with decrees, each one more radical and more "socialist" than the last. But in this exhibition of Socialism on Paper—more likely designed for the stupefaction of our descendants—there appears neither the desire nor the capacity to solve the immediate problems of the day!

Meanwhile the *Vikzhel's* Conference to Form a New Government continued to meet night and day. Both sides had already agreed in principle to the basis of the Government; the composition of the People's Council was being discussed; the Cabinet was tentatively chosen, with Chernov as Premier; the Bolsheviki were admitted in a large minority, but Lenin and Trotsky were barred. The Central Committees of the Menshevik and Socialist Revolutionary parties, the Executive Committee of the Peasants' Soviets, resolved that, although unalterably opposed to the "criminal politics" of the Bolsheviki, they would, "in order to halt the fratricidal bloodshed," not oppose their entrance into the People's Council.

The flight of Kerensky, however, and the astounding success of the Soviets everywhere, altered the situation. On the 16th, in a meeting of the *Tsay-ee-kah,* the Left Socialist Revolutionaries insisted that the Bolsheviki should form a coalition Government with the other Socialist parties; otherwise they would withdraw from the Military Revolutionary Committee and the *Tsay-ee-kah*. Malkin said, "The news from Moscow, where our comrades are dying on both sides of the barricades, determines us to bring up once more the question of organisation of power, and it is not only our right to do so, but our duty. . . . We have won the right to sit with the Bolsheviki here within the walls of Smolny Institute, and to speak from this tribune. After the bitter internal party struggle, we shall be obliged, if you refuse to compromise, to pass to open battle outside. . . . We must propose to the democracy terms of an acceptable compromise. . . ."

After a recess to consider this ultimatum, the Bolsheviki returned with a resolution, read by Kamenev:

The *Tsay-ee-kah* considers it necessary that there enter into the Government representatives of *all the Socialist parties composing the Soviets of Workers', Soldiers' and Peasants' Deputies who recognise the conquests of the Revolution of November 7th—that is to say, the establishment of a Government of Soviets, the decrees on peace, land, workers' control over industry, and the arming of the working-class.* The *Tsay-ee-kah* therefore resolves to propose negotiations concerning the constitution of the Government to all parties *of the Soviet,* and insists upon the following conditions as a basis:

The Government is responsible to the *Tsay-ee-kah.* The *Tsay-ee-kah* shall be enlarged to 150 members. To these 150 delegates of the Soviets of Workers' and Soldiers' Deputies shall be added 75 delegates of the *Provincial* Soviets of Peasants' Deputies, 80 from the Front organisations of the Army and Navy, 40 from the Trade Unions (25 from the various All-Russian Unions, in proportion to their importance, 10 from the *Vikzhel,* and 5 from the Post and Telegraph Workers), and 50 delegates from the Socialist groups in the Petrograd City Duma. In the Ministry itself, at least one-half the portfolios must be reserved to the Bolsheviki. The Ministries of Labour, Interior and Foreign Affairs must be given to

the Bolsheviki. The command of the garrisons of Petrograd
and Moscow must remain in the hands of delegates of the
Moscow and Petrograd Soviets.

The Government undertakes the systematic arming of the
workers of all Russia.

It is resolved to insist upon the candidature of comrades
Lenin and Trotsky.

Kamenev explained. "The so-called 'People's Council,' "
he said, "proposed by the Conference, would consist of
about 420 members, of which about 150 would be Bolsheviki. Besides, there would be delegates from the counter-
revolutionary old *Tsay-ee-kah,* 100 members chosen by
the Municipal Dumas—Kornilovtsi all; 100 delegates from
the Peasants' Soviets—appointed by Avksentiev, and 80
from the old Army Committees, who no longer represent
the soldier masses.

"We refuse to admit the old *Tsay-ee-kah,* and also the
representatives of the Municipal Dumas. The delegates
from the Peasants' Soviets shall be elected by the Congress of Peasants, which we have called, and which will
at the same time elect a new Executive Committee. The
proposal to exclude Lenin and Trotsky is a proposal to
decapitate our party, and we do not accept it. And finally,
we see no necessity for a 'People's Council' anyway; the
Soviets are open to all Socialist parties, and the *Tsay-ee-
kah* represents them in their real proportions among the
masses. . . ."

Karelin, for the Left Socialist Revolutionaries, declared
that his party would vote for the Bolshevik resolution, re-
serving the right to modify certain details, such as the
representation of the peasants, and demanding that the
Ministry of Agriculture be reserved for the Left Socialist
Revolutionaries. This was agreed to. . . .

Later, at a meeting of the Petrograd Soviet, Trotsky answered a question about the formation of the new Government:

"I don't know anything about that. I am not taking part in the negotiations. . . . However, I don't think that they are of great importance. . . ."

That night there was great uneasiness in the Conference. The delegates of the City Duma withdrew. . . .

But at Smolny itself, in the ranks of the Bolshevik party, a formidable opposition to Lenin's policy was growing. On the night of November 17th the great hall was packed and ominous for the meeting of the *Tsay-ee-kah*.

Larin, Bolshevik, declared that the moment of elections to the Constituent Assembly approached, and it was time to do away with "political terrorism."

"The measures taken against the freedom of the press should be modified. They had their reason during the struggle, but now they have no further excuse. The press should be free, except for appeals to riot and insurrection."

In a storm of hisses and hoots from his own party, Larin offered the following resolution:

The decree of the Council of People's Commissars concerning the Press is herewith repealed.

Measures of political repression can only be employed subject to decision of a special tribunal, elected by the *Tsay-ee-kah* proportionally to the strength of the different parties represented; and this tribunal shall have the right also to reconsider measures of repression already taken.

This was met by a thunder of applause, not only from the Left Socialist Revolutionaries, but also from a part of the Bolsheviki.

Avanesov, for the Leninites, hastily proposed that the

question of the Press be postponed until after some compromise between the Socialist parties had been reached.
Overwhelmingly voted down.

"The revolution which is now being accomplished,"
went on Avanesov, "has not hesitated to attack private
property; and it is as private property that we must
examine the question of the Press. . . ."

Thereupon he read the official Bolshevik resolution:

The suppression of the bourgeois press was dictated not
only by purely military needs in the course of the insurrection,
and for the checking of counter-revolutionary action, but it
is also necessary as a measure of transition toward the establishment of a new régime with regard to the Press—a régime
under which the capitalist owners of printing-presses and of
paper cannot be the all-powerful and exclusive manufacturers of public opinion.

We must further proceed to the confiscation of private printing plants and supplies of paper, which should become the
property of the Soviets, both in the capital and in the
provinces, so that the political parties and groups can make
use of the facilities of printing in proportion to the actual
strength of the ideas they represent—in other words, proportionally to the number of their constituents.

The reëstablishment of the so-called "freedom of the
press," the simple return of printing presses and paper to
the capitalists,—poisoners of the mind of the people—this
would be an inadmissible surrender to the will of capital, a
giving up of one of the most important conquests of the
Revolution; in other words, it would be a measure of un-
questionably counter-revolutionary character.

Proceeding from the above, the *Tsay-ee-kah* categorically
rejects all propositions aiming at the reëstablishment of the
old régime in the domain of the Press, and unequivocally
supports the point of view of the Council of People's Commissars on this question, against pretentions and ultimatums

dictated by petty bourgeois prejudices, or by evident surrender to the interests of the counter-revolutionary bourgeoisie.

The reading of this resolution was interrupted by ironical shouts from the Left Socialist Revolutionaries, and
bursts of indignation from the insurgent Bolsheviki. Karelin
was on his feet, protesting. "Three weeks ago the Bolsheviki were the most ardent defenders of the freedom of
the Press. . . The arguments in this resolution suggest
singularly the point of view of the old Black Hundreds
and the censors of the Tsarist régime—for they also talked
of 'poisoners of the mind of the people.'"

Trotsky spoke at length in favour of the resolution. He
distinguished between the Press during the civil war, and
the Press after the victory. "During civil war the right to
use violence belongs only to the oppressed. . . ." (Cries
of "Who's the oppressed now? Cannibal!").

"The victory over our adversaries is not yet achieved,
and the newspapers are arms in their hands. In these conditions, the closing of the newspapers is a legitimate measure of defence. . . ." Then passing to the question of
the Press after the victory, Trotsky continued:

"The attitude of Socialists on the question of freedom
of the Press should be the same as their attitude toward
the freedom of business. . . . The rule of the democracy
which is being established in Russia demands that the
domination of the Press by private property must be
abolished, just as the domination of industry by private
property. . . . The power of the Soviets should confiscate
all printing-plants." (Cries, "Confiscate the printing-shop
of *Pravda!*")

"The monopoly of the Press by the bourgeoisie must
be abolished. Otherwise it isn't worth while for us to take

the power! Each group of citizens should have access to printshops and paper. . . . The ownership of print-type and of paper belongs first to the workers and peasants, and only afterwards to the bourgeois parties, which are in a minority. . . . The passing of the power into the hands of the Soviets will bring about a radical transformation of the essential conditions of existence, and this transformation will necessarily be evident in the Press. . . . If we are going to nationalise the banks, can we then tolerate the financial journals? The old régime must die; that must be understood once and for all. . . ." Applause and angry cries.

Karelin declared that the *Tsay-ee-kah* had no right to pass upon this important question, which should be left to a special committee. Again, passionately, he demanded that the Press be free.

Then Lenin, calm, unemotional, his forehead wrinkled, as he spoke slowly, choosing his words; each sentence falling like a hammer-blow. "The civil war is not yet finished; the enemy is still with us; consequently it is impossible to abolish the measures of repression against the Press.

"We Bolsheviki have always said that when we reached a position of power we would close the bourgeois press. To tolerate the bourgeois newspapers would mean to cease being a Socialist. When one makes a Revolution, one cannot mark time; one must always go forward—or go back. He who now talks about the 'freedom of the Press' goes backward, and halts our headlong course toward Socialism.

"We have thrown off the yoke of capitalism, just as the first revolution threw off the yoke of Tsarism. *If the first revolution had the right to suppress the Monarchist papers,* then we have the right to suppress the bourgeois press. It is impossible to separate the question of the freedom of the Press from the other questions of the class struggle. We have promised to close these newspapers, and we shall do it. The immense majority of the people is with us!

"Now that the insurrection is over, we have absolutely no desire to suppress the papers of the other Socialist parties, except inasmuch as they appeal to armed insurrection, or to disobedience to the Soviet Government. However, we shall not permit them, under the pretence of freedom of the Socialist press, to obtain, through the secret support of the bourgeoisie, a monopoly of printing-presses, ink and paper. . . . These essentials must become the property of the Soviet Government, and be apportioned, first of all, to the Socialist parties in strict proportion to their voting strength. . . ." *

Then the vote. The resolution of Larin and the Left Socialist Revolutionaries was defeated by 31 to 22; the Lenin motion was carried by 34 to 24. Among the minority were the Bolsheviki Riazanov and Lozovsky, who declared that it was impossible for them to vote against any restriction on the freedom of the Press.

Upon this the Left Socialist Revolutionaries declared they could no longer be responsible for what was being done, and withdrew from the Military Revolutionary Committee and all other positions of executive responsibility.

Five members—Nogin, Rykov, Miliutin, Teodorovich and Shliapnikov—resigned from the Council of People's Commissars, declaring:

We are in favour of a Socialist Government composed of all the parties in the Soviets. We consider that only the creation of such a Government can possibly guarantee the results of the heroic struggle of the working-class and the revolution-

* For some reason, the speech as reported by Reed differs considerably from the version of it to be found in Lenin's *Works*. Reed's version is more coherent and logical and less menacing than the original.—*Ed.*

ary army. Outside of that, there remains only one way: the constitution of a purely Bolshevik Government by means of political terrorism. This last is the road taken by the Council of People's Commissars. We cannot and will not follow it. We see that this leads directly to the elimination from political life of many proletarian organisations, to the establishment of an irresponsible régime, and to the destruction of the Revolution and the country. We cannot take the responsibility for such a policy, and we renounce before the *Tsay-ee-kah* our function as People's Commissars.

Other Commissars, without resigning their positions, signed the declaration—Riazanov, Derbychev of the Press Department, Arbuzov, of the Government Printing-plant, Yurenev, of the Red Guard, Feodorov, of the Commissariat of Labour, and Larin, secretary of the Section of Elaboration of Decrees.

At the same time Kamenev, Rykov, Miliutin, Zinoviev and Nogin resigned from the Central Committee of the Bolshevik party, making public their reasons:

. . . The constitution of such a Government (composed of all the parties of the Soviet) is indispensable to prevent a new flow of blood, the coming famine, the destruction of the Revolution by the Kaledinists, to assure the convocation of the Constituent Assembly at the proper time, and to apply effectively the programme adopted by the Congress of Soviets. . . .

We cannot accept the responsibility for the disastrous policy of the Central Committee, carried on against the will of an enormous majority of the proletariat and the soldiers, who are eager to see the rapid end of the bloodshed between the different political parties of the democracy. . . . We renounce our title as members of the Central Committee, in order to be able to say openly our opinion to the masses of workers and soldiers. . . .

We leave the Central Committee at the moment of victory; we cannot calmly look on while the policy of the chiefs of the Central Committee leads toward the loss of the fruits of victory and the crushing of the proletariat. . . .

The masses of the workers, the soldiers of the garrison, stirred restlessly, sending their delegations to Smolny, to the Conference for Formation of the New Government, where the break in the ranks of the Bolsheviki caused the liveliest joy.

But the answer of the Leninites was swift and ruthless. Shliapnikov and Teodorovich submitted to party discipline and returned to their posts. Kamenev was stripped of his powers as president of the *Tsay-ee-kah,* and Sverdlov elected in his place. Zinoviev was deposed as president of the Petrograd Soviet. On the morning of the 5th, *Pravda* contained a ferocious proclamation to the people of Russia, written by Lenin, which was printed in hundreds of thousands of copies, posted on the walls everywhere, and distributed over the face of Russia.

The second All-Russian Congress of Soviets gave the majority to the Bolshevik party. Only a Government formed by this party can therefore be a Soviet Government. And it is known to all that the Central Committee of the Bolshevik party, a few hours before the formation of the new Government and before proposing the list of its members to the All-Russian Congress of Soviets, invited to its meeting three of the most eminent members of the Left Socialist Revolutionary group, comrades Kamkov, Spiro and Karelin, and ASKED THEM to participate in the new Government. We regret infinitely that the invited comrades refused; we consider their refusal inadmissible for revolutionists and champions of the working-class; we are willing at any time to include the Left Socialist Revolutionaries in the Government; but we declare that, as the party of the majority at the second All-

Russian Congress of Soviets, we are entitled and BOUND before the people to form a Government. . . .

. . . Comrades! Several members of the Central Committee of our party and the Council of People's Commissars, Kamenev, Zinoviev, Nogin, Rykov, Miliutin and a few others left yesterday, November 17th, the Central Committee of our party, and the last three, the Council of People's Commissars. . . .

The comrades who left us acted like deserters, because they not only abandoned the posts entrusted to them, but also disobeyed the direct instructions of the Central Committee of our party, to the effect that they should await the decisions of the Petrograd and Moscow party organisations before retiring. We blame decisively such desertion. We are firmly convinced that all conscious workers, soldiers and peasants, belonging to our party or sympathising with it, will also disapprove of the behaviour of the deserters. . . .

Remember, comrades, that two of these deserters, Kamenev and Zinoviev, even before the uprising in Petrograd, appeared as deserters and strike-breakers, by voting at the decisive meeting of the Central Committee, October 23d, 1917, against the insurrection; and even AFTER the resolution passed by the Central Committee, they continued their campaign at a meeting of the party workers. . . . But the great impulse of the masses, the great heroism of millions of workers, soldiers and peasants, in Moscow, Petrograd, at the front, in the trenches, in the villages, pushed aside the deserters as a railway train scatters saw-dust. . . .

Shame upon those who are of little faith, who hesitate, who doubt, who allow themselves to be frightened by the bourgeoisie, or who succumb before the cries of the latter's direct or indirect accomplices! There is NOT A SHADOW of hesitation in the MASSES of Petrograd, Moscow, and the rest of Russia. . . .

. . . We shall not submit to any ultimatums from small groups of intellectuals which are not followed by the masses,

which are PRACTICALLY only supported by Kornilovists, Sa-
vinkovists, *yunkers,* and so forth. . . .*

The response from the whole country was like a blast
of hot storm. The insurgents never got a chance to "say
openly their opinion of the masses of workers and soldiers." Upon the *Tsay-ee-kah* rolled in like breakers the
fierce popular condemnation of the "deserters." For days
Smolny was thronged with angry delegations and committees, from the front, from the Volga, from the Petrograd factories. "Why did they dare leave the Government? Were they paid by the bourgeoisie to destroy the
Revolution? They must return and submit to the decisions
of the Central Committee!"

Only in the Petrograd garrison was there still un-
certainty. A great soldier meeting was held on November
24th, addressed by representatives of all the political
parties. By a vast majority Lenin's policy was sustained,
and the Left Socialist Revolutionaries were told that they
must enter the government. . . . *See page 363.*

The Mensheviki delivered a final ultimatum, demanding that all Ministers and *yunkers* be released, that all
newspapers be allowed full freedom, that the Red Guard
be disarmed and the garrison put under command of the
Duma. To this Smolny answered that all the Socialist
Ministers and also all but a very few *yunkers* had been
already set free, that all newspapers were free except the
bourgeois press, and that the Soviet would remain in command of the armed forces. . . . On the 19th the Conference to Form a New Government disbanded, and the
opposition one by one slipped away to Moghilev, where,
under the wing of the General Staff, they continued to

* The full text is to be found in Lenin, *Works,* Vol. XXVI, pp. 269-79.—*Ed.*

form Government after Government, until the end. . . .*

Meanwhile the Bolsheviki had been undermining the power of the *Vikzhel.* An appeal of the Petrograd Soviet to all railway workers called upon them to force the *Vikzhel* to surrender its powers. On the 15th, the *Tsay-ee-kah,* following its procedure toward the peasants, called an All-Russian Congress of Railway Workers for December 1st; the *Vikzhel* immediately called its own Congress for two weeks later. On November 16th, the *Vikzhel* members took their seats in the *Tsay-ee-kah.* On the night of December 2d, at the opening session of the All-Russian Congress of Railway Workers, the *Tsay-ee-kah* formally offered the post of Commissar of Ways and Communications to the *Vikzhel*—which accepted. . . .**

Having settled the question of power, the Bolsheviki turned their attention to problems of practical administration. First of all the city, the country, the Army must be fed. Bands of sailors and Red Guards scoured the warehouses, the railway terminals, even the barges in the canals, unearthing and confiscating thousands of *poods****

* The "ultimatum" was a demand drafted by Martov and Abramovich that real negotiations for an all-socialist government required the stopping of the terror against the other socialist parties and the press. Reed is mistaken on the matter of "slipping away to Moghilev." None of the leading negotiators for the Menshevik Internationalists nor of any other group that entered seriously into the negotiations went to Moghilev.—*Ed.*

** The Bolsheviks did not succeed in winning *Vikzhel* and the Railway Union in the form Reed relates. At the Extraordinary All-Russian Congress of Railwaymen, held in January 1918, *Vikzhel* secured a small majority (273-261) which favored the Constituent Assembly as against a government by the Bolshevik controlled Soviets. The minority supporting the Bolshevik then bolted and formed an All-Russian Executive Committee of Railwaymen (*Vikzheldor*), consisting of 25 Bolsheviks, 12 Left SR's and three Social Democrat Internationalists. The government then recognized the split off organization, and began to use administrative and terror measures against the majority union. It was from *Vikzheldor* that Rogov was named Commissar of Ways and Communications. Then a second Commissar, Nevsky, made it a duumvirate. On March 26, 1918, the control of the railways was taken away from the new organization and those railroads where the old union still controlled were put under military dictatorship.—*Ed.*

*** A *pood* is thirty-six pounds.

КЪ ВОПРОСУ О СОГЛАШЕНІИ.

Вниманію всѣхъ рабочихъ и всѣхъ солдатъ.

11-го Ноября въ клубѣ Преображенскаго полка состоялось чрезвычайное собраніе представителей всѣхъ частей Петроградскаго гарнизона.

Собраніе это было созвано по иниціативѣ Преображенскаго и Семеновскаго полковъ для обсужденія вопроса о томъ, какія соціалистическія партіи стоятъ за совѣтскую власть, какія противъ совѣтской власти, какія стоятъ за народъ, какія противъ него, и возможно ли соглашеніе.

На собраніе были приглашены представители Центральнаго Исполнительнаго Комитета Совѣтовъ, Городской думы, Авксентьевскаго крестьянскаго совѣта и всѣхъ политическихъ партій отъ большевиковъ до народныхъ соціалистовъ включительно.

Послѣ долгаго обсужденія, заслушавъ рѣчи всѣхъ партій и организацій, собраніе подавляющимъ большинствомъ голосовъ признало, что только большевики и лѣвые эс-эры стоятъ за народъ, а всѣ остальныя партіи только прикрываются лозунгомъ соглашенія для того, чтобы лишить народъ тѣхъ завоеваній, которыя были сдѣланы въ дни великой октябрьской рабочей и солдатской революціи.

Вотъ текстъ резолюціи, принятой на этомъ собраніи Петроградскаго гарнизона 61 голосомъ противъ 1 при 12 воздержавшихся:

„Гарнизонное собраніе, созванное по иниціативѣ Преображенскаго и Семеновскаго полковъ, выслушавъ представителей всѣхъ соціалистическихъ партій и общественныхъ организацій по вопросу о соглашеніи политическихъ партій, находитъ, что:

1) Представители Центральнаго Исполнительнаго Комитета Совѣтовъ (2-го созыва), представители партіи большевиковъ и лѣвыхъ эс-эровъ опредѣленно заявили, что они за власть совѣтовъ, за декреты о землѣ, мирѣ и контролѣ надъ производствомъ и что на этой платформѣ они допускаютъ соглашеніе соціалистическихъ партій.

2) Въ то же время представители другихъ партій (эс-эровъ и меньшевиковъ) или не дали отвѣта или прямо заявили, что они противъ совѣтской власти и противъ декретовъ о землѣ, мирѣ и контролѣ.

Въ виду чего совѣщаніе постановляетъ:

1) Вынести рѣзкое порицаніе тѣмъ партіямъ, которыя, прикрываясь лозунгомъ соглашенія, на самомъ дѣлѣ хотятъ сорвать завоеванія, добытыя народомъ въ дни октябрьской революціи.

2) Выразить полное довѣріе Центральному Исполнительному Комитету и Совѣту народныхъ Комиссаровъ и обѣщать имъ полную поддержку.

Въ то же время собраніе находитъ необходимымъ, чтобы товарищи лѣвые эс-эры вступили въ составъ Народнаго Правительства.

Совѣщаніе представителей воинскихъ частей Петроградскаго гарнизона.

Литографія «Кольцъ», Петроградъ, Сабанн пер., 6, соб. домъ.

Announcement, posted on the walls of Petrograd, of the result of a meeting of representatives of the garrison regiments, called to consider the question of forming a new Government. For translation see Note 6, p. 387.

of food held by private speculators. Emissaries were sent
to the provinces, where with the assistance of the Land
Committees they seized the store-houses of the great grain-
dealers. Expeditions of sailors, heavily armed, were sent
out in groups of five thousand, to the South, to Siberia,
with roving commissions to capture cities still held
by the White Guards, establish order, and *get food*. Pas-
senger traffic on the Trans-Siberian Railroad was suspended for two weeks, while thirteen trains, loaded with
bolts of cloth and bars of iron assembled by the Factory-
Shop Committees, were sent out eastward, each in charge
of a Commissar, to barter with the Siberian peasants for
grain and potatoes. . . .

Kaledin being in possession of the coal-mines of the
Don, the fuel question became urgent. Smolny shut off
all electric lights in theatres, shops and restaurants, cut
down the number of street cars, and confiscated the private
stores of fire-wood held by the fuel-dealers. . . . And
when the factories of Petrograd were about to close down
for lack of coal, the sailors of the Baltic Fleet turned
over to the workers two hundred thousand *poods* from the
bunkers of battle-ships. . . .

Toward the end of November occurred the "wine-pog-
roms" [7]—looting of the wine-cellars—beginning with the
plundering of the Winter Palace vaults. For days there
were drunken soldiers on the streets. . . . In all this was
evident the hand of the counter-revolutionists, who distributed among the regiments plans showing the location
of the stores of liquor. The Commissars of Smolny began
by pleading and arguing, which did not stop the growing
disorder, followed by pitched battles between soldiers and
Red Guards. . . . Finally the Military Revolutionary
Committee sent out companies of sailors with machine-
guns, who fired mercilessly upon the rioters, killing many;

and by executive order the wine-cellars were invaded by Committees with hatchets, who smashed the bottles—or blew them up with dynamite. . . .

Companies of Red Guards, disciplined and well-paid, were on duty at the headquarters of the Ward Soviets day and night, replacing the old Militia. In all quarters of the city small elective Revolutionary Tribunals were set up by the workers and soldiers to deal with petty crime. . . .

The great hotels, where the speculators still did a thriving business, were surrounded by Red Guards, and the speculators thrown into jail.[8] . . .

Alert and suspicious, the working-class of the city constituted itself a vast spy system, through the servants prying into bourgeois households, and reporting all information to the Military Revolutionary Committee, which struck with an iron hand, unceasing. In this way was discovered the Monarchist plot led by former Duma-member Purishkevich and a group of nobles and officers, who had planned an officers' uprising, and had written a letter inviting Kaledin to Petrograd.[9] . . . In this way was unearthed the conspiracy of the Petrograd Cadets, who were sending money and recruits to Kaledin. . . .

Neratov, frightened at the outburst of popular fury provoked by his flight, returned and surrendered the Secret Treaties to Trotsky, who began their publication in *Pravda,* scandalising the world. . . .

The restrictions on the Press were increased by a decree[10] making advertisements a monopoly of the official Government newspaper. At this all the other papers suspended publication as a protest, or disobeyed the law and were closed. . . . Only three weeks later did they finally submit.

Still the strike of the Ministries went on, still the sabotage of the old officials, the stoppage of normal economic

ОБЯЗАТЕЛЬНОЕ ПОСТАНОВЛЕНІЕ.

1) Городъ Петроградъ объявленъ на осадномъ положеніи.

2) Всякія собранія, митинги, сборища и т. п. на улицахъ и площадяхъ воспрещается.

3) Попытки разгромовъ винныхъ погребовъ, складовъ, заводовъ, лавокъ, магазиновъ, частныхъ квартиръ и проч. и т. п. будутъ прекращаемы пулеметнымъ огнемъ безъ всякаго предупрежденія.

4) Домовымъ комитетамъ, швейцарамъ, дворникамъ и милиціи вмѣняется въ безусловную обязанность поддерживать самый строжайшій порядокъ въ домахъ, дворахъ и на улицахъ, причемъ ворота и подъѣзды домовъ должны запираться въ 9 час. вечера и открываться въ 7 час. утра. Послѣ 9 час. вечера выпускать только жильцовъ подъ контролемъ домовыхъ комитетовъ.

5) Виновные въ раздачѣ, продажѣ или пріобрѣтеніи всякихъ спиртныхъ напитковъ, а также въ нарушеніи пунктовъ 2-го и 4-го будутъ немедленно арестованы и подвергнуты самому тяжкому наказанію.

Петроградъ 6-го декабря, 3 часа ночи.

Комитетъ по борьбѣ съ погромами при Исполнительномъ Комитетѣ Совѣта Рабочихъ и Солдатскихъ Депутатовъ.

Типографія «Копейка», Петроградъ. Садовая пер. 4, соб. домъ.

Bolshevik order. A proclamation of the Committee to Fight against Pogroms attached to the Petrograd Soviet. For translation see Note 11, p. 392.

life. Behind Smolny was only the will of the vast, un-organised popular masses; and with them the Council of People's Commissars dealt, directing revolutionary mass-action against its enemies. In eloquent proclamations,[12] couched in simple words and spread over Russia, Lenin explained the Revolution, urged the people to take the power into their own hands, by force to break down the resistance of the propertied classes, by force to take over the institutions of Government. Revolutionary order. Revolutionary discipline! Strict accounting and control! No strikes! No loafing!

On the 20th of November the Military Revolutionary Committee issued a warning:

The rich classes oppose the power of the Soviets—the Government of workers, soldiers and peasants. Their sympathisers halt the work of the employees of the Government and the Duma, incite strikes in the banks, try to interrupt communication by the railways, the post and the telegraph. . . .

We warn them that they are playing with fire. The country and the Army are threatened with famine. To fight against it, the regular functioning of all services is indispensable. The Workers' and Peasants' Government is taking every measure to assure the country and the Army all that is necessary. Opposition to these measures is a crime against the People. We warn the rich classes and their sympathisers that, if they do not cease their sabotage and their provocation in halting the transportation of food, they will be the first to suffer. They will be deprived of the right of receiving food. All the reserves which they possess will be requisitioned. The property of the principal criminals will be confiscated.

We have done our duty in warning those who play with fire.

We are convinced that in case decisive measures become necessary, we shall be solidly supported by all workers, soldiers, and peasants.

Ко всѣмъ рабочимъ
ПЕТРОГРАДА!

Товарищи! Революція побѣждаетъ—революція побѣдила. Вся власть перешла къ нашимъ Совѣтамъ. Первыя недѣли самыя трудныя. Надо раздавить до конца сломленную уже реакцію, надо обезпечить полное торжество нашимъ стремленіямъ. Рабочій классъ долженъ, обязанъ проявить въ эти дни

величайшую выдержку и выносливость,

чтобы облегчить Новому Народному Правительству Совѣтовъ выполненіе всѣхъ задачъ. На этихъ же дняхъ будутъ изданы новые законы по рабочему вопросу и въ томъ числѣ одинъ изъ самыхъ горячихъ законъ о рабочемъ контролѣ надъ производствомъ и объ регулированіи промышленности.

Забастовки и выступленія рабочихъ массъ въ Петроградѣ теперь только вредятъ.

Мы просимъ васъ немедленно прекратить всѣ экономическія и политическія забастовки, всѣмъ стать на работу и производить ее въ полномъ порядкѣ. Работа на заводахъ и во всѣхъ предпріятіяхъ необходима новому правительству Совѣтовъ, потому что всякое разстройство работъ создаетъ для насъ новыя затрудненія которыхъ и безъ того довольно. Всѣ къ своему мѣсту.

Лучшее средство поддержать новое правительство Совѣтовъ въ эти дни— исполнять свое дѣло.

Да здравствуетъ твердая выдержка пролетаріата! Да здравствуетъ революція!

Петроградскій Совѣтъ Р. и С. Д.
Петроградскій Совѣтъ Профессіональныхъ Союзовъ.
Центральный Совѣтъ Фабрично-Заводскихъ Комитетовъ.

Appeal of the Petrograd Soviet, the Petrograd Council of Professional Unions and the Petrograd Council of Factory Shop Committees, to the Workers of Petrograd, urging them to work hard and not to strike. For translation see Note 13, p. 394.

On the 22d of November the walls of the city were placarded with a sheet headed "EXTRAORDINARY COMMUNICATION":

The Council of People's Commissars has received an urgent telegram from the Staff of the Northern Front. . . .

"There must be no further delay; do not let the Army die of hunger; the armies of the Northern Front have not received a crust of bread now for several days, and in two or three days they will not have any more biscuits—which are being doled out to them from reserve supplies until now never touched. . . . Already delegates from all parts of the Front are talking of a necessary removal of part of the Army to the rear, foreseeing that in a few days there will be headlong flight of the soldiers, dying from hunger, ravaged by the three years' war in the trenches, sick, insufficiently clothed, bare-footed, driven mad by superhuman misery."

The Military Revolutionary Committee brings this to the notice of the Petrograd garrison and the workers of Petrograd. The situation at the Front demands the most urgent and decisive measures. . . . Meanwhile the higher functionaries of the Government institutions, banks, railroads, post and telegraph, are on strike and impeding the work of the Government in supplying the Front with provisions. . . . Each hour of delay may cost the life of thousands of soldiers. The counter-revolutionary functionaries are the most dishonest criminals toward their hungry and dying brethren on the Front. . . .

The MILITARY REVOLUTIONARY COMMITTEE GIVES THESE CRIMINALS A LAST WARNING. In event of the least resistance or opposition on their part, the harshness of the measures which will be adopted against them will correspond to the seriousness of their crime. . . .

The masses of workers and soldiers responded by a savage tremor of rage, which swept all Russia. In the capital the Government and bank employees got out hundreds of proclamations and appeals,[14] protesting, defending themselves, such as this one:

To the Attention of All Citizens.
The State Bank Is Closed!
Why?

Because the violence exercised by the Bolsheviki against the State Bank has made it impossible for us to work. The first act of the People's Commissars was to DEMAND TEN MILLION RUBLES, and on November 27th THEY DEMANDED TWENTY-FIVE MILLIONS, without any indication as to where this money was to go.

. . . We functionaries cannot take part in plundering the people's property. We stopped work.

CITIZENS! The money in the State Bank is yours, the people's money, acquired by your labour, your sweat and blood. CITIZENS! Save the people's property from robbery, and us from violence, and we shall immediately resume work.

EMPLOYEES OF THE STATE BANK.

From the Ministry of Supplies, the Ministry of Finance, from the Special Supply Committee, declarations that the Military Revolutionary Committee made it impossible for the employees to work, appeals to the population to support them against Smolny. . . . But the dominant worker and soldier did not believe them; it was firmly fixed in the popular mind that the employees were sabotaging, starving the Army, starving the people. . . . In the long bread lines, which as formerly stood in the iron winter streets, it was not *the Government* which was blamed, as it had been under Kerensky, but the *chinovniki,* the sabotageurs; for the Government was *their* Government, *their* Soviets—and the functionaries of the Ministries were against it. . . .

At the centre of all this opposition was the Duma, and its militant organ, the Committee for Salvation, protesting against all the decrees of the Council of People's Commissars, voting again and again not to recognise the Soviet Government, openly cooperating with the new counter-revolutionary "Governments" set up at Moghilev. . . . On the 17th of November, for example, the Committee for Salvation addressed "all Municipal Governments, Zemstvos, and all democratic and revolutionary organisations of peasants, workers, soldiers and other citizens," in these words:

Do not recognize the Government of the Bolsheviki, and struggle against it.

Form local Committees for Salvation of Country and Revolution, who will unite all democratic forces, so as to aid the All-Russian Committee for Salvation in the tasks which it has set itself. . . .

Meanwhile the elections for the Constituent Assembly in Petrograd[15] gave an enormous plurality to the Bolsheviki; so that even the Mensheviki Internationalists pointed out that the Duma ought to be re-elected, as it no longer represented the political composition of the Petrograd population. . . . At the same time floods of resolutions from workers' organisations, from military units, even from the peasants in the surrounding country, poured in upon the Duma, calling it "counter-revolutionary, Kornilovets," and demanding that it resign. The last days of the Duma were stormy with the bitter demands of the Municipal workers for decent living wages, and the threat of strikes. . . .

On the 23d a formal decree of the Military Revolutionary Committee dissolved the Committee for Salvation. On the 29th, the Council of People's Commissars ordered the dissolution and re-election of the Petrograd City Duma:

In view of the fact that the Central Duma of Petrograd, elected September 2d, . . . has definitely lost the right to represent the population of Petrograd, being in complete disaccord with its state of mind and its aspirations . . . and in view of the fact that the personnel of the Duma majority, although having lost all political following, continues to make use of its prerogatives to resist in a counter-revolutionary manner the will of the workers, soldiers and peasants, to sabotage and obstruct the normal work of the Government—the Council of People's Commissars considers it its duty to invite the population of the capital to pronounce judgment on the policy of the organ of Municipal autonomy.

To this end the Council of People's Commissars resolves:

(1) To dissolve the Municipal Duma; the dissolution to take effect November 30th, 1917.

(2) All functionaries elected or appointed by the present Duma shall remain at their posts and fulfil the duties confided to them, until their places shall be filled by representatives of the new Duma.

(3) All Municipal employees shall continue to fulfil their duties; those who leave the service of their own accord shall be considered discharged.

(4) The new elections for the Municipal Duma of Petrograd are fixed for December 9th, 1917. . . .

(5) The Municipal Duma of Petrograd shall meet December 11th, 1917, at two o'clock.

(6) Those who disobey this decree, as well as those who intentionally harm or destroy the property of the Municipality, shall be immediately arrested and brought before the Revolutionary Tribunals. . . .

The Duma met defiantly, passing resolutions to the effect that it would "defend its position to the last drop of its blood," and appealing desperately to the population to save their "own elected City Government." But the population remained indifferent or hostile. On the 31st Mayor Schreider and several members were arrested, interrogated, and released. That day and the next the Duma continued to meet, interrupted frequently by Red Guards and sailors, who politely requested the assembly to disperse. At the meeting of December 2d, an officer and some sailors entered the Nicolai Hall while a member was speaking, and ordered the members to leave, or force would be used. They did so, protesting to the last, but finally "ceding to violence."

The new Duma, which was elected ten days later, and for which the "Moderate" Socialists refused to vote, was almost entirely Bolshevik. . . .

There remained several centres of dangerous opposition, such as the "republics" of Ukraine and Finland, which were showing definitely anti-Soviet tendencies. Both at Helsingfors and at Kiev the Governments were gathering troops which could be depended upon, and entering upon campaigns of crushing Bolshevism, and of disarming and expelling Russian troops. The Ukrainian Rada had taken command of all southern Russia, and was furnishing Kaledin reinforcements and supplies. Both Finland and Ukraine were beginning secret negotiations with the Germans, and were promptly recognised by the Allied Governments, which loaned them huge sums of money, joining with the propertied classes to create counter-revolutionary centres of attack upon Soviet Russia. In the end, when Bolshevism had conquered in both these countries, the defeated bourgeoisie called in the Germans to restore them to power. . . .

But the most formidable menace to the Soviet Government was internal and two-headed—the Kaledin movement, and the Staff at Moghilev, where General Dukhonin had assumed command.

The ubiquitous Muraviov was appointed commander of the war against the Cossacks, and a Red Army was recruited from among the factory workers. Hundreds of propagandists were sent to the Don. The Council of People's Commissars issued a proclamation to the Cossacks,[16] explaining what the Soviet Government was, how the propertied classes, the *chinovniki,* landlords, bankers and their allies, the Cossack princes, land-owners and Generals, were trying to destroy the Revolution, and prevent the confiscation of their wealth by the people.

On November 27th a committee of Cossacks came to Smolny to see Trotsky and Lenin. They demanded if it were true that the Soviet Government did not intend to divide the Cossack lands among the peasants of Great Russia? "No," answered Trotsky. The Cossacks deliberated for a while. "Well," they asked, "does the Soviet Government intend to confiscate the estates of our great Cossack land-owners and divide them among the working Cossacks?" To this Lenin replied. "That," he said, "is for *you* to do. We shall support the working Cossacks in all their actions. . . . The best way to begin is to form Cossack Soviets; you will be given representation in the *Tsay-ee-kah,* and then it will be *your* Government, too. . . ."

The Cossacks departed, thinking hard. Two weeks later General Kaledin received a deputation from his troops. "Will you," they asked, "promise to divide the great estates of the Cossack landlords among the working Cossacks?"

"Only over my dead body," responded Kaledin. A month later, seeing his army melt away before his eyes,

Отъ Комиссіи по Народному Образованію при Центральной Городской Думѣ.

Товарищи рабочіе и работницы!

За нѣсколько дней до праздника была объявлена забастовка учащими городскихъ училищъ. Учащія оказались на сторонѣ буржуазіи противъ рабочаго и крестьянскаго Правительства.

Товарищи, организуйте родительскіе комитеты и выносите резолюціи противъ забастовки учащихъ. Обращайтесь въ районные Совѣты Рабочихъ и Солдатскихъ Депутатовъ, профессіональные союзы, фабрично-заводскіе и партійные комитеты съ предложеніемъ устраивать митинги протеста. Устраивайте собственными силами елки и развлеченія для дѣтей, требуйте возобновленія занятій послѣ праздника въ срокъ, который укажетъ Центральная Дума.

Товарищи, укрѣпляйте свои позиціи въ дѣлѣ народнаго образованія, настаивайте на контролѣ пролетарскихъ организацій надъ школой.

Комиссія по Народному Образованію при Центральной Городской Думѣ.

Proclamation of the Commission on Public Education attached to the City Duma, concerning the strike of school-teachers, just before the Christmas holidays. The Duma had been reelected, and was composed almost entirely of Bolsheviki. For translation see Note 17, p. 402.

Kaledin blew out his brains. And the Cossack movement was no more. . . .

Meanwhile at Moghilev were gathered the old *Tsay-ee-kah,* the "moderate" Socialist leaders—from Avksentiev to Chernov*—the active chiefs of the old Army Committees, and the reactionary officers. The Staff steadily refused to recognise the Council of People's Commissars. It had united about it the Death Battalions, the Knights of St. George, and the Cossacks of the Front, and was in close and secret touch with the Allied military attachés, and with the Kaledin movement and the Ukrainian Rada. . . .

The Allied Governments had made no reply to the Peace decree of November 8th, in which the Congress of Soviets had asked for a general armistice.

On November 20th Trotsky addressed a note to the Allied Ambassadors:[18]

I have the honour to inform you, Mr. Ambassador, that the All-Russian Congress of Soviets . . . on November 8th constituted a new Government of the Russian Republic, in the form of the Council of People's Commissars. The President of this Government is Vladimir Ilyitch Lenin. The direction of Foreign Affairs has been entrusted to me, as People's Commissar for Foreign Affairs. . . .

In drawing your attention to the text, approved by the All-Russian Congress, of the proposition for an armistice and a democratic peace without annexations or indemnities, based on the right of self-determination of peoples, I have the honour to request you to consider that document as a formal proposal of an immediate armistice on all fronts, and the

* Chernov went to Moghilev only to try to stop the fighting and to work for the convocation of the Peasant Soviet. Then he returned to Petrograd for the All-Russian Peasant Soviet Congress and the Constituent Assembly, of which he was elected chairman.

opening of immediate peace negotiations; a proposal which the authorised Government of the Russian Republic addresses at the same time to all the belligerent peoples and their Governments.

Please accept, Mr. Ambassador, the profound assurance of the esteem of the Soviet Government toward your people, who cannot but wish for peace, like all the other peoples exhausted and drained by this unexampled butchery. . . .

The same night the Council of People's Commissars telegraphed to General Dukhonin:

. . . The Council of People's Commissars considers it indispensable without delay to make a formal proposal of armistice to all the powers, both enemy and Allied. A declaration conforming to this decision has been sent by the Commissar for Foreign Affairs to the representatives of the Allied powers at Petrograd.

The Council of People's Commissars orders you, Citizen Commander, . . . to propose to the enemy military authorities immediately to cease hostilities, and enter into negotiations for peace. In charging you with the conduct of these preliminary pourparlers, the Council of People's Commissars orders you:

1. To inform the Council by direct wire immediately of any and all steps in the pourparlers with the representatives of the enemy armies.

2. Not to sign the act of armistice until it has been passed upon by the Council of People's Commissars.

The Allied Ambassadors received Trotsky's note with contemptuous silence, accompanied by anonymous interviews in the newspapers, full of spite and ridicule. The order to Dukhonin was characterised openly as an act of treason. . . .

As for Dukhonin, he gave no sign. On the night of

November 22nd he was communicated with by telephone, and asked if he intended to obey the order. Dukhonin answered that he could not, unless it emanated from "a Government sustained by the Army and the country."

By telegraph he was immediately dismissed from the post of Supreme Commander, and Krylenko appointed in his place. Following his tactics of appealing to the masses, Lenin sent a radiogram to all regimental, divisional and corps Committees, to all soldiers and sailors of the Army and the Fleet, acquainting them with Dukhonin's refusal, and ordering that "the regiments on the front shall elect delegates to begin negotiations with the enemy detachments opposite their positions. . . ."

On the 23d, the military attachés of the Allied nations, acting on instructions from their Governments, presented a note to Dukhonin, in which he was solemnly warned not to "violate the conditions of the treaties concluded between the Powers of the Entente." The note went on to say that if a separate armistice with Germany were concluded, that act "would result in the most serious consequences" to Russia. This communication Dukhonin at once sent out to all the soldiers' Committees. . . .

Next morning Trotsky made another appeal to the troops, characterising the note of the Allied representatives as a flagrant interference in the internal affairs of Russia, and a bald attempt "to force by threats the Russian Army and the Russian people to continue the war in execution of the treaties concluded by the Tsar. . . ."

From Smolny poured out proclamation after proclamation,[19] denouncing Dukhonin and the counter-revolutionary officers about him, denouncing the reactionary politicians gathered at Moghilev, rousing, from one end of the thousand-mile Front to the other, millions of angry, suspicious soldiers. And at the same time Krylenko, accompanied by three detachments of fanatical sailors, set out for the *Stavka,* breathing threats of vengeance,[20] and received by the soldiers everywhere with tremendous ovations—a triumphal progress. The Central Army Committee issued a declaration in favour of Dukhonin; and at once ten thousand troops moved upon Moghilev. . . .

On December 2d the garrison of Moghilev rose and seized the city, arresting Dukhonin and the Army Committee, and going out with victorious red banners to meet the new Supreme Commander. Krylenko entered Moghilev next morning, to find a howling mob gathered about the railway-car in which Dukhonin had been imprisoned. Krylenko made a speech in which he implored the soldiers not to harm Dukhonin, as he was to be taken to Petrograd and judged by the Revolutionary Tribunal. When he had finished, suddenly Dukhonin himself appeared at the window, as if to address the throng. But with a savage roar the people rushed the car, and falling upon the old General, dragged him out and beat him to death on the platform. . . .

So ended the revolt of the *Stavka.* . . .

Immensely strengthened by the collapse of the last important stronghold of hostile military power in Russia, the Soviet Government began with confidence the organisation of the state. Many of the old functionaries flocked to its banner, and many members of other parties entered the Government service. The financially ambitious, however, were checked by the decree on Salaries of Government Employees, fixing the salaries of the People's Commissars —the highest—at five hundred rubles (about fifty dollars) a month. . . . The strike of Government Employees, led by the Union of Unions, collapsed, deserted by the financial and commercial interests which had been backing it. The bank clerks returned to their jobs. . . .

With the decree on the Nationalisation of Banks, the formation of the Supreme Council of People's Economy, the putting into practical operation of the Land decree in the villages, the democratic reorganisation of the Army, and the sweeping changes in all branches of the Government and of life,—with all these, effective only by the will of the masses of workers, soldiers and peasants, slowly began, with many mistakes and hitches, the moulding of proletarian Russia.

Not by compromise with the propertied classes, or with the other political leaders; not by conciliating the old Government mechanism, did the Bolsheviki conquer the power. Nor by the organized violence of a small clique. If the masses all over Russia had not been ready for insurrection it must have failed. The only reason for Bolshevik success lay in their accomplishing the vast and simple desires of the most profound strata of the people, calling them to the work of tearing down and destroying the old, and afterward, in the smoke of falling ruins, cooperating with them to erect the frame-work of the new. . . .

NOTES TO CHAPTER XI

1 Limitations of This Chapter

This chapter extends over a period of two months, more or less. It covers the time of negotiations with the Allies, the negotiations and armistice with the Germans, and the beginning of the Peace negotiations at Brest-Litovsk, as well as the period in which were laid the foundations of the Soviet State.

However, it is no part of my purpose in this book to describe and interpret these very important historical events, which require more space. They are therefore reserved for another volume, "Kornilov to Brest-Litovsk."

In this chapter, then, I have confined myself to the Soviet Government's attempts to consolidate its political power at home, and sketched its successive conquests of hostile domestic elements —which process was temporarily interrupted by the disastrous Peace of Brest-Litovsk.

2 Preamble—Declaration of the Rights of the Peoples of Russia

The October Revolution of the workers and peasants began under the common banner of Emancipation.

The peasants are being emancipated from the power of the landowners, for there is no longer the landowner's property right in the land—it has been abolished. The soldiers and sailors are being emancipated from the power of autocratic generals, for generals will henceforth be elective and subject to recall. The workingmen are being emancipated from the whims and arbitrary will of the capitalists, for henceforth there will be established the control of the workers over mills and factories. Everything living and capable of life is being emancipated from the hateful shackles.

There remain only the peoples of Russia, who have suffered and are suffering oppression and arbitrariness, and whose emancipation must immediately be begun, whose liberation must be effected resolutely and definitely.

During the period of Tsarism the peoples of Russia were systematically incited against one another. The result of such a policy are known: massacres and *pogroms* on the one hand, slavery of peoples on the other.

There can be and there must be no return to this disgraceful policy. Henceforth the policy of a voluntary and honest union of the peoples of Russia must be substituted.

In the period of imperialism, after the March revolution, when the power was transferred into the hands of the Cadet bourgeoisie, the naked policy of provocation gave way to one of cowardly distrust of the peoples of Russia, to a policy of fault-finding, of meaningless "freedom" and "equality" of peoples. The results of such a policy are known: the growth of national enmity, the impairment of mutual confidence.

An end must be put to this unworthy policy of falsehood and distrust, of fault-finding and provocation. Henceforth it must be replaced by an open and honest policy leading to the complete mutual confidence of the peoples of Russia. Only as the result of such a trust can there be formed an honest and lasting union of the peoples of Russia. Only as the result of such a union can the workers and peasants of the peoples of Russia be cemented into one revolutionary force able to resist all attempts on the part of the imperialist-annexationist bourgeoisie.

3 Decrees

On the Nationalisation of the Banks

In the interest of the regular organisation of the national economy, of the thorough eradication of bank speculation and the complete emancipation of the workers, peasants, and the whole labouring population from the exploitation of banking capital, and with a view to the establishment of a single national bank of the Russian Republic which shall serve the real interests of the people and the poorer classes, the Central Executive Committee (*Tsay-ee-kah*) resolves:

1. The banking business is declared a state monopoly.

2. All existing private joint-stock banks and banking offices are merged in the State Bank.

3. The assets and liabilities of the liquidated establishments are taken over by the State Bank.

4. The order of the merger of private banks in the State Bank is to be determined by a special decree.

5. The temporary administration of the affairs of the private banks is entrusted to the board of the State Bank.

6. The interests of the small depositors will be safeguarded.

On the Equality of Rank of All Military Men

In realisation of the will of the revolutionary people regarding the prompt and decisive abolition of all remnants of former inequality in the Army, the Council of People's Commissars decrees:

1. All ranks and grades in the Army, beginning with the rank of Corporal and ending with the rank of General, are abolished. The Army of the Russian Republic consists now of free and equal citizens, bearing the honourable title of Soldiers of the Revolutionary Army.

2. All privileges connected with the former ranks and grades, also all outward marks of distinction, are abolished.

3. All addressing by titles is abolished.

4. All decorations, orders, and other marks of distinction are abolished.

5. With the abolition of the rank of officer, all separate officers' organisations are abolished.

Note.—Orderlies are left only for headquarters, chanceries, Committees and other Army organisations.

President of the Council of People's Commissars,
VL. ULIANOV (LENIN).
People's Commissar for Military and Naval Affairs,
N. KRYLENKO.
People's Commissar for Military Affairs,
N. PODVOISKY.
Secretary of the Council,
N. GORBUNOV.

*　　*　　*　　*

On the Elective Principle and the Organisation of Authority in the Army

1. The army serving the will of the toiling people is subject to its supreme representative—the Council of People's Commissars.

2. Full authority within the limits of military units and combinations is vested in the respective Soldiers' Committees and Soviets.

3. Those phases of the life and activity of the troops which are already under the jurisdiction of the Committees are now formally placed in their direct control. Over such branches of activity which the Committees cannot assume, the control of the Soldiers' Soviets is established.

4. The election of commanding Staff and officers is introduced. All commanders up to the commanders of regiments, inclusive, are elected by general suffrage of squads, platoons, companies, squadrons, batteries, divisions (artillery, 2-3 batteries), and regiments. All commanders higher than the commander of a regiment, and up to the Supreme Commander, inclusive, are elected by congresses or conferences of Committees.

Note.—By the term "conference" must be understood a meeting of the respective Committees together with delegates of committees one degree lower in rank. (Such as a "conference" of Regimental Committees with delegates from Company Committees.—Author.)

5. The elected commanders above the rank of commander of regiment must be confirmed by the nearest Supreme Committee.

Note. In the event of a refusal by a Supreme Committee to confirm an elected commander, with a statement of reasons for such refusal, a commander elected by the lower Committee a second time must be confirmed.

6. The commanders of Armies are elected by Army congresses. Commanders of Fronts are elected by congresses of the respective Fronts.

7. To posts of a technical character, demanding special knowledge or other practical preparation, namely: doctors, engineers, technicians, telegraph and wireless operators, aviators, automobilists, etc., only such persons as possess the required special knowledge may be elected, by the Committees of the units of the respective services.

8. Chiefs of Staff must be chosen from among persons with special military training for that post.

9. All other members of the Staff are appointed by the Chief of Staff, and confirmed by the respective congresses.

Note.—All persons with special training must be listed in a special list.

10. The right is reserved to retire from the service all commanders on active service who are not elected by the soldiers to any post, and who consequently are ranked as privates.

11. All other functions beside those pertaining to the command, with the exception of posts in the economic departments, are filled by appointment of the respective elected commanders.

12. Detailed instructions regarding the elections of the commanding Staff will be published separately.

President of the Council of People's Commissars,
VL. ULIANOV (LENIN).

People's Commissar for Military and Naval Affairs,
N. KRYLENKO.

People's Commissar for Military Affairs,
N. PODVOISKY.

Secretary of the Council,
N. GORBUNOV.

*   *   *   *

On the Abolition of Classes and Titles

1. All classes and class divisions, all class privileges and de-limitations, all class organisations and institutions and all civil ranks are abolished.

2. All classes of society (nobles, merchants, petty bourgeois, etc.), and all titles (Prince, Count and others), and all denominations of civil rank (Privy State Councillor, and others), are abolished, and there is established the general denomination of Citizen of the Russian Republic.

3. The property and institutions of the classes of nobility are transferred to the corresponding autonomous Zemstvos.

4. The property of merchant and bourgeois organisations is transferred immediately to the Municipal Self-Governments.

5. All class institutions of any sort, with their property, their rules of procedure, and their archives, are transferred to the administration of the Municipalities and Zemstvos.

6. All articles of existing laws applying to these matters are herewith repealed.

7. The present decree becomes effective on the day it is published and applied by the Soviets of Workers', Soldiers', and Peasants' Deputies.

The present decree has been confirmed by the *Tsay-ee-kah* at the meeting of November 23d, 1917, and signed by:

President of the Tsay-ee-kah,
SVERDLOV.
President of the Council of People's Commissars,
VL. ULIANOV (LENIN).
Executive of the Council of People's Commissars,
V. BONCH-BRUEVICH.
Secretary of the Council,
N. GORBUNOV.

*   *   *   *

On December 3d the Council of People's Commissars resolved "to reduce the salaries of functionaries and employees in all Government institutions and establishments, general or special, without exception."

To begin with, the Council fixed the salary of a People's Commissar at 500 rubles per month, with 100 rubles additional for each grown member of the family incapable of work. . . .

This was the highest salary paid to any Government official. . . .

4.

Countess Panina was arrested and brought to trial before the first Supreme Revolutionary Tribunal. The trial is described in the chapter on "Revolutionary Justice" in my forthcoming volume, "Kornilov to Brest-Litovsk." The prisoner was sentenced to "return the money, and then be liberated to the public contempt." In other words, she was set free!

5 Ridicule of the New Régime

From *Drug Naroda* (Menshevik), November 18th:

"The story of the 'immediate peace' of the Bolsheviki reminds us of a joyous moving-picture film. . . . Neratov runs—Trotsky pursues; Neratov climbs a wall, Trotsky too; Neratov dives into the water—Trotsky follows; Neratov climbs onto the roof—Trotsky right behind him; Neratov hides under the bed—and Trotsky has him! He has him! Naturally, peace is immediately signed. . . .

"All is empty and silent at the Ministry of Foreign Affairs. The couriers are respectful, but their faces wear a caustic expression. . . .

"How about arresting an ambassador and signing an armistice or a Peace Treaty with him? But they are strange folk, these ambassadors. They keep silent just as if they had heard nothing. Hola, hola, England, France, Germany! We have signed an armistice with you! Is it possible that you know nothing about it? Nevertheless, it has been published in all the papers and posted on all the walls. On a Bolshevik's word of honour, Peace has been signed. We're not asking much of you; you just have to write two words. . . .

"The ambassadors remain silent. The Powers remain silent. All is empty and silent in the office of the Minister of Foreign Affairs.

" 'Listen,' says Robespierre-Trotsky to his assistant Marat-Uritsky, 'run over to the British Ambassador's, tell him we're proposing peace!'

" 'Go yourself,' says Marat-Uritsky. 'He's not receiving.'

" 'Telephone him, then.'

" 'I've tried. The receiver's off the hook.'

" 'Send him a telegram.'

" 'I did.'

" 'Well, with what result?'

"Marat-Uritsky sighs and does not answer. Robespierre-Trotsky spits furiously into the corner. . . .

" 'Listen, Marat,' recommences Trotsky, after a moment. 'We must absolutely show that we're conducting an active foreign policy. How can we do that?'

" 'Launch another decree about arresting Neratov,' answers Uritsky, with a profound air.

" 'Marat, you're a blockhead!' cries Trotsky. All of a sudden he arises, terrible and majestic, looking at this moment like Robespierre.

" 'Write, Uritsky!' he says with severity. 'Write a letter to the British ambassador, a registered letter with receipt demanded. Write! I also will write! The peoples of the world await an immediate peace!'

"In the enormous and empty Ministry of Foreign Affairs are to be heard only the sound of two typewriters. With his own hands Trotsky is conducting an active foreign policy. . . ."

6 On the Question of an Agreement

To the Attention of All Workers and All Soldiers.

November 11th, in the club of the Preobrazhensky Regiment, was held an extraordinary meeting of representatives of all the units of the Petrograd garrison.

The meeting was called upon the initiative of the Preobrazhensky and Semionovsky Regiments, for the discussion of the question as to which Socialist parties are for the power of the Soviets, which are against, which are for the people, which against, and if an agreement between them is possible.

The representatives of the *Tsay-ee-kah,* of the Municipal Duma, of the Avksentiev Peasants' Soviets, and of all the political parties from the Bolsheviki to the Populist Socialists, were invited to the meeting.

After long deliberation, having heard the declarations of all parties and organisations, the meeting by a tremendous majority of votes agreed that only the Bolsheviki and the Left Socialist Revolutionaries are for the people, and that all the other parties are only attempting, under cover of seeking an agreement, to deprive the people of the conquests won in the days of the great Workers' and Peasants' Revolution of November.

Here is the text of the resolution carried at this meeting of the Petrograd garrison, by 61 votes against 11, and 12 not voting:

"The garrison conference, summoned at the initiative of the Semionovsky and Preobrazhensky Regiments, on hearing the representatives of all the Socialist parties and popular organisations on the question of an agreement between the different political parties finds that:

"1. The representatives of the *Tsay-ee-kah,* the representatives of the Bolshevik party and the Left Socialist Revolutionaries, declared definitely that they stand for a Government of the Soviets, for the decrees on Land, Peace and Workers' Control of Industry, and that upon this platform they are willing to agree with all the Socialist parties.

"2. At the same time the representatives of the other parties (Mensheviki, Socialist Revolutionaries) either gave no answer at all, or declared simply that they were opposed to the power of the Soviets and against the decrees on Land, Peace and Workers' Control.

"In view of this the meeting resolves:

" '1. To express severe censure of all parties which, under cover of an agreement, wish practically to annul the popular conquests of the Revolution of November.

" '2. To express full confidence in the *Tsay-ee-kah* and the Council of People's Commissars, and to promise them complete support.'

"At the same time the meeting deems it necessary that the comrades Left Socialist Revolutionaries should enter the People's Government."

7   Wine "Pogroms"

It was afterward discovered that there was a regular organisation, maintained by the Cadets, for provoking rioting among the soldiers. There would be telephone messages to the different barracks, announcing that wine was being given away at such and such an address, and when the soldiers arrived at the spot an individual would point out the location of the cellar. . . .

The Council of People's Commissars appointed a Commissar

for the Fight Against Drunkenness, who, besides mercilessly putting down the wine riots, destroyed hundreds of thousands of
bottles of liquor. The Winter Palace cellars, containing rare
vintages valued at more than five million dollars, were at first
flooded, and then the liquor was removed to Cronstadt and destroyed.

In this work the Cronstadt sailors, "flower and pride of the
revolutionary forces," as Trotsky called them, acquitted themselves with iron self-discipline. . . .

8 Speculators

Two orders concerning them:

Council of People's Commissars
To the Military Revolutionary Committee
The disorganisation of the food supply created by the war, and
the lack of system, is becoming to the last degree acute, thanks
to the speculators, marauders and their followers on the railways,
in the steamship offices, forwarding offices, etc.

Taking advantage of the nation's greatest misfortunes, these
criminal spoliators are playing with the health and life of millions
of soldiers and workers, for their own benefit.

Such a situation cannot be borne a single day longer.

The Council of People's Commissars proposes to the Military
Revolutionary Committee to take the most decisive measures towards the uprooting of speculation, sabotage, hiding of supplies,
fraudulent detention of cargoes, etc.

All persons guilty of such actions shall be subject, by special
orders of the Military Revolutionary Committee, to immediate
arrest and confinement in the prisons of Cronstadt, pending their
arraignment before the Revolutionary Tribunal.

All the popular organisations are invited to cooperate in the
struggle against the spoliators of food supplies.
                    President of the Council of People's Commissars.
                              V. ULIANOV (LENIN).

Accepted for execution,
            Military Revolutionary Committee attached to the
                C. E. C. of the Soviets of W. & S. Deputies.
Petrograd, Nov. 23d, 1917.

*   *   *   *

To All Honest Citizens

The Military Revolutionary Committee Decrees:

Spoliators, marauders, speculators, are declared to be enemies of the People. . . .

The Military Revolutionary Committee proposes to all public organisations, to all honest citizens: to inform the Military Revolutionary Committee immediately of all cases of spoliation, marauding, speculation, which become known to them.

The struggle against this evil is the business of all honest people. The Military Revolutionary Committee expects the support of all to whom the interests of the People are dear.

The Military Revolutionary Committee will be merciless in pursuit of speculators and marauders.

THE MILITARY REVOLUTIONARY COMMITTEE.

Petrograd, Dec. 2d, 1917.

9   Purishkevich's Letter to Kaledin

"The situation at Petrograd is desperate. The city is cut off from the outside world and is entirely in the power of the Bolsheviki. . . . People are arrested in the streets, thrown into the Neva, drowned and imprisoned without any charge. Even Burtzev is shut up in Peter-Paul fortress, under strict guard.

"The organisation at whose head I am is working without rest to unite all the officers and what is left of the *yunker* schools, and to arm them. The situation cannot be saved except by creating regiments of officers and *yunkers.* Attacking with these regiments, and having gained a first success, we could later gain the aid of the garrison troops; but without that first success it is impossible to count on a single soldier, because thousands of them are divided and terrorised by the scum which exists in every regiment. Most of the Cossacks are tainted by Bolshevik propaganda, thanks to the strange policy of General Dutov, who allowed to pass the moment when by decisive action something could have been obtained. The policy of negotiations and concessions has borne its fruits: all that is respectable is persecuted, and it is the *plebe* and the criminals who dominate—and nothing can be done except by shooting and hanging them.

"We are awaiting you here, General, and at the moment of your arrival, we shall advance with all the forces at our disposal. But for that we must establish some communication with you, and before all, clear up the following points:

"(1) Do you know that in your name all officers who could take part in the fight are being invited to leave Petrograd on the pretext of joining you?

"(2) About when can we count on your arrival at Petrograd? We should like to know in order to coordinate our actions.

"In spite of the criminal inaction of the conscious people here, which allowed the yoke of Bolshevism to be laid upon us—in spite of the extraordinary pig-headedness of the majority of officers, so difficult to organise—we believe in spite of all that Truth is on our side, and that we shall conquer the vicious and criminal forces who say that they are acting for motives of love of country and in order to save it. Whatever comes, we shall not permit ourselves to be struck down, and shall remain firm until the end."

Purishkevich, being brought to trial before the Revolutionary Tribunal, was given a short prison term. . . .

10   Decree on the Monopoly of Advertisements

1. The printing of advertisements, in newspapers, books, billboards, kiosks, in offices and other establishments is declared to be a State monopoly.

2. Advertisements may only be published in the organs of the Provisional Workers' and Peasants' Government at Petrograd, and in the organs of local Soviets.

3. The proprietors of newspapers and advertising offices, as well as all employees of such establishments, should remain at their posts until the transfer of the advertisement business to the Government . . . superintending the uninterrupted continuation of their houses, and turning over to the Soviets all private advertising and the sums received therefor, as well as all accounts and copy.

4. All managers of publications and businesses dealing with paid advertising, as well as their employees and workers, shall agree to hold a City Congress, and to join, first the City Trade Unions, and then the All-Russian Unions, to organise more thoroughly and justly the advertising business in the Soviet publications, as well as to prepare better rules for the public utility of advertising.

5. All persons found guilty of having concealed documents or

money, or having sabotaged the regulations indicated in paragraphs 3 and 4, will be punished by a sentence of not more than three years' imprisonment, and all their property will be confiscated.

6. The paid insertion of advertisements . . . in private publications, or under a masqued form, will also be severely penalised.

7. Advertising offices are confiscated by the Government, the owners being entitled to compensation in cases of necessity. Small proprietors, depositors and stock-holders of the confiscated establishments will be reimbursed for all moneys held by them in the concern.

8. All buildings, officers, counters, and in general every establishment doing a business in advertising, should immediately inform the Soviet of Workers' and Soldiers' Deputies of its address, and proceed to the transfer of its business, under penalty of the punishment indicated in paragraph 5.

President of the Council of People's Commissars,
VL. ULIANOV (LENIN).
People's Commissar for Public Instruction,
A. V. LUNACHARSKY.
Secretary of the Council,
N. GORBUNOV.

11   Obligatory Ordinance

1. The city of Petrograd is declared to be in a state of siege.

2. All assemblies, meetings and congregations on the streets and squares are prohibited.

3. Attempts to loot wine-cellars, warehouses, factories, stores, business premises, private dwellings, etc., etc., *will be stopped by machine-gun fire without warning.*

4. House Committees, doormen, janitors and Militiamen are charged with the duty of keeping strict order in all houses, courtyards and in the streets, and house-doors and carriage-entrances must be locked at 9 o'clock in the evening, and opened at 7 o'clock in the morning. After 9 o'clock in the evening only tenants may leave the house, under strict control of the House Committees.

5. Those guilty of the distribution, sale or purchase of any kind of alcoholic liquor, and also those guilty of the violation of

sections 2 and 4, will be immediately arrested and subjected to the most severe punishment.

Petrograd, 6th of December, 3 o'clock in the night.

Committee to Fight Against Pogroms, attached to the Executive Committee of the Soviet of Workers' and Soldiers' Deputies.

12   Two Proclamations

Lenin, *To the People of Russia:*

"Comrades workers, soldiers, peasants—all toilers!

"The Workers' and Peasants' Revolution has won at Petrograd, at Moscow. . . . From the Front and the villages arrive every day, every hour, greetings to the new Government. . . . The victory of the Revolution . . . is assured, seeing that it is sustained by the majority of the people.

"It is entirely understandable that the proprietors and the capitalists, the employees and functionaries closely allied with the bourgeoisie—in a word, all the rich and all those who join hands with them—regard the new Revolution with hostility, oppose its success, threaten to halt the activity of the banks, and sabotage or obstruct the work of other establishments. . . . Every conscious worker understands perfectly that we cannot avoid this hostility, because the high officials have set themselves against the People and do not wish to abandon their posts without resistance. But the working-classes are not for one moment afraid of that resistance. The majority of the people are for us. For us are the majority of the workers and the oppressed of the whole world. We have justice on our side. Our ultimate victory is certain.

"The resistance of the capitalists and high officials will be broken. No one will be deprived of his property without a special law on the nationalisation of banks and financial syndicates. This law is in preparation. Not a worker will lose a single kopek; on the contrary, he will be assisted. Without at this moment establishing the new taxes, the new Government considers one of its primary duties to make a severe accounting and control on the reception of taxes decreed by the former régime. . . .

"Comrades workers! Remember that you yourselves direct the Government. No one will help you unless you organise yourselves and take into your own hands the affairs of the State. Your Soviets are now the organs of governmental power. . . . Strengthen them, establish a severe revolutionary control, pitilessly crush the attempts at anarchy on the part of drunkards, brigands, counter-revolutionary *yunkers* and Kornilovists.

"Establish a strict control over production and the accounting for products. Arrest and turn over to the Revolutionary Tribunal of the People every one who injures the property of the People, by sabotage in production, by concealment of grain-reserves, reserves of other products, by retarding the shipments of grain, by bringing confusion into the railroads, the posts and the telegraphs, or in general opposing the great work of bringing Peace and transferring the Land to the peasants. . . .

"Comrades workers, soldiers, peasants—all toilers!

"Take immediately all local power into your hands. . . . Little by little, with the consent of the majority of peasants, we shall march firmly and unhesitatingly toward the victory of Socialism, which will fortify the advance-guards of the working-class of the most civilised countries, and give to the peoples an enduring peace, and free them from every slavery and every exploitation."

13.

"To All Workers of Petrograd!

"Comrades! The Revolution is winning—the revolution has won. All the power has passed over to our Soviets. The first weeks are the most difficult ones. The broken reaction must be finally crushed, a full triumph must be secured to our endeavours. The working-class ought to—must—show in these days THE GREATEST FIRMNESS AND ENDURANCE, in order to facilitate the execution of all the aims of the new People's Government of Soviets. In the next few days decrees on the Labour question will be issued, and among the very first will be the decree on Workers' Control over the production and regulation of Industry.

"STRIKES AND DEMONSTRATIONS OF THE WORKER MASSES IN PETROGRAD NOW CAN ONLY DO HARM.

"We ask you to cease immediately all economic and political strikes, to take up your work, and do it in perfect order. The work in the factories and all the industries is necessary for the new Government of Soviets, because any interruption of this work will only create new difficulties for us, and we have enough as it is. All to your places.

"The best way to support the new Government of Soviets in these days—is by doing your job.

"LONG LIVE THE IRON FIRMNESS OF THE PROLETARIAT! LONG LIVE THE REVOLUTION!"

> Petrograd Soviet of W. & S. D.
> Petrograd Council of Trade Unions.
> Petrograd Council of Factory-Shop Committees.

14 Appeals and Counter-Appeals

From the Employees of the State and private Banks
To the Population of Petrograd:

"Comrades workers, soldiers and citizens!

"The Military Revolutionary Committee in an 'extraordinary notice' is accusing the workers of the State and private banking and other institutions of 'impeding the work of the Government, directed towards the ensuring of the Front with provisions.'

"Comrades and citizens, do not believe this calumny, brought against us, who are part of the general army of labour.

"However difficult it be for us to work under the constant threat of interference by acts of violence in our hard-working life, however depressing it be to know that our Country and the Revolution are on the verge of ruin, we, nevertheless, all of us, from the highest to the lowest, employees, *artelshtchiki,* counters, labourers, couriers, etc., are continuing to fulfil our duties which are connected with the ensuring of provisions and munitions to the Front and country.

"Counting upon your lack of information, comrades workers and soldiers, in questions of finance and banking, you are being incited against workers like yourselves, because it is desirable to divert the responsibility for the starving and dying brother-soldiers at the Front from the guilty persons to the innocent workers who are accomplishing their duty under the burden of general poverty and disorganisation.

"REMEMBER, WORKERS AND SOLDIERS! THE EMPLOYEES HAVE ALWAYS STOOD UP FOR AND WILL ALWAYS STAND UP FOR THE INTERESTS OF THE TOILING PEOPLE, PART OF WHICH THEY ARE THEMSELVES, AND NOT A SINGLE KOPEK NECESSARY FOR THE FRONT AND THE WORKERS HAS EVER BEEN DETAINED AND WILL NOT BE DETAINED BY THE EMPLOYEES.

"From November 6th to November 23d, i.e., during 17 days, 500 million rubles were dispatched to the Front, and 120 millions to Moscow, besides the sums sent to other towns.

"Keeping guard over the wealth of the people, the master of

which can be only the Constituent Assembly, representing the whole nation, the employees refuse to give out money for purposes which are unknown to them.

"DO NOT BELIEVE THE CALUMNIATORS CALLING YOU TO TAKE THE LAW INTO YOUR OWN HANDS!"

Central Board of the All-Russian Union of Employees of the State Bank.

Central Board of the All-Russian Trade Union of Employees of Credit Institutions.

*   *   *   *

To the Population of Petrograd

"CITIZENS: Do not believe the falsehood which irresponsible people are trying to suggest to you by spreading terrible calumnies against the employees of the Ministry of Supplies and the workers in other Supply organisations who are labouring in these dark days for the salvation of Russia. Citizens! In posted placards you are called upon to lynch us, we are accused falsely of sabotage and strikes, we are blamed for all the woes and misfortunes that the people are suffering, although we have been striving indefatigably and uninterruptedly, and are still striving, to save the Russian people from the horrors of starvation. Notwithstanding all that we are bearing as citizens of unhappy Russia, we have not for one hour abandoned our heavy and responsible work of supplying the Army and population with provisions.

"The image of the Army, cold and hungry, saving our very existence by its blood and its tortures, does not leave us for a single moment.

"Citizens! If we have survived the blackest days in the life and history of our people, if we have succeeded in preventing famine in Petrograd, if we have managed to procure to the suffering army bread and forage by means of enormous, almost superhuman, efforts, it is because we have honestly continued and are still continuing to do our work. . . .

"To the 'last warning' of the usurpers of the power we reply: It is not for you who are leading the country to ruin to threaten us who are doing all we can not to allow the country to perish. We are not afraid of threats; before us stands the sacred image of tortured Russia. We will continue our work of supplying the Army and the people with bread to our last efforts, so long as you will not prevent us from accomplishing our duty to our country.

In the contrary case the Army and the people will stand before the horrors of famine, but the responsibility therefor belongs to the perpetrators of violence.

> *Executive Committee of the Employees of the Ministry of Supplies.*

*   *   *   *

To the Chinovniki (*Government Officials*)

It is notified hereby, that all officials and persons who have quitted the service in Government and public institutions or have been dismissed for sabotage or for having failed to report for work on the day fixed, and who have nevertheless received their salary paid in advance for the time they have not served, are bound to return such salary not later than on November 27th, 1917, to those institutions where they were in service.

In the event of this not being done, these persons will be rendered answerable for stealing the Treasury's property and tried by the Military Revolutionary Court.

> *The Military-Revolutionary Committee.*

December 7th, 1917.

*   *   *   *

From the Special Board for the Supplies

CITIZENS

"The conditions of our work for the supplying of Petrograd are getting more and more difficult every day.

"The interference with our work—which is so ruinous to our business—of the Commissars of the Military Revolutionary Committee is still continuing.

"THEIR ARBITRARY ACTS, their annulling of our orders, MAY LEAD TO A CATASTROPHE.

"Seals have been affixed to one of the cold storages where the meat and butter destined for the population are kept, and we cannot regulate the temperature SO THAT THE PRODUCTS WOULD NOT BE SPOILT.

"One carload of potatoes and one carload of cabbages have been seized and carried away no one knows where to.

"Cargoes which are not liable to requisition (*khalva*) are requisitioned by the Commissars and, as was the case one day, five boxes of *khalva* were seized by the Commissar for his own use.

"WE ARE NOT IN A POSITION TO DISPOSE OF OUR STORAGES, where the self-appointed Commissars do not allow the cargoes to be taken out, and terrorise our employees, threatening them with arrest.

"ALL THAT IS GOING ON IN PETROGRAD IS KNOWN IN THE PROVINCES, AND FROM THE DON, FROM SIBERIA, FROM VORONEZH AND OTHER PLACES PEOPLE ARE REFUSING TO SEND FLOUR AND BREAD.

"THIS CANNOT GO ON MUCH LONGER.

"The work is simply falling out of our hands.

"OUR DUTY is to let the population know of this.

"To the last possibility we will remain on guard of the interests of the population.

"WE WILL DO EVERYTHING TO AVOID THE ONCOMING FAMINE, BUT IF UNDER THESE DIFFICULT CONDITIONS OUR WORK IS COMPELLED TO STOP, LET THE PEOPLE KNOW THAT IT IS NOT OUR FAULT. . . ."

*   *   *   *

15   Elections to the Constituent Assembly in Petrograd

There were nineteen tickets in Petrograd. The results are as follows, published November 30th:

Party	Vote
Populist Socialists	19,109
Cadets	245,006
Christian Democrats	3,707
Bolsheviki	424,027
Socialist Universalists	158
S. D. and S. R. Ukrainian and Jewish Workers	4,219
League of Women's Rights	5,310
Socialist Revolutionaries (*oborontsi*)	4,696
Left Socialist Revolutionaries	152,230
League of the People's Development	385
Radical Democrats	413
Orthodox Parishes	24,139
Feminine League for Salvation of Country	318
Independent League of Workers, Soldiers, Peasants	4,942
Christian Democrats (Catholic)	14,382
Unified Social Democrats	11,740
Mensheviki	17,427
Yedinstvo group	1,823
League of Cossack Troops	6,712

16 From the Council of People's Commissars to the Toiling Cossacks

"Brothers-Cossacks.

"You are being deceived. You are being incited against the People. You are told that the Soviets of Workers', Soldiers' and Peasants' Deputies are your enemies, that they want to take away your Cossack land, your Cossack 'liberty.' Don't believe it, Cossacks. . . . Your own Generals and landowners are deceiving you, in order to keep you in darkness and slavery. We, the Council of People's Commissars, address ourselves to you, Cossacks, with these words. Read them attentively and judge yourselves which is the truth and which is cruel deceit. The life and service of a Cossack were always bondage and penal servitude. At the first call of the authorities a Cossack always had to saddle his horse and ride out on campaign. All his military equipment a Cossack had to provide with his own hardly earned means. A Cossack is on service, his farm is going to rack and ruin. Is such a condition fair? No, it must be altered for ever. THE COSSACKS MUST BE FREED FROM BONDAGE. The new People's Soviet power is willing to come to the assistance of the toiling Cossacks. It is only necessary that the Cossacks themselves should resolve to abolish the old order, that they should refuse submission to their slave-driver officers, land-owners, rich men, that they should throw off the cursed yoke from their necks. Arise, Cossacks! Unite! The Council of People's Commissars calls upon you to enter a new, fresh, more happy life.

"In November and December in Petrograd there were All-Russian Congresses of Soviets of Soldiers', Workers', and Peasants' Deputies. These Congresses transferred all the authority in the different localities into the hands of the Soviets, i.e., into the hands of men elected by the People. From now on there must be in Russia no rulers or functionaries who command the People from above and drive them. The People create the authority themselves. A General has no more rights than a soldier. All are equal. Consider, Cossacks, is this wrong or right? We are calling upon you, Cossacks, to join this new order and to create your own Soviets of Cossacks' Deputies. To such Soviets all the power must belong in the different localities. Not to *hetmans* with the rank of General, but to the elected representatives of the toiling Cossacks, to your own trustworthy reliable men.

"The All-Russian Congresses of Soldiers', Workers', and Peasants' Deputies have passed a resolution to transfer all landowners' land into the possession of the toiling people. Is not that fair, Cossacks? The Kornilovs, Kaledins, Dutovs, Karaulovs, Bardizhes, all defend with their whole souls the interests of the rich men, and they are ready to drown Russia in blood if only the lands remain in the hands of the landowners. But you, the toiling Cossacks, do not you suffer yourselves from poverty, oppression and lack of land? How many Cossacks are there who have more than 4-5 *dessiatins* per head? But the landowners, who have thousands of *dessiatins* of their own land, wish besides to get into their hands the lands of the Cossack Army. According to the new Soviet laws, the lands of Cossack landowners must pass without compensation into the hands of the Cossack workers, the poorer Cossacks. You are being told that the Soviets wish to take away your lands from you. Who is frightening you? The rich Cossacks, who know that the Soviet AUTHORITY WISHES TO transfer the landowners' lands to you. Choose then, Cossacks, for whom will you stand: for the Kornilovs and Kaledins, for the Generals and rich men, or for the Soviets of Peasants', Soldiers', Workers' and Cossacks' Deputies.

"THE COUNCIL OF PEOPLE'S COMMISSARS elected by the All-Russian Congress HAS PROPOSED TO ALL NATIONS AN IMMEDIATE ARMISTICE AND AN HONOURABLE DEMOCRATIC PEACE WITHOUT LOSS OR DETRIMENT TO ANY NATION. All the capitalists, landowners, Generals-Kornilovists have risen against the peaceful policy of the Soviets. The war was bringing them profits, power, distinctions. And to you, Cossack privates? You were perishing without reason, without purpose, like your brothers-soldiers and sailors. It will soon be three years and a half that this accursed war has gone on, a war devised by the capitalists and landowners of all countries for their own profit, their world robberies. To the toiling Cossacks the war has only brought ruin and death. The war has drained all the resources from Cossack farm life. The only salvation for the whole of our country and for the Cossacks in particular is a prompt and honest peace. The Council of People's Commissars has declared to all Governments and peoples: We do not want other people's property, and we do not wish to give away our own. Peace without annexations and without indemnities. Every nation must decide its own fate. There must be no oppressing of one nation by another. Such is the honest, democratic, People's peace

which the Council of People's Commissars is proposing to all
Governments, to all peoples, allies and enemies. And the results
are visible: ON THE RUSSIAN FRONT AN ARMISTICE HAS BEEN CON-
CLUDED.

"The soldier's and the Cossack's blood is not flowing there any
more. Now, Cossacks, decide: do you wish to continue this
ruinous, senseless, criminal slaughter? Then support the Cadets,
the enemies of the people, support Chernov, Tseretelli, Skobelev, who drove you into the offensive of July 1st; support Kornilov,
who introduced capital punishment for soldiers and Cossacks at
the front. BUT IF YOU WISH A PROMPT AND HONEST PEACE, THEN
ENTER THE RANKS OF THE SOVIETS AND SUPPORT THE COUNCIL OF
PEOPLE'S COMMISSARS.

"Your fate, Cossacks, lies in your own hands. Our common
foes, the landowners, capitalists, officers-Kornilovists, bourgeois
newspapers, are deceiving you and driving you along the road to
ruin. In Orenburg, Dutov has arrested the Soviet and disarmed
the garrison. Kaledin is threatening the Soviets in the province of
the Don. He has declared the province to be in a state of war and
is assembling his troops. Karaulov is shooting the local tribes in
the Caucasus. The Cadet bourgeoisie is supplying them with its
millions. Their common aim is to suppress the People's Soviets,
to crush the workers and peasants, to introduce again the discipline of the whip in the army, and to eternalise the bondage of
the toiling Cossacks.

"Our revolutionary troops are moving to the Don and the Ural
in order to put an end to this criminal revolt against the people.
The commanders of the revolutionary troops have received orders
not to enter into any negotiations with the mutinous Generals, to
act decisively and mercilessly.

"Cossacks! On you depends now whether your brothers' blood
is to flow still. We are holding out our hand to you. Join the
whole people against its enemies. Declare Kaledin, Kornilov,
Dutov, Karaulov and all their aiders and abettors to be the
enemies of the people, traitors and betrayers. Arrest them with
your own forces and turn them over into the hands of the Soviet
authority, which will judge them in open and public Revolutionary
Tribunal. Cossacks! Form Soviets of Cossacks' Deputies. Take
into your toil-worn hands the management of all the affairs of the
Cossacks. Take away the lands of your own wealthy landowners.
Take over their grain, their inventoried property and live-stock

for the cultivation of the lands of the toiling Cossacks, who are ruined by the war.

"Forward, Cossacks, to the fight for the common cause of the people!

"Long live the toiling Cossacks!

"Long live the union of the Cossacks, the soldiers, peasants and workers!

"Long live the power of the Soviets of Cossacks', Soldiers', Workers' and Peasants' Deputies.

"Down with the war! Down with the landowners and the Kornilovist-Generals!

"Long live Peace and the Brotherhood of peoples!"

Council of People's Commissars.

17 From the Commission on Public Education attached to the Central City Duma

"Comrades Workingmen and Workingwomen!

"A few days before the holidays, a strike has been declared by the teachers of the public schools. The teachers side with the bourgeoisie against the Workers' and Peasants' Government.

"Comrades, organise parents' committees and pass resolutions against the strike of the teachers. Propose to the Ward Soviets of Workers' and Soldiers' Deputies, the Trade Unions, the Factory-Shop and Party Committees, to organise protest meetings. Arrange with your own resources Christmas trees and entertainments for the children, and demand the opening of the schools, after the holidays, at the date which will be set by the Duma.

"Comrades, strengthen your position in matters of public education, insist on the control of the proletarian organisations over the schools."

*Commission on Public Education attached
to the Central City Duma.*

18 Diplomatic Correspondence of the Soviet Government

The notes issued by Trotsky to the Allies and to the neutral powers, as well as the note of the Allied military Attachés to General Dukhonin, are too voluminous to give here. Moreover they belong to another phase of the history of the Soviet Republic, with which this book has nothing to do—the foreign relations of the Soviet Government. This I treat at length in the next volume, "Kornilov to Brest-Litovsk."

19 Appeals to the Front Against Dukhonin

". . . The struggle for peace has met with the resistance of the bourgeoisie and the counter-revolutionary Generals. . . . From the acounts in the newspapers, at the *Stavka* of former Supreme Commander Dukhonin are gathering the agents and allies of the bourgeoisie, Verkhovski, Avksentiev, Chernov, Gotz, Tseretelli, etc. It seems even that they want to form a new power against the Soviets.

"Comrades soldiers! All the persons we have mentioned have been Ministers already. They have acted in accord with Kerensky and the bourgeoisie. They are responsible for the offensive of July 1st and for the prolongation of the war. They promised the land to the peasants and then arrested the Land Committees. They reestablished capital punishment for soldiers. They obey the orders of French, English and American financiers. . . .

"General Dukhonin, for having refused to obey orders of the Council of People's Commissars, has been dismissed from his position as Supreme Commander. . . . For answer he is circulating among the troops the note from the Military Attachés of the Allied imperialist Powers, and attempting to provoke a counter-revolution. . . .

"Do not obey Dukhonin! Pay no attention to his provocation! Watch him and his group of counter-revolutionary Generals carefully. . . ."

20 From Krylenko

Order Number Two

". . . The ex-Supreme Commander, General Dukhonin, for having opposed resistance to the execution of orders, for criminal action susceptible of provoking a new civil war, is declared enemy of the People. All persons who support Dukhonin will be arrested, without respect to their social or political position or their past. Persons equipped with special authority will operate these arrests. I charge General Manikhovsky with the execution of the above-mentioned dispositions. . . ."

CHAPTER XII

THE PEASANTS' CONGRESS

It was on November 18th that the snow came. In the morning we woke to window-ledges heaped white, and snowflakes falling so whirling thick that it was impossible to see ten feet ahead. The mud was gone; in a twinkling the gloomy city became white, dazzling. The *droshki* with their padded coachmen turned into sleighs, bounding along the uneven street at headlong speed, their drivers' beards stiff and frozen. . . . In spite of Revolution, all Russia plunging dizzily into the unknown and terrible future, joy swept the city with the coming of the snow. Everybody was smiling; people ran into the streets, holding out their arms to the soft, falling flakes, laughing. Hidden was all the greyness; only the gold and coloured spires and cupolas, with heightened barbaric splendour, gleamed through the white snow.

Even the sun came out, pale and watery, at noon. The colds and rheumatism of the rainy months vanished. The life of the city grew gay, and the very Revolution ran swifter. . . .

I sat one evening in a *traktir*—a kind of lower-class inn —across the street from the gates of Smolny; a low-ceilinged, loud place called "Uncle Tom's Cabin," much frequented by Red Guards. They crowded it now, packed close around the little tables with their dirty table-cloths and enormous china tea-pots, filling the place with foul cigarette-smoke, while the harassed waiters ran about crying "*Seichass! Seichass!* In a minute! Right away!"

In one corner sat a man in the uniform of a captain, addressing the assembly, which interrupted him at every few words.

"You are no better than murderers!" he cried. "Shooting down your Russian brothers on the streets!"

"When did we do that?" asked a worker.

"Last Sunday you did it, when the *yunkers*——"

"Well, didn't they shoot us?" One man exhibited his arm in a sling. "Haven't I got something to remember them by, the devils?"

The captain shouted at the top of his voice. "You should remain neutral! You should remain neutral! Who are you to destroy the legal Government? Who is Lenin? A German——"

"Who are you? A counter-revolutionist! A provocator!" they bellowed at him.

When he could make himself heard the captain stood up. "All right!" said he. "You call yourselves the people of Russia. But you're *not* the people of Russia. The *peasants* are the people of Russia. Wait until the peasants ——"

"Yes," they cried, "wait until the peasants speak. We know what the peasants will say. . . . Aren't they workingmen like ourselves?"

In the long run, everything depended upon the peasants. While the peasants had been politically backward, still they had their own peculiar ideas, and they constituted more than eighty per cent of the people of Russia. The Bolsheviki had a comparatively small following among the peasants; and a permanent dictatorship of Russia by the industrial workers was impossible. . . . The traditional peasant party was the Socialist Revolutionary party; of all the parties now supporting the Soviet Government, the Left Socialist Revolutionaries were the logical inheritors of peasant leadership—and the Left Socialist Revolutionaries, who were at the mercy of the organised city proletariat, desperately needed the backing of the peasants. . . .

Meanwhile Smolny had not neglected the peasants. After the Land decree, one of the first actions of the new *Tsay-ee-kah* had been to call a Congress of Peasants, over the head of the Executive Committee of the Peasants' Soviets. A few days later was issued detailed Regulations for the *Volost* (Township) Land Committees, followed by Lenin's "Instruction to Peasants," [1] which explained the Bolshevik revolution and the new Government in simple terms; and on November 16th, Lenin and Miliutin published the "Instructions to Provincial Emissaries," * of whom thousands were sent by the Soviet Government into the villages.

1. Upon his arrival in the province to which he is accredited, the emissary should call a joint meeting of the Central Executive Committees of the Soviets of Workers', Soldiers' and Peasants' Deputies, to whom he should make a report on the agrarian laws, and then demand that a joint plenary session of the Soviets be summoned. . . .

2. He must study the aspects of the agrarian problem in the province.

a. Has the land-owners' property been taken over, and if so, in what districts?

b. Who administers the confiscated land—the former proprietor, or the Land Committees?

c. What has been done with the agricultural machinery and with the farm-animals?

---

* This questionnaire bears the earmarks of Lenin's style but has not been included in his *Collected Works.—Ed.*

3. Has the ground cultivated by the peasants been augmented?

4. How much and in what respect does the amount of land now under cultivation differ from the amount fixed by the Government as an average minimum?

5. The emissary must insist that, after the peasants have received the land, it is imperative that they increase the amount of cultivated land as quickly as possible, and that they hasten the sending of grain to the cities, as the only means of avoiding famine.

6. What are the measures projected or put into effect for the transfer of land from the land-owners to the Land Committees and similar bodies appointed by the Soviets?

7. It is desirable that agricultural properties well appointed and well organised should be administered by Soviets composed of the regular employees of those properties, under the direction of competent agricultural scientists.

All through the villages a ferment of change was going on, caused not only by the electrifying action of the Land decree, but also by thousands of revolutionary-minded peasant-soldiers returning from the front. . . . These men, especially, welcomed the call to a Congress of Peasants.

Like the old *Tsay-ee-kah* in the matter of the second Congress of Workers' and Soldiers' Soviets, the Executive Committee tried to prevent the Peasant Congress summoned by Smolny. And like the old *Tsay-ee-kah,* finding its resistance futile, the Executive Committee sent frantic telegrams ordering the election of Conservative delegates. Word was even spread among the peasants that the Congress would meet at Moghilev, and some delegates went there; but by November 23d about four hundred had gathered in Petrograd, and the party caucuses had begun. . . .

The first session took place in the Alexander Hall of

the Duma building, and the first vote showed that more
than half of all the delegates were Left Socialist Revolutionaries, while the Bolsheviki controlled a bare fifth, the
conservative Socialist Revolutionaries a quarter, and all
the rest were united only in their opposition to the old
Executive Committee, dominated by Avksentiev, Chaikovsky and Peshekhonov. . . .

The great hall was jammed with people and shaken with
continual clamour; deep, stubborn bitterness divided the
delegates into angry groups. To the right was a sprinkling
of officers' epaulettes, and the patriarchal, bearded faces
of the older, more substantial peasants; in the centre were
a few peasants, non-commissioned officers, and some
soldiers; and on the left almost all the delegates wore the
uniforms of common soldiers. These last were the young
generation, who had been serving in the army. . . . The
galleries were thronged with workers—who, in Russia,
still remember their peasant origin. . . .

Unlike the old *Tsay-ee-kah,* the Executive Committee,
in opening the session, did not recognise the Congress as
official; the official Congress was called for December 13th;
amid a hurricane of applause and angry cries, the speaker
declared that this gathering was merely "Extraordinary
Conference". . . . But the "Extraordinary Conference"
soon showed its attitude toward the Executive Committee
by electing as presiding officer Maria Spiridonova, leader
of the Left Socialist Revolutionaries.

Most of the first day was taken up by a violent debate
as to whether the representatives of *Volost* Soviets should
be seated, or only delegates from the Provincial bodies;
and just as in the Workers' and Soldiers' Congress, an overwhelming majority declared in favour of the widest possible representation. Whereupon the old Executive Committee left the hall. . . .

Almost immediately it was evident that most of the delegates were hostile to the Government of the People's Commissars. Zinoviev, attempting to speak for the Bolsheviki, was hooted down, and as he left the platform, amid laughter, there were cries, "There's how a People's Commissar sits in a mud-puddle!"

"We Left Socialist Revolutionaries refuse," cried Nazariev, a delegate from the Provinces, "to recognise this so-called Workers' and Peasants' Government until the peasants are represented in it. At present it is nothing but a dictatorship of the workers. . . . We insist upon the formation of a new Government which will represent the entire democracy!"

The reactionary delegates shrewdly fostered this feeling, declaring, in the face of protests from the Bolshevik benches, that the Council of People's Commissars intended either to control the Congress or dissolve it by force of arms—an announcement which was received by the peasants with bursts of fury. . . .

On the third day Lenin suddenly mounted the tribune; for ten minutes the room went mad. "Down with him!" they shrieked. "We will not listen to any of your People's Commissars! We don't recognise your Government!"

Lenin stood there quite calmly, gripping the desk with both hands, his little eyes thoughtfully surveying the tumult beneath. Finally, except for the right side of the hall, the demonstration wore itself out somewhat.

"I do not come here as a member of the Council of People's Commissars," said Lenin, and waited again for the noise to subside, "but as a member of the Bolshevik faction, duly elected to this Congress." And he held his credentials up so that all might see them.

"However," he went on, in an unmoved voice, "nobody will deny that the present Government of Russia has been formed by the Bolshevik party—" he had to wait a moment, "so that for all purposes it is the same thing. . . ." Here the right benches broke into deafening clamour, but the centre and left were curious, and compelled silence.

Lenin's argument was simple. "Tell me frankly, you peasants, to whom we have given the lands of the *pomieshchiki;* do you want now to prevent the workers from getting control of industry? This is class war. The *pomieshchiki* of course oppose the peasants, and the manufacturers oppose the workers. Are you going to allow the ranks of the proletariat to be divided? Which side will you be on?

"We, the Bolsheviki, are the party of the proletariat— of the peasant proletariat as well as the industrial proletariat. We, the Bolsheviki, are the protectors of the Soviets —of the Peasants' Soviets as well as those of the Workers and Soldiers. The present Government is a Government of Soviets; we have not only invited the Peasants' Soviets to join that Government, but we have also invited representatives of the Left Socialist Revolutionaries to enter the Council of People's Commissars. . . .

"The Soviets are the most perfect representatives of the people—of the workers in the factories and mines, of the workers in the fields. Anybody who attempts to destroy the Soviets is guilty of an anti-democratic and counter-revolutionary act. And I serve notice here on you, comrades *Right* Socialist Revolutionaries—and on you, Messrs. Cadets—that if the Constituent Assembly attempts to destroy the Soviets, we shall not permit the Constituent Assembly to do this thing!"

On the afternoon of November 25th Chernov arrived in hot haste from Moghilev, summoned by the Executive Committee. Only two months before considered an extreme revolutionist, and very popular with the peasants, he was now called to check the dangerous drift of the Congress toward the Left. Upon his arrival Chernov was arrested and taken to Smolny, where, after a short conversation, he was released.

His first act was to bitterly rebuke the Executive Committee for leaving the Congress. They agreed to return, and Chernov entered the hall, welcomed with great applause by the majority, and the hoots and jeers of the Bolsheviki.

"Comrades! I have been away. I participated in the Conference of the Twelfth Army on the question of calling a Congress of all the Peasant delegates of the armies of the Western Front, and I know very little about the insurrection which occurred here——"

Zinoviev rose in his seat, and shouted, "Yes, you were away—for a few minutes!" Fearful tumult. Cries, "Down with the Bolsheviki!"

Chernov continued. "The accusation that I helped lead an army on Petrograd has no foundation, and is entirely false. Where does such an accusation come from? Show me the source!"

Zinoviev: *"Izvestia* and *Dielo Naroda*—your own paper —that's where it comes from!"

Chernov's wide face, with the small eyes, waving hair and greyish beard, became red with wrath, but he controlled himself and went on. "I repeat, I know practically nothing about what has happened here, and I did not lead any army except this army, (he pointed to the peasant delegates), which I am largely responsible for bringing here!" Laughter, and shouts of "Bravo!"

"Upon my return I visited Smolny. No such accusation was made against me there. . . . After a brief conversation I left—and that's all! Let any one present make such an accusation!"

An uproar followed, in which the Bolsheviki and some of the Left Socialist Revolutionaries were on their feet all at once, shaking their fists and yelling, and the rest of the assembly tried to yell them down.

"This is an outrage, not a session!" cried Chernov, and he left the hall; the meeting was adjourned because of the noise and disorder. . . .

Meanwhile, the question of the status of the Executive Committee was agitating all minds. By declaring the assembly "Extraordinary Conference," it had been planned to block the reelection of the Executive Committee. But this worked both ways; the Left Socialist Revolutionists decided that if the Congress had no power over the Executive Committee, then the Executive Committee had no power over the Congress. On November 25th the assembly resolved that the powers of the Executive Committee be assumed by the Extraordinary Conference, in which only members of the Executive who had had been elected as delegates might vote. . . .

The next day, in spite of the bitter opposition of the Bolsheviki, the resolution was amended to give all the members of the Executive Committee, whether elected as delegates or not, voice and vote in the assembly.

On the 27th occurred the debate on the Land question, which revealed the differences between the agrarian programme of the Bolsheviki and the Left Socialist Revolutionaries.

Kolchinsky, for the Left Socialist Revolutionaries, outlined the history of the Land question during the Revolution. The first Congress of Peasants' Soviets, he said, had voted a precise and formal resolution in favour of putting the landed estates immediately into the hands of the Land Committees. But the directors of the Revolution, and the bourgeois in the Government, had insisted that the question could not be solved until the Constituent Assembly met. . . . The second period of the Revolution, the period of "compromise," was signalled by the entrance of Chernov into the Cabinet. The peasants were convinced that now the practical solution of the Land question would begin; but in spite of the imperative decision of the first Peasant Congress, the reactionaries and conciliators in the Executive Committee had prevented any action. This policy provoked a series of agrarian disorders, which appeared as the natural expression of impatience and thwarted energy on the part of the peasants. The peasants understood the exact meaning of the Revolution—they tried to turn words into action. . . .

"The recent events," said the orator, "do not indicate a simple riot, or a 'Bolshevik adventure,' but on the contrary, a real popular rising, which has been greeted with sympathy by the whole country. . . .

"The Bolsheviki in general took the correct attitude toward the Land question; but in recommending that the peasants seize the land by force, they committed a profound error. . . . From the first days, the Bolsheviki declared that the peasants should take over the land 'by revolutionary mass-action." This is nothing but anarchy; the land can be taken over in an organized manner. . . . For the Bolsheviki it was important that the problems of the Revolution should be solved in the quickest possible manner—but the Bolsheviki were not interested in *how* these problems were to be solved. . . .

"The Land decree of the Congress of Soviets is identical in its fundamentals with the decisions of the first Peasants' Congress. Why then did not the new Government follow the tactics outlined by that Congress? Because the Council of People's Commissars wanted to hasten the settlement of the Land question, so that the Constituent Assembly would have nothing to do. . . .

"But also the Government saw that it was necessary to adopt practical measures, so without further reflection, it adopted the Regulations for Land Committees, thus creating a strange situation; for the Council of People's Commissars abolished private property in land, but the Regulations drawn up by the Land Committees are based on private property. . . . However, no harm has been done by that; for the Land Committees are paying no attention to the Soviet decrees, but are putting into operation their own practical decisions—decisions based on the will of the vast majority of the peasants. . . .

"These Land Committees are not attempting the legislative solution of the Land question, which belongs to the Constituent Assembly alone. . . . But will the Constituent Assembly desire to do the will of the Russian peasants? Of that we cannot be sure. . . . All we can be sure of is that the revolutionary determination of the peasants is now aroused, and that the Constituent will be *forced* to settle the Land question the way the peasants want it settled. . . . The Constituent Assembly will not dare to break with the will of the people. . . ."

Followed him Lenin, listened to now with absorbing intensity. "At this moment we are not only trying to solve the Land question, but the question of Social Revolution—not only here in Russia, but all over the world. The Land question cannot be solved independently of the other problems of the Social Revolution. . . . For example, the confiscation of the landed estates will provoke the resistance not only of Russian land-owners, but also of foreign capital—with whom the great landed properties are connected through the intermediary of the banks. . . .

"The ownership of the land in Russia is the basis for

immense oppression, and the confiscation of the land by the peasants is the most important step of our Revolution. But it cannot be separated from the other steps, as is clearly manifested by the stages through which the Revolution has had to pass. The first stage was the crushing of autocracy and the crushing of the power of the industrial capitalists and land-owners, whose interests are closely related. The second stage was the strengthening of the Soviets and the political compromise with the bourgeoisie. The mistake of the Left Socialist Revolutionaries lies in the fact that at that time they did not oppose the policy of compromise, because they held the theory that the consciousness of the masses was not yet fully developed. . . .

*"If Socialism can only be realised when the intellectual development of all the people permits it, then we shall not see Socialism for at least five hundred years. . . . The So-*cialist political party—this is the vanguard of the working-class; it must not allow itself to be halted by the lack of education of the mass average, but it must lead the masses, using the Soviets as organs of revolutionary initiative. . . . But in order to lead the wavering, the comrades Left Socialist Revolutionaries themselves must stop hesitating. . . .

"In July last a series of open breaks began between the popular masses and the 'compromisers'; but now, in November, the Left Socialist Revolutionaries are still holding out their hand to Avksentiev, who is pulling the people with his little finger. . . . If Compromise continues, the Revolution disappears. No compromise with the bourgeoisie is possible; its power must be absolutely crushed. . . .

"We Bolsheviki have not changed our Land programme; we have not given up the abolition of private property in the land, and we do not intend to do so. We adopted the

Regulations for Land Committees,—which are *not* based
on private property at all—because we want to accomplish
the popular will in the way the people have themselves
decided to do it, so as to draw closer the coalition of all
the elements who are fighting for the Social Revolution.

"We invite the Left Socialist Revolutionaries to enter
that coalition, insisting, however, that they cease looking
backward, and that they break with the 'conciliators' of
their party. . . .

"As far as the Constituent Assembly is concerned, it is
true, as the preceding speaker has said, that the work of
the Constituent will depend on the revolutionary determination of the masses. I say, 'Count on that revolutionary
determination, but don't forget your gun!' " *

Lenin then read the Bolshevik resolution:

The Peasants' Congress, fully supporting the Land decree
of November 8th . . . approves of the Provisional Workers'
and Peasants' Government of the Russian Republic, established by the second All-Russian Congress of Soviets of
Workers' and Soldiers' Deputies.

The Peasants' Congress . . . invites all peasants unanimously to sustain that law, and to apply it immediately themselves; and at the same time invites the peasants to appoint
to posts and positions of responsibility only persons who
have proved, not by words but by acts, their entire devotion
to the interests of the exploited peasant-workers, their desire
and their ability to defend these interests against all resistance
on the part of the great land-owners, the capitalists, their
partisans and accomplices. . . .

The Peasants' Congress, at the same time, expresses its conviction that the complete realisation of all the measures which
make up the Land decree can only be successful through

---

* Reed's report on Lenin's speech is fuller than that included in Lenin's
Works, and concentrates on passages in part missing there. The resolution
Lenin read was drafted by him and appears in full in Vol. XXVI, pp. 290-
91.—*Ed.*

the triumph of the Workers' Social Revolution, which began November 7th, 1917; for only the Social Revolution can accomplish the definite transfer, without possibility of return, of the land to the peasant-workers, the confiscation of model farms and their surrender to the peasant communes, the confiscation of agricultural machinery belonging to the great land-owners, the safe-guarding of the interests of the agricultural workers by the complete abolition of wage-slavery, the regular and methodical distribution among all regions of Russia of the products of agriculture and industry, and the seizure of the banks (without which the possession of land by the whole people would be impossible, after the abolition of private property), and all sorts of assistance by the State to the workers. . . .

For these reasons the Peasants' Congress sustains entirely the Revolution of November 7th . . . as a social revolution, and expresses its unalterable will to put into operation, with whatever modifications are necessary, but without any hesitation, the social transformation of the Russian Republic.

The indispensable conditions of the victory of the Social Revolution, which alone will secure the lasting success and the complete realisation of the Land decree, is the close union of the peasant-workers with the industrial working-class, with the proletariat of all advanced countries. From now on, in the Russian Republic, all the organisation and admiration of the State, from top to bottom, must rest on that union. That union, crushing all attempts, direct or indirect, open or dissimulated, to return to the policy of conciliation with the bourgeoisie—conciliation, damned by experience, with the chiefs of bourgeois politics—can alone insure the victory of Socialism throughout the world. . . .

The reactionaries of the Executive Committee no longer dared openly to appear. Chernov, however, spoke several times, with a modest and winning impartiality. He was invited to sit on the platform. . . . On the second night of the Congress an anonymous note was handed up to the chairman, requesting that Chernov be made honorary President. Ustinov read the note aloud, and immediately Zinoviev was on his feet, screaming that this was a trick of the old Executive Committee to capture the convention; in a moment the hall was one bellowing mass of waving arms and angry faces, on both sides. . . . Nevertheless, Chernov remained very popular.

In the stormy debates on the Land question and the Lenin resolution, the Bolsheviki were twice on the point of quitting the assembly, both times restrained by their leaders. . . . It seemed to me as if the Congress were hopelessly deadlocked.

But none of us knew that a series of secret conferences were already going on between the Left Socialist Revolutionaries and the Bolsheviki at Smolny. At first the Left Socialist Revolutionaries had demanded that there be a Government composed of all the Socialist parties in and out of the Soviets, to be responsible to a People's Council, composed of an equal number of delegates from the Workers' and Soldiers' organisation, and that of the Peasants, and completed by representatives of the City Dumas and the Zemstvos; Lenin and Trotsky were to be eliminated, and the Military Revolutionary Committee and other repressive organs dissolved.

Wednesday morning, November 28th, after a terrible all-night struggle, an agreement was reached. The *Tsay-ee-kah,* composed of 108 members, was to be augmented by 108 members elected proportionally from the Peasants' Congress; by 100 delegates elected directly from the Army and the Fleet; and by 50 representatives of the Trade Unions (35 from the general Unions, 10 Railway Workers, and 5 from the Post and Telegraph Workers). The Dumas and Zemstvos were dropped. Lenin and Trosky remained in the Government, and the Military Revolutionary Committee continued to function.

The sessions of the Congress had now been removed to the Imperial Law School building, Fontanka 6, headquarters of the Peasants' Soviets. There in the great meeting-hall the delegates gathered on Wednesday afternoon. The old Executive Committee had withdrawn, and was holding a rump convention of its own in another room of the same building, made up of bolting delegates and representatives of the Army Committees.

Chernov went from one meeting to the other, keeping a watchful eye on the proceedings. He knew that an agreement with the Bolsheviki was being discussed, but he did not know that it had been concluded.

He spoke to the rump convention. "At present, when everybody is in favour of forming an all-Socialist Government, many people forget the first Ministry, which was *not* a coalition Government, and in which there was only one Socialist—Kerensky; a Government which, in its time, was very popular. Now people accuse Kerensky; they forget that he was raised to power, not only by the Soviets, but also by the popular masses. . . .

"Why did public opinion change toward Kerensky? The savages set up gods to which they pray, and which they punish if one of their prayers is not answered. . . . That is what is happening at this moment. . . . Yesterday Kerensky; today Lenin and Trotsky; another to-morrow. . . .

"We have proposed to both Kerensky and the Bolsheviki to retire from the power. Kerensky has accepted—to-day he announced from his hiding-place that he has resigned as Premier; but the Bolsheviki wish to retain the power, and they do not know how to use it. . . .

"If the Bolsheviki succeed, or if they fail, the fate of Russia will not be changed. The Russian villages understand perfectly what they want, and they are now carrying out their own measures. . . . The villages will save us in the end. . . ."

In the meanwhile, in the great hall Ustinov had announced the agreement between the Peasants' Congress and Smolny, received by the delegates with the wildest joy. Suddenly Chernov appeared, and demanded the floor.

"I understand," he began, "that an agreement is being concluded between the Peasants' Congress and Smolny. Such an agreement would be illegal, seeing that the true Congress of Peasants' Soviets does not meet until next week. . . .

"Moreover, I want to warn you now that the Bolsheviki will never accept your demands. . . ."

He was interrupted by a great burst of laughter; and realising the situation, he left the platform and the room, taking his popularity with him. . . .

Late in the afternoon of Thursday, November 16th, the Congress met in an extraordinary session. There was a holiday feeling in the air; on every face was a smile. . . . The remainder of the business before the assembly was hurried through, and then old Nathanson, the white-bearded dean of the left wing of the Socialist Revolutionaries, his voice trembling and tears in his eyes, read the report of the "wedding" of the Peasants' Soviets with the Workers' and Soldiers' Soviets. At every mention of the word "union" there was ecstatic applause. . . . At the end Ustinov announced the arrival of a delegation from Smolny, accompanied by representatives of the Red Army, greeted with a rising ovation. One after another a workman, a soldier and a sailor took the floor, hailing them.

Then Boris Reinstein, delegate of the American Socialist Labor Party:* "The day of the union of the Congress of Peasants and the Soviets of Workers' and Soldiers' Deputies is one of the great days of the Revolution. The sound of it will ring with resounding echoes throughout the whole world—in Paris, in London, and across the ocean—in New York. This union will fill with happiness the hearts of all toilers.

"A great idea has triumphed. The West, and America, expected from Russia, from the Russian proletariat, something tremendous. . . . The proletariat of the world is waiting for the Russian Revolution, waiting for the great things that it is accomplishing. . . ."

Sverdlov, president of the *Tsay-ee-kah,* greeted them. And with the shout, "Long live the end of civil war! Long live the United Democracy!" the peasants poured out of the building.

It was already dark, and on the ice-covered snow glittered the pale light of moon and star. Along the bank of the canal were drawn up in full marching order the soldiers of the Pavlovsky Regiment, with their band, which broke into the *Marseillaise.* Amid the crashing full-throated shouts of the soldiers, the peasants formed in line, unfurling the great red banner of the Executive Committee of the All-Russian Peasants' Soviets, embroidered newly in gold, "Long live the union of the revolutionary and toiling masses!" Following were other banners; of the District Soviets—of Putilov Factory, which read, "We bow to this flag in order to create the brotherhood of all peoples!"

---

* The Socialist Labor Party had not given him a mandate to represent it, and later specifically repudiated him.—*Ed.*

From somewhere torches appeared, blazing orange in the night, a thousand times reflected in the facets of the ice, streaming out smokily over the throng as it moved down the bank of the Fontanka singing, between crowds that stood in astonished silence.

"Long live the Revolutionary Army! Long live the Red Guard! Long live the Peasants!"

So the great procession wound through the city, growing and unfurling ever new red banners lettered in gold. Two old peasants, bowed with toil, were walking hand in hand, their faces illumined with child-like bliss.

"Well," said one, "I'd like to see them take away our land again, *now!*"

Near Smolny the Red Guard was lined up on both sides of the street, wild with delight. The other old peasant spoke to his comrade, "I am not tired," he said. "I walked on air all the way!"

On the steps of Smolny about a hundred Workers' and Soldiers' Deputies were massed, with their banner, dark against the blaze of light streaming out between the arches. Like a wave they rushed down, clasping the peasants in their arms and kissing them; and the procession poured in through the great door and up the stairs, with a noise like thunder. . . .

In the immense white meeting-room the *Tsay-ee-kah* was waiting, with the whole Petrograd Soviet and a thousand spectators beside, with that solemnity which attends great conscious moments in history.

Zinoviev announced the agreement with the Peasants' Congress, to a shaking roar which rose and burst into storm as the sound of music blared down the corridor, and the head of the procession came in. On the platform the presidium rose and made place for the Peasants' presidium, the two embracing; behind them the two banners were intertwined against the white wall, over the empty frame from which the Tsar's picture had been torn. . . .

Then opened the "triumphal session." After a few words of welcome from Sverdlov, Maria Spiridonova, slight, pale, with spectacles and hair drawn flatly down, and the air of a New England school-teacher, took the tribune—the most loved and the most powerful woman in all Russia.

". . . Before the workers of Russia open now horizons which history has never known. . . . All workers' movements in the past have been defeated. But the present movement is international, and that is why it is invincible. There is no force in the world which can put out the fire of the Revolution! The old world crumbles down, the new world begins. . . ."

Then Trotsky, full of fire: "I wish you welcome, comrades peasants! You come here not as guests, but as masters of this house, which holds the heart of the Russian Revolution. The will of millions of workers is now concentrated in this hall. . . . There is now only one master of the Russian land: the union of the workers, soldiers and peasants. . . ."

With biting sarcasm he went on to speak of the Allied diplomats, till then contemptuous of Russia's invitation to an armistice, which had been accepted by the Central Powers.

"A new humanity will be born of this war. . . . In this hall we swear to workers of all lands to remain at our revolutionary post. If we are broken, then it will be in defending our flag. . . ."

Krylenko followed him, explaining the situation at the front, where Dukhonin was preparing to resist the Council of People's Commissars. "Let Dukhonin and those with him understand well that we shall not deal gently with those who bar the road to peace!"

Dybenko saluted the assembly in the name of the Fleet, and Krushinsky, member of the *Vikzhel,* said, "From this moment, when the union of all true Socialists is realised, the whole army of railway workers places itself absolutely at the disposition of the revolutionary democracy!" And Lunacharsky, almost weeping, and Proshian, for the Left Socialist Revolutionaries, and finally Saharashvili, for the United Social Democrats Internationalists, composed of members of the Martov's and of Gorky's groups, who declared:

"We left the *Tsay-ee-kah* because of the uncompromising policy of the Bolsheviki, and to force them to make concessions in order to realise the union of all the revolutionary democracy. Now that that union is brought about, we consider it a sacred duty to take our places once more in the *Tsay-ee-kah.* . . . We declare that all those who have withdrawn from the *Tsay-ee-kah* should now return."

Stachkov, a dignified old peasant of the presidium of the Peasants' Congress, bowed to the four corners of the room. "I greet you with the christening of a new Russian life and freedom!"

Gronsky, in the name of the Polish Social Democracy; Skrypnik, for the Factory-Shop Committees; Tifonov, for the Russian soldiers at Salonika; and others, interminably, speaking out of full hearts, with the happy eloquence of hopes fulfilled. . . .

It was late in the night when the following resolution was put and passed unanimously:

"The *Tsay-ee-kah,* united in extraordinary session with the Petrograd Soviet and the Peasants' Congress, confirms the Land and Peace decrees adopted by the second Congress of Soviets of Workers' and Soldiers' Deputies, and also the decree on Workers' Control adopted by the *Tsay-ee-kah.*

"The joint session of the *Tsay-ee-kah* and the Peasants' Congress expresses its firm conviction that the union of workers, soldiers and peasants, this fraternal union of all the workers and all the exploited, will consolidate the power conquered by them, that it will take all revolutionary measures to hasten the passing of the power into the hands of the working-class in other countries, and that it will assure in this manner the lasting accomplishment of a just peace and the victory of Socialism." [2]

NOTES TO CHAPTER XII

1 Instruction to Peasants*

In answer to the numerous enquiries coming from peasants, it is hereby explained that the whole power in the country is from now on held by the Soviets of the Workers', Soldiers', and Peasants' Deputies. The Workers' Revolution, after having conquered in Petrograd and in Moscow, is now conquering in all other centres of Russia. The Workers' and Peasants' Government safeguards the interests of the masses of peasantry, the poorest of them; it is with the majority of peasants and workers against the land-owners, and against the capitalists.

Hence the Soviets of Peasants' Deputies, and before all the District Soviets, and subsequently those of the Provinces, are from now on and until the Constituent Assembly meets, full-powered bodies of State authority in their localities. All landlords' titles to the land are cancelled by the second All-Russian Congress of Soviets. A decree regarding the land has already been issued by the present Provisional Workers' and Peasants' Government. On the basis of the above decree all lands hitherto belonging to landlords now pass entirely and wholly into the hands of the Soviets of Peasants' Deputies. The *Volost* (a group of several villages forms a *Volost*) Land Committees are immediately to take over all land from the landlords, and to keep a strict account

* Signed by Lenin, this document was also drafted by him, and is now included in his *Collected Works.*—*Ed.*

over it, watching that order be maintained, and that the whole estate be well guarded, seeing that from now on all private estates become public property and must therefore be protected by the people themselves.

All orders given by the *Volost* Land Committees, adopted with the assent of the District Soviets of Peasants' Deputies, in fulfilment of the decrees issued by the revolutionary power, are absolutely legal and are to be forthwith and irrefutably brought into execution.

The Workers' and Peasants' Government appointed by the second All-Russian Congress of Soviets has received the name of the Council of People's Commissars.

The Council of People's Commissars summons the Peasants to take the whole power into their hands in every locality.

The workers will in every way absolutely and entirely support the peasants, arrange for them all that is required in connection with machines and tools, and in return they request the peasants to help with the transport of grain.

President of the Council of People's Commissars,

V. ULIANOV (LENIN).

Petrograd, November 18th, 1917.

2.

The full-powered Congress of Peasants' Soviets met about a week later, and continued for several weeks. Its history is merely an expanded version of the history of the "Extraordinary Conference." At first the great majority of the delegates were hostile to the Soviet Government, and supported the reactionary wing. Several days later the assembly was supporting the moderates with Chernov. And several days after that the vast majority of the Congress were voting for the faction of Maria Spiridonova, and sending their representatives into the *Tsay-ee-kah* at Smolny. . . . The Right Wing then walked out of the Congress and called a Congress of its own, which went on, dwindling from day to day, until it finally dissolved. . . .

INDEX

MODERN LIBRARY GIANTS

A series of full-sized library editions of books that formerly were available only in cumbersome and expensive sets.
THE MODERN LIBRARY GIANTS REPRESENT A
SELECTION OF THE WORLD'S GREATEST BOOKS

These volumes contain from 600 to 1,400 pages each

DATE DUE

APR 3 0 1997		
MAY 1 2 2000		
APR 2 6 2004		
	261-2500	Printed in USA